AF479131

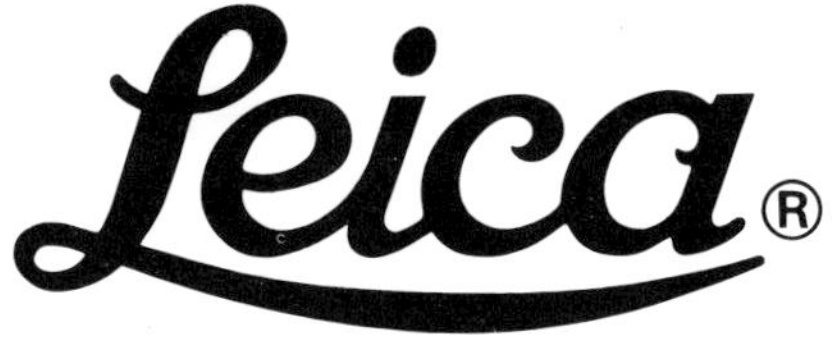

THE FIRST SIXTY YEARS

Gianni Rogliatti

Additional Text and English Editing by Dennis Laney

Hove Foto Books

LEICA THE FIRST 60 YEARS
FIRST EDITION
First Printing August 1985 English
Second Printing January 1989
First Printing October 1985 German
First Printing October 1985 French

LEICA THE FIRST 50 YEARS
FIRST EDITION
First Printing May 1975
Second Printing April 1976
Third Printing July 1976
First Printing 1975 Italian

SECOND EDITION
First Printing June 1977 English
First Printing July 1977 French
Second Printing (Minor Revisions) October 1977 English
First Printing January 1979 German
Third Printing May 1979 English
Fourth Printing April 1982 English

ISBN No 0-906447-32-1

Published by
HOVE FOTO BOOKS
34, Church Road,
Hove, East Sussex, BN3 2GJ,
United Kingdom.

U.S.A. Distributors
Seven Hills Books,
49 Central Avenue,
Suite 300,
Cincinnatti,
Ohio 45202,
Tel: (513) 381 3831
Fax: (513) 381 8839

Trade
U.K. Distribution
Fountain Press Ltd.
45 The Broadway
Tolworth, Surrey, KT6 DW

Printed and Bound by Short Run Press Ltd., Exeter, United Kingdom.

INTRODUCTION

A lot has happened in the ten years that have elapsed since I wrote the Introduction to the book "LEICA – The First Fifty Years", but the Leitz name and the LEICA itself remain synonymous with both high technology and excellence in photography; just as they were in the first fifty years of the camera's life.

For example, we have introduced electronics into our cameras, in both the reflex and rangefinder models, but only when they would be of real practical use to serious photographers, not to satisfy passing fashion or whim.

New systems for recording images, both on film and electronically, have also appeared in the meantime. However, in the face of all these developments the quality of the LEICA image remains unsurpassed and it is very apparent that current image-forming techniques by means of the two LEICA systems will be with us for many years yet.

This book by the same author who wrote the original work on the history of the LEICA should be a welcome addition to any enthusiast's library.

Dr. Knut Kühn-Leitz
Wetzlar, July 1985

CONTENTS

ACKNOWLEDGEMENTS

The Author and Publisher would like to thank Ernst Leitz Wetzlar GmbH for their permission to use the following registered trademarks for this book only.

®

LEICA®
LEICAFLEX®
VISOFLEX®
ELMAR®
ELMARIT®

HEKTOR®
SUMMICRON®
SUMMILUX®
NOCTILUX®
SUMMARON®

TELYT®
SUPER-ANGULON®
PA-CURTAGON®
PRADO®
PRADOVIT®

FOCOMAT®
ELCAN®
LECAVIT®
TELEVIT®
REPROVIT®

They are also most grateful to Leitz, and Rüdy Krauth in particular, for their help in providing information and pictures.

Photographs on the following pages are by John Robert Young: 34-5, 37, 39, 42-5, 50-4, 56, 58-61, 63, 67-9, 73, 77, 84-5, 88-90, 92, 96, 98, 109, 114, 118, 126, 128-9, 135, 139, 140-1, 143-5, 150, 152, 163-5, 168-9, Pl. 3.

Other photographs, and diagrams, are from the following sources:-
    Author's archives; Hove Foto Books archives; Items from the collection of the late John Newton, photographed by Brian Tomkins; Ernst Leitz Wetzlar GmbH.

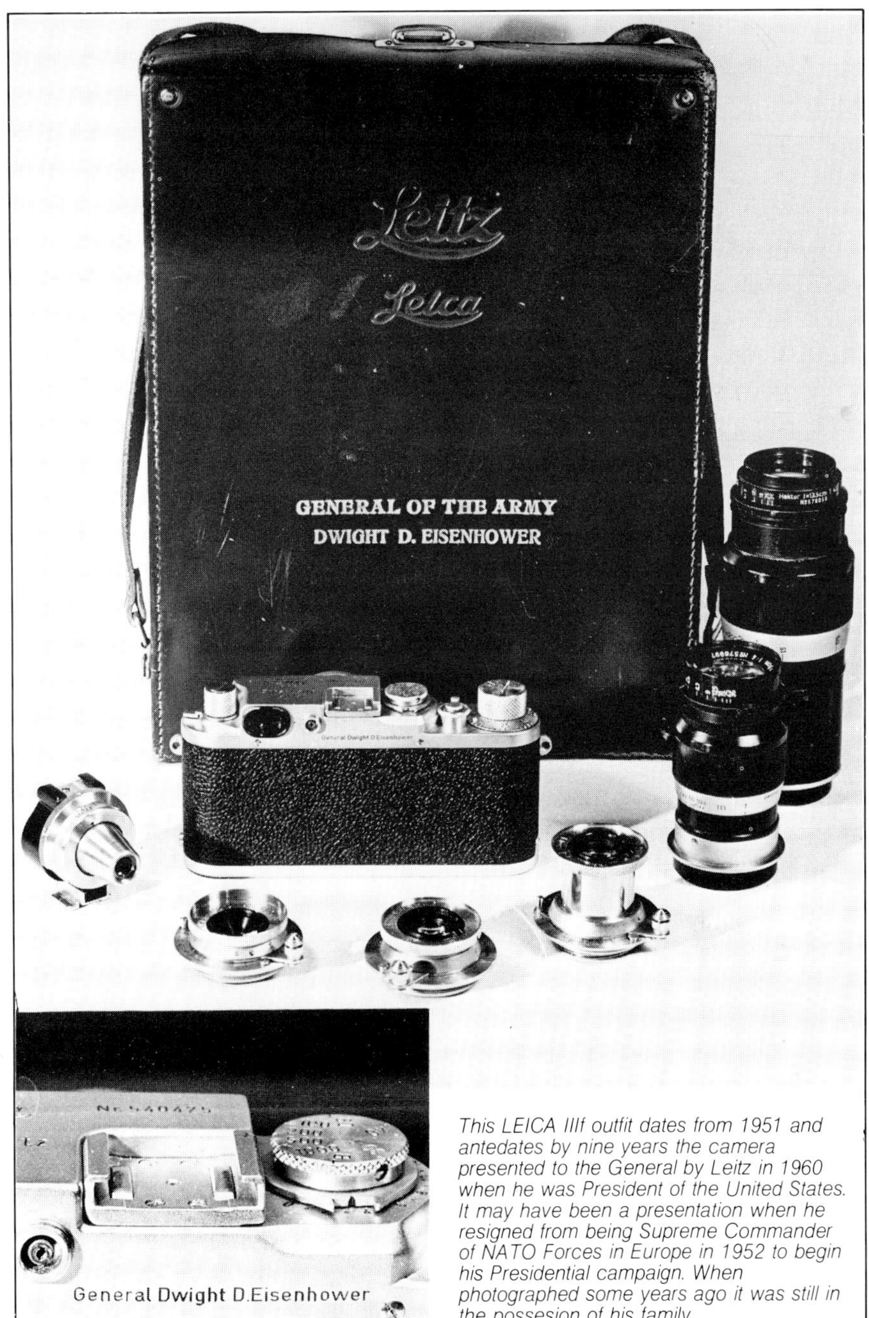

This LEICA IIIf outfit dates from 1951 and antedates by nine years the camera presented to the General by Leitz in 1960 when he was President of the United States. It may have been a presentation when he resigned from being Supreme Commander of NATO Forces in Europe in 1952 to begin his Presidential campaign. When photographed some years ago it was still in the possesion of his family.

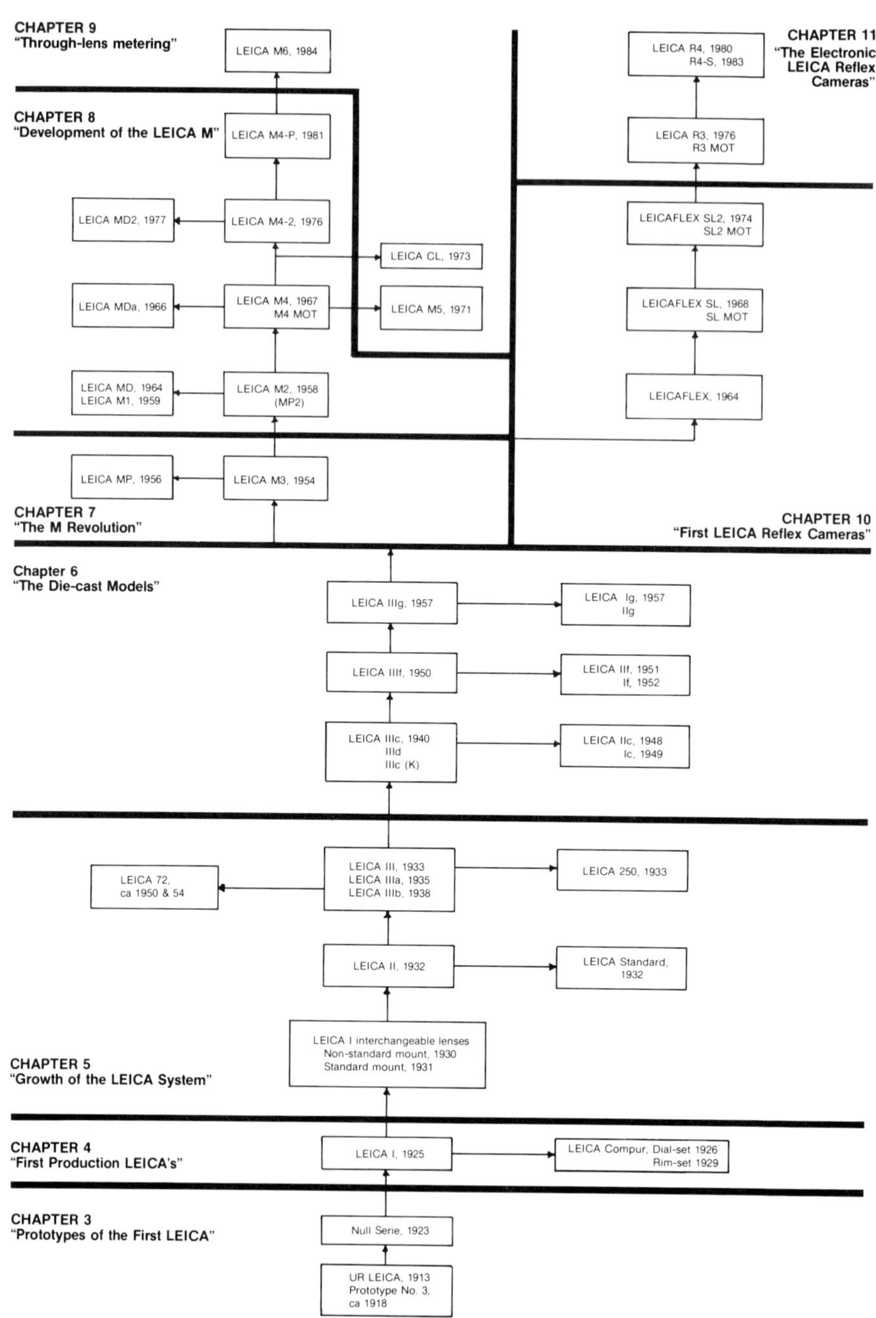

A continuous path of technical development can be traced from the UR LEICA of 1913 to the present day rangefinder M6 and M4-P cameras and the R4 and R4-S reflexes. Leitz had had years of experience of making mirror mechanisms for the VISOFLEX reflex attachment before they designed the first LEICAFLEX. The above chart traces this path, and it also serves as a guide to the chapters dealing with the principle LEICA models. The dates in the boxes are the years of first production.

Chapter 1

The LEICA Story

Looking back over the ten years that have elapsed since the LEICA Golden Anniversary we can see now that on its 50th birthday the LEICA was at the crossroads. The need for rapid development of the reflex cameras to meet fierce Japanese competition, high production costs, the need for capital, and the uncertain market future for the rangefinder type of camera meant that there would either have to be drastic changes or we would see the end of camera production by Letiz. Zeiss had already ceased camera production two years earlier.

At the time there were four current models, and all were issued with special engravings and serial numbers for the 50th Anniversary in 1975. The LEICAFLEX SL2 was the third Leitz reflex model and represented the peak of perfection of a single lens reflex with a purely mechanical shutter and mirror. The LEICA M4 was a camera in the direct tradition and lineage of the classic LEICA. The LEICA M5 was the first rangefinder camera in the world with through-lens metering, the ultimate perfection in convenience but bought at the cost of a considerable increase in bulk. The interesting newcomer was the LEICA CL, the compact LEICA, which incorporated in its small size the same through-lens metering system as the M5 – a photocell mounted on a swinging arm and centered behind the lens for metering and swung up out of the way for picture taking. The CL was one of the first fruits of the co-operative agreement with Minolta and the camera was manufactured in Japan to Leitz' specification, with the lenses being made in Germany.

Of these cameras, the LEICAFLEX SL2 ceased production in 1976, after only three years, and is now much prized as both a user's and a collector's camera; the LEICA M5 likewise, although in its case the anniversary year was its last year of production. There had been initial production problems with the CL, but it was an advanced product and once these were out of the way this Wetzlar designed camera, produced by Minolta, increased in popularity. However, it went out of the Leitz list after only three years, although Minolta continued to produce a similar camera with the LEICA M bayonet for a number of years. The LEICA M4, which at the time looked to be the most obsolescent of the four, was the one whose basic configuration has survived through successive models, the M4-2 and M4-P, until now the M6 has viewfinder frames for six focal lengths from 28 to 135mm, and, above all, through-lens metering with no increase in bulk. Meanwhile electronics took over control of the mechanism in reflex cameras and we had first, in 1976, the LEICA R3 with its electronic Copal shutter and its unique spot or whole field metering, followed in 1980 by the totally electronic LEICA R4, offering a choice of five programmes: spot or integral aperture priority, shutter priority, automatic or manual; as well as interchangeable focusing screens, and latterly the R4-S, similar but limited to three programme modes.

All the events that were to influence the LEICA during the next ten years had taken place just as the company was preparing to celebrate its famous camera's fiftieth anniversary. Financial difficulties had led finally to the Swiss company Wild, a well known manufacturer of microscopes and other technical equipment, acquiring a controlling interest in Leitz. There was a time in the ensuing events when the whole photographic division seemed to be in jeopardy, but luckily a more optimistic appraisal of the situation led to renewed efforts and enthusiastic development of the new family of electronic cameras. Experience of recent years has shown that there is very much a continuing demand for cameras of the LEICA quality.

In 1974 in its search for better operating conditions the company had established a new factory in the small Portuguese town of Vilanova de Famalicao, near Porto. In this modern complex the bodies for the LEICA R4 and R4–S are assembled, along with the TRINOVID binoculars, projection lenses, and even some types of microscope. The new factory is well integrated with the existing ones at Wetzlar and the Canadian one at Midland.

The co-operative agreement with the Japanese company Minolta was also negotiated in the early seventies, as we saw with the LEICA CL. This has given Leitz access to Minolta camera technology for the new generation reflex cameras whilst Leitz can concentrate on their own strengths of superb mechanical design and the unique quality of their lenses.

Now, having reached the venerable age of sixty years the LEICA system, or rather systems because there are two, are securely in charge of photography at the highest level. In the company plans there is a steady output of new lenses, the best corrected that the industry can offer. But let us now see how it all started.

The story of Oskar Barnack and how he came to invent the camera that eventually was called the LEICA has been told before by the late Theo Kisselbach, master of LEICA photography, in "The LEICA Book". Barnack, born near Brandenburg in 1879, arrived at the Leitz company in Wetzlar in 1911 after having worked in Jena, that other great centre of the German optical industry.

Wetzlar is a small, pleasant town with a population of 52,000 situated about 40 miles north of Frankfurt. The river Lahn separates the old medieval burg from the modern part of the town. Hills and woods make it ideal as a holiday resort and, as proudly stated on a plaque on a house in the "Kornmarkt", Goethe himself stayed there. Wetzlar has a long tradition in the optical industry that dates back to the beginning of the eighteenth century. Thus the founder of the Leitz dynasty and company took over the heritage of the Rudersdorf, Engelbert, Kellner and Belthe families, to name but a few. The Leitz company itself dates back to 1849.

Barnack was working on the development of the cine camera at Leitz and, having experienced the toil of carrying around a large view camera, he realised the possibilities of motion picture film for still photography. He would produce a small camera that could use cine film, but it would have to yield negatives of such

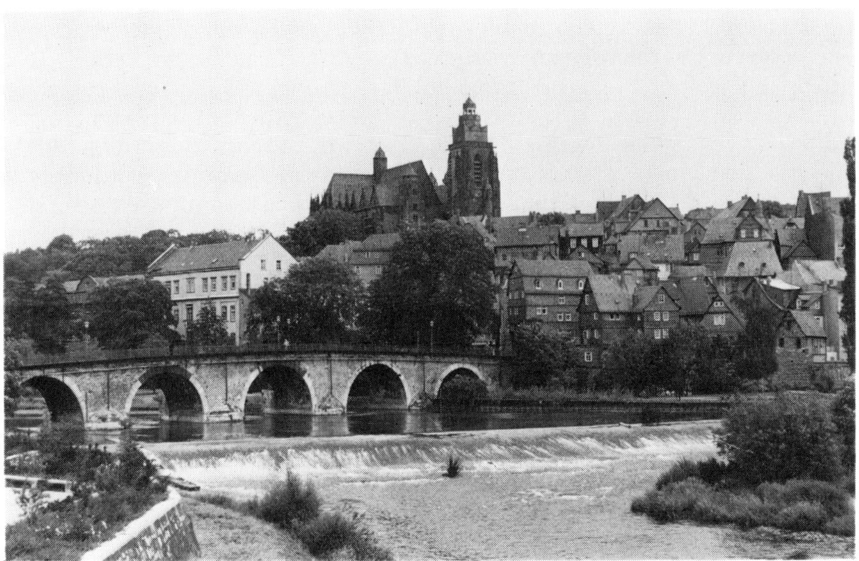

Wetzlar, the old town today.

high quality that a relatively big enlargement could be obtained. This was the origin of the famous Leitz saying "little negative, large print".

The prototype (which was later to be known as the "UR-LEICA") was built by Barnack in 1913: to be exact, two such prototypes were built, one of which was used by Barnack himself and the second by Ernst Leitz II, who took it with him on his trip to America in the spring of 1914, certainly the first Leicaman in his own right.

During the war there was no time for further development of the small camera. Nevertheless, in the long years that passed, whilst using the camera (sometimes even exchanging pictures with the farmers for food) Barnack would have noted the shortcomings of the early design and planned the necessary improvements.

After the war, when the camera came under examination as a possible product for the Leitz factory, many of the improvements were incorporated into the pre-production run of 31 cameras. Other improvements were well defined so that they could be included in the design of the production models. Finally, after much probing around with other names, the actual one was chosen from the initials of LEItz CAmera, although the first choice omitted the "I" as the name in the early advertisements was "LECA".

Of course the most important milestone was the decision to manufacture the camera. Ernst Leitz III was a young man then, and recalls the "longest day" when Leitz directors discussed the issue. Opinions were fairly evenly split between those who were for manufacturing the camera and those who were against. It was known that many opinions against the small camera were

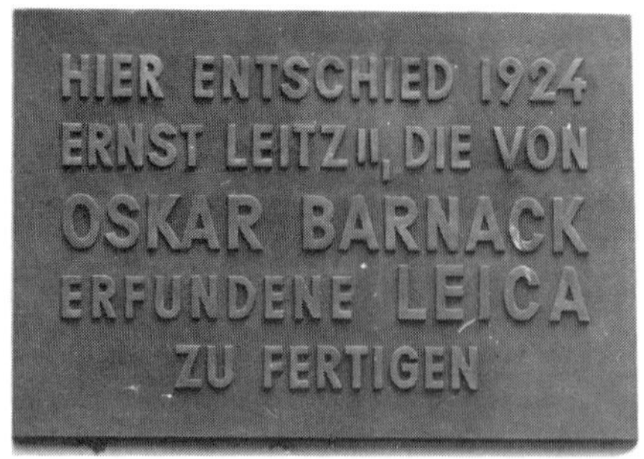

Plaque on the building in which in 1924 the decision was taken to manufacture the LEICA.

influenced by those representatives of the photographic trade who had stocked large quantities of photo glass plate as a defence against inflation (a great danger in Germany at that time). Therefore a camera that used a cheap 35mm film would create a strong demand for that film and a loss of interest for the traditional material. Mounted on the wall of the old Leitz factory building is a plaque which states that in 1924 the decision to build Barnack's LEICA was taken there.

The official date for the start of production is indicated as 1925, since in the same year the camera was introduced to the public at the Leipzig spring fair; however, actual production began in 1924 and in December of that year some cameras were delivered.

There can be no doubt that the LEICA was a success from the start. It was no surprise that it was expensive, as nothing was spared and quality was foremost. After a great deal of organisation and with typical German thoroughness, production was started cautiously. In 1924-25 only 870 cameras were produced, reaching the serial number 1,000 (there are no cameras with numbers under 100 and the first 31 were reserved for the pre-production run). The name "LEICA", although official, was not engraved on the cameras until much later with the coupled rangefinder LEICA II. On each camera there was the name "Ernst Leitz Wetzlar", and the letters "D.R.P." (which represent Deutches Reichs Patent) and also the serial number. This number was also on some part of the internal mechanism, making it simple to check if any major part of the camera has been modified at a later date.

In 1926 production doubled and 1,654 cameras were built, of which some 200 were of the type with the Compur shutter instead of the focal plane shutter. In 1927 the production doubled again, reaching and surpassing the number of 3,000 cameras built in a year, and in 1928 there was yet a bigger jump to more than 7,000 cameras built in a single year. After a modest increase in 1929 the climax came in 1930 when more than 38,000 cameras were produced. 1931 was a model change year and was also hit by depression, as a result only 11,000 cameras were made. By 1932 full camera production was restored and in all the ensuing years on average 30-35,000 LEICA's were built.

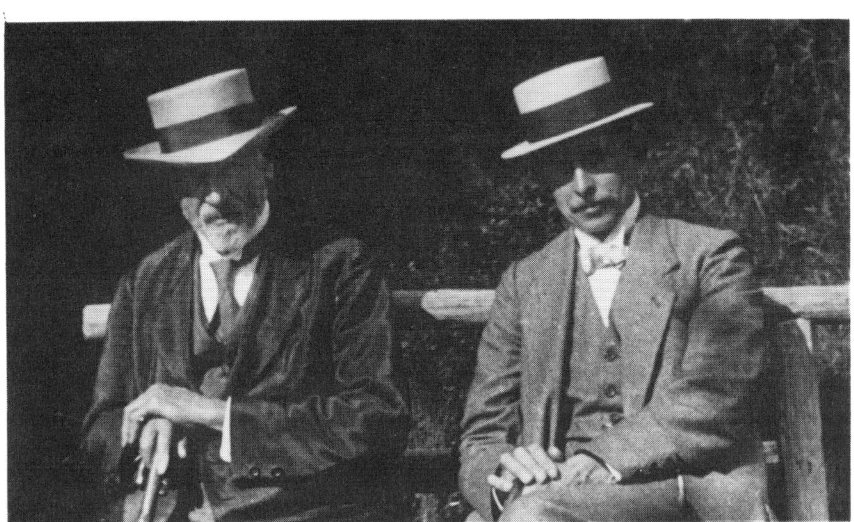

Ernest Leitz I and Oskar Barnack, taken with the Ur-LEICA.

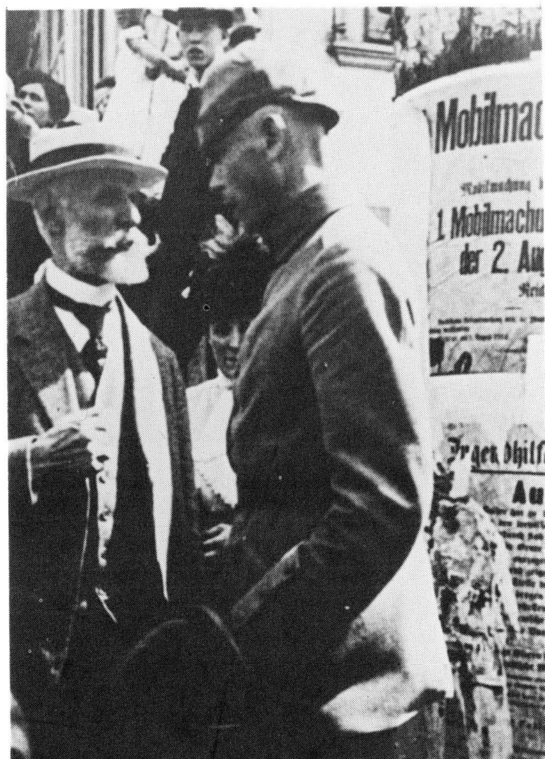

Example of Oskar Barnack's photo-journalistic eye; a civilian commenting on the declaration of war with a soldier, taken with Ur-LEICA.

The most important milestones in the development of the LEICA were the introduction of the two concepts in design of the camera that led the way to all subsequent improvements. These were: first, the inter-changeability of lenses introduced in 1930 (at the beginning restricted to a given set of lenses specially matched to a specific camera, with the last three digits of the camera serial number engraved on the lenses); second, the automatic coupling of all lenses to the built-in rangefinder. This coupling became effective from 1932 onwards, after the flange to film plane distance was standardised in 1931 so that every LEICA lens could be interchanged at will between camera bodies. Earlier lenses could also be modified to ensure correct registration and coupling to rangefinder.

By its very presence on the market the LEICA contributed immensely to the improvement of 35mm film because the requirements of photography and the enormous possibilities offered by the excellent lenses were far superior to the common needs of the motion picture industry. In the beginning there was a search for the best type of film suitable for the LEICA. It was later on that film manufacturers obliged by making a "LEICA film" which gave the best results. Amongst the memories of Ernst Leitz III are trips he made to America in the thirties to share first-hand experiences with Kodak technicians, especially when the film was rolls of Kodachrome which he brought back to Germany and then sent back to America to be processed and returned by airmail, using the service offered by the Zeppelin airships*. The search for better types of black and white film led to the strangest discoveries. For example, a young Leitz executive went to Egypt and discovered that a particular type of Agfa film in tropical packing gave the best results, whilst another man found that the emulsions made by Perutz for aero photography worked very well as LEICA film.

Agfa introduced a special black and white film which yielded colour pictures when used in conjunction with a special Leitz/Agfa tri-colour filter. This astonishing performance was possible thanks to the extremely large aperture of the HEKTOR 73mm lens (f1.9) and the f2.0 SUMMAR, which allowed the use of a dense red-blue-green filter to separate the primary colours on a thin undulated film. The film was then developed and reversed as black and white diapositive. However, when projected through a similar filter system it produced a colour image on a screen. This Agfa process antedated Kodachrome by a year or so, but was killed off by the success of the latter.

---

* It is interesting to note that Kodachrome celebrated its first fifty years in 1985 as the LEICA celebrated its first sixty. It was initially launched as 16mm narrow gauge cine film but 35mm still film followed one year later and became the first production high-grade colour transparency film. It led LEICA photographers into a completely new and exciting type of photography, but it also gave them the ability to project the original 24 x 36mm transparency direct without the intermediate step of printing. This opened up 35mm photography to people who hitherto had not wanted to concern themselves with darkrooms and enlargers. The result was a surge in the popularity of the 35mm format and a demand for faster lenses, because the colour film in the early days was slow compared with black-and-white. No doubt also there was a reciprocal effect in that the establishment of the 35mm format by Leitz over the previous ten years was one of the factors which encouraged Kodak to go ahead with Kodachrome. From the earliest days of the LEICA Leitz had produced projectors for 35mm black-and-white transparencies and had demonstrated that excellent results could be obtained from the very small slides. The equipment was also small and compact and the slides could be easily stored, whereas the otherwise standard slide format of the day was 9 x 9cm (3½ x 3½in) and the slides and their associated projectors were far too heavy and clumsy to ever become a popular medium, even with the benefit of colour. It should be remembered that viable colour print processes suitable for amateur photography only came many years later. (Ed.).

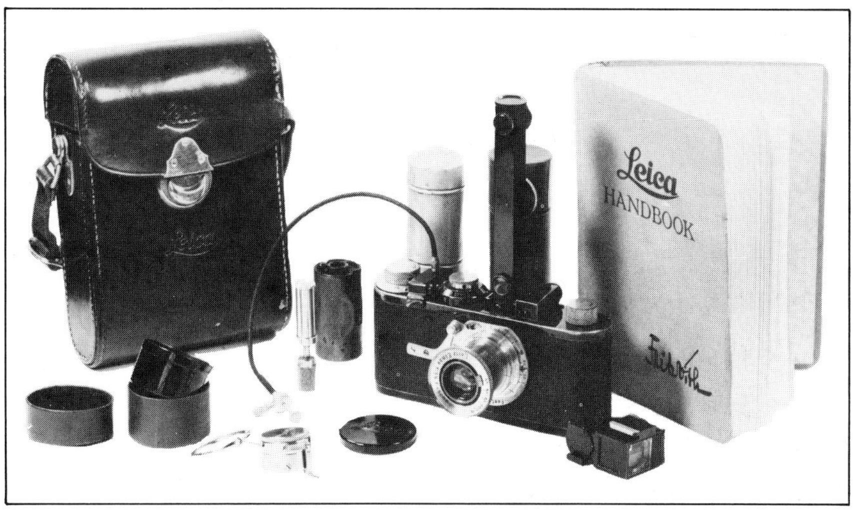

LEICA I outfit, with case, FODIS rangefinder, waist-level viewer AUFSU, FISON lens hood and box, cassette and metal case, the non-Leitz DIREKT delayed action release and RAPIDO rapid winder, together with the famous "Leica Handbook" by Fritz Vith.

Every development of the LEICA and its system resulted from an obvious start in the right direction; every improvement had the advantage of that single but fundamental fact that the LEICA was born with a perfect heart – its two-curtain shutter. In sixty years the basic system has remained unchanged in the rangefinder cameras, but has been constantly improved on, and is now reaching as near to perfection as possible.

On the 18th January 1930, the Leitz company was transformed from a family business to G.m.b.H., which means Gesellshaft mit beschrankter Haftung, a Company Limited (U.S.A. Incorporated) in short. However, those letters would not appear on the cameras until after the second World War, and on the cameras that were also marked with a D.B.P. (for Deutsches Bundesrepublik Patent) in place of D.R.P. It should be noted that these markings appear at the same time on different cameras as the models which were manufactured before and after the war bear the same markings, whilst the new models produced after 1949, bear the new markings.

The designation of camera models is another puzzling matter. At the beginning there were two such designations; the first camera marketed was known as LEICA I to the public, but as type A in the factory and in some other countries. The second model, with the Compur shutter, was type B. A newer model with a screw lens mount was also called LEICA I and was known inside the factory as type C, (and in some foreign countries). Then the LEICA II rangefinder was known a type D, while the Standard LEICA (without rangefinder) type E.

In 1933 the LEICA III or type F was introduced, the main improvement being the introduction of slow speeds set by a front knob, ranging from 1/20th of a

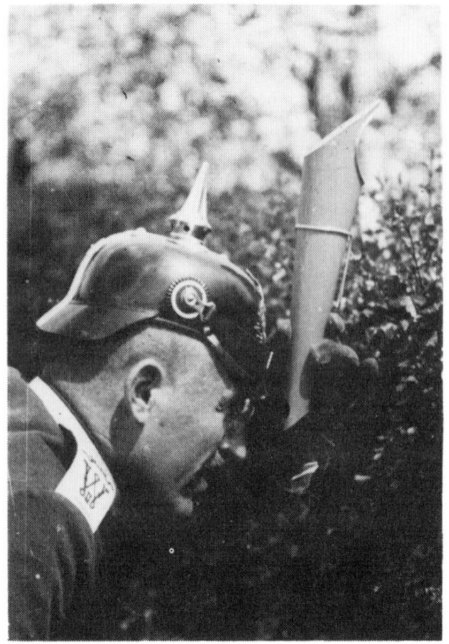

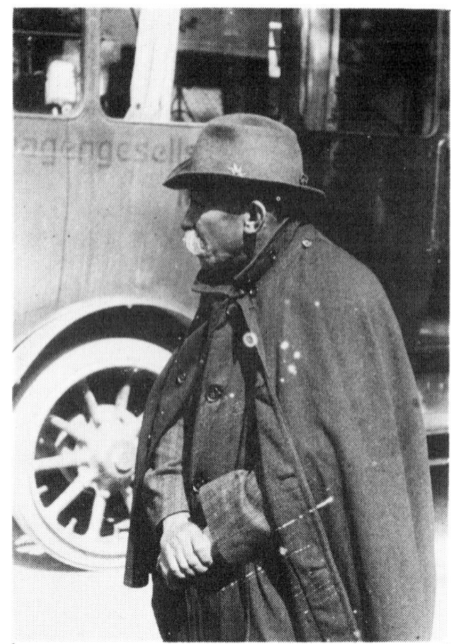

German officer using periscope, taken with Ur-LEICA.

A poor man, taken with Ur-LEICA.

second to a full second, plus time exposure. This obviated the single disadvantage which the shutter could have had in comparison with the Compur. The same problem must have been the reason behind Leitz' decision early in the LEICA career to make the Compur type, which was deemed simpler in construction than the normal model and was therefore less expensive (in 1926 the LEICA sold for 220 Reichsmark and the Compur for 196).

In 1934, Barnack, who was a great photographer and could have been one of the great photo-reporters of his day, judging by his pictures, built a LEICA specially devised for the journalistic trade. This was aptly named the "Reporter", later to be called the "250" due to the picture capacity of its huge film chambers. Care for detail was evident also in this case, because the film chambers were so constructed as to avoid rewinding the film, and the exposed part could simply be removed by changing the receiving chamber. Leitz even devised a special cutting tool for cutting the film in the camera.

It was a relatively simple task to increase the higher shutter speed from 1/500 to the very high 1/1000th of a second; this was accomplished in 1935 with the model IIIa. This was to be the last contribution by Oskar Barnack during his life time. He died at the age of 57 on the 16th January 1936, after celebrating on the 2nd of the same month his 25 years' service with the Leitz company. A frail man, he nevertheless managed to keep working even in bad health and left behind him one of the best examples of modern technology.

The success story of the LEICA continued: its fame having reached every country and continent, the camera was now being made at a sustained rate in the four basic models: Standard (replacing the type I), II, III and IIIa plus the Reporter type, which accounted for only a few hundred cameras per year. The lens range was also being continually expanded from the traditional ELMAR f3.5 50mm lens to the 35mm wide-angle and a range of medium to long-range lenses which included 73mm, 90mm, 105mm, 135mm and 200mm.

1938 saw the introduction of the IIIb (developed in 1937) which was similar to the IIIa except for minor details, the most important of which was the placing of the viewfinder and rangefinder eyepieces close together.

The big change came with the IIIc which did not appear until 1940. Although it looked similar to previous models it had a die-cast main frame which made it much more robust. It also had a slightly longer body to make space for more sophisticated mechanisms, including the delayed action timer that was to come later.

During World War II development continued on special types such as the IIIc K (for Kugel lager or ball bearing equipped mechanism) and the electric drive 250. After the war, with the tremendous job of reconstruction and fulfilling the demand for the LEICA which was increasing, work went full steam ahead. Thus the IIIc was not the only model introduced to the post-war world, the Ic and IIc, which were simpler models, were also added.

However, the older models III, IIIa and IIIb were still being produced until the allocated series were completed. Also some of the older models were converted to modern specifications. For example, the rangefinder added to early type I, and flash synchronization added to types II and III. This practice of updating any LEICA was always honoured by the company and led to the great fame of the camera and the confidence of the customer who did not need to fear planned obsolescence.

But this practice has brought some confusion regarding the numbers; as far as can be ascertained when a type I LEICA was being transformed to a type II, the rangefinder cover was stamped with the original serial number. Later on, however, this was deemed a too long and costly procedure and a new serial number for converted cameras was started, using five digits as in the initial series; this numbering went on also in the immediate postwar period, including cameras which received completely new internal mechanisms.

During the first postwar years and until 1949, 95 per cent of total production went to the U.S.A. After that period production was returned to a world market, but Leitz took the big step in 1952 of opening a new factory in Canada, close to their all important American market.

In 1950 there was a new model with an important addition: the IIIf with built-in flash synchronization; prior to the IIIf flash was actuated by external contacts on top of the speed setting dial, or a special baseplate. There is a missing link between the IIId (actually a IIIc with delayed action) and the IIIf and it is because IIIe would sound strange in German.

The IIIg was to be the last of the screw-mount LEICA's, but it was unique among them in having a bright-line finder which showed frames for 50 and

90mm lenses. The IIIg is now a prized collector's item as a fine example of the last of the screw camera range. The screw-mount cameras were finally discontinued in 1960.

The most important innovation for thirty years was revealed by the unveiling, in 1954, of a completely different LEICA, the M3 with bayonet mount lenses and bright-line viewfinder frames that changed when the lenses were changed. It also offered the facility of direct coupling of an exposure meter to the special dial, making it a semi-automatic camera. This was a welcome camera for professionals and all those who objected to the longish operation of lens changing with the screw-mount cameras. The LEICA M3 started another thirty year story which is documented in this book and is not yet over.

In 1965 the LEICAFLEX was introduced as Leitz' long awaited entry to the SLR market. As expected they made a thoroughly efficient job of it and it set a standard by which others were judged. It was also totally within the Leitz tradition and with its two successor models, the LEICAFLEX SL and SL2, brings us up to where we started this story in 1975.

The two systems, rangefinder and reflex, are fairly complete with accessories such as motors, near focusing devices, and comprehensive sets of lenses. What is more, both systems are still compatible, that is parts from one, particularly lenses, can be used with the other; this is a point that few other systems can match.

During the life of the M series of cameras Leitz had fully developed the VISOFLEX system to give reflex focusing and picture composition, especially for use with long focus lenses and for close-up work. The VISOFLEX has now been discontinued, but paradoxically its biggest single disadvantage would now be overcome with the advent of the M6 with its through-lens metering.

The old debate about which was better, reflex or rangefinder, has been settled in the past decade to the satisfaction of both sides. Each type of camera has a clear and distinct role in modern photography. The LEICA M camera is a robust, relatively light-weight and handy instrument for quick and accurate focusing, particularly in poor lighting conditions and with fast lenses, with focal lengths from 21 to 135mm. These attributes, combined with its near-silent shutter, make it the ideal camera for the photo-reporter. The LEICA R camera is the universal camera, with the widest range of applications from the amateur's general photography to precise scientific work. The reflex screen makes picture composition easy and eliminates the need for additional viewfinders and focusing aids for close-ups.

There is no doubt that the LEICA camera completely changed photography, making it better for the amateur and professional alike. No other camera has done this for photography. Any previous camera has just been a small improvement on existing types, but the LEICA created a completely new way of taking photographs. For the amateur it was the convenience of the automatic cocking of the shutter when the film was advanced, the small size, the feeling that good pictures were possible with little effort. For the professional it was the speed of operation and the number of exposures that could be taken on a single roll, apart from the enormous advantage of the camera's size. The small size in turn made it possible to use both fast and long lenses that were rather impracticable with the larger formats. Photojournalism as we know it today would not exist without the LEICA and all the other cameras which it inspired that use the 35 mm perforated film first used by Barnack in his prototype in 1913.

Although the LEICA was not the first still camera to use 35 mm perforated cine film, it was certainly the most successful, and for a long time the only one. Nobody can dispute the fact that it has played the leading part for the sixty years of its existence. Nor should it be forgotten that the LEICA was not simply a new type of camera, but also the first photographic system of its kind. Everything required from picture-taking to enlarging and projecting was supplied by the same maker, and therefore designed and manufactured with the same and consistent high standard of production.

The number of accessories that were invented and manufactured by Leitz over the years is unbelievable. One has only to leaf through the Code Word list to see that most of the accessories used today on 35 mm cameras were either made by or experimented with by Leitz for the LEICA. Long before the advent of the modern SLR one could change lenses on the LEICA and still focus with the coupled rangefinder of the camera; one could take pictures of the moon with the extreme telephoto lens, or penetrate the inside of the human body with the endoscopic attachment; one could snap on a clockwork motor and take sequence shots, or attach a device for stereo pictures. It may be argued that there are several camera systems on the market today which can perform just as well or are more comprehensive, but the point is that with a LEICA one could do it all thirty or forty years ago. The LEICA was the product of the mechanical genius of one man and the wisdom of another. Oskar Barnack perfected it and Ernst Leitz II took the calculated risk of producing it. Both were equally important for the success of the camera.

Now, of the third generation, Ernst Leitz III sadly is no longer with us, and we have also lost the friendly advice of Theo Kisselbach; but their memory will remain, together with that of Oskar Barnack, and every time we hold a LEICA we must be grateful to men like them who made this possible.

PRESENTATION LEICA CAMERAS

Ever since the beginning in 1925 LEICA cameras with landmark serial numbers have been presented to notable people. These have usually been people who have made a distinguished contribution to photography, or its application, although national leaders also figure in the list. The following is the official Leitz list:

1925   1,000   Prof. Dr. Walther Schultze, Hauptklinik, Giessen
1928   10,000   Dr. Hugo Eckner, pioneer of German aeronautics
1929   25,000   Sven Hedin, Swedish explorer of Asia

1931	50,000	Dr. Wilhelm Filchner, German explorer of Asia
1932	75,000	Prof. Auguste Piccard, deep sea and high altitude explorer
1933	100,000	Prof. Dr. Leo Frobenius, explorer of central Africa
1933	125,000	Prof. Dr. G.O. Dyrenfurth, leader of International Himalayan Expeditions, 1930 and 1934
1935	150,000	Leopold Godowsky } joint inventors of the Kodachrome
	175,000	Leopold Mannes } process
1936	200,000	Dr. Paul Wolff, pioneer LEICA photographer
1937	250,000	Dr. Wilhelm Filchner, to replace 50,000 lost in Asia
1941	300,000	Dr. Gustav Wilmanns } creators of Agfacolor film
	350,000	Dr Wilhelm Schneider }
1946	400,000	Dr. Schneider, to replace 350,000 lost during the war
1949	450,000	Richard Schirmann, founder of German Youth Hostel Association
1950	500,000	Dr. Ernst Leitz II (now in Leitz Museum)
1951	575,000	Dr. Albert Schweitzer, physician, musician and philosopher
1952	600,000	Dr. William Beebe, USA, zoologist and deep sea explorer
1953	650,000	Prof. Dr. Norman Dyrenfurth, photographer on Swiss Everest expedition
1953	675,000	Prof. Dr. Fritz Zernike, physics Nobel Laureate
1955	700,000	Prof. Stephen Kruckenhause, author of many books of LEICA pictures
1955	750,000	Henri Cartier-Bresson, photographer
1956	800,000	Federal Chancellor Dr. Konrad Audenauer, on his 80th birthday
1956	830,000	Pandit Nehru
1957	875,000	Philippe Tiranty, Leitz distributor in France
1958	900,000	Edwin L. Wisherd, Washington, USA
1958	919,000*	H.M. Queen Elizabeth II, on the occasion of the State Visit of President Heuss. M3 outfit
1959	950,000	Fulvio Roiter, Venice
1960	980,000	President Eisenhower
1960	1,000,000	Dr. Ludwig Leitz (the camera was made in September 1960 and is now in the Leitz Museum)
1961	1,000,001	Alfred Eisenataadt, photographer "Life" magazine
1961	1,084,900*	H.M. Queen Elizabeth II, presented on a State Visit to Germany by Minister President of Hesse G. A. Zinn. LEICAFLEX outfit
1965	1,100,000	Emil Schulthess, photographer and author of many books
1965	1,111,111	A. Rothstein, Chief Photographer of American "Look" magazine
1979	1,500,000	Dr. Hans Friderichs, President of German Photographic Society
1979	1,500,001	Dr. Max Kreis, Chairman of the Board of Ernst Leitz Wetzlar GmbH

* These two cameras bear no external number, but are engraved with the royal monogram "E II R"

Chapter 2

Technical Background

With a good idea and a sound basic design one is only at the beginning of the hard path that leads to an efficient machine that can be produced consistently and will function reliably. It takes a lot of development and meticulous attention to detail in making those step-by-step improvements that result in a successful product. The LEICA system is a classic example of such a process leading to success.

One of the main features that has given the LEICA its reputation is its shutter. All LEICA mechanical shutters have been derived from Barnack's original prototype. These have been fitted to every LEICA model, including the latest M6, except for the R3 and R4/R4-S which have electronic shutters. Barnack's idea for a small camera was based on the principle that the shutter would run on the long side of the frame, that is horizontally when the camera was used in the normal position. His focal plane shutter system compensated for acceleration which ensured evenly exposed negatives. The first two prototypes had shutters with a fixed slit. This meant that shortcomings in the design would become apparent during use, including the need to cover the lens when the shutter was set, but ample time was to elapse for development from the primitive idea to the actual production of the LEICA.

The remarkable fact is that Barnack's first prototype had all the features that make a modern 35mm camera so practical: its size and shape and general layout, the simple arrangement of the controls, and the ease with which they could be used. Even the accessory shoe as we know it was utilised by Barnack to carry interchangeable viewfinders, and later a rangefinder.

The other secret of success lay in the simplicity and perfection of design and the way in which the camera was made. The LEICA shutter has always been rugged and made with the best materials for the purpose. For this reason a LEICA has never been cheap, but on the other hand a LEICA can be expected to perform faithfully after decades of use, or of neglect.

The gears are of bronze alloy formed on hobbing machines, spindles are of selected alloy steel, all bearings have large surfaces and from 1940 there have been ball bearings at critical points. From the take-up spool shaft, which is connected with the winding knob (or lever on the M type), the motion is transmitted via a train of gears to the shutter spindle.

The operation of winding the camera on advances the film the required amount and tensions the shutter automatically (thus preventing double exposure). With screw cameras the user then sets the shutter speed. M cameras have the advantage that the shutter speed can be set before or after winding.

The operation of the shutter is simplicity itself. Upon depressing the shutter release button, the film advance mechanism is disengaged and at the same time the second shutter blind is arrested by the locking lever whilst the first blind begins its traverse across the focal plane. As the first blind moves across, it starts to expose the film visible in the filmgate aperture and at the required position it releases the second blind by the action of the release arm (controlled by the first blind) pushing the locking lever backwards, thus permitting the second blind to run free. The position of release of the second blind varies, depending upon the required shutter speed. The longer the exposure the greater the delay between the first blind starting its traverse and the releasing of the second blind. For example; at 1/20th of a second the blinds follow one another at that interval. In the case of higher shutter speeds, say 1/500, the second blind will follow the first after a delay of 1/500. sec.

At the end of the traverse the first blind stops followed by the second; this then caps (closes) the shutter and remains in place during the retensioning of the shutter as the camera is wound on.

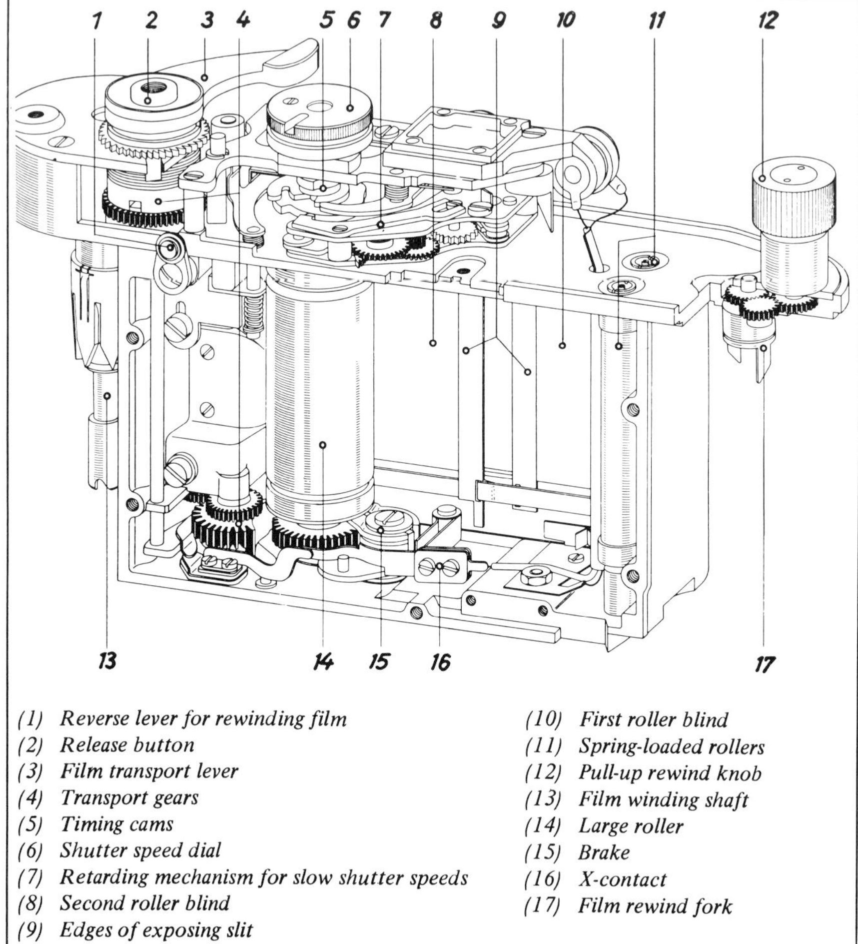

(1)	Reverse lever for rewinding film	(10)	First roller blind
(2)	Release button	(11)	Spring-loaded rollers
(3)	Film transport lever	(12)	Pull-up rewind knob
(4)	Transport gears	(13)	Film winding shaft
(5)	Timing cams	(14)	Large roller
(6)	Shutter speed dial	(15)	Brake
(7)	Retarding mechanism for slow shutter speeds	(16)	X-contact
(8)	Second roller blind	(17)	Film rewind fork
(9)	Edges of exposing slit		

Exploded view of the LEICA shutter mechanism, as fitted to an M camera

On the first LEICA's the traverse speed was 1/20th of a second across the gate (36mm). This speed was later increased to 1/30 (IIIc and IIIf black dial) (from IIIf red dial, IIIg, M cameras, this was 1/50) and finally 1/100 on the LEICAFLEX. (Slower speeds in all cases were obtained by an escapement mechanism).

Incidentally, the speed of travel of the blinds governs the shutter speeds which can be used in conjunction with electronic flash. It is only when the first blind is fully open and the second has not yet begun to move that the flash can be triggered and the whole picture area is illuminated; flash bulbs on the contrary can be used at any speed as they burn long enough to illuminate the picture, even with a narrow slit.

To begin with a maximum exposure of 1/20 of a second only could be used, as there was no way then of obtaining longer exposures with this design of shutter. This was obviated later with an external slow speed escapement, "Heboo", sold as an accessory; then, with the advent of the LEICA III, by an internal escapement which was located in the base of the shutter assembly. When the main speed dial was set on the lowest speed (i.e. 1/20 of a second) the slow speed dial could be set to any speed up to a second. The escapement mechanism was controlled by a cam and shaft linkage from the slow speed dial. In the M series and LEICAFLEX the escapement is actuated by the single speed dial. It was necessary to increase the speed of travel of the blind when the maximum shutter speed was increased to 1/2000 of a second on the LEICAFLEX, and to achieve this with the curtain travelling at 1/30 or 1/50 of a second would require too narrow a slit, less precise control.

Up until the model IIIb, the frame counter was simple; the frame counter disc was connected to the winding knob by friction so that it could be set by hand for initial settings. The internal gearing is such that when the film advancing sprocket rotates one full turn, the knob rotates one turn minus 1/40 so the counter, in effect, is advanced by one division; from the IIIc onward there is a reciprocating gear activated by cam on the winding shaft. The winding of the camera thus permits the counter to advance by one division at a time. On the M series (except the M1 and M2 where resetting is manual) the frame counter resets itself automatically, as do the counters of the reflex cameras.

The coupled rangefinder of the LEICA was, and still is, a miniature optical and mechanical achievement. With a base (distance between centres of the front windows) of only 38mm it is nevertheless capable of accurately measuring distances from one metre (3.3ft) to some 100 metres (330ft) and infinity. Unless the camera has been subjected to abuse, the rangefinder can be expected to perform satisfactorily after many years of use.

For all screw-mount cameras, the eyepiece of the rangefinder and viewfinder were separate, though they were brought close together with the introduction of the IIIb; Leitz preferred to have slight magnification on the rangefinder (1.5 x, thus giving more critical range-finding) from the LEICA III onward for use with high speed and longer lenses.

The most fascinating feature is the serviceability of the camera: all parts are secured by screws so that everything can be disassembled for repair, adjustment or replacement. On cameras up to the IIIb the main mechanical components were mounted on to the top plate which in turn was secured on the body shell. From the IIIc onwards there was an important change. A main casting formed both the top and the support for all the internal mechanism, thus assuring quicker adjustment and much improved alignment. This change was also needed because the camera was becoming more complex in order to keep up with the requirements of an expanding range of users. For example, space had to be made for the self timer, and for an improved mechanism for the shutter which inevitably was larger. It is a tribute to the ability of the Leitz technicians that almost every improvement was compatible with the cameras already in use so that a LEICA virtually never became out-dated.

Total compatability is also evident in the use of fixed distances from the lens flange to focal plane (28.8mm from camera No. 60,001). The first batch of cameras with interchangeable lenses had no fixed lens-flange-to-focal-plane distance (so every camera had to have its own set of individually adjusted lenses).

With the introduction of the new M series cameras the distance from flange to film plane was reduced by 1mm to 27.8mm. This permitted a thin intermediate flange to be made which could be inserted into the bayonet mount and had a standard screw thread inside. With this adaptor all lenses made for the screw mount LEICA's could be used on the M type camera. Compatability was again the main feature when the new LEICAFLEX was brought on the market and the possibility of using earlier lenses (still valued for their performance) was extended.

Any lens that could be used on the VISOFLEX II-III can be used on the LEICAFLEX via the adapter 14127 or on the LEICAFLEX SL and later reflex models via adapter 14167. These adapters adapt the M bayonet of the lenses to the reflex bayonet and provide the extra length needed to make up for the thickness of the VISOFLEX (Lens to film plane distance is 68.8mm with VISOFLEX compared to 47mm for LEICA reflex cameras). If the lens to be used was originally for the VISOFLEX I an additional ring is needed, 16466, which converts from screw to bayonet mount. Of course, if any particular lens needed a special ring to adapt it to the VISOFLEX, that ring should also be used. Only M and screw lenses with adequate back focus could be used on the VISOFLEX and hence on the reflex cameras. The shortest was the 65mm, f3.5 ELMAR-V that was made specially for the VISOFLEX II and III. Lenses of 90mm and longer focal length that had lens heads that unscrewed from the barrel could also be used with appropriate focusing mounts. It should be noted that with the advent of different models of the reflex cameras one has to remember certain restrictions on the use of types or vintage of lens.

The LEICAFLEX and LEICA R models are a series of reflex cameras built to the same standards as those set by the rangefinder LEICA. The first LEICAFLEX had an external light metering photocell, but in all subsequent models the metering has been TTL. After three series of LEICAFLEX's with mechanical shutters, the electronic system was finally chosen. This was not so much because of better precision (a properly adjusted LEICAFLEX shutter can be taken as a standard) but because of the many possibilities offered by electronics in terms of automatic exposure.

Thus the LEICA R3 in 1976 and the LEICA R4 in 1980 offered what can be considered the best set of characteristics with no-nonsense gadgetry.

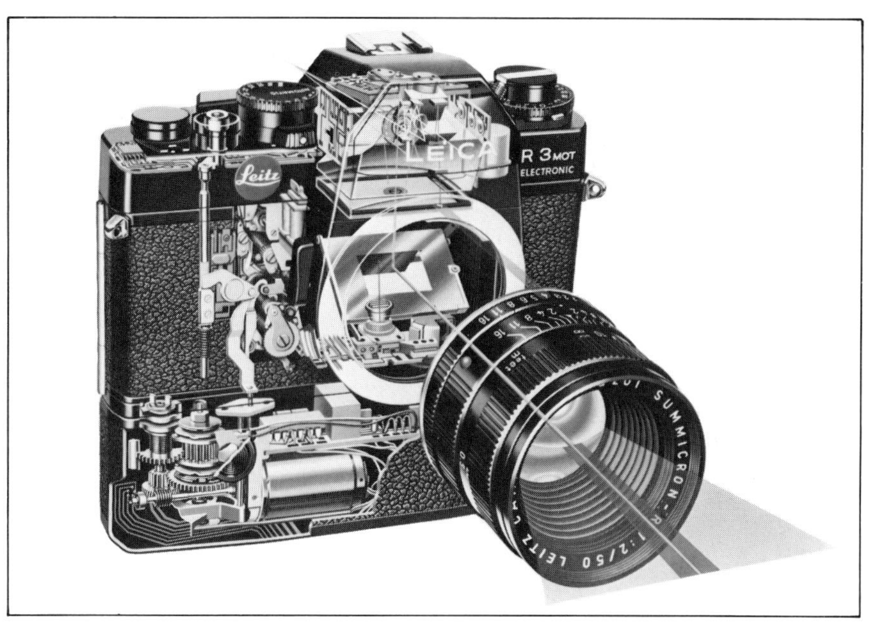

Cutaway diagram of Leitz' first camera with an electronic shutter – the R3 in its motorised form, the R3-MOT.

After a short period in which the goals of the company in rangefinder cameras was concentrated simply in maintaining production of the M4 and its updated versions, an interesting step was taken in 1984 by introducing the M6. This camera is externally identical to the M4 but by a clever use of the available space a TTL metering system has been added. Unlike the previous system employed on the M5 and CL models, the new one has neither a swinging arm nor a galvanometer, it promises therefore to be even more reliable than before. An extremely sensitive photoelement is pointed to a spot in the centre of the first curtain and "reads" the light entering the lens and reflected by this spot. An electronic circuit interprets this reading, taking into consideration the speed setting and the film sensitivity. A pair of triangular-shaped LEDs shows when the exposure is correct by both being evenly illuminated, or point to the direction the shutter dial or diaphragm ring must be turned to achieve best results when only one is illuminated.

With this type of metering the rangefinder LEICA now has the same degree of convenience as the LEICA R. Distance can be measured more accurately with

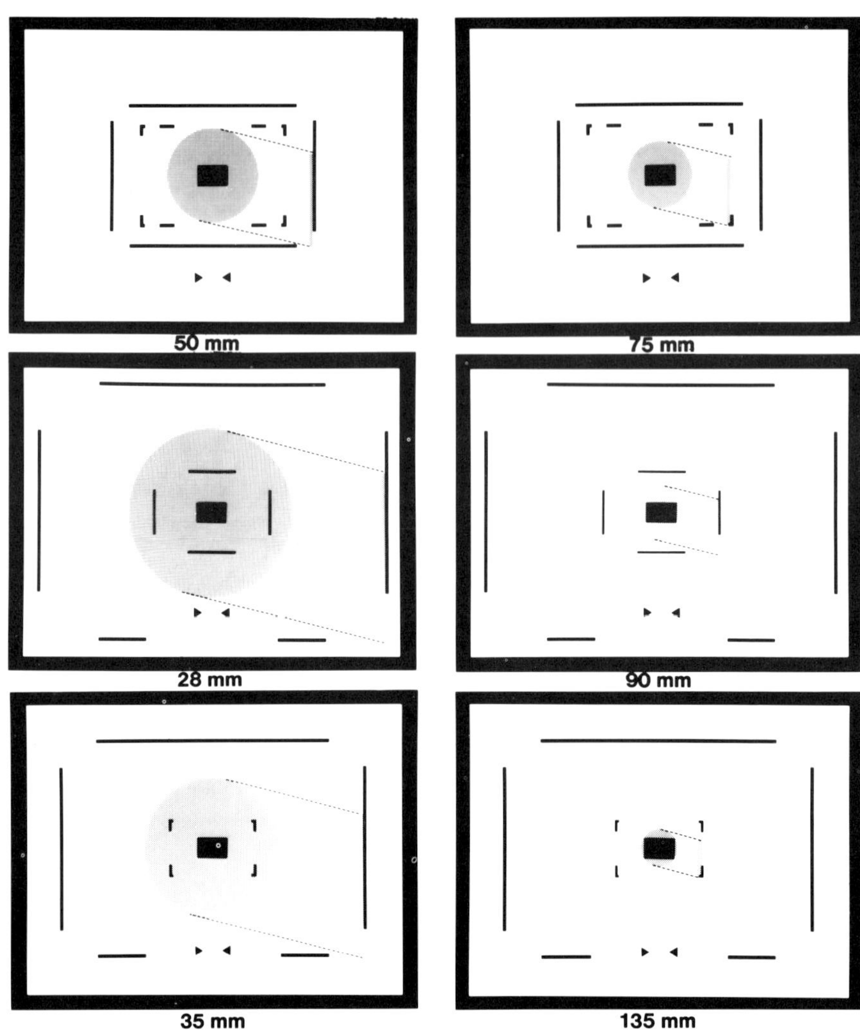

Viewfinder frames of the LEICA M6 showing the area of spot metering for each lens.

the rangefinder when using shorter focal length lenses (up to 135mm) than with the reflex screen, even with the latter's focusing aids. This is a very important consideration with wide aperture lenses used at full aperture, especially the f1 NOCTILUX when the depth of field will be wafer thin. It is also possible to focus accurately with the rangefinder when the light is too poor for detail to be seen on the screen of a reflex. The shutter of the LEICA M is much quieter than that of the LEICA R which has a mirror to move as well. Thus the LEICA M6 is now the only camera in the world for unobtrusive work in dim light with very fast lenses.

On the other hand the LEICA R is the more versatile and universal camera and the reflex screen makes it easier to compose the picture and one can use very long and very wide-angle lenses with it and easily switch from distant to 1:1 reproduction with very little fuss.

The modern photographer, whether amateur or professional, will select the system, R or M, that suits his personal likings and type of photography and knowing that both are equally convenient. No matter which one he chooses, he will obtain a superb piece of workmanship. As one LEICA user once said "After all, a LEICA is just an assembly of glass, brass parts, black and chrome, but to hold it in one's hand, to feel it, to use it and hear the sound of the smooth mechanism inside, one finally realises that there is no other camera quite like the LEICA – except another LEICA."

This certainly applied to the old types which appeal to the collector, and it can be safely said of the modern types because of the continuing quality of each camera. Just to name two points which are exclusive to the modern LEICA: the electrical contacts in the flash wiring are made of an 80 per cent gold alloy and the breaker points of the contacts are made of a platinum-iridium alloy. All LEICA's can perform satisfactorily at temperatures of at least 20° centigrade below zero but if necessary they can be "winterized" to –40° of cold, by changing the standard lubricant with a silicone based type. The several operations of fastening and securing of screws and parts require no less than five types of adhesives; the material that covers the body and which is called "Vulcanite" has been tested to a

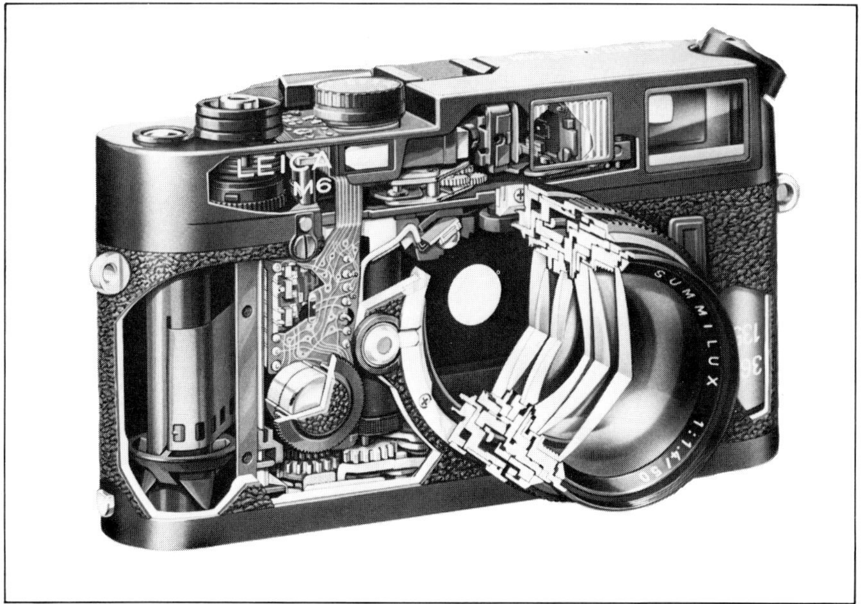

The electronics of the LEICA M6 have been packed into the space traditionally reserved for the self timer on M cameras. The system of reflecting the light from the white spot on the shutter blind to a fixed photocell means there are no moving parts in the metering system.

very high standard and even in the field of the metal finish Leitz has lead the way with the "black chrome" finish, much more durable than black enamel.

As well as the perfection of its mechanism, the reputation of the LEICA has rested in equal parts on its lenses. There are only a few manufacturers of high quality optical glass in the world and Leitz are one of them, although they only produce it for themselves. Glass for LEICA lenses is carefully selected from these makers, but it is supplemented by other special glasses made in Leitz' own glass laboratory. Over the years since the last war they have developed new glasses with high refractive index and very low dispersion which have been incorporated in the notable lenses that have appeared since then. These glasses made possible the apochromatic telephotos, the flare- and coma-free wide aperture lenses, the reduction in number of elements, and hence weight, of many lenses, and the increase in speed from f1.2 to f1 whilst at the same time eliminating the aspherical surfaces of the NOCTILUX. The mounts and diaphragm mechanisms of LEICA lenses are made to the same standards as the cameras themselves. All the cams and coupling links with the camera body are kept safely within the mount, protected from damage, unlike many rivals, and the automatic diaphragms of the R lenses are made to close very fast and without bounce, whatever the aperture set, so that exposure will always be accurate.

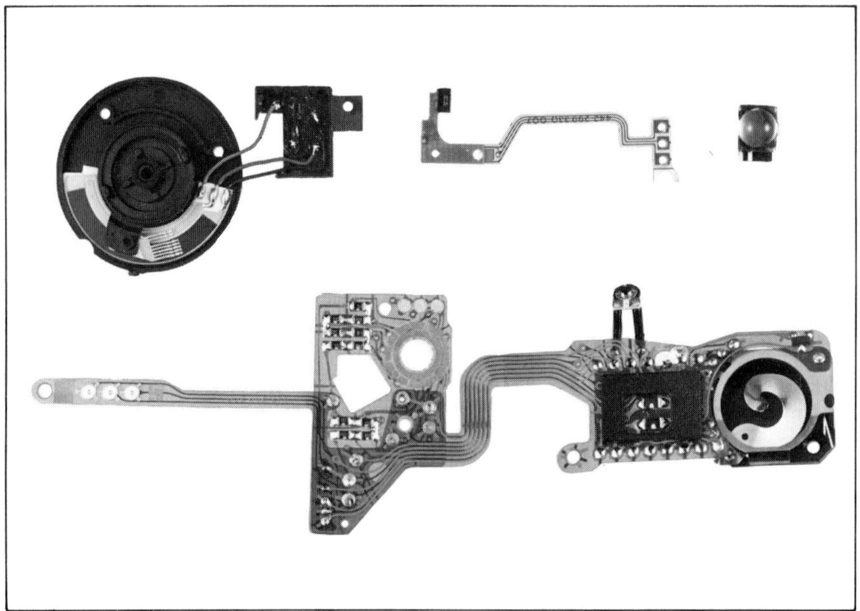

Electronic components of LEICA M6.

Chapter 3

Prototypes of the First LEICA

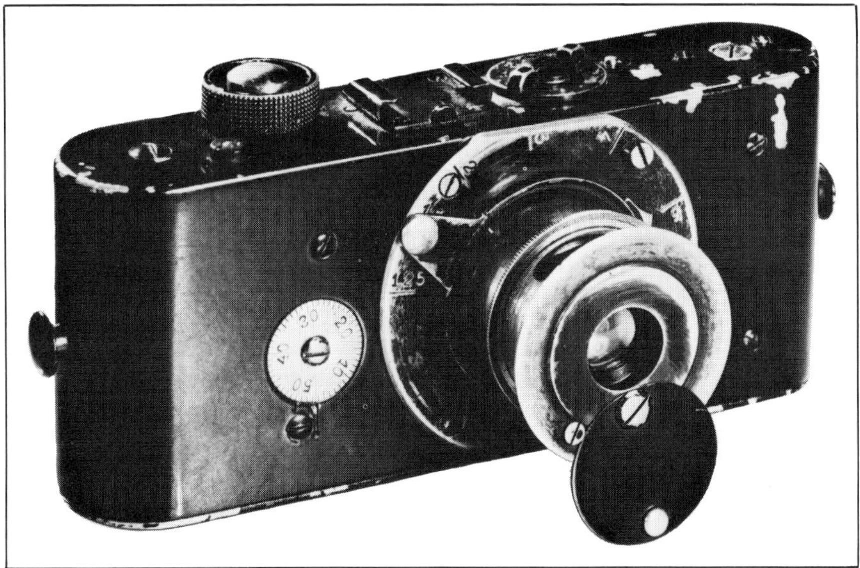

The Ur-LEICA.

The grandfather of them all is a small camera that Oskar Barnack built between 1913 and 1914: it is certain that two such cameras were built (there was a rumour also of a third prototype) and of these one is kept in the Wetzlar museum while the other (the one used by Barnack himself) was sold at an auction after having survived the war in the museum of Munich. It is most certainly well hidden in some unknown collection.

Even if at the beginning the camera may have appeared as an experiment towards a simpler and lighter photographic device, there is no doubt that someone at Leitz thought it a possible commercial venture, because in May 1914 a patent application was filed covering the main features of such a camera.

The mechanism was both simple and efficient: the winding knob advanced the film by the space of a frame, and at the end of the cycle cocked the shutter. The camera body was completely of metal and also compact, thanks to the telescoping lens mount, and the shape and dimensions made it a very handy apparatus. As we would say today, the ergonomics were sound.

In practice though, the use of the camera was not without problems as it was necessary to load the film in a darkroom. It was necessary also to cap the lens when winding the film because the slit in the blind remained open when running back towards the cocked position. But the fundamental features of the future LEICA were present: the image size of 24 x 36mm obtained on 35mm perforated film; the main mechanical system; the layout of the controls on top of the camera; the accessory shoe which in the prototype served to carry the viewfinder.

The camera was built within the smallest dimensions that were compatible with the need to house the few parts of its simple mechanism, so that it was smaller than the production model. In detail, the body depth was 28mm against the 29mm of the LEICA I, the height was 53mm against the 55mm of the LEICA I (excluding the knobs in both cases) and the body length of the prototype was 128mm compared to 133mm on the production model. The prototype in the Leitz museum has two strap lugs at the sides to attach a leather neck strap; a feature that would not appear on the production models until much later and then in a different form on the LEICA III. As mentioned, the shutter consisted of a single blind with a slit 38mm wide, which is slightly wider than the picture; the blind winds on a drum on each side of its travel and is powered by a spring. The exposure time is determined by the tension of the spring which in turn fixes the speed of travel of the curtain. The spring tension is adjustable by means of the winder knob by the accessory shoe. This prototype is not in working order so it is impossible to establish exactly the exposure times, but it is possible that there were two speeds about 1/25th and 1/40th of a second. Higher speeds are unlikely because of the rather large slit. The exposure counter is on the camera front and is marked for up to 50 frames. The release button is in the centre of the winding knob which is situated on top of the sprocket drum. It is worth noting that this feature was due to reappear many years later on the M3 (in 1954). The bottom of the camera opens to load the film and is retained in position by a large screw.

The lens was one of the main problems that Barnack had to solve. The size of the picture being exactly double that of the cine frame cine lenses were not very suitable, as it was evident when a Kino Tessar was first tried.

The lens was fixed to the camera in a collapsible mount with helical focusing. The diaphragm was set by means of a small lever that protruded behind the front flange of the lens mount. In front there was a swivel cap that covered the lens during the tensioning of shutter and transport of film. Even with the impracticability of the lens (it needed to be covered after every picture was taken) Barnack used this camera to take many good quality pictures of exceptional journalistic value. A forerunner of the modern photo-reporter, the inventor of the LEICA himself, demonstrated the great potential of 35mm photography.

On the back of the body there is the Leitz trademark, in the shape of a special condenser which they patented in 1911. It is worth noting that the back of the prototype is removable, probably to allow the exact focusing for different lenses under test. To remove the back, four screws had to be removed.

It is not certain which type of viewfinder was used on this prototype, but the possibility of changing it, thanks to the accessory shoe, seems to suggest that many types were tried, from the simpler frame types to optical ones.

Realising the interest in this historic camera, the Leitz company produced some hundreds of replicas of it during the late 1960's and early 70's, with the marking "Nachbildung der Ur-Leica" on top of it. "Ur" comes from the German "Urbild", meaning "prototype".

Prototype No. 3

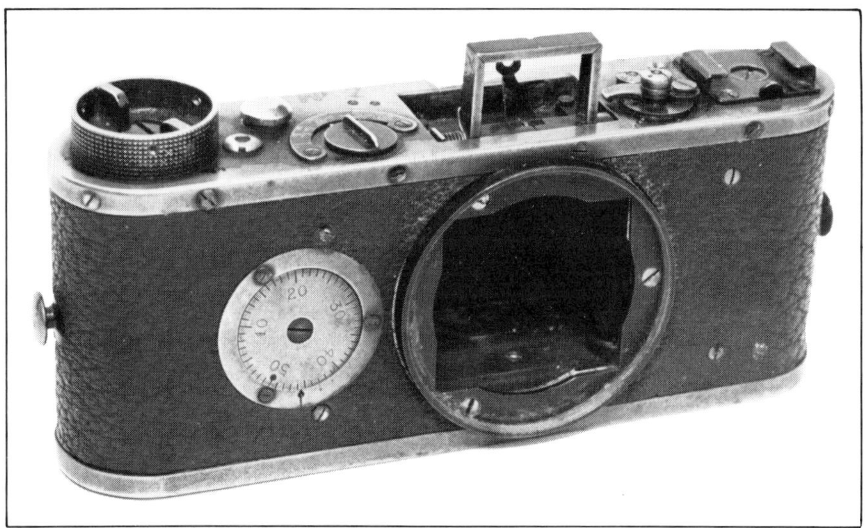

Prototype camera No. 3 without lens.

From practical experience of his 35mm Hand Camera (later to be referred to as the UR LEICA) Barnack was soon aware of the camera's limitations. He continued to use his camera recording life about him and at the same time toyed with ideas for his second series camera.

One of the major problems was the limitations of the shutter, as it operated only at approximate speeds from 1/20th to 1/40th of a second, depending upon the adjustment of the shutter tension. The Ur LEICA shutter had a measured fixed slit size of 38 x 25mm, which ensured minimal capping of approximately 1mm of the filmgate in both the wound-on and released positions.

Barnack set about designing another camera, possibly with a view to seeing his ideas form the basis of a subsequent production model. He decided to redesign the camera drastically, yet still have it fit within the basic envelope of his earlier design which had proved ideal.

The new camera provided the actual stepping stone for the development of the production LEICA as so much of its constructional detail was adopted later in various forms. This camera has been somewhat neglected in respect of the LEICA history, yet so much is owed to its existence.

The date of the camera's origin is doubtful, but it would appear that its design, although a hybrid, is allied closer to the production LEICA's than to the Ur

LEICA, but some of its features are a development of those of the original camera. A reference in "Leica Fotografie" 1960, No. 2, under the chapter "From first Prototype to M3", mentions that Barnack was developing a camera of new design sometime after 1918 and that he had used the Ur LEICA by then for a number of years.

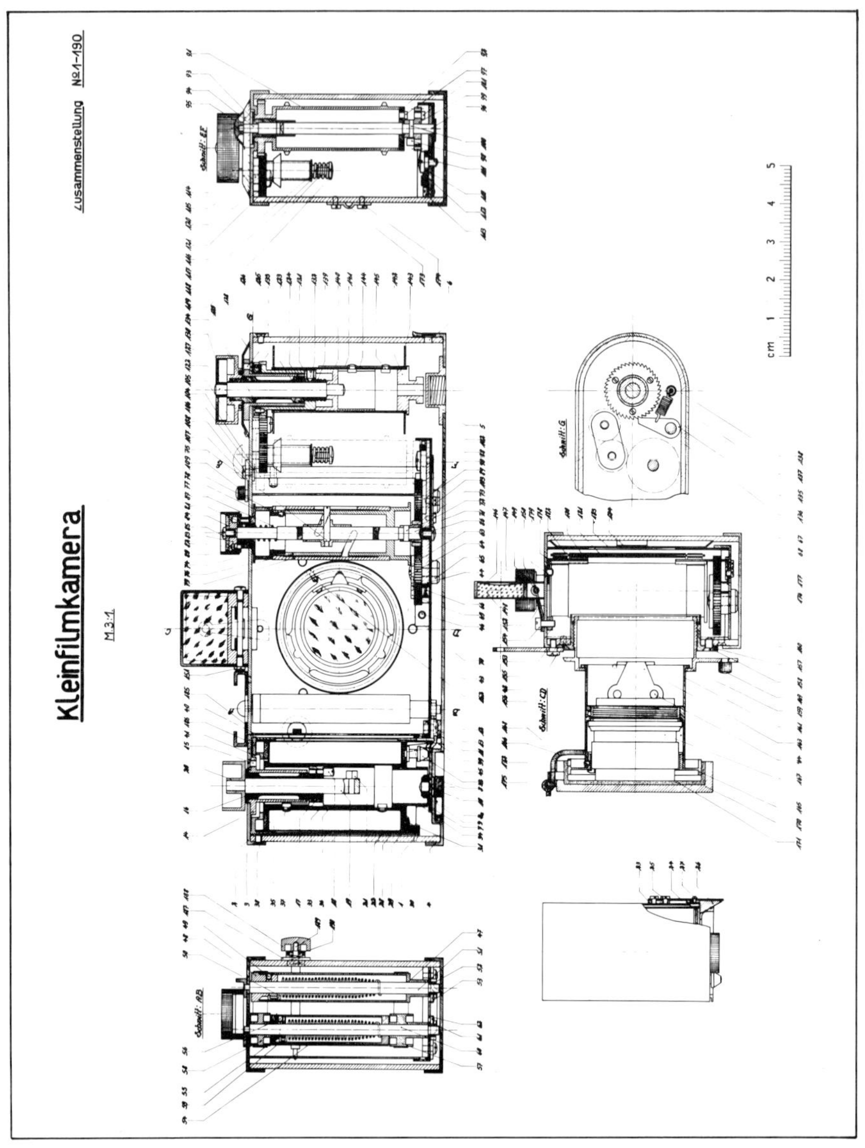

Drawing of one version of the "Null Serie" batch of cameras, dated 23rd June 1923.

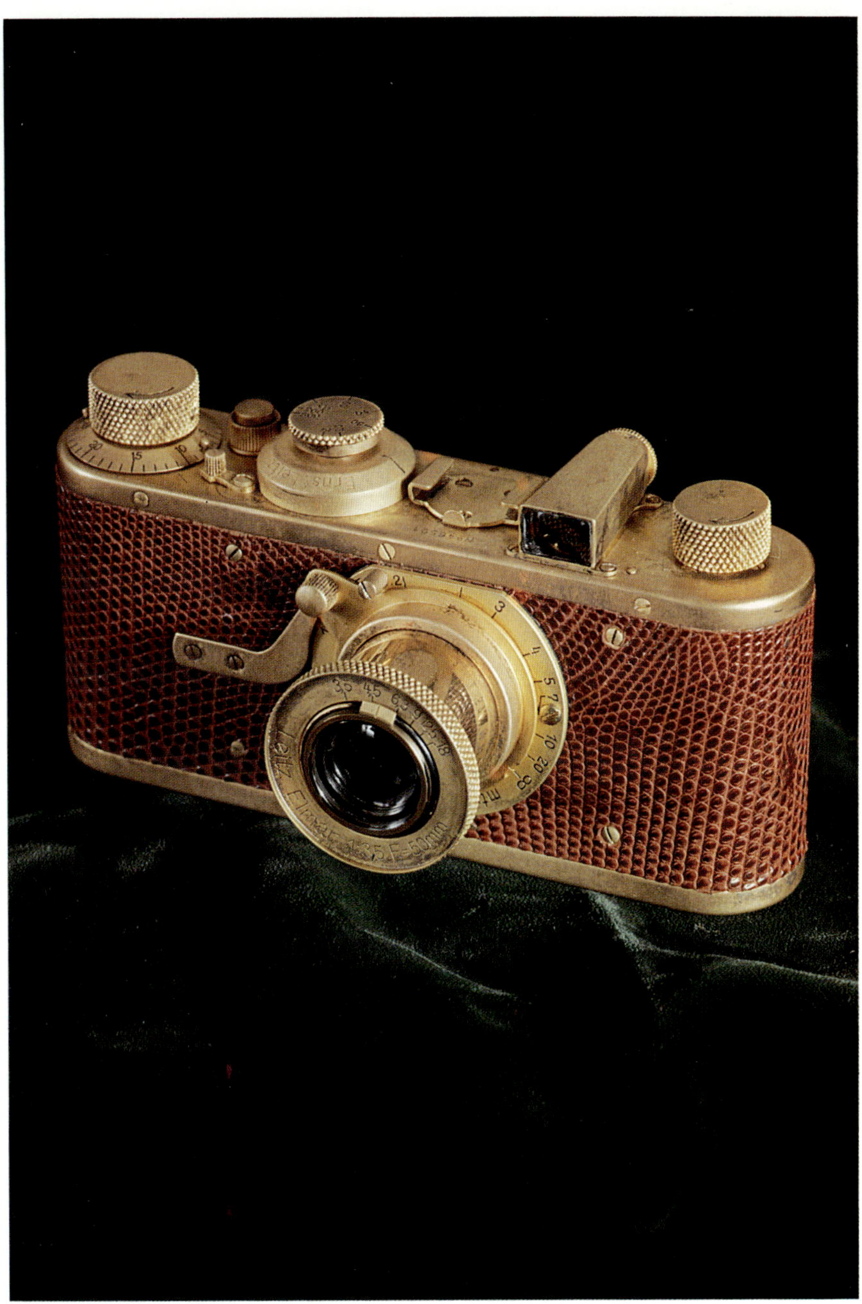

LEICA "Luxus". The finish was a dull gilt and the body covering was lizard skin, available coloured green, blue, red or brown.

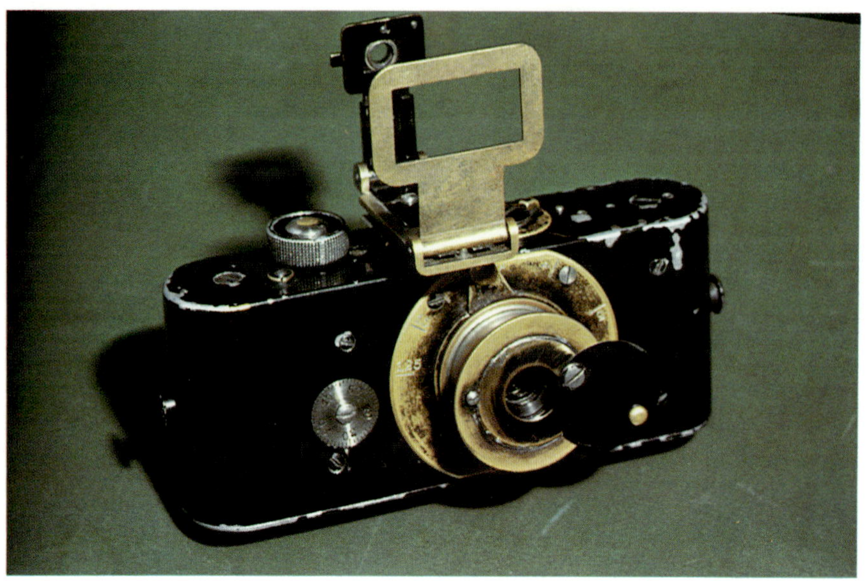

The original Ur LECIA made by Oskar Barnack, with rebuilt frame finder. Now in the Leitz museum.

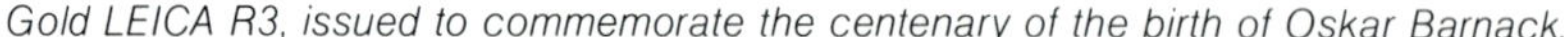

Gold LEICA R3, issued to commemorate the centenary of the birth of Oskar Barnack.

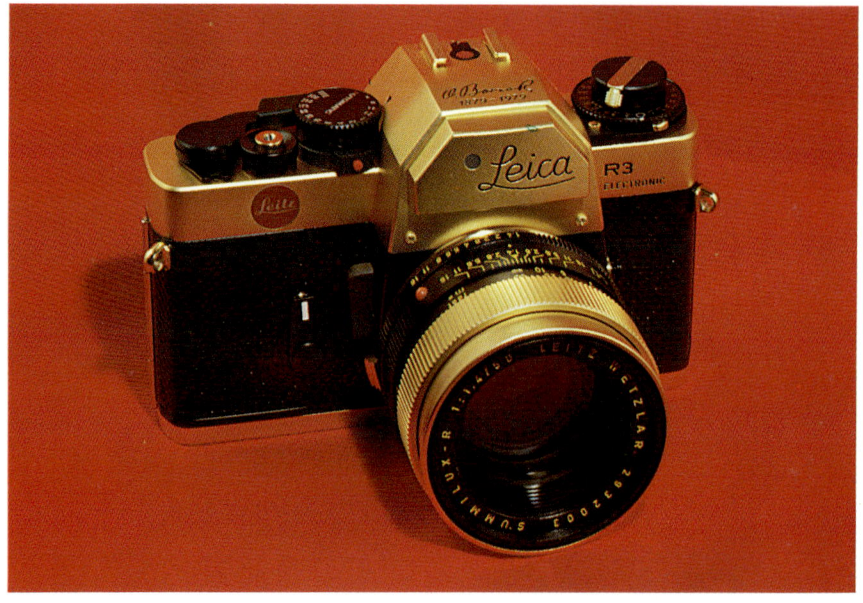

The basic construction of the camera used a brass top and base plate, with vulcanite covered alloy body shell. This assembly contained all the mechanism for shutter and film advance.

The shutter was of a non-capping focal plane type running between two spindles, as in the Ur LEICA, namely a main drum and tensioning drum. The shutter differed from that of the original camera in that it had provision for adjusting the shutter slit width from 2mm to 38mm, thus providing exposures over a greater range. The slit setting mechanism was graduated 2, 5, 10, 20, 50 and "0". When the slit width was set to 50 the opening measured 38mm. The numbers 2 to 50 indicated relative exposure settings equal to a variation of 25 times. It is apparent that the widths do not comply with scale however, since as the slit is reduced the tension increases, thus compensating for this deviation, just as on the "0" series LEICA's.

The shutter consisted of two rubberised cloth blinds, linked together by a pair of adjustable tapes. The required speeds were obtained by a combination of setting the shutter speed selector and the slit adjusting knob. The winding knob rotated anti-clockwise as with the Ur LEICA. However this camera wound the film emulsion side in, the opposite way to the Ur LEICA and all other LEICA's. The camera had no provision for rewind as it was loaded spool to spool in a darkroom.

The layout of the top plate was as follows: Winding knob, Release Button, Slit selector stop, Recess for folding optical viewfinder, Slit regulator knob and locking lever, Accessory shoe (this appears to have been added later).

The frame counter mechanism, which registered up to 50 exposures, was operated by a geared drive from a helix cut on the sprocket drum. A threaded brass lens fixing flange permitted interchangeability of lenses. No lens is fitted to the camera now, but it is evident that a collapsible lens had been fitted at some time with its own integral focusing mount.

The baseplate was of a push-on fit secured by a thumb screw to the base of the shutter crate. The baseplate also had the film pressure plate attached.

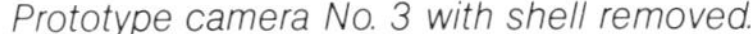

Prototype camera No. 3 with shell removed.

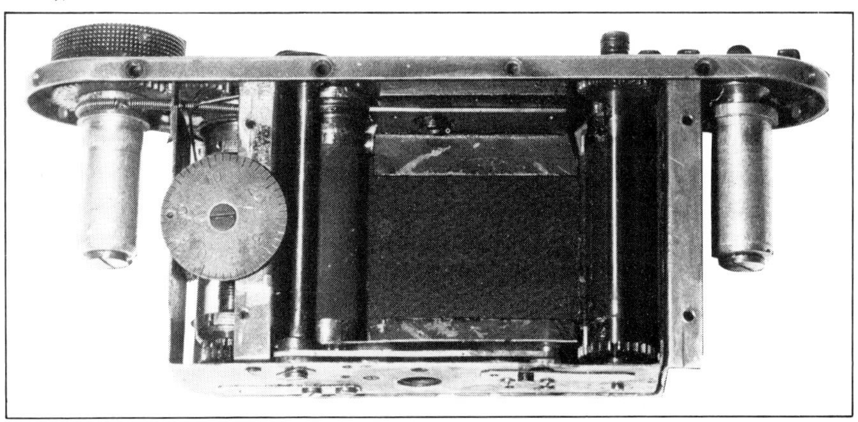

LEICA "Model 0" – "NULLSERIE"

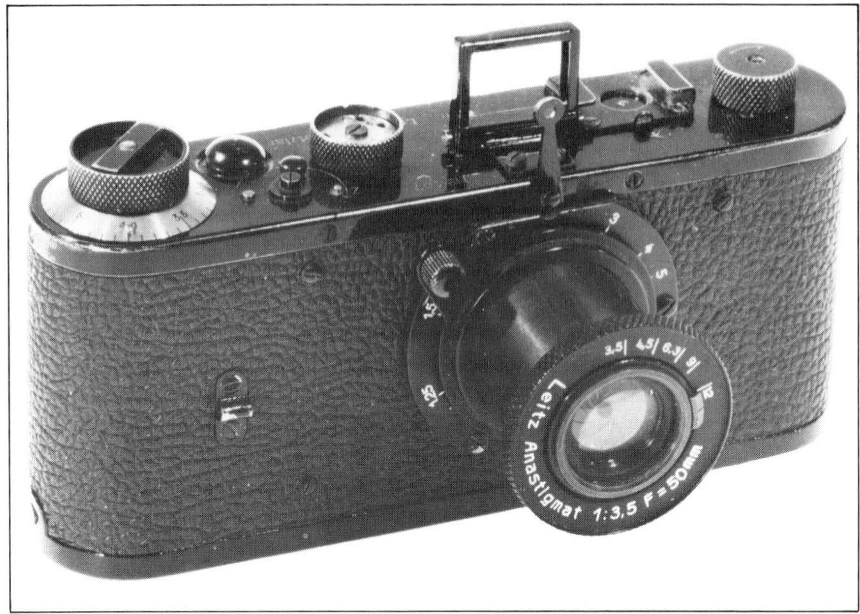

LEICA "0"

The LEICA type "0" (or "nullserie" in German) was made as the preproduction model to test reactions and also to check production methods. Cameras of this series were numbered 100-130 inclusive and so there were 31, but not all of them still exist. We would be fortunate indeed if we could trace half of them.

This type had all the main features of the production model except one, the self capping shutter. For this reason cameras of this series still have the lens cap, although not of the hinged type as on the Ur-LEICA. They were simply attached with a short cord to the camera body. Some surviving cameras have lost the lens cap but there is still the small bracket to which the cord was attached.

The camera body is a section of light alloy extrusion with the shape which is so familiar and with similar dimensions to the LEICA I. The covering is in thin vulcanite and the top and base plates are painted black. The bottom plate opens to load the film. On the top plate are all the controls in the classic positions: the release button in the shape of a hemisphere; the rewind and function lever with three position setting; the shutter slit width control knob; the viewfinder; the accessory shoe and the rewind knob. It is interesting to note that in this range of cameras the viewfinder is located centrally over the lens so that no lateral parallax correction is necessary, but in the production models the viewfinder was always to the left of the lens axis.

The shutter consisted of two blinds whose relative distance can be changed. To set the shutter the procedure was as follows: the winding knob was turned until the index mark on the speed dial came in line with the fixed mark on the camera top; the speed dial was then turned for the required setting, and finally the winding knob was turned all the way to complete the advance of the film and fully tension the shutter. There was, however, an important improvement to the shutter system which had a constant spring tension and a variable slit width; but the shutter winding system was complicated and still lacked the self capping action. This could come however in the production models.

Shutter speeds were not indicated directly, but rather the slit widths instead, in this order:

2 = approx. 1/500	20 = approx. 1/50
5 = approx. 1/200	50 = approx. 1/20
10 = approx. 1/100	

50 was the widest opening and thus the slowest speed, about 1/20th of a second. 2 was the fastest, about 1/500th.

Further control of the shutter was via the reverse, or function lever which had three positions instead of the two of the production models. The R position was for rewind; M for normal use; and the third position Z (zeit) for time exposures, because the shutter remained open for as long as the button was depressed. For this last setting the slit width dial had to be set to "50".

In the original drawings for the camera there is a detail that doesn't appear in any of the models known. This was a sort of button in front of the camera, near to the top, that operated what appears to be a punch to mark the film. Nobody at the factory seems to remember having seen such a detail, nor does anyone know for sure what it was about.

On some cameras, probably the first ones, there was a simple viewfinder formed by a negative lens with a pointer in front of it. When not in use the lens folded back and the pointer moved sideways (specimen No. 109 in the Eastman museum in Rochester has this finder). Other cameras have the standard finder of

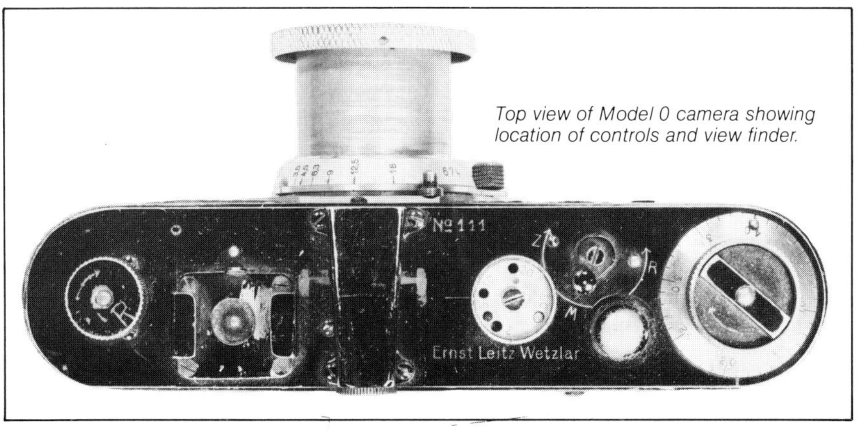

Top view of Model 0 camera showing location of controls and view finder.

the reversed Galilean telescope type (specimen No. 116 in the Leitz museum, Wetzlar).

The frame counter was marked from 5-40 (40 being equal to 0 in this case) because this was the number originally planned for a film length of about 1.75 metres; however it was soon discovered that film bases varied in thickness and so a standard of 36 pictures per roll was finally set for a somewhat shorter film length of 1.60 metres.

On all the pre-production cameras the Leitz Anastigmat 50mm lens was used. This had a maximum aperture of f3.5 and a collapsible barrel in a helical focusing mount. The rewind knob was extensible in most cases.

From information available, most of the preproduction cameras were built in 1923, and from early 1924 the possibility of marketing a new product was being actively discussed.

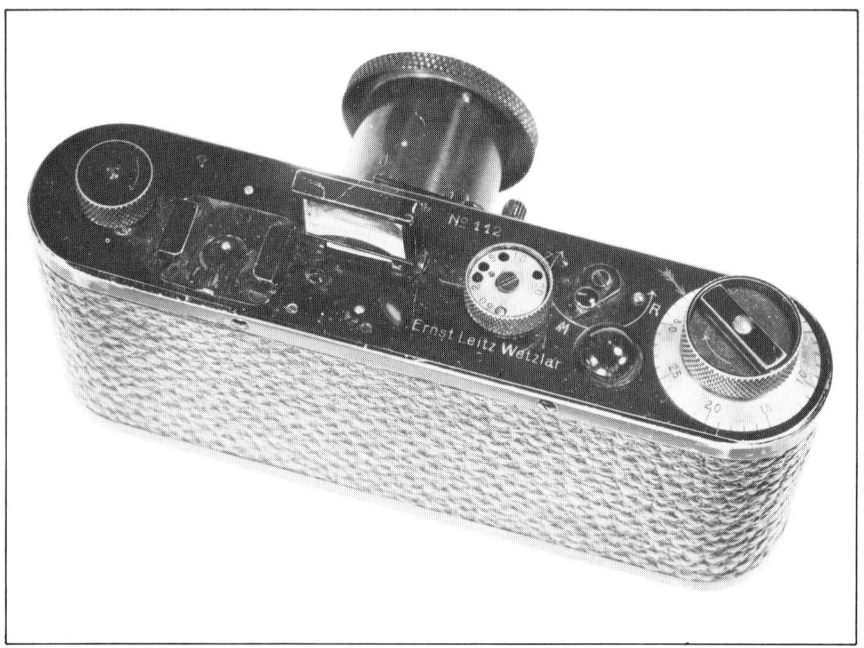

'O' Series No.112.

Chapter 4

First Production LEICA's – A New System of Photography is Launched

LEICA I, "Model A"

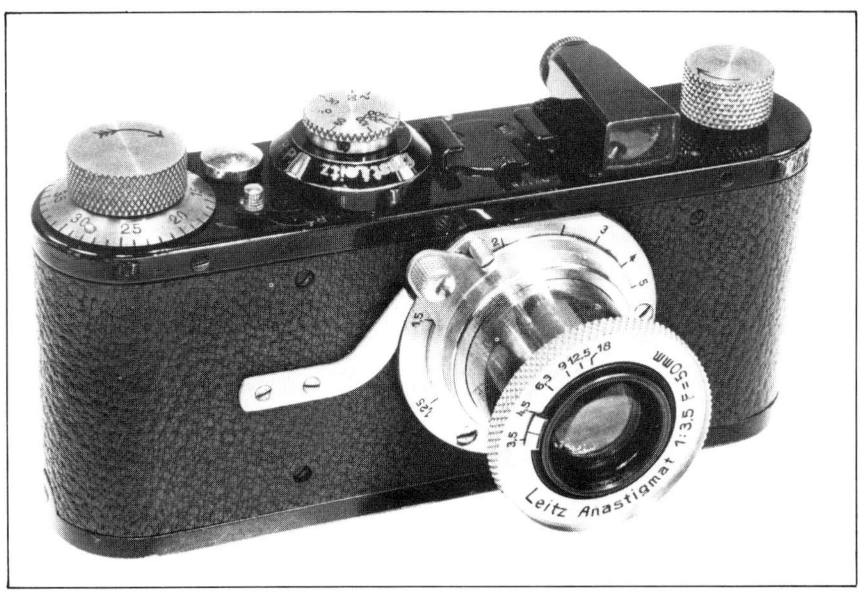

LEICA I (Anastigmat)

In 1924 the LEICA as we know it was born, but it was in 1925 that it made its debut to society and was introduced to the public at the Leipzig spring fair.

The model shown was the regular production type and it was named "LEICA" from the initials of *Leitz Camera*. The name was not engraved, only mentioned in the advertising; on the camera there was the manufacturer's name "Ernst Leitz Wetzlar" and the letters D.R.P. meaning Deutsches Reichs Patent.

The new camera was similar to the "0" Series, except for the interchange of position of the viewfinder and the accessory shoe and the addition of a small housing beneath the speed dial for the self-capping shutter mechanism. The main improvement was the self-capping of the shutter. This meant it remained capped when tensioning the shutter thus avoiding the need for covering the lens.

The external dimensions were similar but the winding knob was a more practical shape. The body was covered by vulcanite which had the appearance of leather, and was often mistaken for it. On the shutter mehanism housing there was an index line which served as a reference mark for setting the shutter speed after advancing the film. The speed change was effected by lifting and rotating the dial. This system was to remain unchanged right through to the model IIIg.

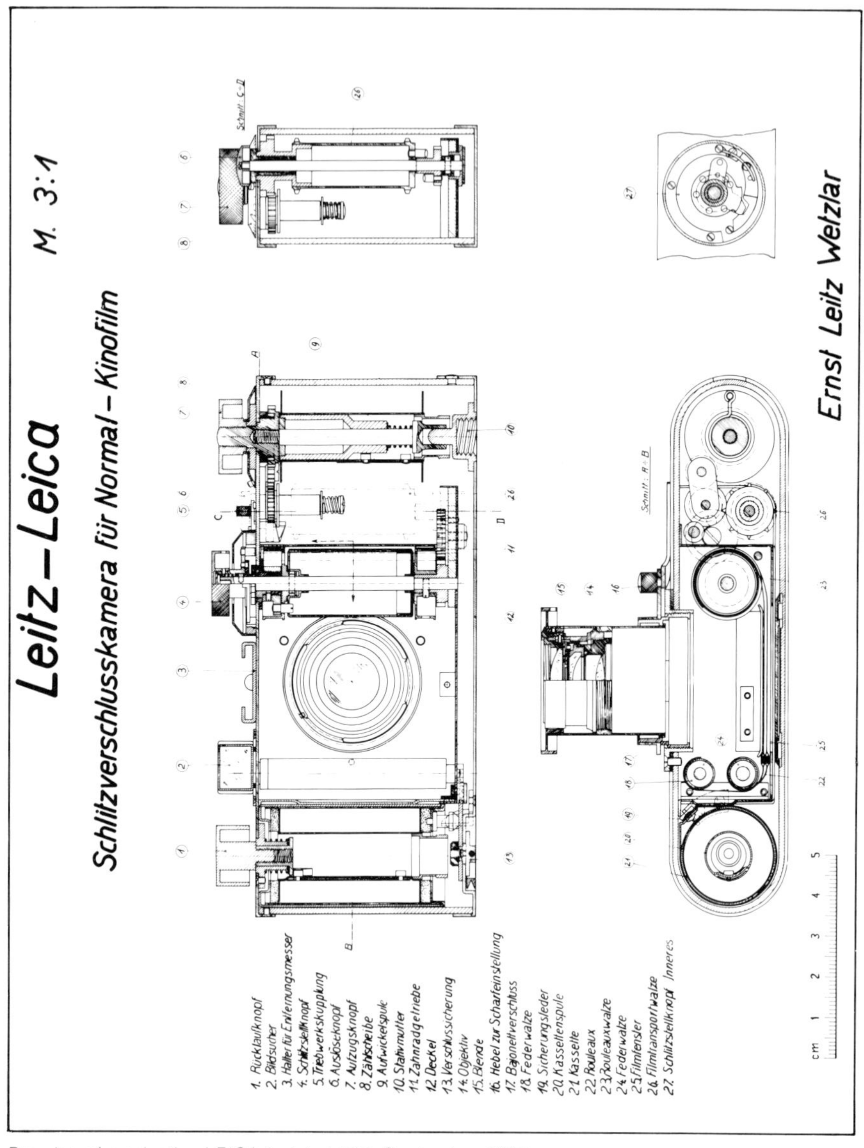

Drawing of production LEICA I, dated 12th September 1927.

The first 500 cameras made in 1925 had the speed steps in the order: 1/25 – 1/40 – 1/60 – 1/100 – 1/200 – 1/500th of a second; later the steps were to be: 1/20 – 1/30 – 1/40 – 1/60 – 1/100 – 1/200 – 1/500 plus time exposure, marked Z for zeit.

In the first year two different lenses were fitted on the cameras, first the Leitz Anastigmat, followed by the Elmax, and later in 1926 the ELMAR, which was to become the standard LEICA lens. All these lenses had the same focal length, 50mm, and the same aperture, f3.5. The lenses were fixed to the camera body in a collapsible mount with helical focusing.

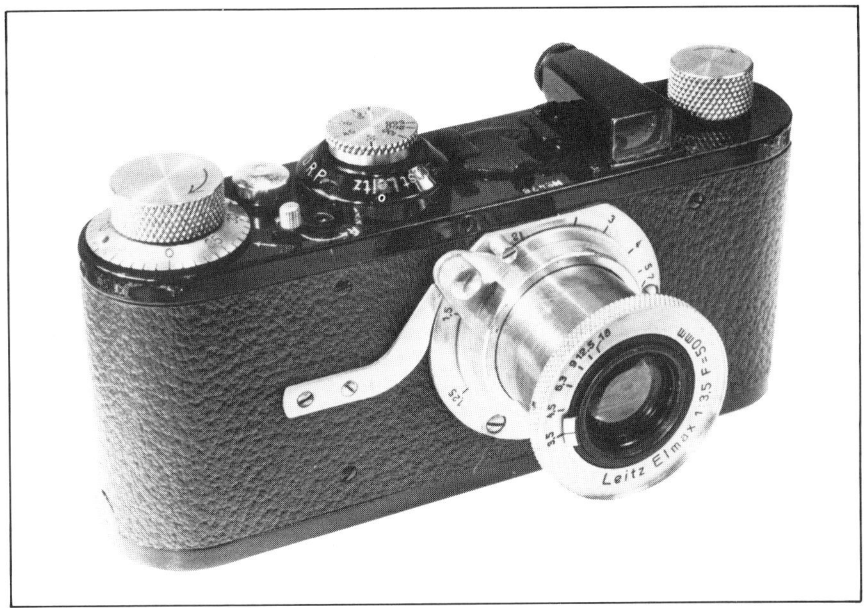

LEICA I (Elmax)

The minimum focusing distance was one metre, but from 1926 some ELMAR lenses were introduced with a nearer focusing distance of 20in. Towards the end of the series a fourth lens was introduced, this was the 50mm HEKTOR f2.5. This lens probably equipped some 1,000 cameras. We thus have four variants concerning the lens, of which the ELMAR was by far the most common.

There are other variations. The initial run of approximately 17,000 cameras were equipped with the mushroom shaped release button. Later this button was changed to allow for a screw-on cable release. Cameras which went back to the factory were updated in this respect, but it is not certain how many remain in the original form.

During the first year camera production serial numbers reached the figure of 1,000, but to be exact 869 cameras were made, as the first camera in this production run was No. 131. At the end of 1927 the serial number reached 5,500, and by the end of 1928 it was slightly over 13,000 (in the meantime a few hundred

Compur shutter LEICA's were also built). At the end of 1929 the serial number was already past the 21,000 mark, proving the success of the camera.

In 1930 the serial number reached 60,000 and of these no less than 58,291 were LEICA I's. These were also known as Model A to distinguish them from the Compur shutter type, which was known on Model B. Model C (with interchangeable lenses) started limited production at about 54,000, and Model A itself was produced in very small quantities from 54,000-60,000.

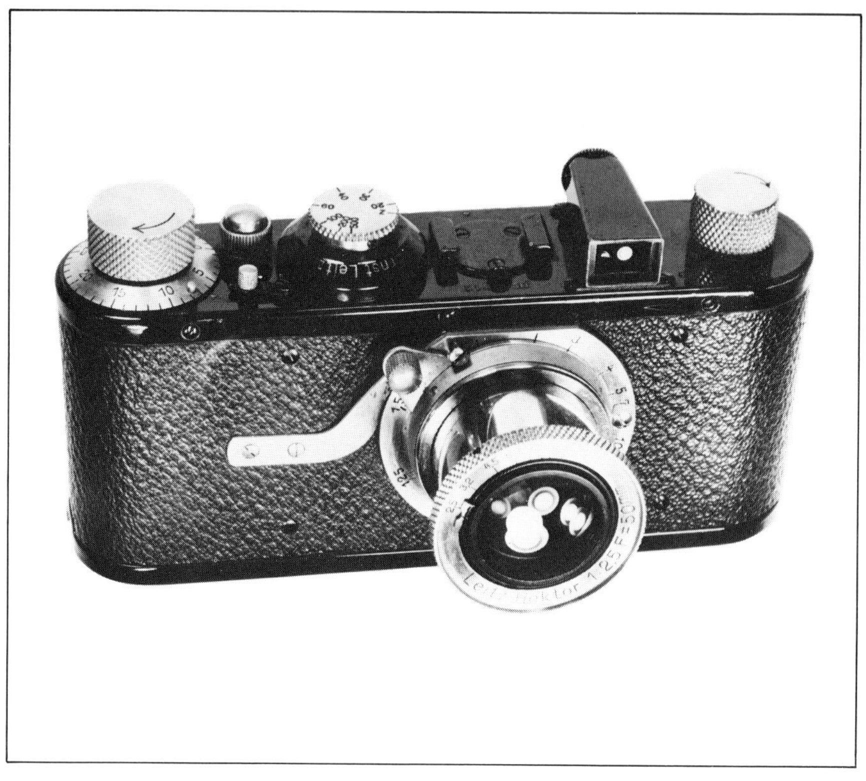

LEICA I with f2.5 HEKTOR and the later style threaded shutter release button to take a screw-on cable release.

There was another variant built in small batches. This was the "Luxus", identical to the LEICA I in every respect except for the fact that all metal parts were gold plated and the camera body was covered with lizard skin, with a camera case of alligator skin. The recorded serial numbers for these cameras were fifteen between 34,803 and 34,817 but at Wetzlar there is Luxus No. 9,781 perhaps the prototype of the variant. A total of 87 Luxus are recorded at Wetzlar small batches being manufactured to demand during the run of the LEICA I. Further research suggests a figure nearer to 115 for total Luxus production.

Apart from Luxus there was another type covered with calf skin but otherwise normal with black covers and nickel plated knobs and lens mounts. No. 35,000 was normal except for a lizard skin cover.

On display at Wetzlar are also LEICA I No. 245 with Anastigmat lens, No. 372 with Elmax lens, and No. 4404 with ELMAR.

Apart from the variants mentioned, there were many lesser differences introduced in a continuous effort to improve the camera so that a great many different LEICA I's are known to exist. Among them are: two different shapes of the viewfinder eyepiece; two different rewind levers (one black, one with nickel knob); two different shapes of the rewind knob. Four securing screws for the top plate on earlier cameras and six on later ones.

Probably the most interesting change, and one that was to affect all production was the one regarding the one-way movement of the winding knob. On the first 600 or so cameras it was a ratchet type, identical to the one used on the "Null serie" cameras. Afterwards it was a simpler, spring type that wound on the shaft and prevented this from turning backwards. The difference is easy to detect because of the peculiar noise a ratchet makes.

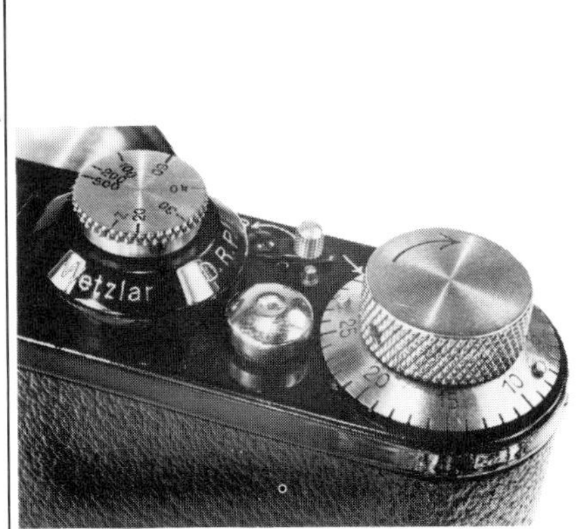

Detail showing mushroom release with indent for cable release.

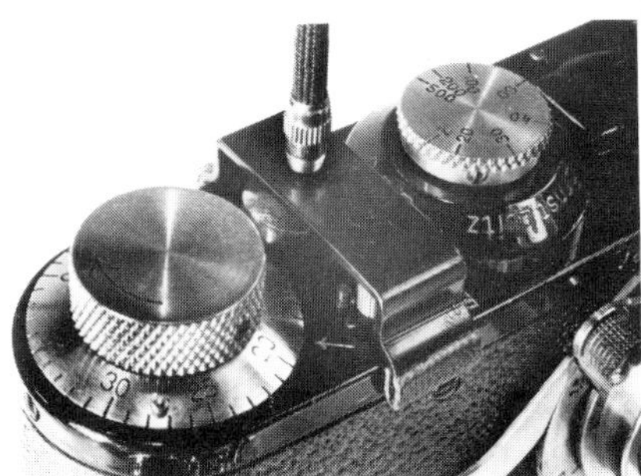

Cable release mounted on bridge piece.

Finally two variants are known to exist regarding the baseplate: one is the piece that unlocks the film holder and the other is the shape of the locking catch. These are differences hard to define in relation to the other variations because it is easy to switch baseplates from camera to camera.

General production of the LEICA I type A ceased in 1930 when the new model was available, however a few were still made in 1931, up to serial number 60,000.

With regular production and sale of the camera established, small accessories were also manufactured. Leitz adopted the fascinating five letter codes to list the products in their catalogues and this system continued until 1960 when numbers were substituted. These codes were soon to become the trademark of the real LEICA expert and a source of amusement. Sometimes the original five letters codeword would receive a suffix to indicate a variant of the same item. So, for example, the LEICA I with Elmar lens was LEANE, if complete with leather case ETRUX it became LETTO but if the ever-ready case ESNEL was used the same camera was LENEL; if however a special case with spare rolls of film was used with the name ETRIN, the whole outfit was called "LEICA", so we must assume that this latter was the classic outfit. The Luxus model was LELUX and the calf skin covered type was LEANEKALB, and so on. The accessory rangefinder was FOFER.

When production of the differing types increased and the range of accessories specially made for them came to an astonishing number of items, Leitz really went wild over the names, as will be seen at the back of the book.

As early as 1928 the LEICA I had an "interchangeable" lens. This was a conversion by Meyer who fitted one of their own f1.5 lenses by means of a screw mount. As far as can be ascertained they originated the LEICA screw mount. These cameras were advertised from 1928. Other conversions to interchangeable lenses are also known.

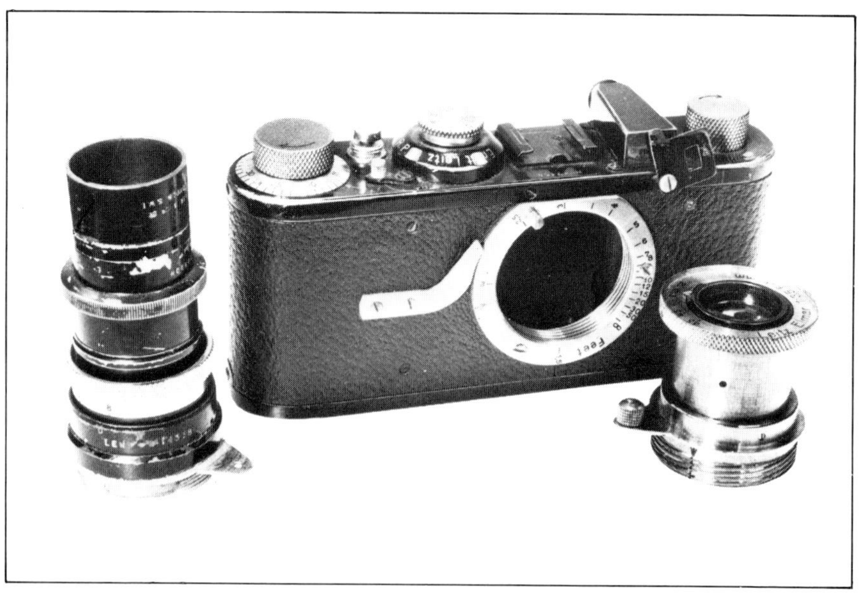

Early Model I non-interchangeable converted to removable lens for using 4 inch focal length lens with swing-over mask on viewfinder. This conversion was available before Leitz introduced Model "C".

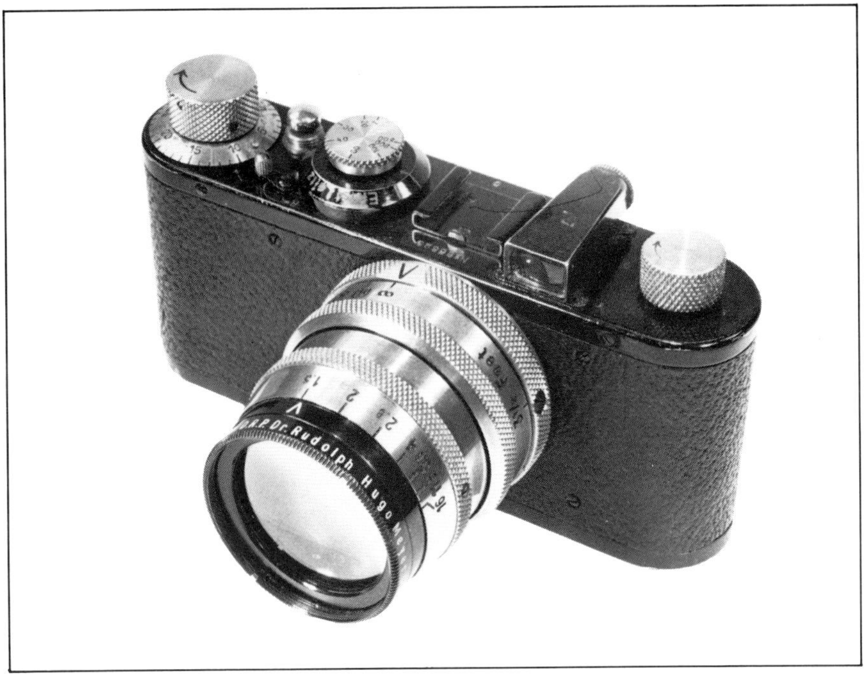

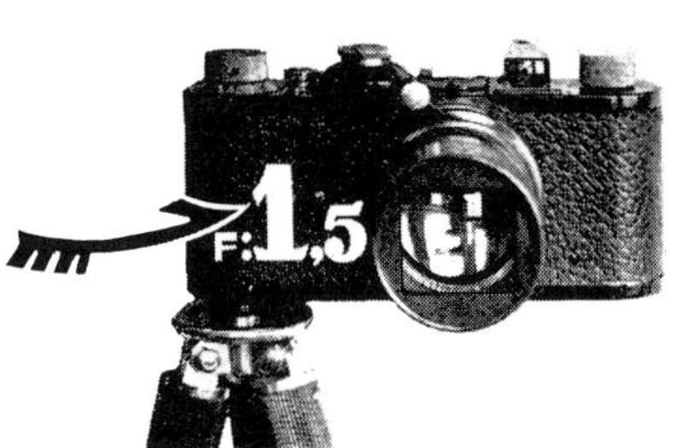

LEICA I with Meyer "interchangeable" lens

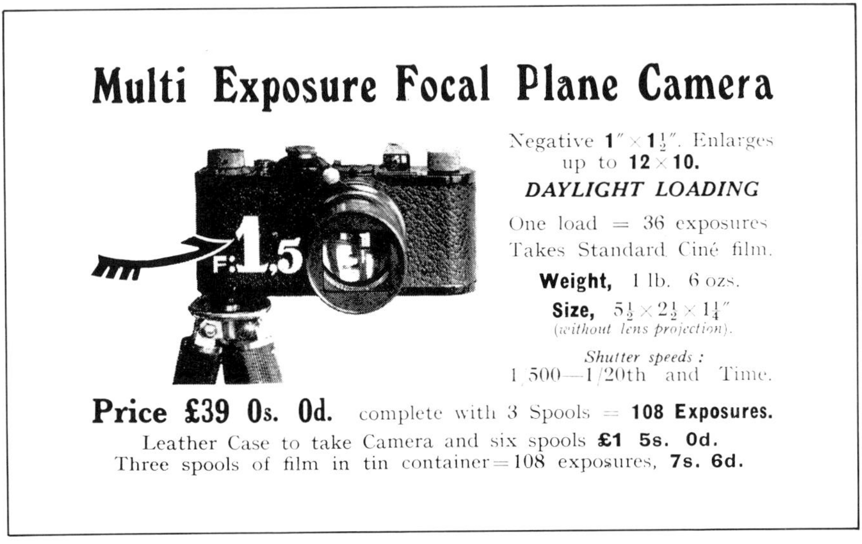

Advertisement for LEICA with Meyer f1.5 lens by Meyer's British Distributor, A. O. Roth. Notice that the camera's name is not mentioned. (The British Journal Photographic Almanac, 1928).

LEICA Compur, "Model B"

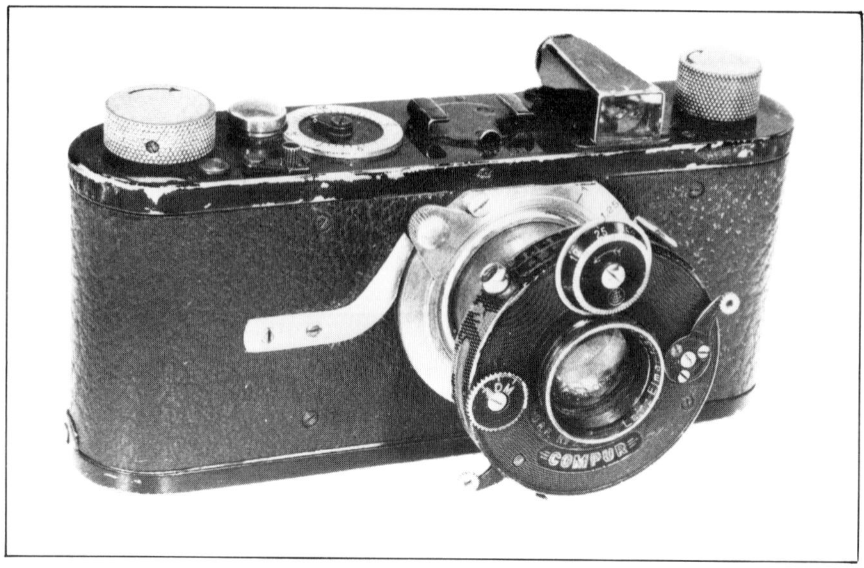

LEICA Compur (B) Dial Set shutter

In 1926 Leitz introduced a variant of the LEICA equipped with an ELMAR lens in a Compur shutter in place of the characteristic focal plane shutter. It is not easy to establish the reason for this move. It could have been to provide a camera with a full range of slow speeds, or some customers may have liked the camera but distrusted the novel shutter, or maybe it was to produce a cheaper model – the Compur LEICA cost 196 marks against 220 for the normal LEICA I.

Compur models were manufactured in two variants, according to the type of shutter fitted. The first variant, produced from 1926 to 1929 and with serial numbers from 5,701 to 6,300 and 13,101 to 13,139, had the dial-set shutter. One dial set the speeds from 1 second to 1/300th of a second, the other, smaller dial had three settings: for instantaneous speeds, for manually controlled time, B; and for time exposure, T. Apart from this there were two levers, one to cock and the other to release the shutter. This shutter was manually set and not linked to the film advance mechanism. The handling of the levers and dials on the front of the lens could alter the focusing. In any case this camera was not a success in comparison with the regular model.

In 1929 and 1930 a second type of LEICA Compur was made, using the new type of rim-set Compur shutter with rim settings comprising B and T and speeds 1 second – 1/2 – 1/5 – 1/10 – 1/25 – 1/50 and 1/300th second.

According to the list of serial numbers a possible total of 1,481 Compur cameras were made, including the 639 of the dial-set type. The rim-set models were made in small batches from serial numbers 13,140 and 51,715.

Apart from the shutters, both types of camera were similar in most other details, except that they differed from the LEICA I by the frame counter being on top of the body where the speed dial was normally placed; the winding knob was simpler and similar to the rewind knob. The ELMAR lens was of the type used for Compur mounting by other camera manufacturers. The release button was of mushroom type. As can be seen from the pictures, the accessory shoe changed from round to square, apparently with the change from dial to rim set Compur shutter.

Code name for the Compur LEICA was LECUR and with the case ETROS it became LECOM.

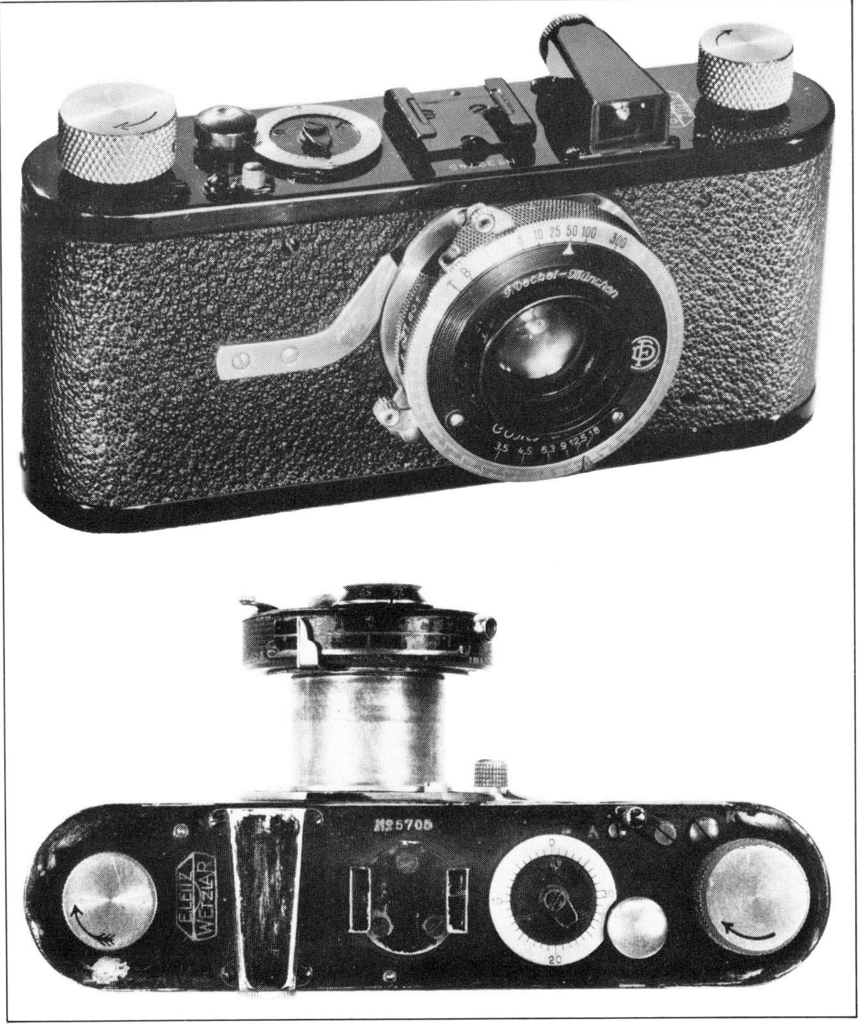

Chapter 5

Versatility and Speed – Growth of the LEICA System

LEICA I Interchangeable, "Model C"

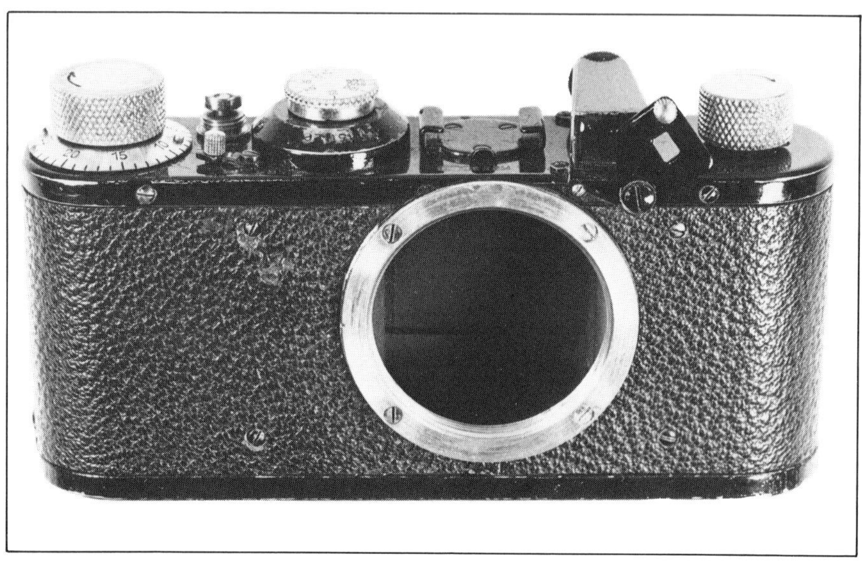

LEICA I, Model C, with non-standardised lens mount and swing-over mask on the viewfinder for 135mm lens.

The first LEICA from Wetzlar with a screw-mount, interchangeable lens was the LEICA I, type C, made in 1931; it was also a short lived model because it was soon superseded by new and improved types. It differed from the previous model I by its lens mounting flange, a threaded ring with a pitch of 1mm x 39mm. With it came new accessory lenses: a wide angle 35mm, f/3.5 ELMAR, a long focus 135mm, f/4.5 ELMAR, the 50mm, f/2.5 HEKTOR and, later in 1931, a new lens was added, the 90mm, f/4 ELMAR.

The first cameras of the new type could not offer total interchangeability, only the possibility of using a set of lenses specifically matched to a particular camera and bearing the last three digits of the same camera's serial number.

Some cameras with interchangeable lenses were made with numbers beginning with No. 37280, and then the main production cameras would start with No. 55,404. There is some mixing of fixed lens type and screw mount up to No. 60,500.

However, the problem of full interchangeability was soon solved with the standardisation of the front-flange-to-film-plane-distance at 28.8mm and thus later lenses could be used on all cameras. To make this clear the cameras that were made in this fashion bore an 'O' marking on the top centre of the lens mounting flange. This "zero" setting was used for a long time on the following models also; earlier lenses and cameras could be modified. The production run of this camera type was in 1931, from approximate number 60,001 to 71,199 at the end of the year.

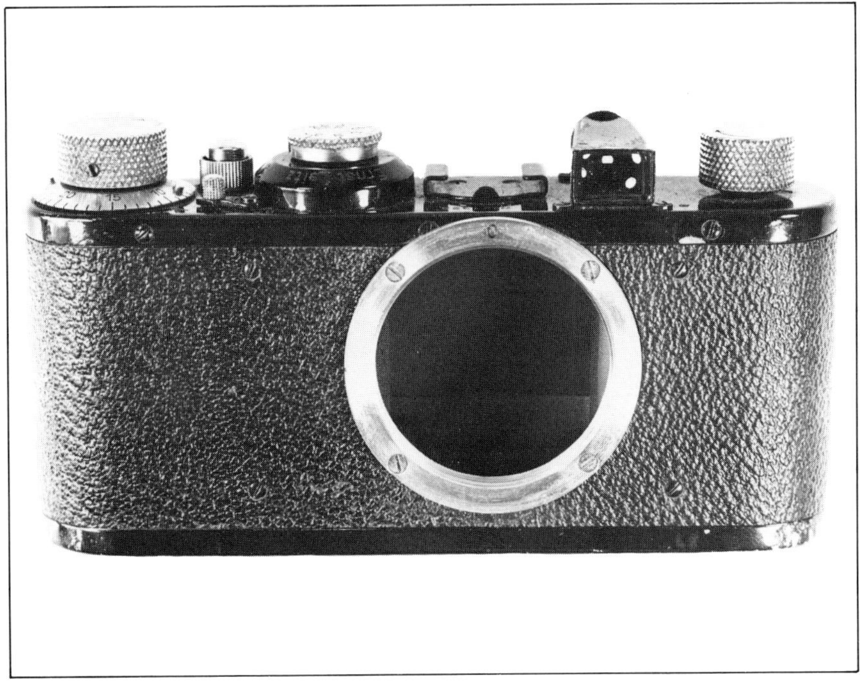

LEICA I, Model C, with standardised lens mount with flange-to-film-plane distance of 28.8mm, indicated by 'O' engraved at twelve o'clock on the mount.

The camera can be immediately distinguished from the fixed lens LEICA I as it no longer has the spring "hockey stick", which locks the lens when it is focused at infinity. Apart from this and the shape of the lens mount there is very little other difference. The release button is the well known type as on the LEICA I after the first 17,000 cameras. All cameras had the viewfinder for the standard 50mm lens but on some of them the viewfinder had a swinging mask corresponding to the field of view of the 135mm lens.

Code name for the camera without lens was LENEU, the same but with three film cassettes was LENIX and with ELMAR 3.5 lens was LEOMU;

appropriately enough the code name for the 50mm lens was ELMAR, for the 135mm was EFERN ("fern" meaning "far" in German) and the wide-angle was EKURZ. The universal viewfinder was VISOR. The HEKTOR 50mm, f/2.5 lens broke the rule by being called HEKTOR which has six letters. (Later coded HEKTO).

As to how many of these cameras still exist in their original form is open to speculation: many were converted to more fashionable LEICA II type with the coupled rangefinder.

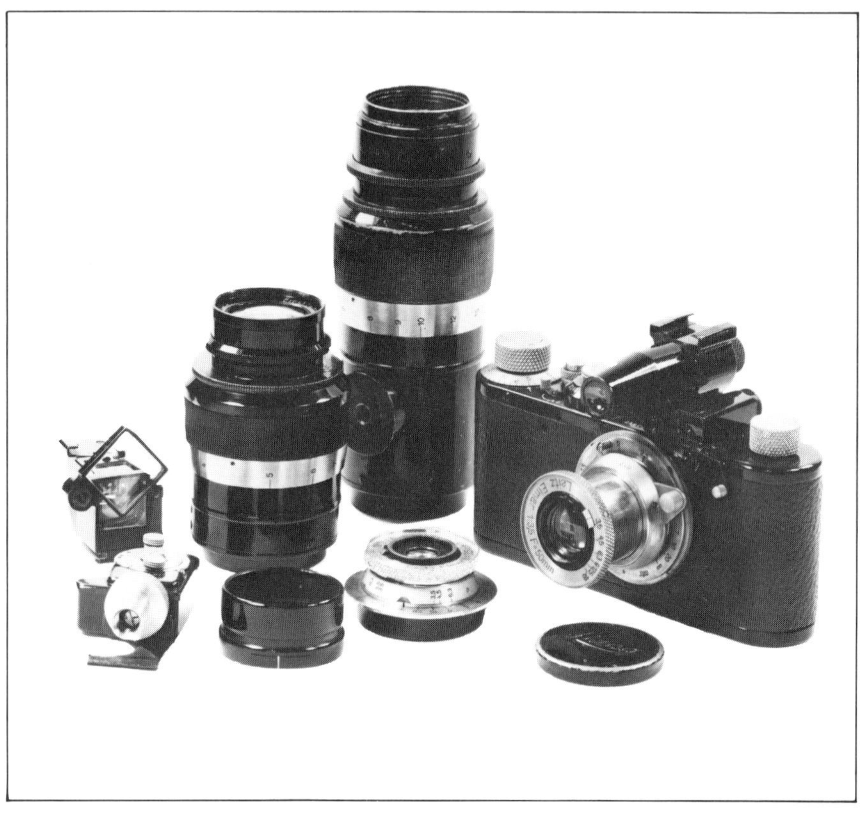

The first interchangeable lenses. LEICA I (Model C) with ELMAR 3.5/50 on camera, together with ELMAR 3.5/35, ELMAR 4/90 ("fat" ELMAR), ELMAR 4.5/135 and lens hood FISON. The "torpedo" finder for these focal lengths would be VISET. This camera also has a swing-over mask for 135mm. Also in the picture are the waist-level finder AYOOC with swing-over lens to show 35mm view, and slow speed attachment HEBOO.

LEICA II, "Model D"

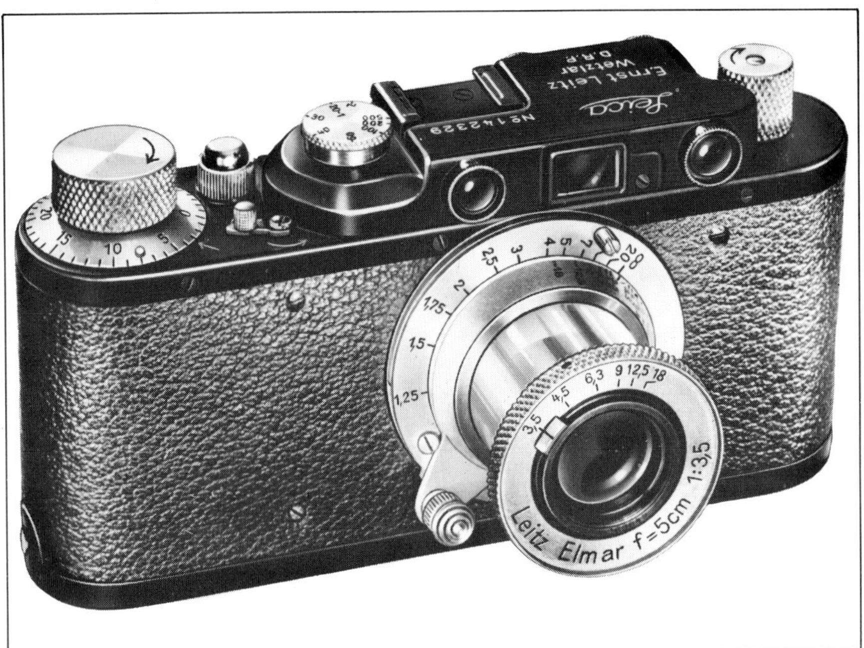

LEICA II

From early 1932 Leitz introduced a model which set new standards for 35 mm photography; the first 35 mm camera with a rangefinder which coupled automatically to lenses from 35 mm to 135 mm. This was no mean feat considering that the LEICA was being produced in quantity and the precision required of the rangefinder demanded a sure way of maintaining this precision in every camera. The roller-actuated arm of the rangefinder is a simple arrangement, but built to the utmost precision.

On 1st February 1932 production of the LEICA II commenced, from serial number 71,200 continuously until number 101,000. It is very unlikely that all cameras in this series were produced in the eleven months of 1932, some were probably built in 1933 when only 3,330 LEICA II's are accounted for by serial numbers allocated in that year, and such an output seems rather low compared to that of 1932.

The main feature of the LEICA II, or type D, was of course the rangefinder. This dictated the use of a new top cover for the range and view finders that goes on the normal top plate, which was still used to carry all the mechanical components. At the back of the cover there were two eye-pieces, the left-hand one (looking from behind the camera) for the rangefinder, and the right-hand one for the viewfinder.

By then the LEICA was a true "system camera" as no less than seven lenses were available. They were the standard 50mm ELMAR f3.5, the wide angle 35mm ELMAR f3.5, the long focus 73mm HEKTOR f1.9, the 90mm ELMAR f4, the 105mm ELMAR f6.3 and the 135mm ELMAR f4.5; also the faster 50mm HEKTOR f2.5 soon to be joined by the 50mm SUMMAR f2.0.

The LEICA II is one of the longer lived models as it stayed in regular production until 1940 and was then produced in smaller batches until 1948. After the initial run of 30,000 cameras, the factory adopted another method of allocating the serial numbers. Because there were several models in production at the same time, batches were usually of a few hundred cameras of a given type.

The first batch of chrome LEICA II's was made in 1933, with serial numbers starting at 111,551. There were still a few black LEICA II's after that; the last batch made during the war ended with the serial number 352,900, after the war, in 1947, more came with numbers 354,076 to 354,100, but there seems also to be a batch 354,201 to 400 made prior to that. The last of the official LEICA II's was made in 1948 and bore the number 358,650. There may be cameras with different numbers from those officially recognised that were converted at a later date. The inside of the camera changed with time. The shutter speed range was, as in the LEICA I, confined to the speeds 1/20, 1/30, 1/40, 1/60, 1/100, 1/200 and 1/500. The camera could be converted to the improved LEICA III or IIIa with the addition of slow speeds with the setting knob in front.

The code name for the early LEICA II was LYKAN when sold without lens; with the ELMAR 3.5 it became LYKUP with the HEKTOR LYHEK; if it was the chrome model the letters CHROM were added. In 1934 however the code names were changed and the LEICA II became AIROO without lens and ABOOT with the ELMAR 3.5 if black and with CHROM added if chrome plated.

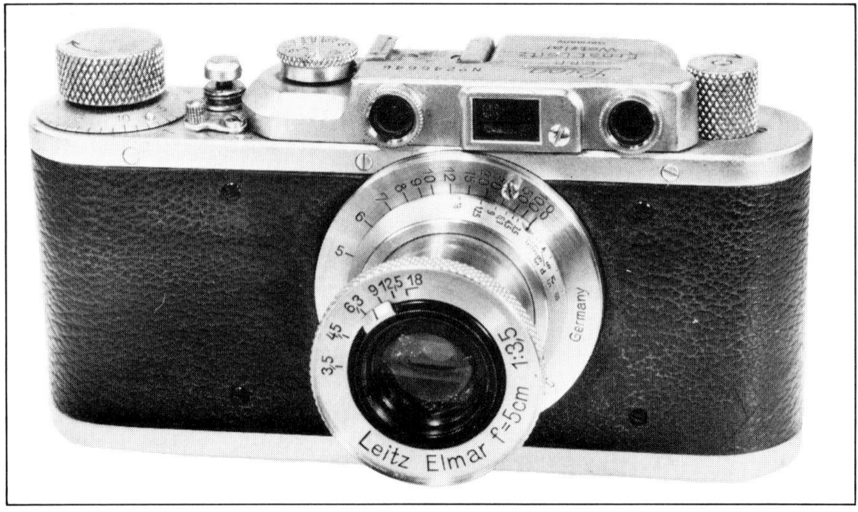

LEICA II chrome

LEICA Standard "Model E"

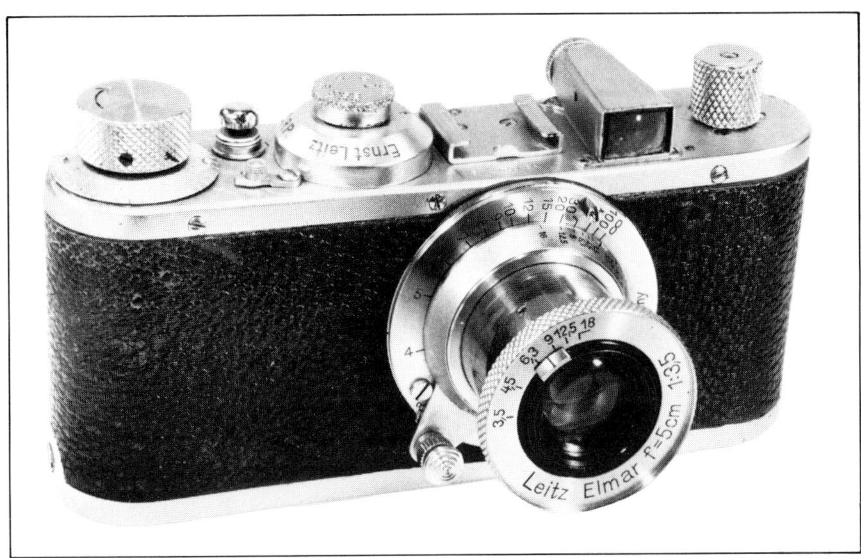

LEICA Standard pre-war

Along with the LEICA II another model was introduced in 1932, the LEICA Standard, or type E. It was similar to the LEICA I, model C, but it had a feature in common with the LEICA II, namely the rewind knob which could be extended to make its operation easier.

The new model was officially introduced in October 1932 and the first models were enamelled black. The serial number of the starting series was 101,001 and in 1932 5,000 cameras were made. Some of these were presumably sold in 1933 because in that year only 50 were registered in the serial number list. In the following years between three and four thousand Standard cameras were made each year.

The first Standard chrome camera was made in 1933, with serial number 114,001. The majority of later cameras of this model were the chrome version.

Although production was continued until 1948, the bulk of the cameras were manufactured before the war. From 1940 onwards only a few hundred were made each year. The last serial number of the Standards was 355,650.

This camera was the simplest of the models made by Leitz and only had a simple viewfinder. However, it could be converted later to model II, and subsequently III and IIIa.

The Standard LEICA only had speeds from 1/20th of a second followed by 1/30 – 1/40 – 1/60 – 1/100 – 1/200 – 1/500, plus Z for time. Strangely enough, the Standard was the only model at the time which did not have "Leica" engraved on the top plate. Only the lens cap had the name on it. Body lugs were fitted on later models, as well as other modifications as they were adopted on other models and if they were applicable to the Standard.

The post war model sported the place for the slow speed dial in front of the camera. In some examples this was covered by an aluminium plate with three screws, in others with a vulcanite covered plate.

The code name for the LEICA Standard in black enamel was ALVOO without lens, and AROOG with ELMAR lens. Chromium plated Standard was ALVOO CHROM, and with lens AROOG CHROM.

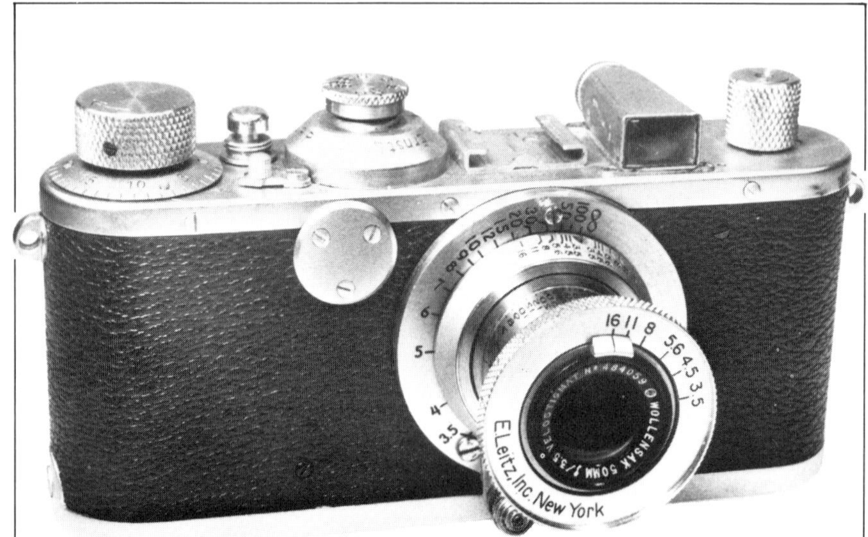

LEICA Standard post-war, shown with Leitz N.Y. Wollensak lens

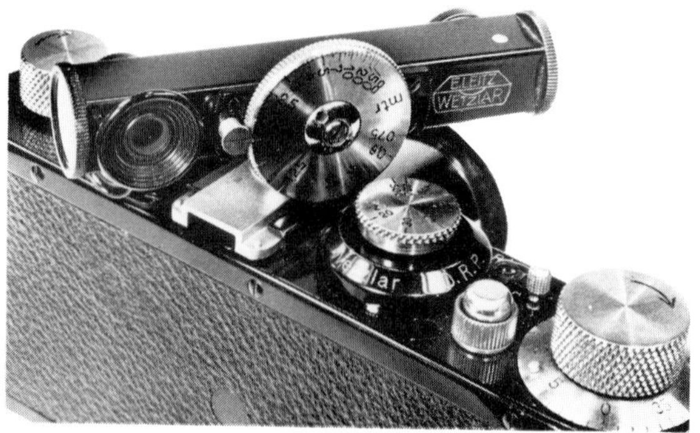

LEICA III, "Model F"

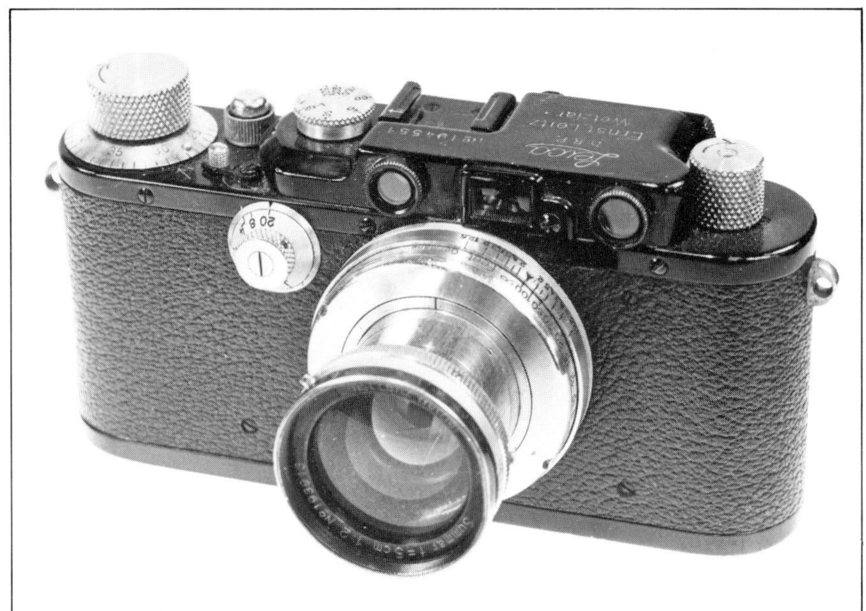

LEICA III

A year after the LEICA II appeared a new and most comprehensive model was introduced with a full range of shutter speeds, from one second to 1/500 of a second; it was the LEICA III. It had a separate dial on the front of the body to set the additional slow speeds of 1 second, 1/2–1/4–1/8 and 1/20, plus Z which held the shutter open until released. The first serial numbers registered for the LEICA III comprised numbers from 107,601 to 107,757 but that series was used on cameras made in 1934. Thus the first LEICA III's made in 1933 were in the series from 108,651 to 108,700. (Early lists of the model had indicated that the first LEICA III was No. 109,001). Production of Model III ceased in 1939 with No. 343,100.

Apart from the important addition of the slow shutter speeds, which made the LEICA competitive with any Compur shutter camera, there were subtle changes in other parts. Firstly there was the welcome addition of a lug on each side of the body to fasten the neckstrap. Secondly was the improvement to the optical system of the rangefinder which now had a magnification ratio of 1.5, which helped more accurate rangefinding with high speed and long lenses, moreover the rangefinder eyepiece had a focusing adjustment whereby a lever worked round the eyepiece itself, in order that the user could adjust the optical system to suit his own eyesight. Also on the LEICA III was added accommodation for the rapid advance baseplate: this required modification of the take-up spool shaft, with a notch to engage the SCNOO device.

On the rangefinder top plate was engraved the name "Leica" (as on the LEICA II), the maker's name "Ernst Leitz Wetzlar" and "D.R.P." The serial number was also on the rangefinder cover.

The LEICA II and LEICA III were similar in most details, since LEICA II's made after the introduction of the LEICA III had the same improvements. At first the LEICA III was made in black but it was soon also made in chrome, this from serial number 116,001. It must be added that when a camera was finished in chrome all other parts were too, including the knobs, which on the black cameras were nickel plated.

A black LEICA III was coded AFOOV, and with ELMAR f3.5 lens was ACOOS; with the fast SUMMAR f2 lens, introduced with the camera, it was ACHOO. Chrome models had the same names with CHROM added, as usual.

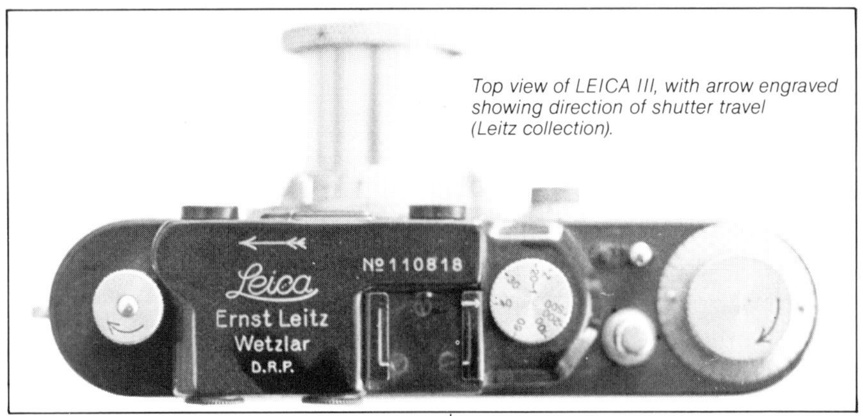

Top view of LEICA III, with arrow engraved showing direction of shutter travel (Leitz collection).

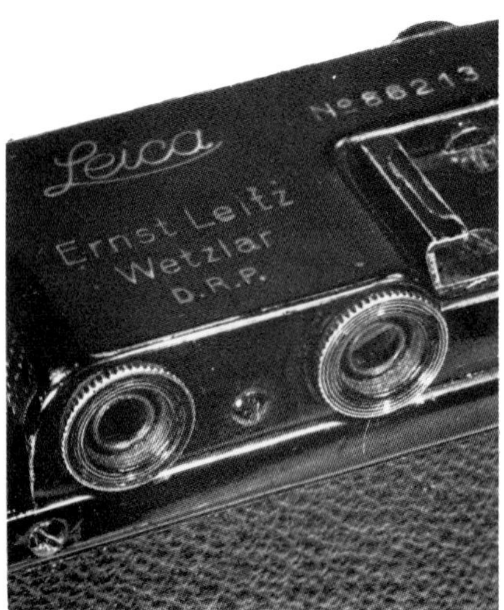

Viewfinder/Rangefinder on LEICA II

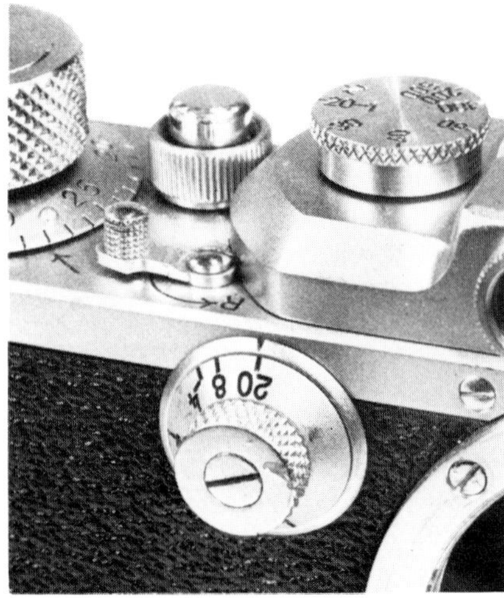

Detail of slow speed dial on LEICA III

LEICA 250, "Model FF" and "GG"

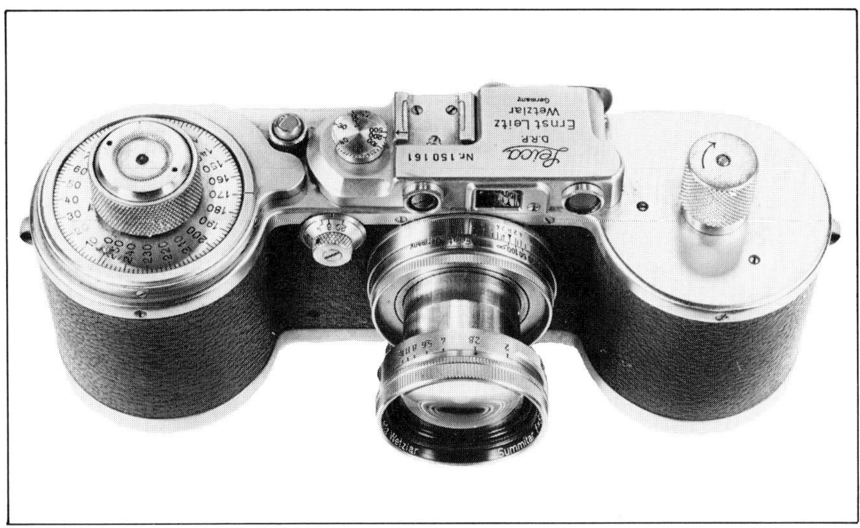

LEICA 250 in chrome, "FF" model.

The big LEICA, LEICA 250 or Reporter LEICA, was developed in 1933 when the first two cameras were made. This was known in the factory as type FF, as it followed the LEICA III which was the type F. This is a good example of the early system of indicating the models with successive letters of the alphabet.

The most noticeable feature of this camera was the increased size, to hold special containers for ten metres of film, which enabled one to take up to 250 exposures, hence the name of the camera. It was also called "Reporter" because it was felt that this camera would be useful to the photo-journalist, who could either take up to 250 pictures or partially use the film and then remove only the exposed film if required. For using the remaining film an empty cassette could then be inserted into the take-up end of the camera. The film cassettes were made to automatically open and close when opening and closing the bottom of the camera. A point worth noting is that this was the only LEICA with cassette to cassette operation.

The shutter mechanism of the production "250" was similar to that of the LEICA III with slow speeds of one second, $1/2 - 1/4 - 1/8 -$ and $1/20$ on the front knob (plus T) and speeds from $1/20$ to $1/500$ selected by the top dial. When the LEICA IIIa was introduced with a top speed of $1/1000$ sec. the "250" was also given this speed and referred to as the "GG".

The production run of the big LEICA started in 1934 with 60 cameras, then in 1935 70 were made, and also in 1936. The following years an average of 100 cameras were made annually, including the wartime years. Production totalled 952, including two prototypes.

The cameras were originally black. A prominent feature, apart from size, was the frame counter, located as usual round the winding knob. It had a special epicyclic gearing which allowed the dial to move slowly, and only after two exposures, instead of as in the normal LEICA's where the exposure counter turned all the way with the knob. Eventually this system was introduced on the normal LEICA's as well.

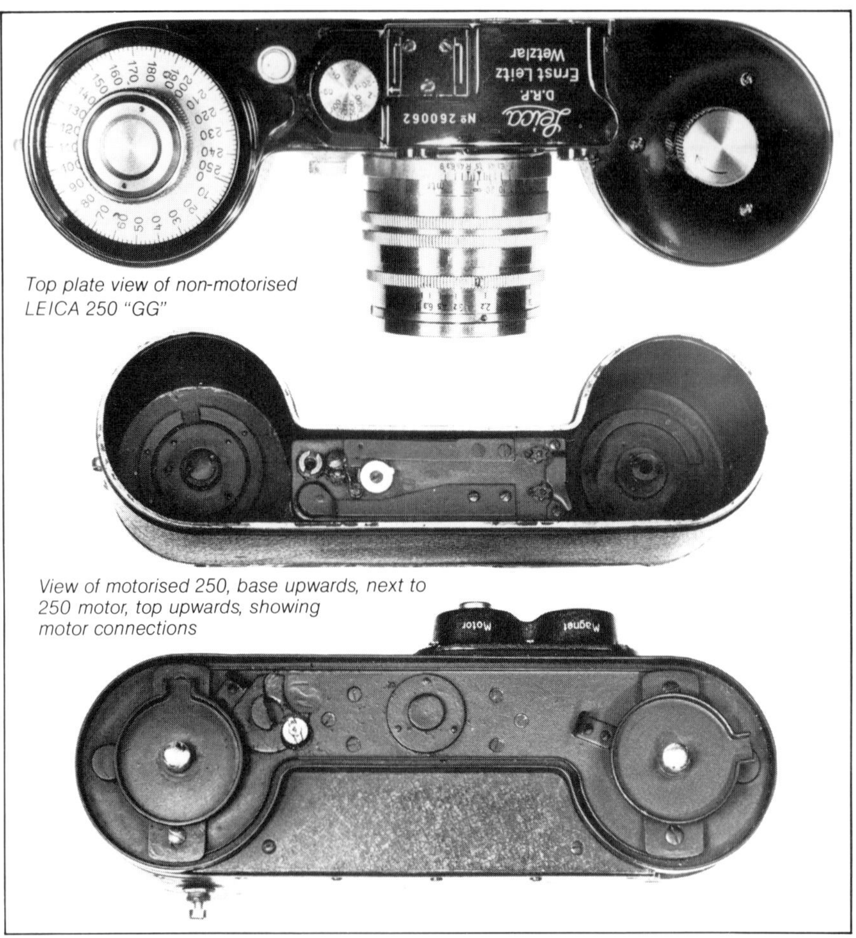

Top plate view of non-motorised LEICA 250 "GG"

View of motorised 250, base upwards, next to 250 motor, top upwards, showing motor connections

The first two cameras were 114,051 and 114,052 (without slow speeds as the LEICA II). After that serial numbers corresponded to the years in which they were made. The one kept at the Leitz museum in Wetzlar bears the number 353,753 and is therefore in the last batch (ending with No. 353,800 made in 1943). Some cameras, destined for the American market, were disassembled and chromed; but there were very few of these cameras.

Before World War II the "250" was specially prepared to take an electric motor drive, which made full advantage of the long film charge. There were probably less than 200 of these motor drive cameras made, which are externally indistinguishable from the normal camera, except that an "M" is engraved before the serial number. It is not certain that all motorised cameras have the M, but at least some do. Internal coupling to the motor was by means of a slotted shaft. There are also examples of the 250 with IIIf type flash synchronisation which would have been installed when the camera was returned to Wetzlar in later years for upgrading.

The code name for the "250" was LOOMY without lens, and LOOYE with ELMAR f3.5 lens. Also a special ever-ready case ESFOO was supplied and with this the camera, complete with two cassettes, was ready to use.

LEICA IIIa, "Model G"

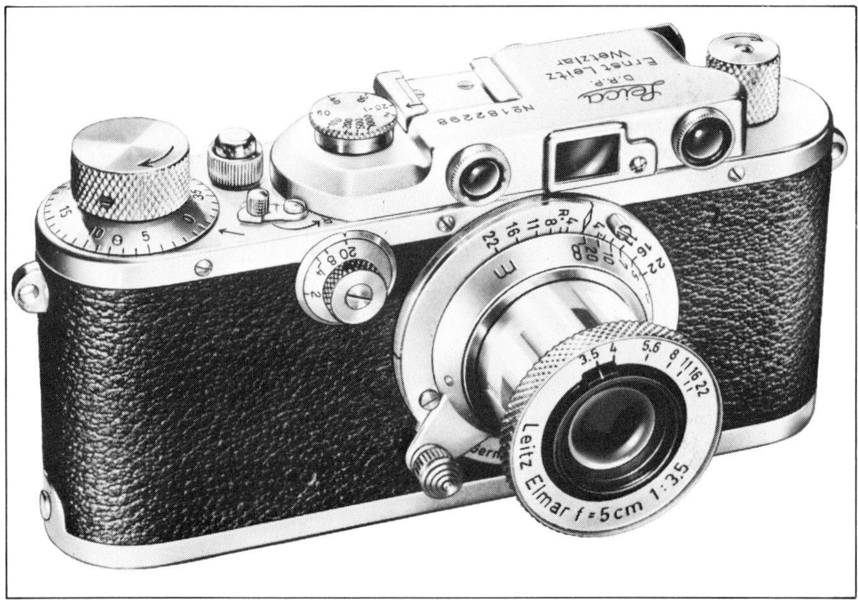

LEICA IIIa

The next improvement on the LEICA was the addition of a top speed of 1/1000 of a second. The camera became a necessity for sports photographers who wanted to obtain action shots. It was perhaps no coincidence that in 1935 when the LEICA IIIa was introduced, German racing cars were also at their fastest.

The IIIa was also called type G, (although model IIIb introduced in 1938 was also named type G). This was to be the last time letters of the alphabet were used in this way.

The first serial number in 1935 was 156,201. Later the camera was built in batches intermixed with other types and 200-300 cameras of each type were produced per batch. The first two years' production of models III and IIIa were about equal, but in the following years production of the IIIa was twice of that of III. Up to 1939 a total of 91,000 IIIa's were built, against 80,000 III's, 53,000 II's and 27,000 Standards. The model IIIb, which was the latest model at that time, accounted for some 20,000 cameras. The model IIIa was produced in diminishing quantities during and after the war, until production ceased in 1950 with serial number 357,200.

The main feature of the LEICA IIIa was the shutter speed range from T (the shutter remains open) 1 second – 1/2 – 1/4 – 1/8 – 1/20 on the front dial, 1/20 – 1/40 – 1/60 – 1/100 – 1/200 – 1/500 – 1/1000 and Z (shutter remains open while release button is depressed) on the speed dial on top.

The top cover of the rangefinder and viewfinder was still separate from the top plate and the two eyepieces were still well apart, as on the LEICA III.

The model IIIa served also as a basis for a half format camera (vertical frame of 18 x 24mm), and in fact one of the experimental models in Wetzlar bears the serial number 357,151 which belongs to the last batch of IIIa's. These half frame cameras made mainly by Ernst Leitz Canada, had numbers of a series immediately following the last IIIa, ie 357,201, that had not been allotted elsewhere.

The LEICA IIIa was produced only in chrome finish. However, if an earlier model black camera was sent back to the factory for conversion to IIIa, the finished rebuild would be a black IIIa synchronized model.

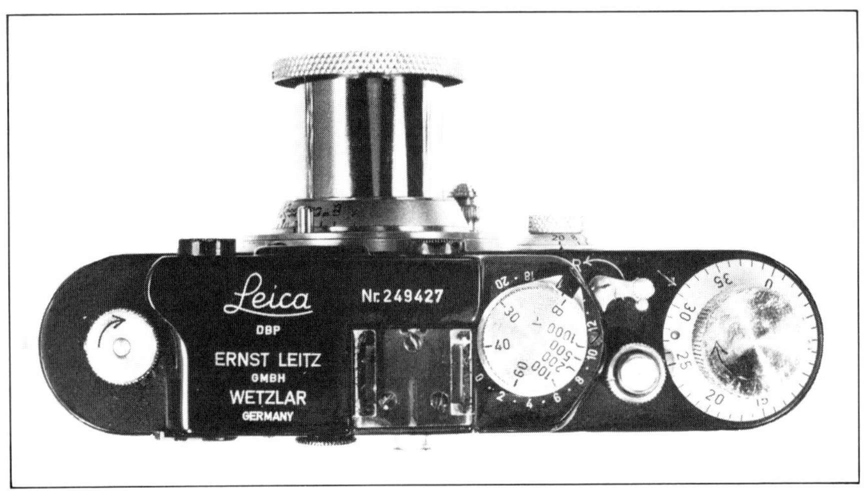

Post-war IIIa flash snyc. conversion

During the 1950's, after the introduction of the IIIf, Leitz at Wetzlar offered the service of converting earlier LEICA models to the IIIf black sync. Leitz would also upgrade the camera and the owner would in fact have an almost new camera returned to him. The top plate and main shutter had to be replaced. The above photograph is an example.

When an earlier camera such as a II was returned to the factory for upgrading, strap eyelets would also be fitted.

Some of these cameras have a particular value to collectors because of special engravings, such as the "Monté en Sarre" ones described below, and the military version which are dealt with in a later chapter.

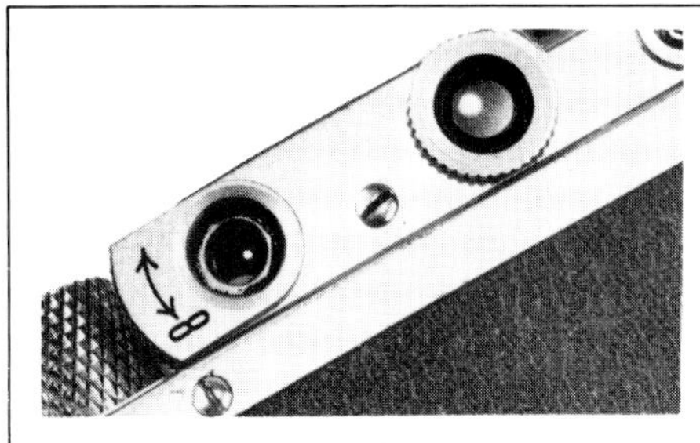

Dioptre adjustment on rangefinder eye-piece of LEICA IIIa

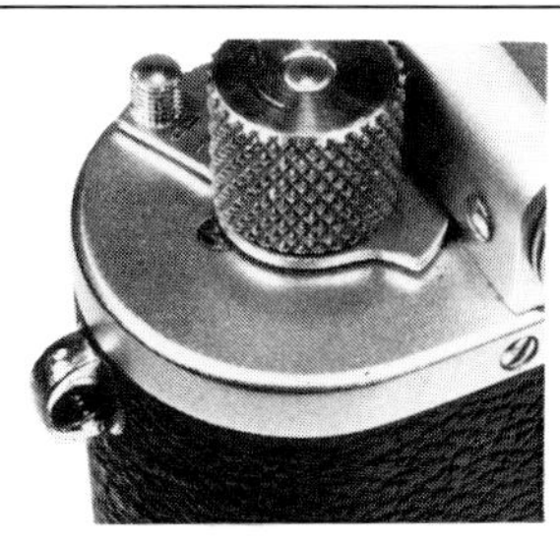

Dioptre adjustment under rewind knob on LEICA IIIb

After the war in 1949-1951 a number of LEICA IIIa's were assembled in the French occupied zone of Germany at St. Ingbert in the Saar by the optical firm of Saroptico. These cameras carried the inscription "Monté en Saar". In this way the high tariffs imposed in France on imported cameras were avoided. They were all sold in France or the French colonies. It seems that about 500 were made. Serial numbers have been recorded from 359,000 to 359,504. Later examples have a film speed reminder on the wind-on knob – a feature that was characteristic of the IIIf.

On the example illustrated a "past owner" has altered the first digit of the serial number from 3 to 8. A small number of IIIf "Monté en Sarre" cameras with IIIf synchronising exist. Whether these are originals or factory conversions cannot be ascertained.

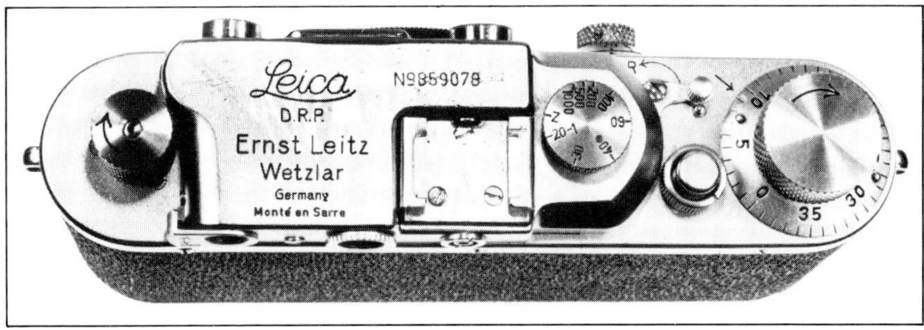

LEICA IIIa "Monté en Sarre"

LEICA IIIb

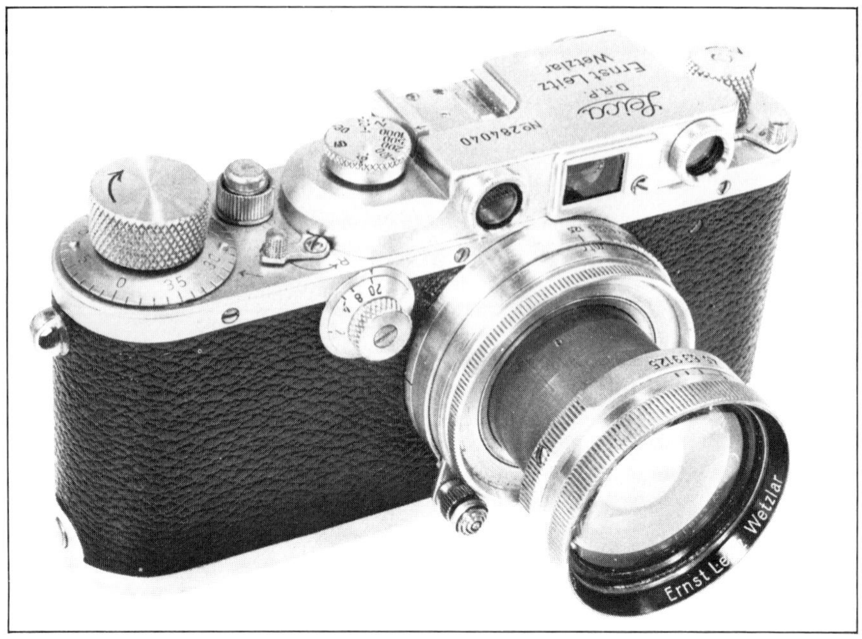

LEICA IIIb

The LEICA IIIb could be called an interim model between the most popular model, which was the IIIa, and the coming model IIIc. In fact the IIIb (also called model G 1938) had the main technical features of the IIIa, including the overall external dimensions, but had the big improvement of the combined eyepieces for the rangefinder and viewfinder. These were placed close together so that it was quicker to pass from focusing to framing. Because of the change in the layout, the rangefinder focusing system also had to be altered with the correction lever now placed under the rewind knob (see illustration on page 59). The cover of the rangefinder was slightly taller, so the total height of the camera was 68mm against 67 for the III and IIIa. The accessory shoe was also different, it was held in place by four screws instead of three and had two small pressure rails. The camera was chrome finished.

The first IIIb in 1937 had the serial number 240,001 and 10,000 cameras a year were built for the next 2 years. Although the camera was still being made in 1946, production had dwindled and between 1940 and 1946 less than 10,000 cameras were produced. Altogether 30,000 cameras of this type were produced, the last serial number being 355,000. Two versions of this camera exist with slightly different rangefinder covers.

The code name for LEICA IIIb without lens was ATOOH, with ELMAR f3.5 lens ARHOO and with SUMMAR f2 lens AZOOB.

II, IIIa & Models, General Arrangement

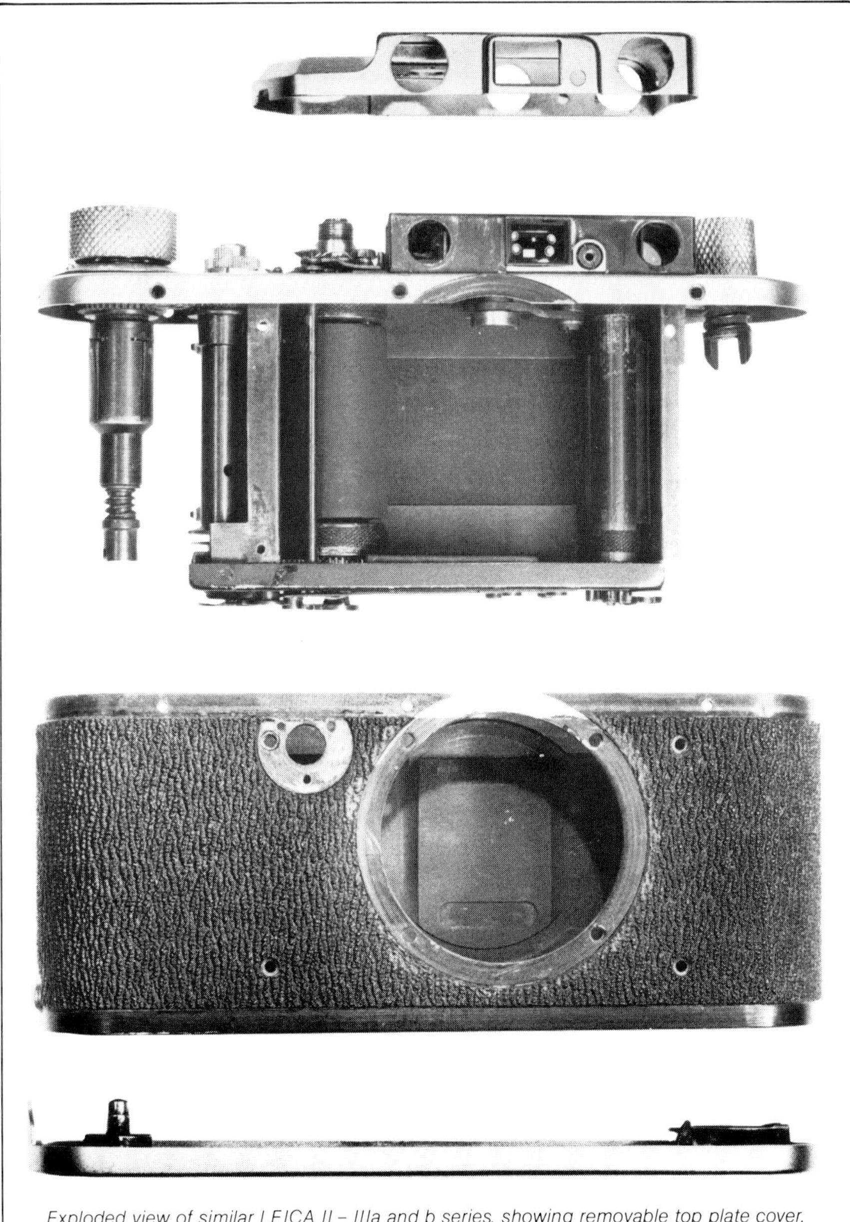

Exploded view of similar LEICA II – IIIa and b series, showing removable top plate cover, range finder combined with main shutter crate, removed shell and base plate.

LEICA 72

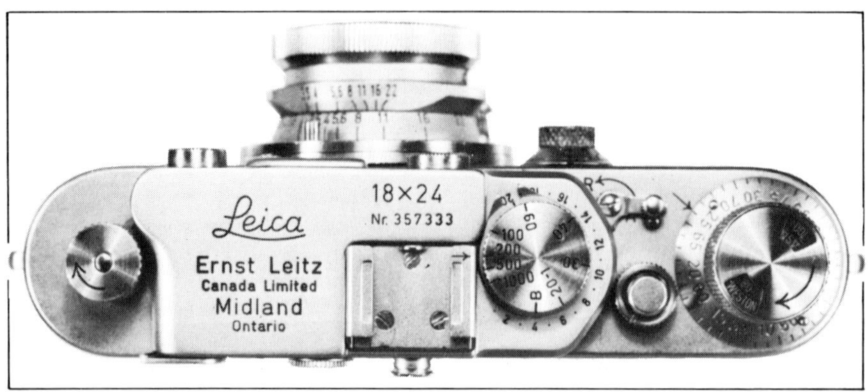

LEICA 72 (Canada)

Leitz at Wetzlar were interested in developing a half-frame, 18 x 24mm format camera for archive work and scientific use in the early 50's. Later they were to design and build a prototype pocket camera in this format but it never went into production. The LEICA 72, as it was known, was based on the LEICA IIIa. It was distinguishable from the IIIa by the exposure counter, which for exposures up to 75 had additional red markings intermixed with the normal ones, and the viewfinder which had a smaller window of the appropriate frame shape.

If the lens is removed and the shutter opened the internal 18 x 24mm mask may be seen. The rest of the internal mechanism is similar to the normal IIIa LEICA, except for the sprocket drum.

Some of these cameras were made at Wetzlar and some 35 are known to exist. However, serious production was undertaken by Leitz in Canada and these are engraved "Ernst Leitz Canada Limited Midland Ontario". Serial numbers started at 357,301. Some of the Canadian cameras have IIIf flash synchronisation.

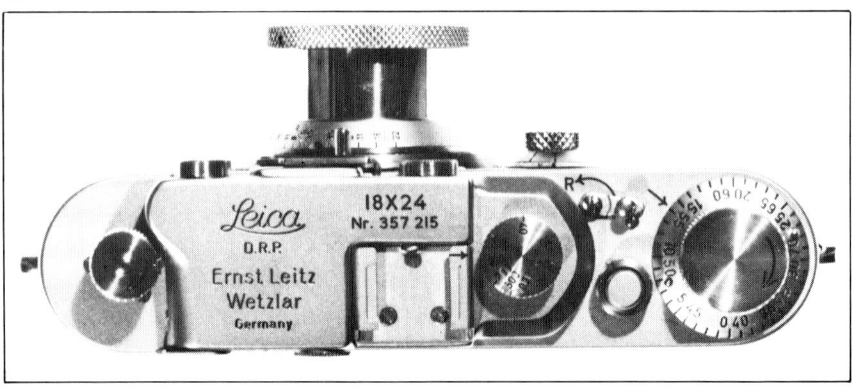

LEICA 72 (Wetzlar)

The LEICA 72 was produced for only a short time and the total number produced is probably the smallest of all LEICA types. It is also the only LEICA ever made available to the general public with a different size format to the standard 24 x 36mm. It is true that from time to time non-standard formats were produced for special purposes, such as the 24 x 24mm X-ray cameras and the 24 x 27mm post camera (q.v.).

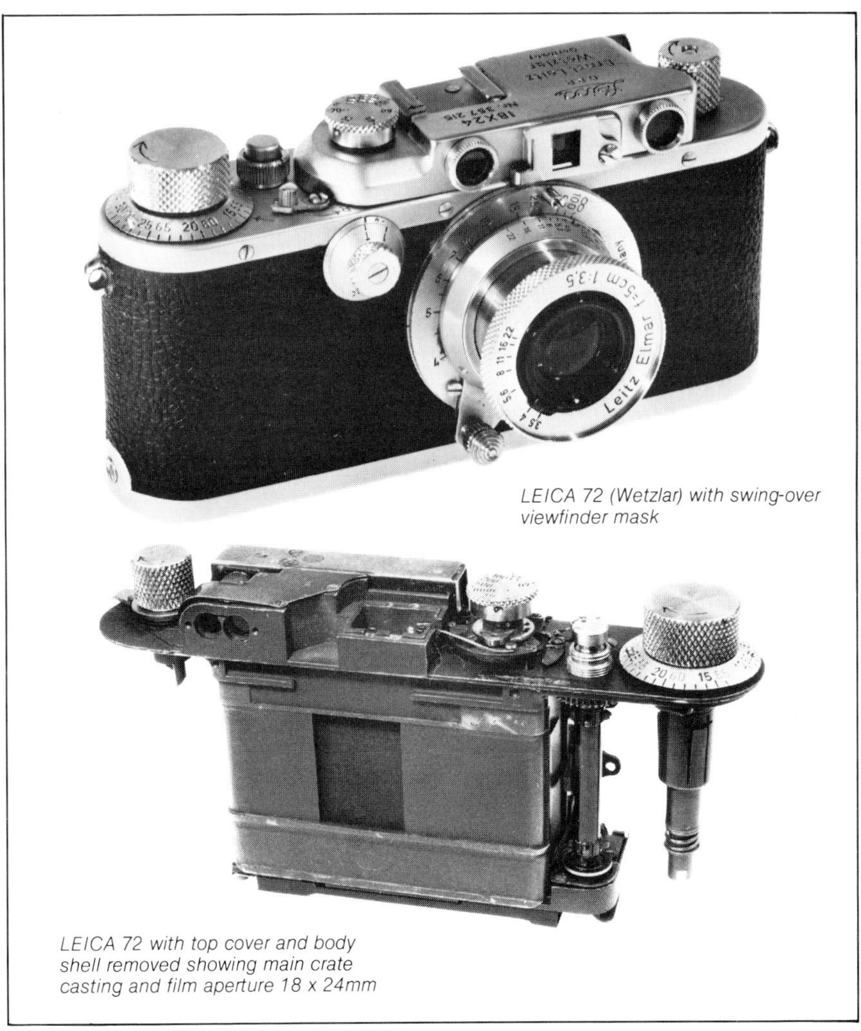

LEICA 72 (Wetzlar) with swing-over viewfinder mask

LEICA 72 with top cover and body shell removed showing main crate casting and film aperture 18 x 24mm

Code word for the "72" model was LKOOM without lens and LMOOK with the ELMAR 3.5/50mm lens. Those made in Wetzlar were not advertised and apparently had no codeword; they were numbered at random, the camera on display at the factory being No. 357,151.

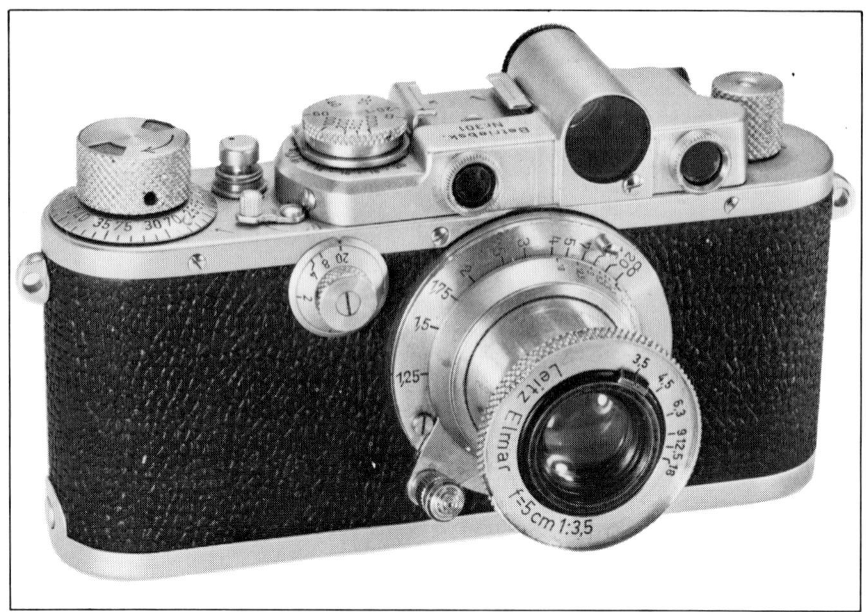

LEICA 72 prototype with special finder that was never put into production.

One or two LEICA 72's based on a IIIc chassis are known, but their serial numbers suggest they were made in 1945 and they were probably prototypes.

As a curiosity can be mentioned the fact that the author owns a 72 No. 357,169, bought many years ago at the factory. A picture of a different 72 with the same number has appeared in a Japanese magazine, leading one to wonder where this second camera might have come from.

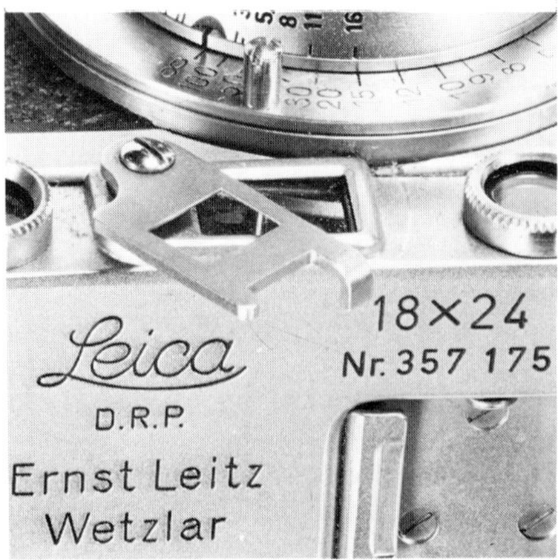

Swing-over viewfinder mask on LEICA 72.

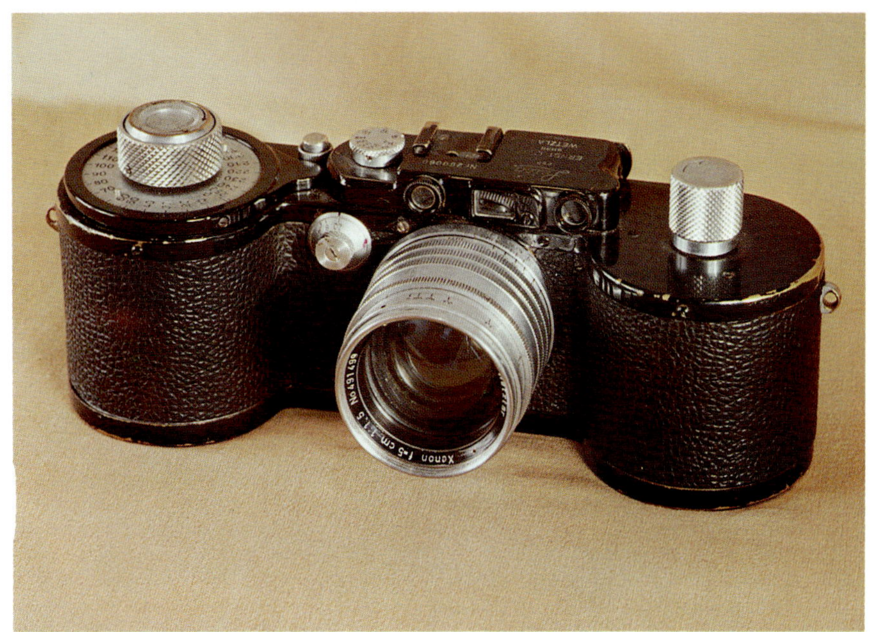

LEICA 250 "Reporter".

LEICA 72.

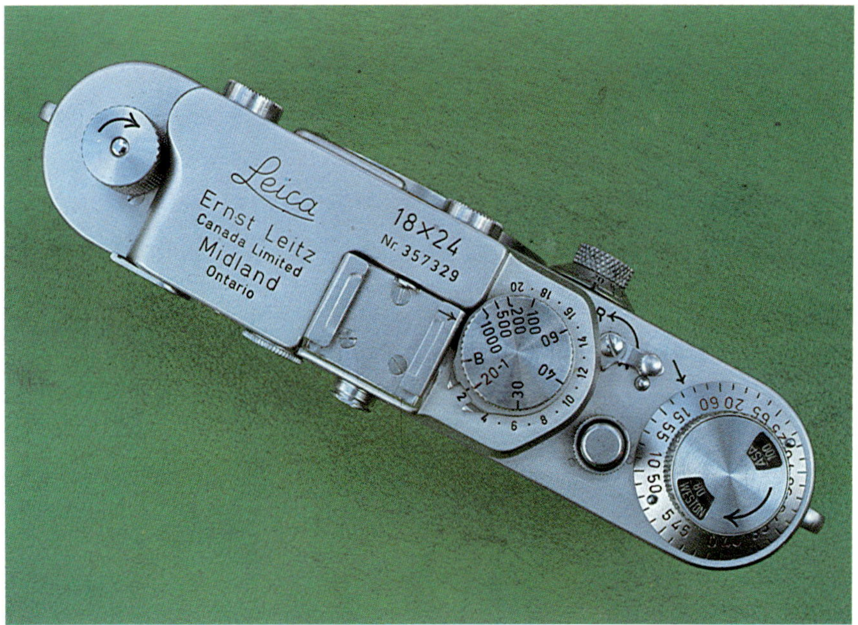

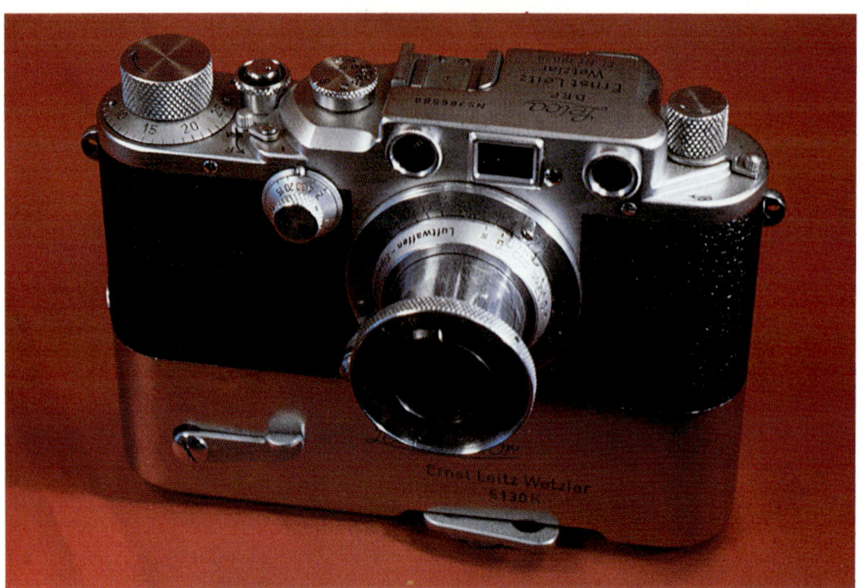

Two wartime military IIIc's, each fitted with MOOLY motor.
Top: Luftwaffe model (note "Fl" number on top-plate). This one has a black body and chrome finish. The motor is of the K type which has additional ball-races for low temperature use.
Bottom: Army model with ball bearing shutter (note the "K" after the serial number). This one is in grey paint finish and is engraved with "W.H." for "Wehrmacht Heer", it also has two fiducial points on the film gate which registered as notches on the negative to indicate the precise centre line from which measurements could be made.

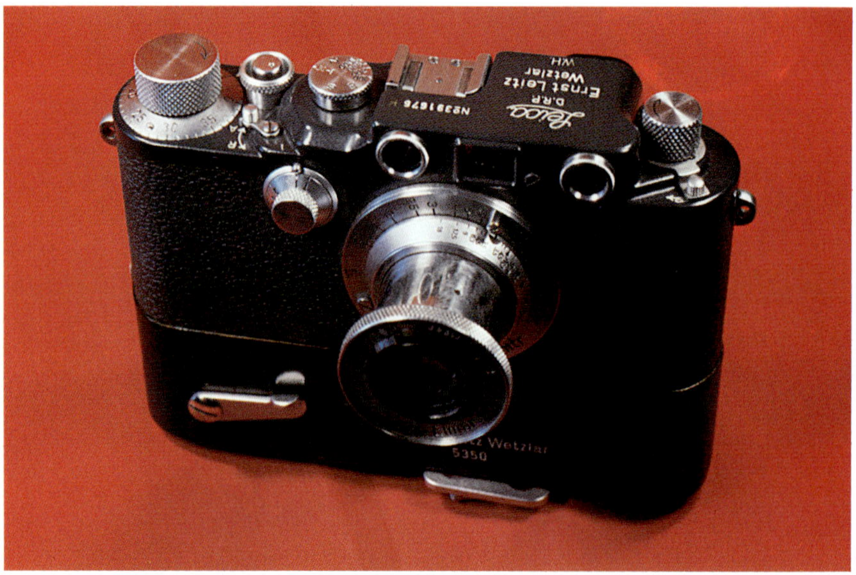

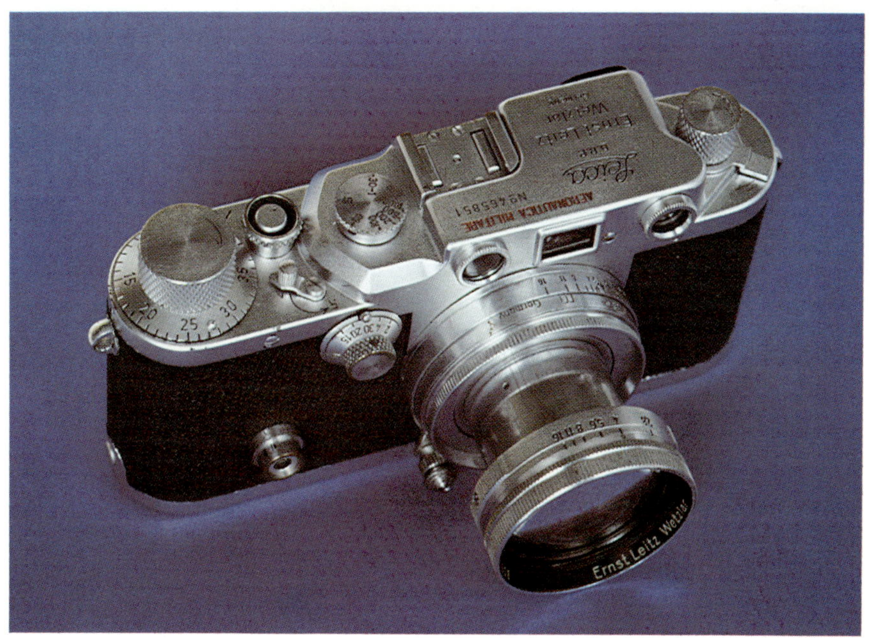

Post-war IIIc supplied to the Italian Air Force.

M3 in olive paint as supplied to the German Army.

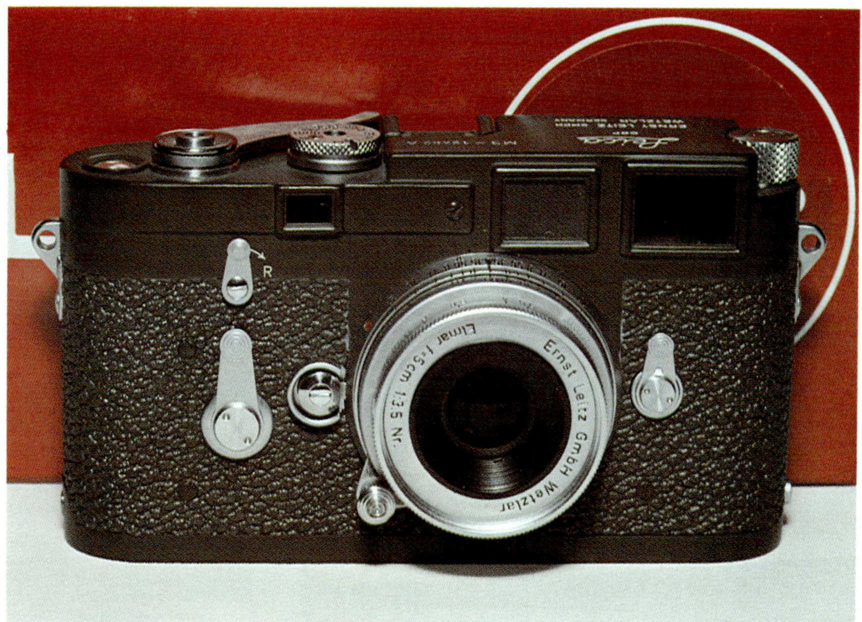

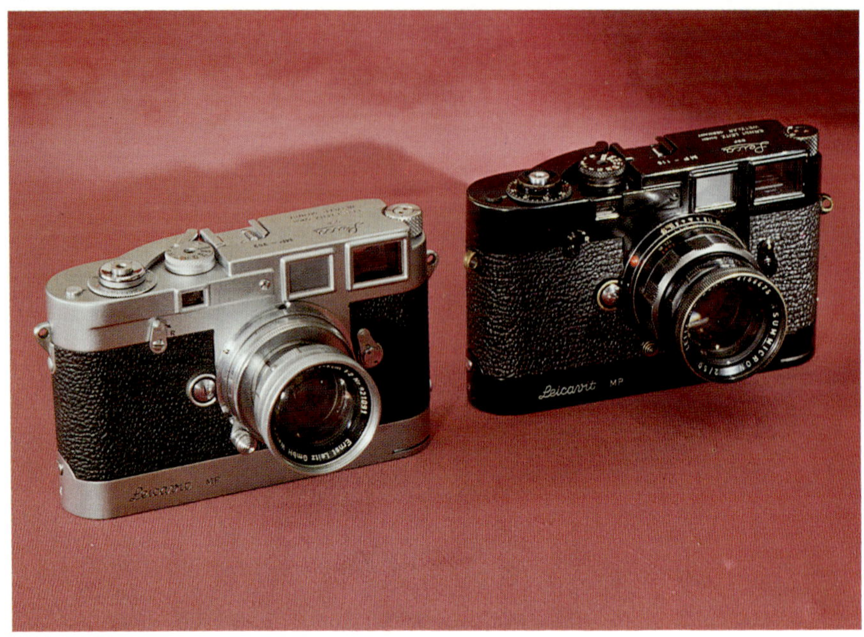

Two *LEICA MP's*.

50th Anniversary *LEICA M4*.

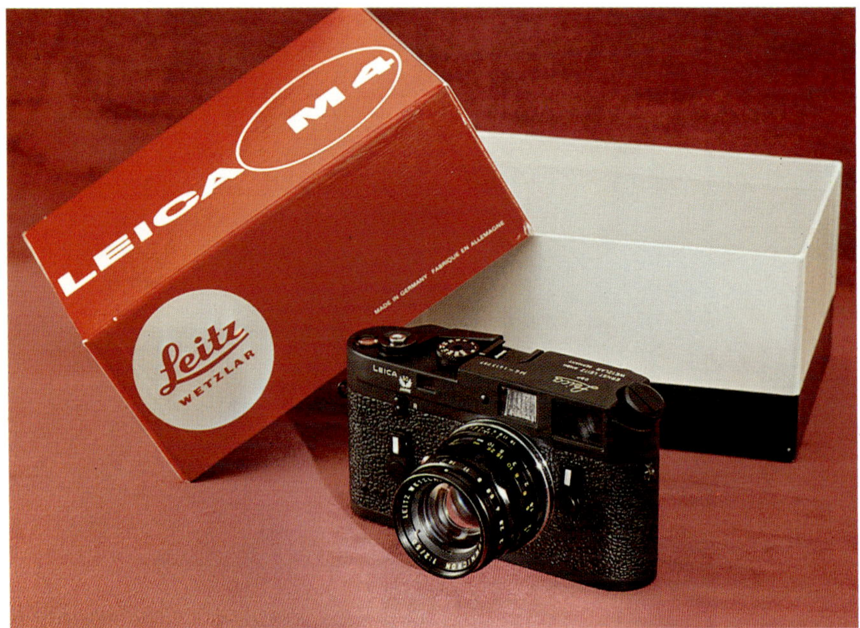

Chapter 6
Perfection of the Screw LEICA – The Die-cast Models

LEICA IIIc

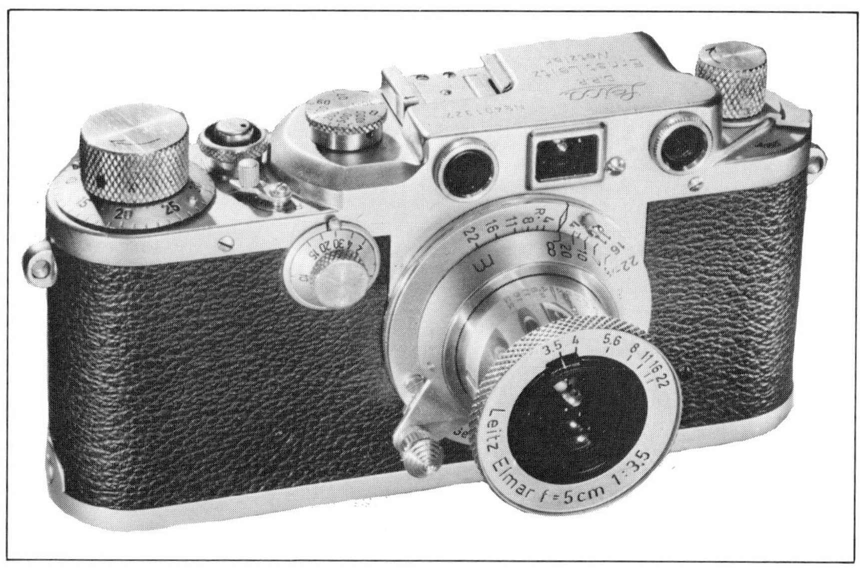

LEICA IIIc, post war model

At first glance there appears to be little difference between the model IIIb and the following model IIIc – there was in fact a great improvement.

The LEICA IIIc, introduced in 1940, was completely new. It had a die cast frame instead of an assembly of small parts. This design required, of course, a major retooling for casting and machining, but it was worth all the expense as it improve the camera, eased the production process, and laid the basis for yet further developments.

Externally, a IIIc can be recognised readily from a IIIb. The cover of the rangefinder is no longer separate from the top plate but is a single unit that affords greater protection to the internal mechanism.

The camera is also longer than previous types by 3mm, the total length being 136mm. All early LEICA IIIc's seem to have been finished in chrome, but the models for military use were finished in blue-grey.

Other minor differences from previous models are in the collar around the release button, which is larger and does not need to be removed when fitting a flexible release cable. The exposure counter, although similar in appearance, works differently from previous models due to an epicyclic gearing that makes it move only one notch at a time.

The serial numbers of the IIIc model started from 360,101 in 1940 and ran continuously until 397,650 in 1946; then, missing the following numbers (they were not allotted to any camera) numbering for the IIIc started again at 400,000 and went up to 525,000. Cameras in the 1940-46 batch were distinguishable by a raised step on which was mounted the release lever for rewind.

An interesting feature was the use of shutter blinds that were red on one side and black on the other; thus one curtain appeared red and the other black because the two curtains are used in opposite positions in the camera, but are actually identical.

This cloth was apparently from a supply used previously for some experimental purpose, as there are reports of earlier model LEICA's with the same blind material. Thus it may be that in a period of shortage this material was utilised and was later found to be unsatisfactory, as all cameras which went back to the factory for checks were fitted with new all-black blinds. From records it appears that red cloth cameras were those made with serial numbers from 362,401 to 379,226.

Also during the war there were batches of cameras with military engravings, and others with grey paint finish. Not every non-chromed LEICA IIIc qualifies as military, as at the end of the war there was an acute shortage of chrome and so paint was used instead.

Wartime LEICA IIIc in grey paint and with early f1.5/8.5cm SUMMAREX

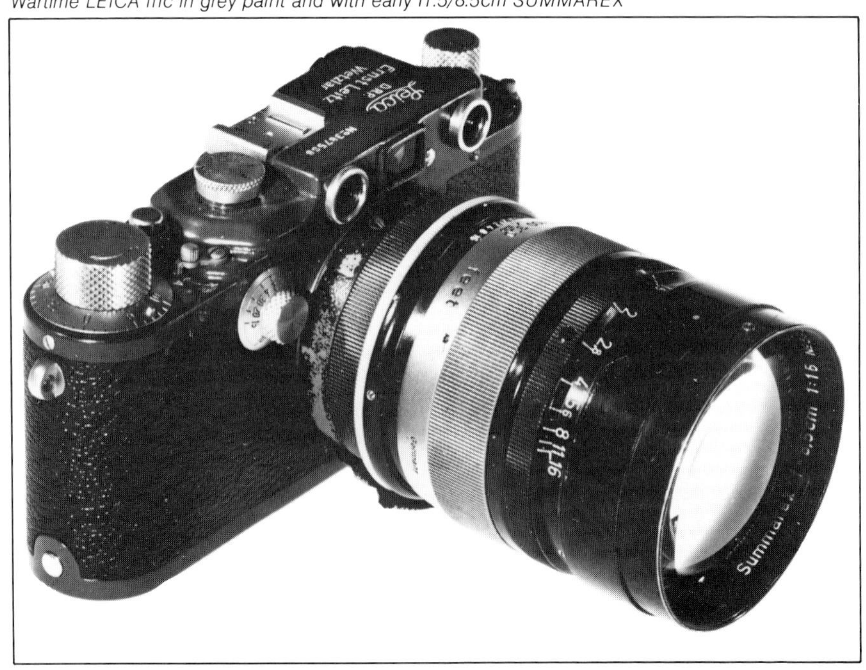

In the same wartime period the IIIc K type was produced. Undoubtedly several prototypes were made in the years before, but the "Kugellaler", or ball-bearing equipped cameras, were used first by the German armed forces, mainly the Luftwaffe, and therefore this type is also mentioned in the chapter on military cameras.

The ballbearings were adopted for the blind rollers to obtain a smoother movement, even at very low temperatures. From this model evolved the new type IIIc manufactured from 1946.

The postwar LEICA IIIc, or those with numbers over 400,000, are different from the first batch. They no longer have the raised step under the reverse lever and the focusing lever for the rangefinder has no knob. Internally the mechanism was improved, and there was space for later installation of ballbearings in the roller shafts. It is evident that the mechanics of the LEICA IIIc model are different by the arrangement of its shutter speed. The front dial has settings of T, one second, $1/2 - 1/4 - 1/10 - 1/15$; $1/20$ and $1/30$th of a second. The traverse speed of the shutter was shortened to $1/30$ of a second, assuring more efficient operation, especially at higher speeds.

Later there was a positive lock on the slow speed dial at the $1/30$ position to prevent accidental changes in the setting. The high speed dial on top of the camera was smaller than on some previous models and had the usual markings of $1/30 - 1/40 - 1/60 - 1/100 - 1/200 - 1/500$ and $1/1000$, plus Z.

The viewfinder had the reduction ratio of about 1:2, whereas the rangefinder had the 1.5 x magnification.

The code word for early IIIc with ELMAR 3.5 was LOOGI, with SUMMITAR f2 it was LOODU, and with XENON 1.5 LOOSB. After the war the IIIc with SUMMARIT 1.5 was LOOIT, with coated ELMAR LOOPN, with coated SUMMITAR LOOKX and without lens LOOHW.

Later the model IIIc had the word "Germany" added, but all other markings were similar to those of the earlier model.

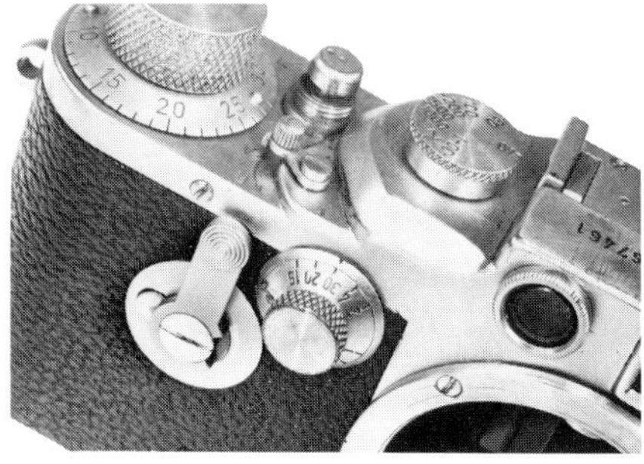

LEICA IIIc, under number 400,000, showing advance rewind lever on step (IIId illustrated)

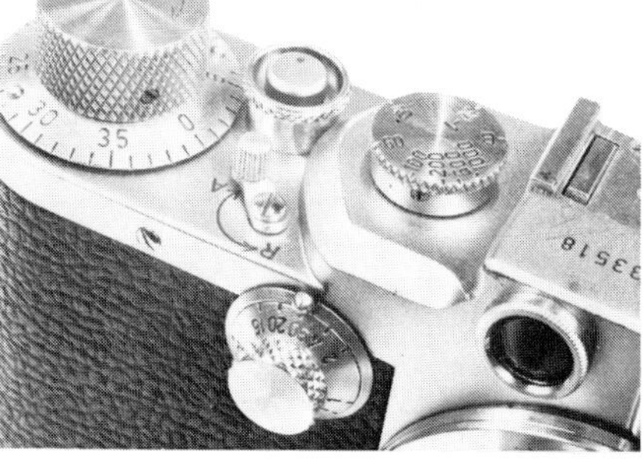

LEICA IIIc, number above 400,000, showing advance rewind lever flat on top plate, and slow shutter speed lock

As mentioned in the previous chapter, one or two IIIc's in half-frame format are known.

LEICA IIId

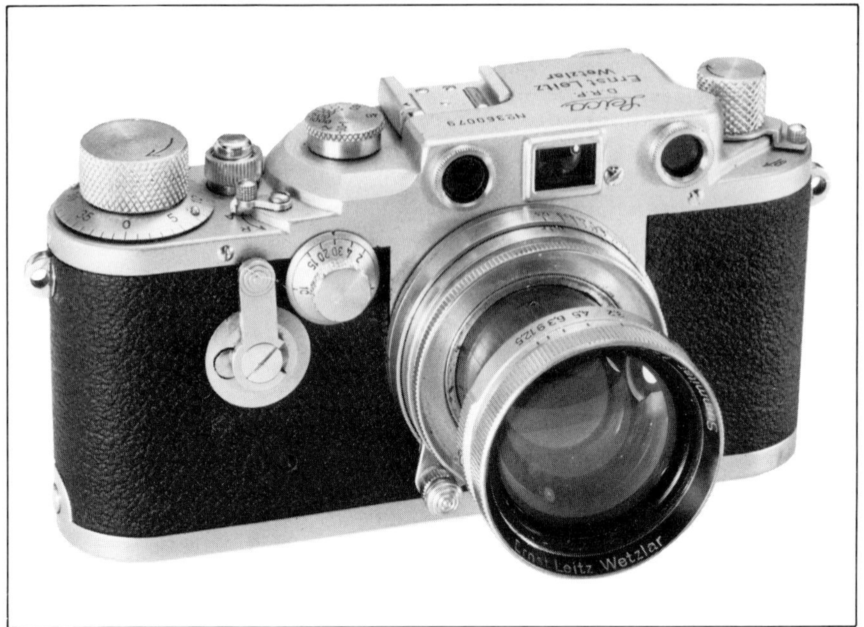

LEICA IIId

The model IIId camera was essentially a model IIIc with delayed action timer. It had the characteristics of the first run of the IIIc, that is with the raised step under the reverse lever.

Two variants are known, one with black curtains and no slow speed dial lock (the first batch) and another with red curtain and slow speed dial lock.

The delayed action mechanism was similar to the type later used on the IIIf and IIIg, but the internal actuating mechanism from the timer to the release action was different, this of course is not noticeable from the outside. The escapement for the delayed action is similar but the case is different, so that although the fixing screws are located at the same place on the IIIc and IIIf and IIIg, the mechanisms cannot be interchanged. There were also minor differences in the actuating arm which had a different number of concentric rings at the tip.

The technical details of this camera were the same as those of the first series of the IIIc. Only a few cameras of this type were made in the very first run of IIIc in the 360,000 series, then 400 more from the 367,000. Nevertheless the LEICA IIId was advertised from 1940 and duly given its code names as follows: camera alone LOOTP (price 255 marks in 1940), camera with ELMAR f3.5 lens LOOUC (332 marks), camera with SUMMAR f2 LAQOO (435 marks) and camera with XENON f1.5 LOOWD at 587 marks.

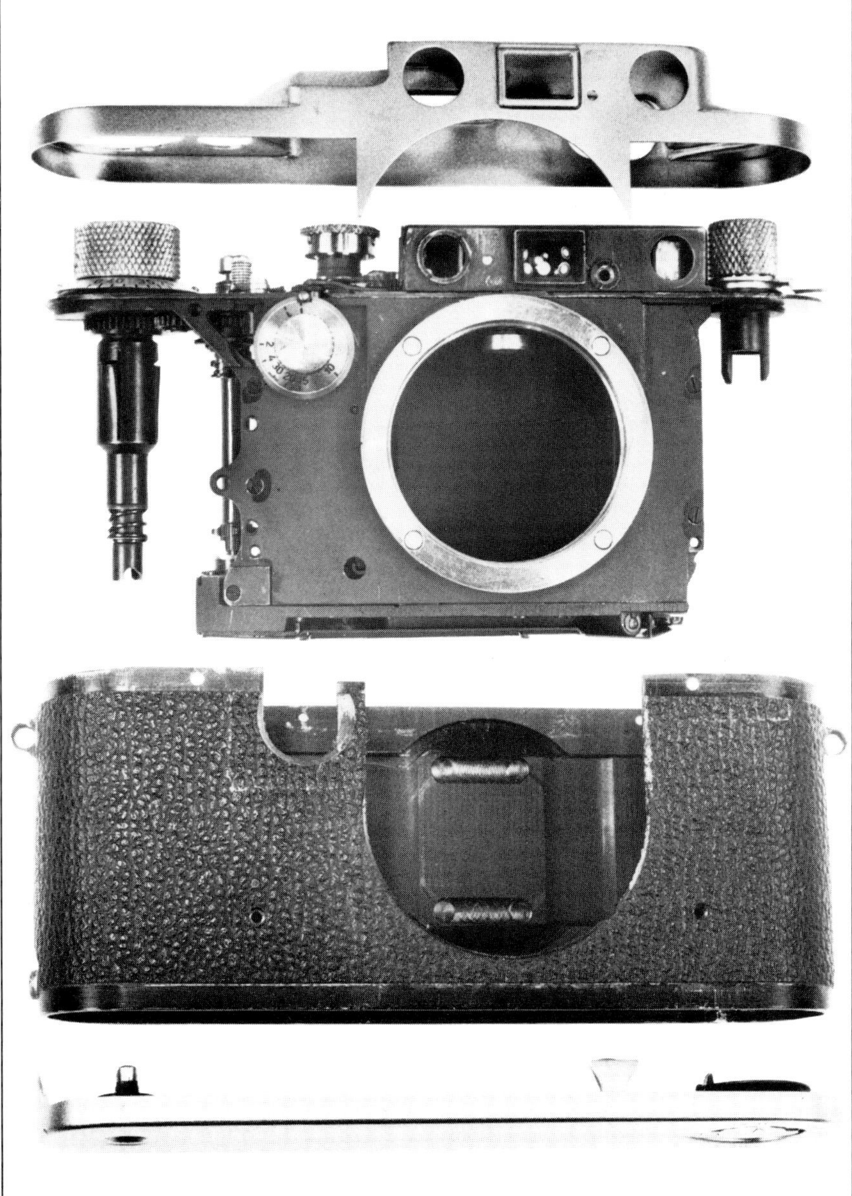

IIIc, f & g Series General Arrangement

Exploded view of similar layout models IIIc, d, f and g showing top plate removed, main shutter crate casting with rangefinder, body shell and base plate.

LEICA IIc

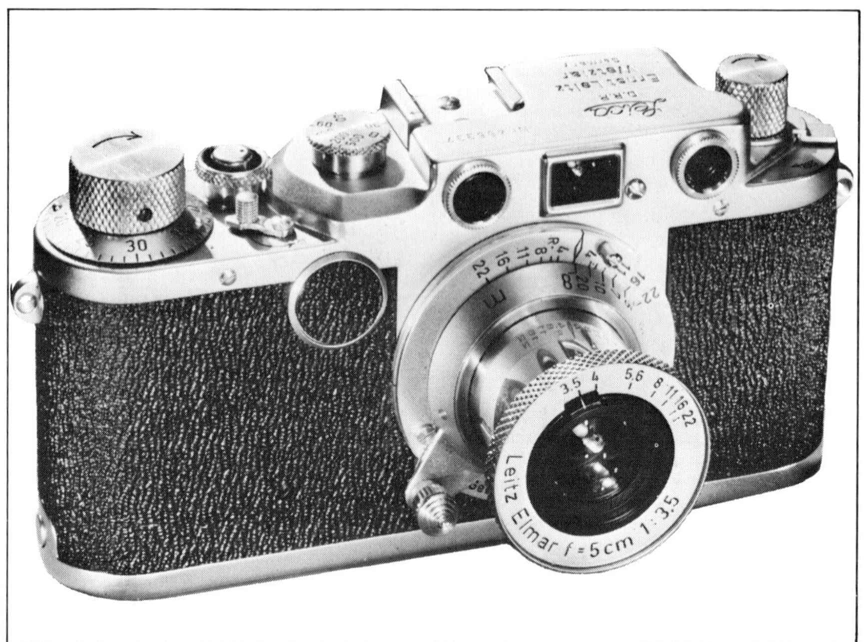

LEICA IIc

After the war there was a strong demand for LEICA's of any type. So the model IIc was produced, being simply a IIIc minus the slow speeds.

The camera was first made in 1948, starting from serial number 440,001 and with an allotment of 9,999 pieces up to 1951. An additional series of 1,000 cameras was then made, numbered from 450,001 to 451,000. A total of 10,999 cameras of this type were built, but there may be a few missing as some of them may have been converted to IIIc models. However it should be easy to recognise a converted IIc camera as they were only made in the above mentioned two batches. All models were chrome finished.

The body of the camera was the normal post-war IIIc, without the step under the reverse lever. Apart from the absence of the slow speed dial in front (which was blanked off) there is another difference: the accessory clip on top is different from that used on the LEICA IIIc and had a spring (similar to a leaf spring) fixed in the middle by two rather large screws. Some cameras were fitted with IIIf type synchronization.

The shutter was speeded 1/30 – 1/40 – 1/60 – 1/100 – 1/200 – 1/500 of a second, + B, Markings on top are still the pre-war type with Leica D.R.P. and Ernst Leitz Wetzlar; however "Germany" is added.

LEICA Ic

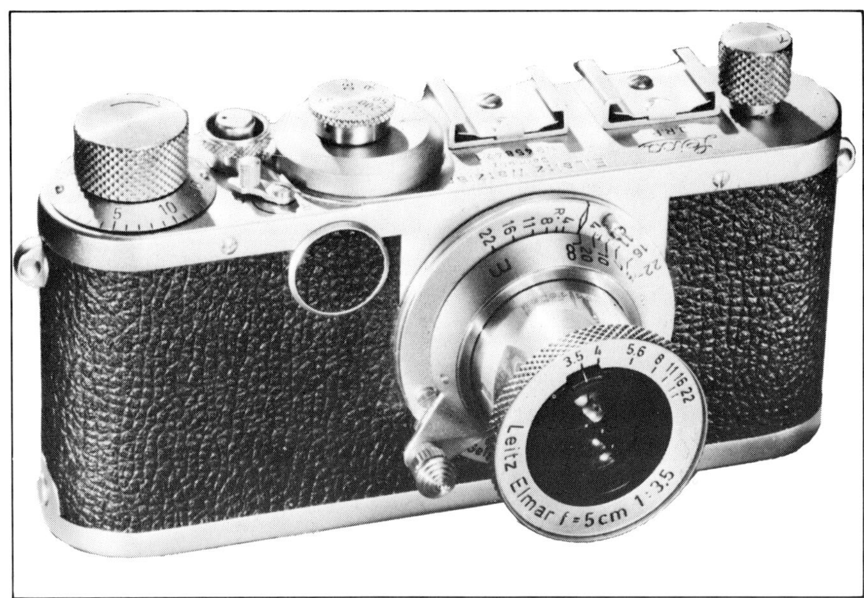

LEICA Ic

When the LEICA Standard was discontinued in 1948, it was replaced with a similar model based on the LEICA IIIc chassis. It was intended for scientific purposes, such as with microscopes where neither rangefinder nor viewfinder were necessary.

It was produced from 1949 to 1951, starting with serial number 455,001; an initial batch of 5,000 was made followed by another of 4,000, finally ending in 1951 with a batch of 2,800, the last serial number being 562,800. A total of 11,800 cameras of this model were produced.

The body was very simple; it had a flat top on which were fixed two accessory shoes. These could accommodate a separate viewfinder and the rangefinder FOKOS if necessary. The shutter speed control was covered by a round housing, flatter and wider than the one on the Standard camera. The speed dial was, like the one on the IIc model, limited to the speeds from 1/30 to 1/500 of a second.

The name "Leica" was engraved to the extreme left of the camera (looking from the top) and had the letters "D.R.P." under it; to the right was the script "E. LEITZ WETZLAR" with "GERMANY" and the serial number under it. These markings were different from other models.

Code names were: OEGIO for the camera body only, but supplied with reflecting viewfinder for the 50mm lenses; camera bare was OEFGO, with ELMAR f3.5 was OEINO and with SUMMITAR f2 it was OESFO. Accessory rangefinder in chrome finish (as the camera) was FOKOS.

LEICA IIIf

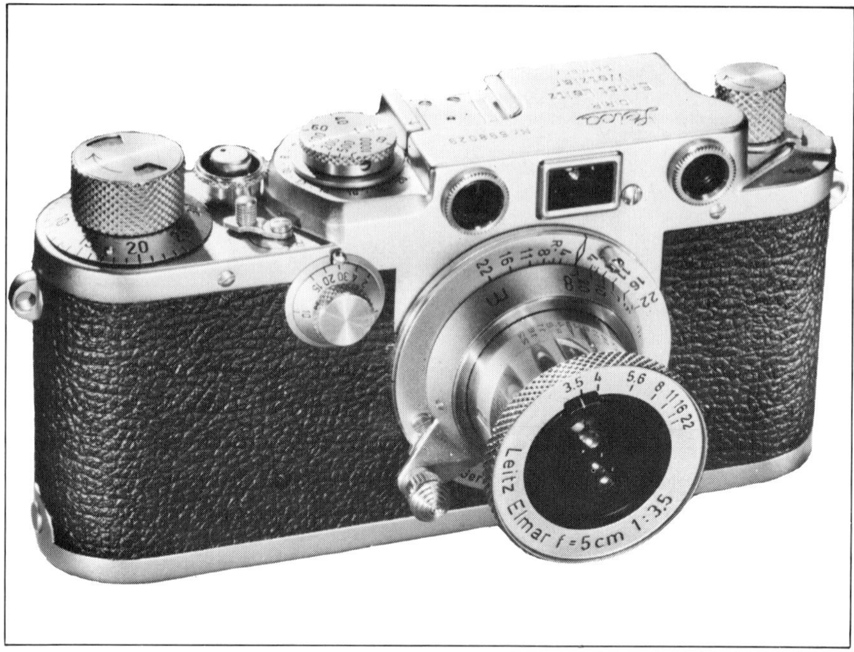

LEICA IIIf

The LEICA IIIf model produced from 1950 was the next improvement to the rangefinder camera. Externally similar to the IIIc, it had the added feature of flash synchronisation. A film type indicator was also situated within the winding knob.

There were at least 15,000 cameras in the first batch of IIIf's, starting from serial number 525, 001, followed in 1951 by a batch of 20,000 and another of 5,000 and, between 1951 and 1952, 30,000 more, making a total of 70,000 cameras. This did not include the 1,000 which were made in Canada, serial numbers 610,001 to 611,000, but which used the normal Wetzlar top-plate. A few IIIf's exist with Leitz Canada engraving. These must be considered rare items as Leitz Canada engraving did not appear on cameras until the M4 was produced in Canada in 1974. (see page 81).

All these cameras had what is commonly known as the "black dial", meaning the numbers 0 to 20 in black form the scale of synchronisation under the speed setting dial; this scale was used by moving a ring with an index point to set the number indicated for different forms of flash, either electronic or bulb; the latter could be used at all shutter speeds, depending on the setting of the synchronisation dial. The "black dial" LEICA IIIf also had the traditional speeds scale; the slow speed dial had the settings from T to one second, 1/2 – 1/4 – 1/10 – 1/15 – 1/20 and 1/30 of a second, with the locking catch at 1/30; the high speed dial had 1/30 – 1/40 – 1/60 – 1/100 – 1/200 – 1/500 – 1/1000 and B settings.

In 1952 a new type of shutter with lighter design was introduced and this new type was used to make a slightly different version of the IIIf called the "red dial", because the numbers on the synchronisation dial were red. But the important change was in the shutter speeds sequence which conformed to international standards; the slow speed dial had the speeds: T – 1 second, 1/2 – 1/5 – 1/10 – 1/15; 1/25, and the upper dial had 1/25 – 1/50 – 1/75 – 1/100 – 1/200 – 1/500 and 1/1000, plus B.

The camera was chrome, had the two eyepieces close together, as on the IIIc, and the focusing lever for the rangefinder under the rewind knob. From the black to the red dials, the engraving changed on top of the camera, which had in the meantime come under new patents; consequently under the name LEICA there was now "D.B.P." (for Deutsches Bundersrepublik Patent), and under "Ernst Leitz" there was "G.M.B.H.", then "Wetzlar" and finally "Germany".

Cameras with the new engravings had serial numbers starting with 615,001 and the first run produced 35,000 cameras followed by another of 18,000. Another batch of 1,000 from 684,001 to 685,000 was allocated to Canada and cameras from 685,001 to 699,999 had the added feature of the self timer. (Some black dial cameras also had this feature added). This feature was to remain on all the IIIf's produced thereafter and all cameras of this type were chrome finished, except some small batches made for military use. The black military LEICA's had no delayed action timer and had black ELMAR 50mm lenses. Production of the IIIf ceased in 1956 with serial number 825,000. (Final total for Canada of 4,265; last No. 839610).

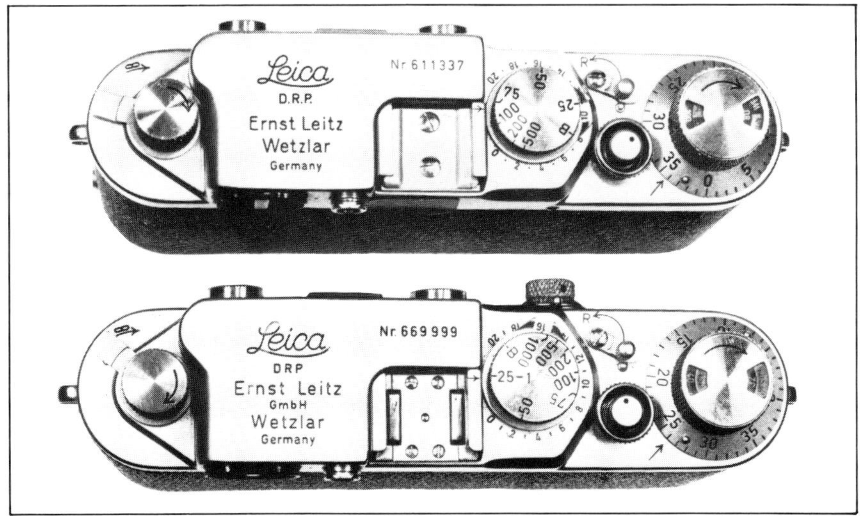

Examples of F top plates showing early and later style of engraving Black Dial IIIf (top) Red Dial IIIf (bottom).

A rather mysterious black variant with delayed action and with serial numbers far removed from those of the "Swedish" cameras in the 680,000 group have also appeared: no exact data are available, but some technicians at the factory seem to remember that a small batch of these black, tropicalised cameras was made at the request of a dealer in India.

A small number of IIIf cameras exist engraved "Montè en Saar". Whether these are originals or conversions cannot be ascertained.

Code names did not change with the improvements and were LOOHW for the LEICA IIIf without lens, LOOPN with ELMAR f3.5, LOOKX with SUMMITAR f2 and later, when the SUMMICRON became available, LUOOX; with fast SUMMARIT f1.5 lens the code was LOOIT.

LEICA If

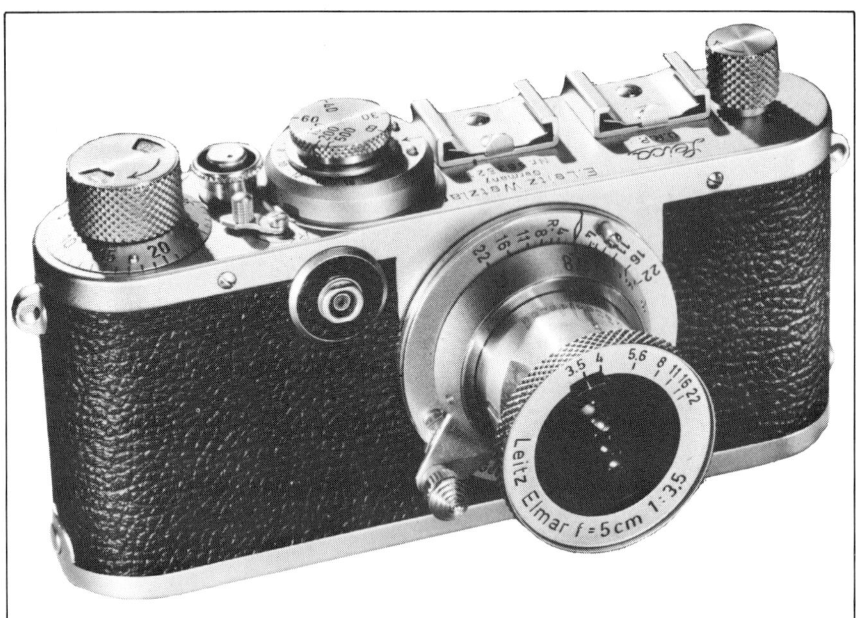

LEICA If

The LEICA If was introduced in 1951 and remained in production until 1956. It was the basic model of the "f" series and replaced the LEICA Ic. It had neither viewfinder nor rangefinder but had a flat top with two accessory shoes. It had a similar housing covering the shutter mechanism, with the speed dial on top, but with the addition of the synchronising ring. The outlet for the flash connecting cable was not on the back of the rangefinder housing, as on the IIIf and IIf models, but in the centre of the round cover of the absent slow speed dial socket.

The LEICA If had the winding knob of the IIIf with the film type indicator and the same speed dial, with speeds up to 1/500 of a second plus B; but there was in due time the change from the old series of speeds to the new one with 1/25 – 1/50 – 1/75 etc.

The first run started from No. 562,801 in 1951 with 2,200 cameras equipped with black dial IIIf shutter. After that another 13,000 LEICA If's appeared up to 1956, with an odd ten cameras still indicated for 1957, these were based on the IIIf red dial shutter and had the marking D.R.P.

The code name for the LEICA If body with reflecting viewfinder for 50mm lenses was OEGIO and with ELMAR f3.5 lens OEINO; the body alone was OEFGO and there was a small accessory to raise the flashgun so it could fit the accessory shoe, and clear the rewind knob and speed dial, code name ZIOOQ.

LEICA IIf

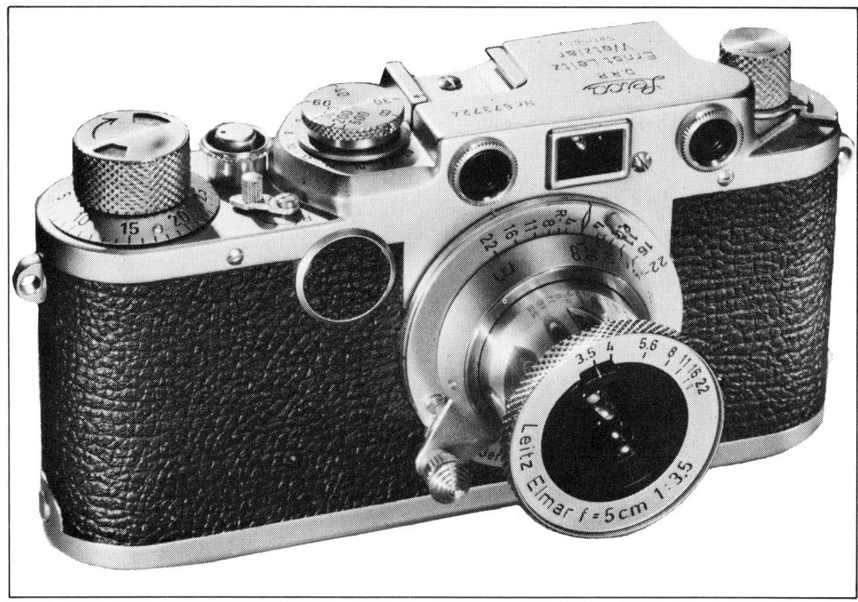

LEICA IIf

In 1951, a year after the introduction of the model IIIf, the LEICA IIf was introduced. It was identical to the IIIf model except for the absence of the slow shutter speeds, and the accessory shoe which was fixed by only two screws and had a large spring similar to that of the IIc.

In 1951 the first batch of LEICA IIf's started with serial number 451,001. Production of the first two batches of this model totalled 9,000 cameras.

These first two batches of IIf serial numbers 451,001 to 455,000, 570,001 to 575,000 had shutter speeds from 1/30 to 1/500 + B, as the black dial IIIf. From the third batch, with serial numbers from 611,001 to 615,000, the new shutter was fitted, with the scale of speed as follows: 1/25 – 1/50 – 1/75 – 1/100 – 1/200 – 1/500 + B. As with the red dial IIIf, later models had a top speed of 1/1000. Altogether some 34,000 cameras of this type were made.

The code name for the LEICA IIf alone was LOOSE, with ELMAR f3.5 lens it was LOOEL and with the faster SUMMICRON lens LOOUN. The camera had, of course, the same type of flash synchronisation as used on the IIIf model. The first two batches (9,000 cameras) had a black dial but others were red dial.

On some of the cameras made in 1952/53 there is an interesting change in markings; these cameras still bear the D.R.P. mark (instead of D.B.P.) but have the letters G.M.B.H. added under Ernst Leitz, as in later models. The production of model IIf ceased in 1956.

LEICA IIIg

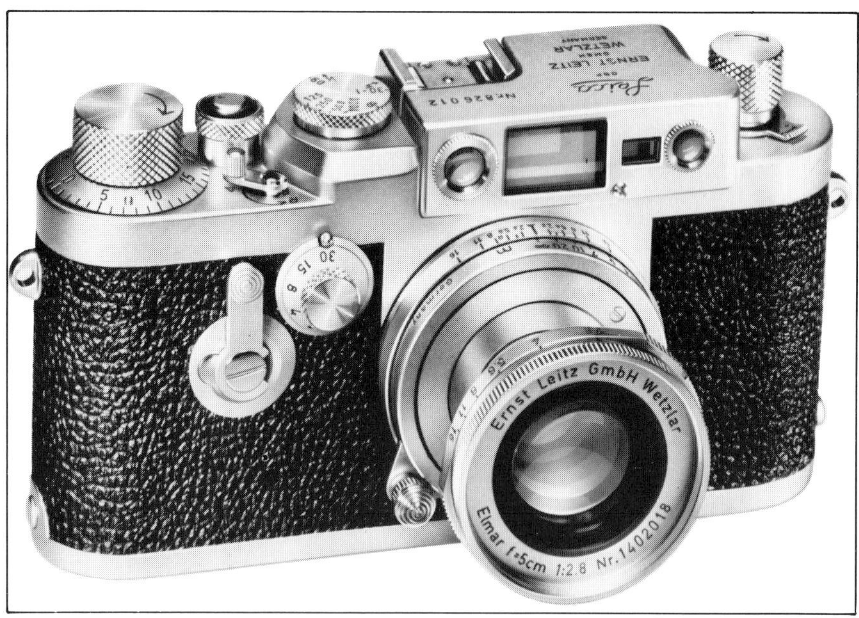

LEICA IIIg

The model IIIg was the last of the screw mount LEICA's and was introduced after the bayonet mount M3 was already in production. Serial numbers for the IIIg started from 825,001 and are registered as manufactured in 1956, both in Germany and Canada. (ELC had a batch from 845,001 to 845,380), but the camera was available to the public from 1957 to 1960 (some cameras in the shops may have been sold after that). Production ended with serial number 988,350. All normal production cameras were chrome. Altogether some 40,000 LEICA IIIg's were made, plus 1,780 in Canada and 125 of a special type finished in black for the Swedish Air Force.

The camera had many improvements over the previous model: the viewfinder was of the suspended frame type with a larger image equal to half life size, it also had a moving frame that was actuated by the rangefinder mechanism and corrected for parallax. The frame showed the image formed by a 50mm lens and it also had four small triangles that indicated the 90mm lens field of view. Characteristic of the camera front was the large viewfinder window and the smaller window to illuminate the frame. The rangefinder windows were round.

The shutter control was still by two dials, one in front and one on top; shutter speeds: T, 1 second, 1/2 – 1/4 – 1/8 – 1/15 – 1/30 – 1/60 – 1/125 – 1/250 – 1/500 – 1/1000, and B, were in geometric progression. Thus each speed was twice as fast as the preceding one and half the following, adding much to the simplicity of setting shutter and diaphragm controls. A lock operated on the slow speeds at 1/30.

The speed dial also had two arrows ($\downarrow$), one black by the 1/60 for the electronic flash synchronisation and the one red by the 1/30 for the lower speeds. There was a single flash contact on the back near the eyepieces.

The camera was fitted with a delayed action release, the frame counter moved a frame at a time, and the lever for eyesight adjustment of the rangefinder had + and – markings. The accessory shoe was fixed by four small screws and had spring loaded rails to fasten the accessories securely.

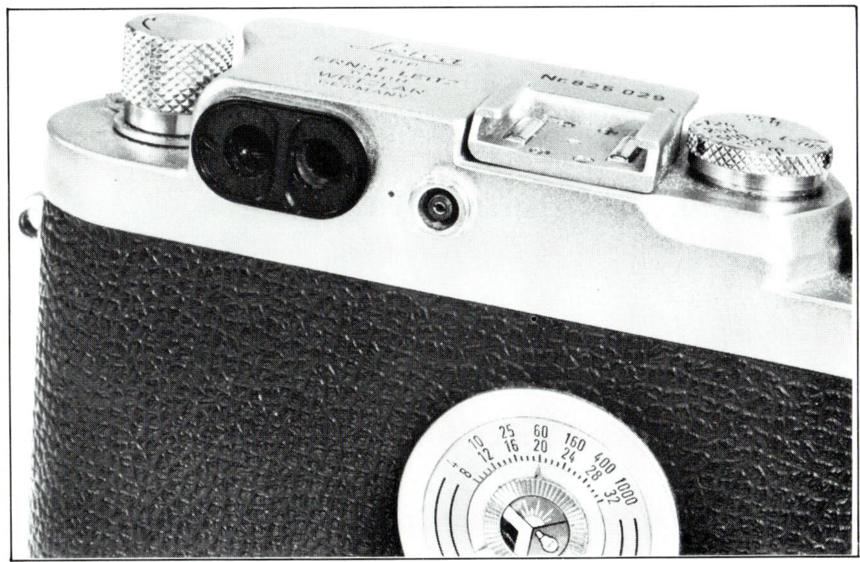

Rear view of LEICA IIIg showing viewfinder, rangefinder, flash connection and film indicator.

The inside of the camera was similar to the IIIf, however in some cases the serial number was also engraved on the lower part of the mechanism and is visible by opening the bottom and looking in the film cassette space.

The film type indicator was no longer on the winding knob but on the camera back as on the M3.

When the last of the LEICA IIIg's left the assembly room it could use a wide range of lenses, ranging from the extreme wide-angle 21mm f4 SUPER ANGULON to the 400mm f5 TELYT. A new ELMAR 50mm was also available with an f2.8 aperture. The code word of the LEICA IIIg with this lens was GOOEL, without lens it was GOOEF, and with the standard SUMMICRON f2 lens was GOOMI.

LEICA Ig

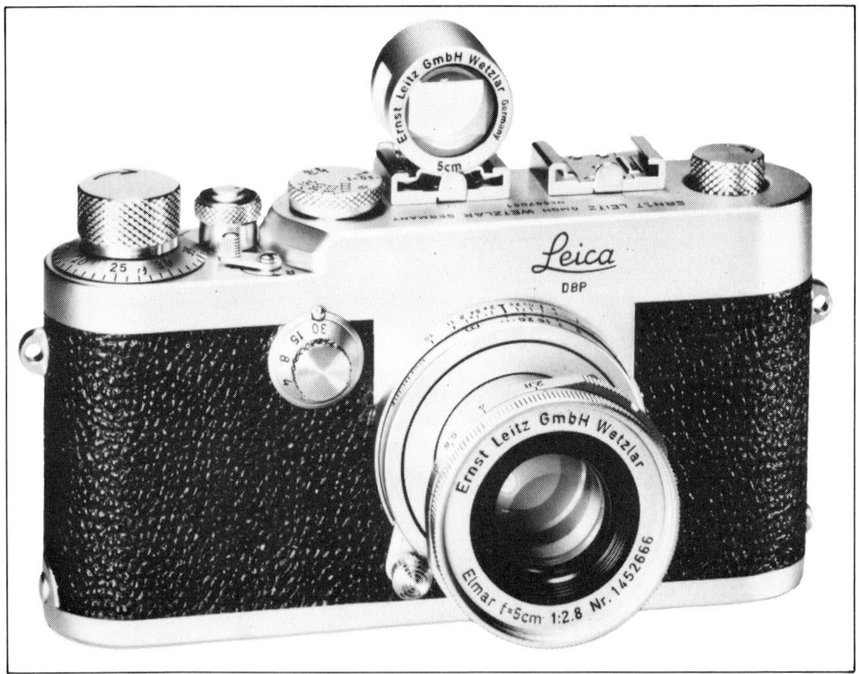

LEICA Ig

In 1957, at the same time as the model IIIg, the simplified LEICA Ig was introduced to replace the If. The first serial number was 887,001. Production continued until 1960 with several batches and a total of 6,300 cameras. The last one had the serial number 987,600.

The LEICA Ig differed from the Ic and If in that it followed the normal camera outline. In order to house the IIIg synchronisation mechanism the top cover was extended round the rewind knob, the latter was partly sunk but could be raised for use. There were two accessory shoes, of the same type as the IIIg with four fixing screws. The shutter had the same speeds as the IIIg, 1 second to 1/1000 + B and T.

The film type indicator was on the back of the body as on the IIIg, and also all other details both inside and outside the camera were the same as those of the IIIg, with the exception that no self timer was fitted.

Unlike other LEICA's, it has the name engraved on the front, with the letters "D.B.P." beneath it; on top of the camera there was the script "Ernst Leitz G.M.B.H. Wetzlar Germany" in a single line with the serial number under it. It was listed, complete with ELMAR f2.8 and viewfinder, as OADGO, minus lens OGILO, and camera alone OCEGO.

Some special models of these cameras were made. Some 68 units were of the so-called "Post" type, ie with a fixed focus lens and a front plate designed to snap the camera into a frame that moved in front of telephone meters. Some other cameras were made without the accessory shoes for special uses. See chapter on special models.

LEICA IIg

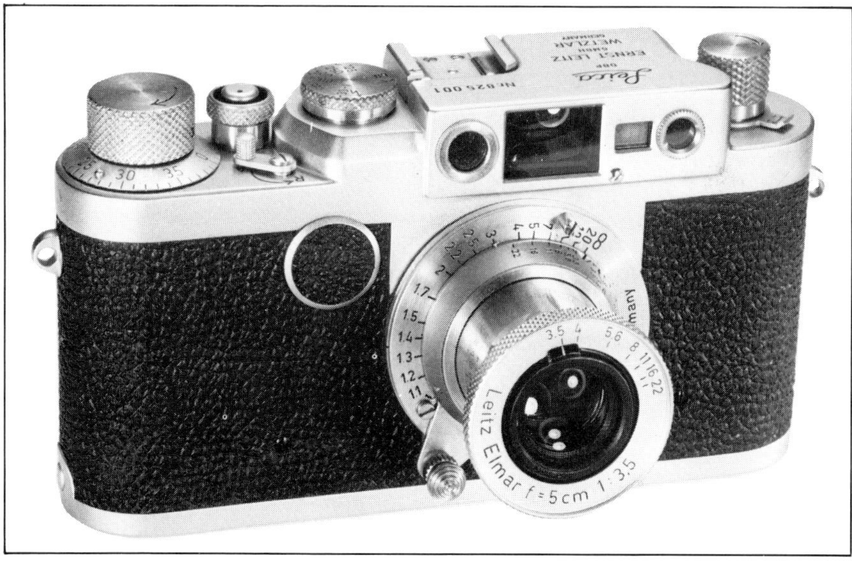

LEICA IIg

In 1956 a very small quantity of LEICA IIg's were manufactured. These in most respects were the same as the LEICA IIIg, with the exception of no slow speeds or self timer. As far as can be ascertained a possible 12-15 cameras were manufactured and very few are known to exist today. The camera illustrated above is from the collection at Wetzlar.

One could argue that these were made in prototype form only, but we now know that a few of these cameras were sold, therefore they must be placed among the production cameras, although it is probably the model with the lowest production quantities. There is also the possibility that the LEICA IIg was devised as an upscaling of the Ig rather than downscaling of the IIIg.

In any case, the increasing interest towards the bayonet-type cameras made impractical the whole project of enlarging the range of the "g" series cameras. It can be gathered from the dates of appearance of the several M models that full priority was given to this new series from its debut with the M3 in 1954.

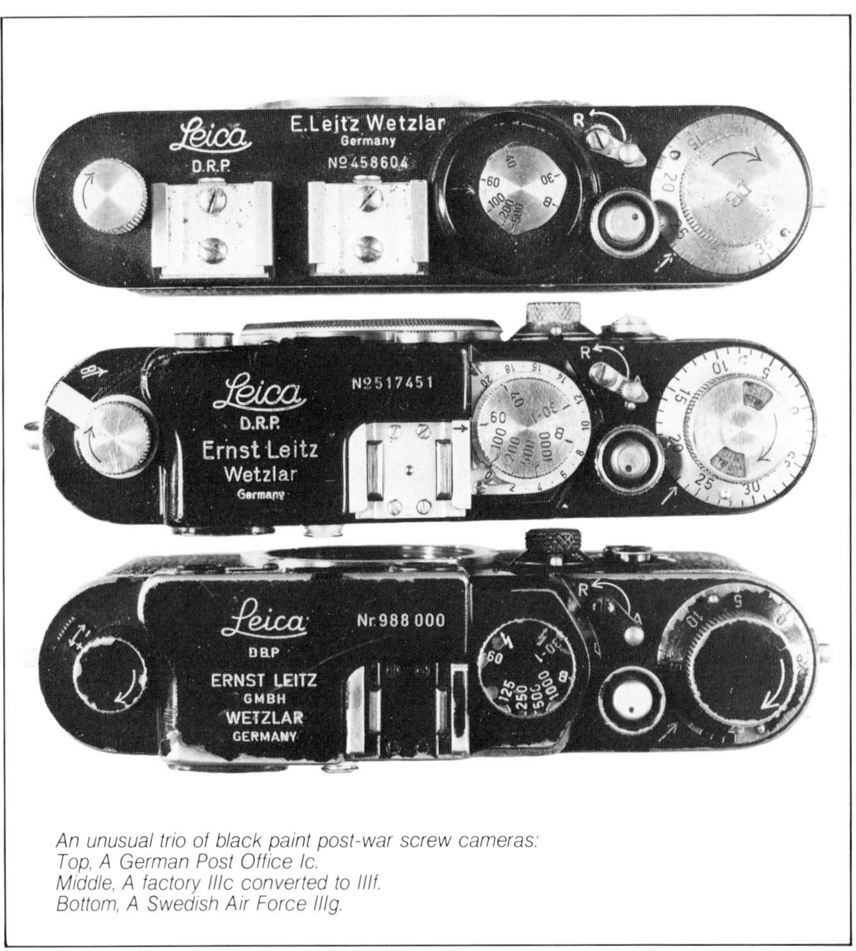

An unusual trio of black paint post-war screw cameras:
Top, A German Post Office Ic.
Middle, A factory IIIc converted to IIIf.
Bottom, A Swedish Air Force IIIg.

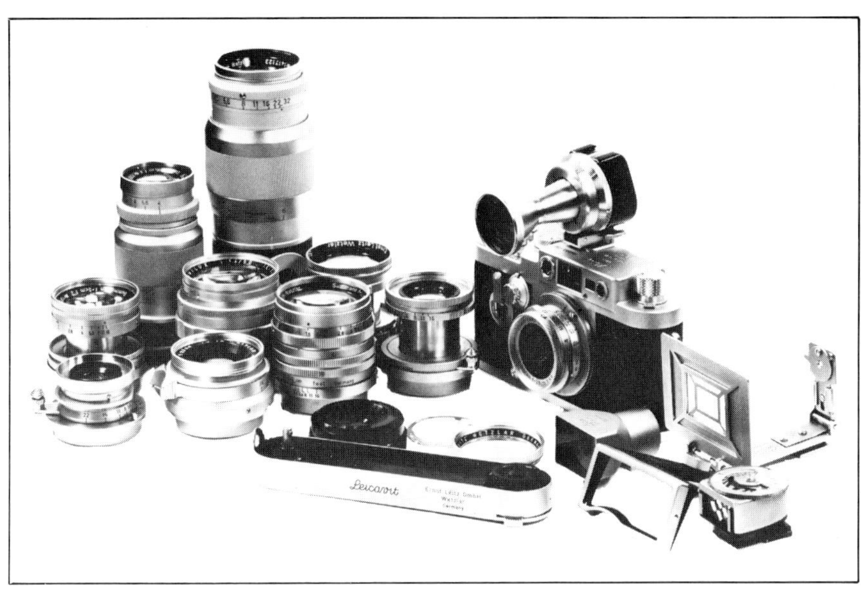

The zenith of the LEICA screw system. LEICA IIIg with contemporary lenses, most of which were also available in bayonet mount for the new LEICA M3. Also shown are the LEICAVIT rapid wind base, framefinder ROSOL, universal viewfinder VIOOH with adapter for 28mm lensesTUVOO, close focusing device ADVOO, 35mm finder SBLOO, and eyepiece for converting a 50 or 90mm lens into a telescope OSBLO.

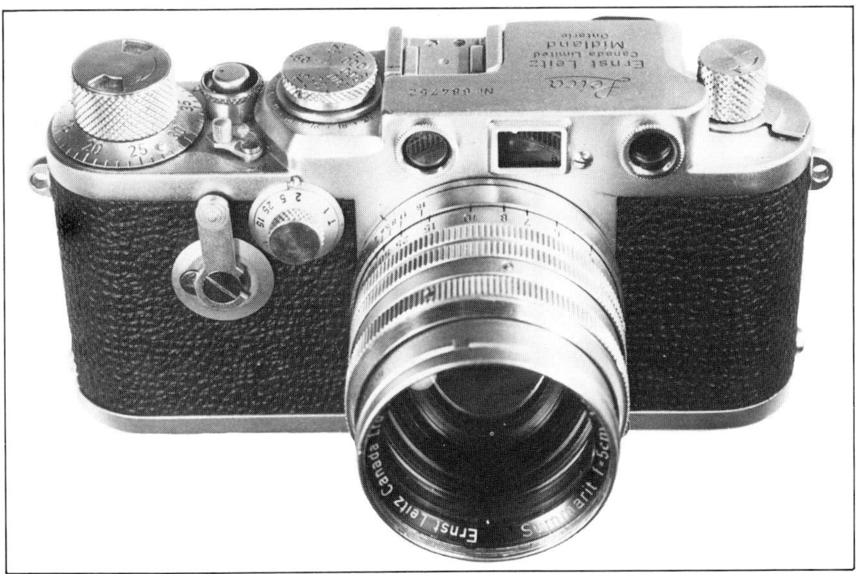

The very rare IIIf with Leitz Canada engraving (see page 72).

Chapter 7

The M Revolution – Beginning of another Thirty Year Saga

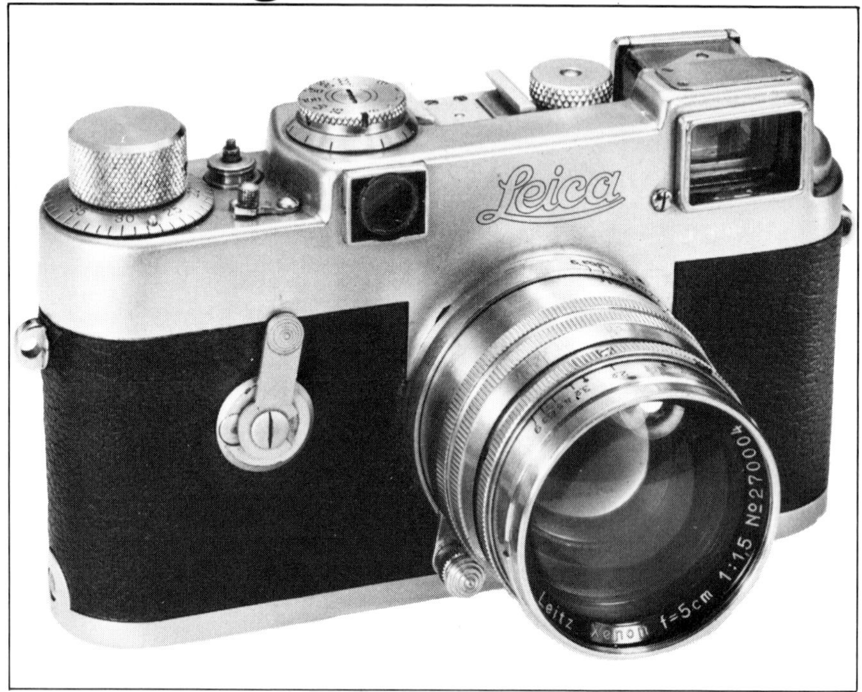

LEICA IV

In 1954, thirty years after the LEICA was born, a completely new model was introduced, without the time honoured screw lens mount. It was called the M3. It differed from the screw-mount cameras in many important respects:

- the bayonet lens mount that locked when the lens was turned 30° clockwise. This was much quicker than the screw system.
- the opening back which allowed for easier insertion of the film.
- the film advance operated by a lever.
- all shutter speeds on a single, non-rotating knob on the top of the camera, with equally spaced positions from B to 1/1000 second.
- the automatic frame counter that reset when a new film was inserted.
- automatic synchronisation for electronic flash and bulbs.

–   above all, the bright-line viewfinder with frames for 50mm, 90mm and 135mm lenses that automatically appeared when the appropriate lens was inserted. Furthermore the rangefinder image appeared in the centre of the viewfinder as a bright rectangle. The viewfinder had parallax correction down to 1 metre and the image was virtually life size (0.9x).

–   a longer rangefinder base, leading to greater accuracy in focusing.

Work on this camera was begun in the late thirties, as evidenced by some drawings for the single knob shutter mechanism and rangefinder-viewfinder system. Prototypes of the single knob shutter were assembled on IIIc bodies around 1942.

In the museum at Wetzlar is the so-called LEICA IV, made even earlier in 1935-36. It has some of the features of the M3, such as the single, non-rotating shutter speed dial, the enlarged rangefinder base, and an opening back flap. It also has interchangeable bright-line viewfinders that slipped into a clip behind the rangefinder window.

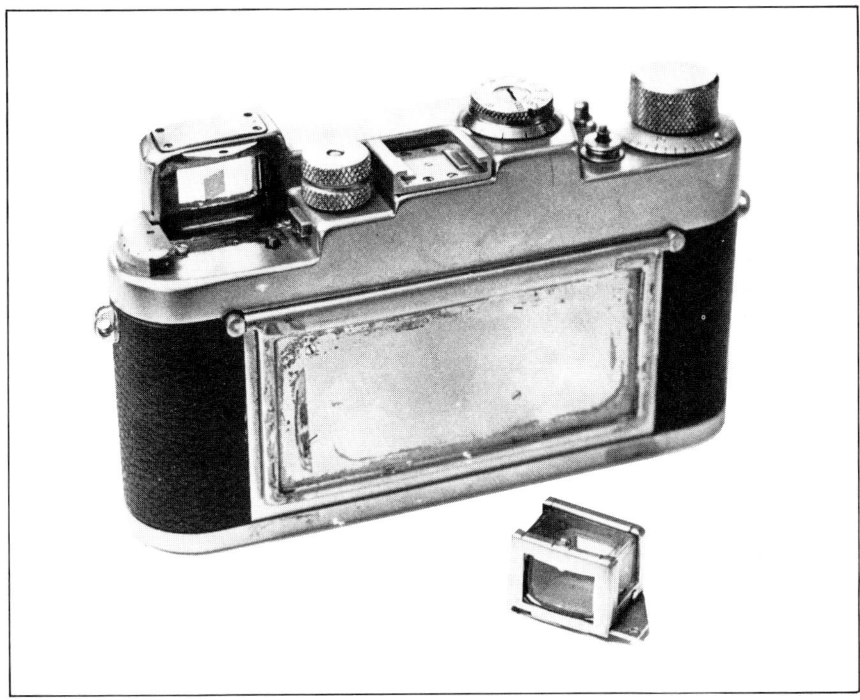

LEICA IV back view showing viewfinder removed

Proof of the perfection reached with this new design can be found in the fact that the basic M3 configuration and mechanism has been retained for over thirty years and is to be found still in the latest M6.

Null Series M3

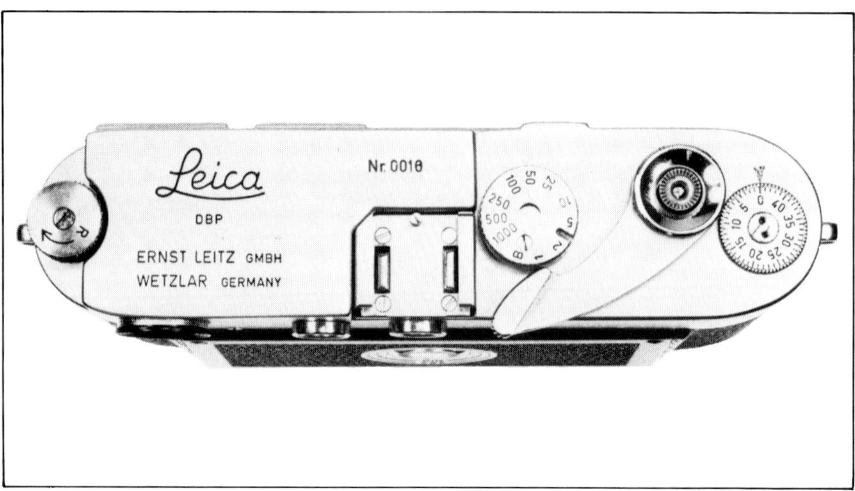

Top plate view of "Null" Model M3

A "Null" series of cameras is the pre-production run of prototypes of a new model. Leitz produced a number before the M3 was introduced in 1954. The exact number made is not known but a few lucky collectors have managed to obtain examples. These cameras were used by Leitz as working examples before making the commitment to production, and for determining any minor problems. Cameras were also loaned to selected LEICA users for evaluation. The example illustrated has a different type external film counter and different self-timer lever.

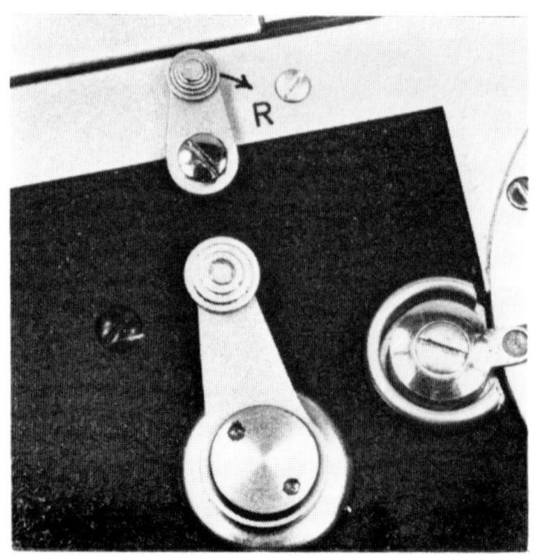

Detail of self-timer lever on "Null" Model M3

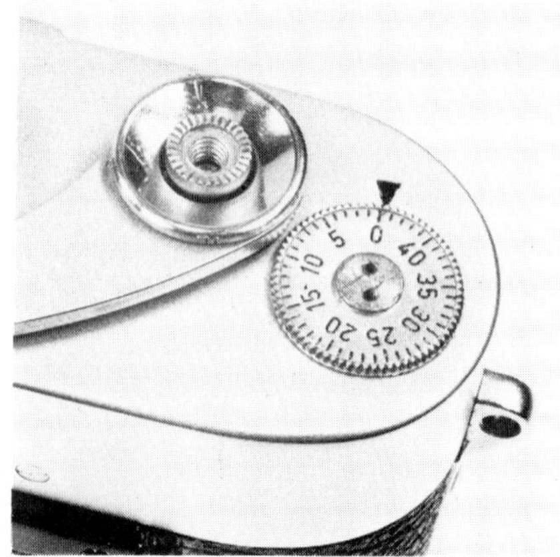

Detail of film counter on "Null" Model M3

LEICA M3

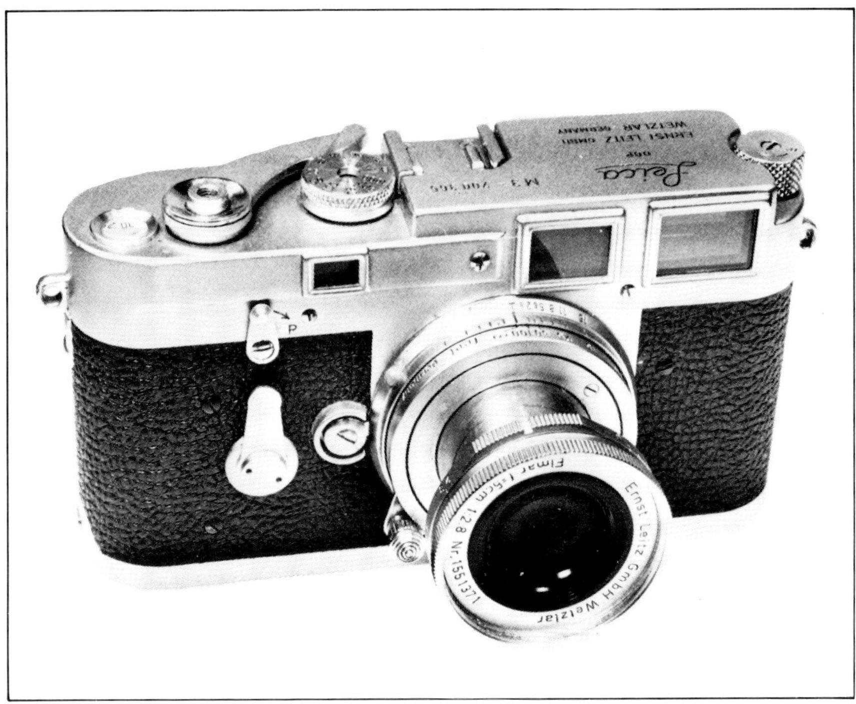

LEICA M3, early series, No. 700,365

The new model, to be known as the M3, was introduced in 1954. The first camera in the production series was No. 700,000 and the model remained in production until 1966, ending with No. 1,164,865.

The front of the camera had three rectangular windows, the smallest one at the left of the camera (looking from the front) for the rangefinder, the central one with ground glass to illuminate the frames, and the biggest one at the right side of the camera for the viewfinder. In the viewfinder (apart from the rangefinder image in the centre) there was also a frame which corresponded with the lens being used; the 50mm lens had the biggest frame, with a small border around the edges to make sure that nothing important was left out of the picture; the frames for 90mm and 135mm lenses appeared when the respective lenses were inserted. Leitz made a special wide-angle 35mm lens, with correcting objectives which were positioned in front of both the rangefinder and viewfinder windows.

The film-type indicator was a disc and was located on the back of the camera (one for daylight colour, one for artificial light colour and one for b/w) and an ASA/DIN scale. This indicator was also applied to the IIIg type.

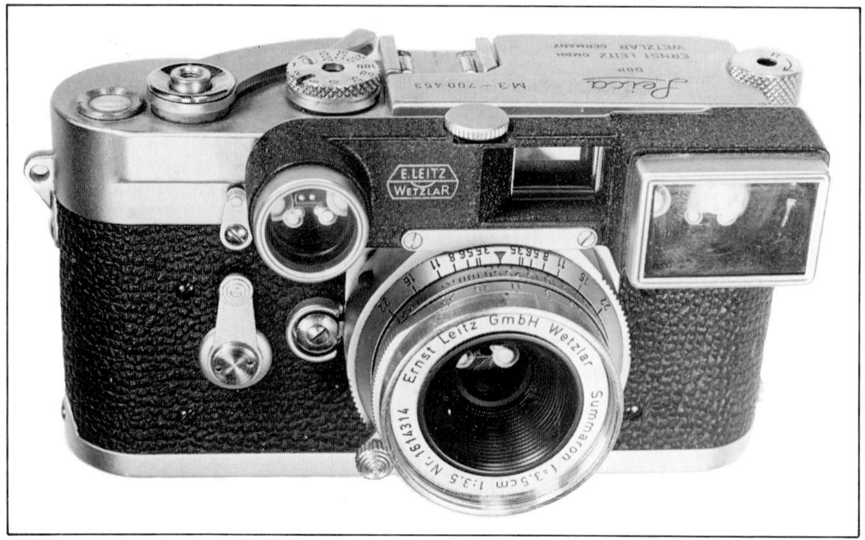

Above: One of the first production batch LEICA M3's with triangular strap lugs and no frame selector. It is fitted with a 35mm SUMMARON which has a converting lens in front of the viewfinder so that the camera's 50mm frame will show the field of view of the 35mm lens, and a compensating objective in front of the rangefinder window.
Below: An M3 of ten years later in the rare black paint finish, with round lugs and frame selector. The lens is the M3 version of the 35mm SUMMICRON.

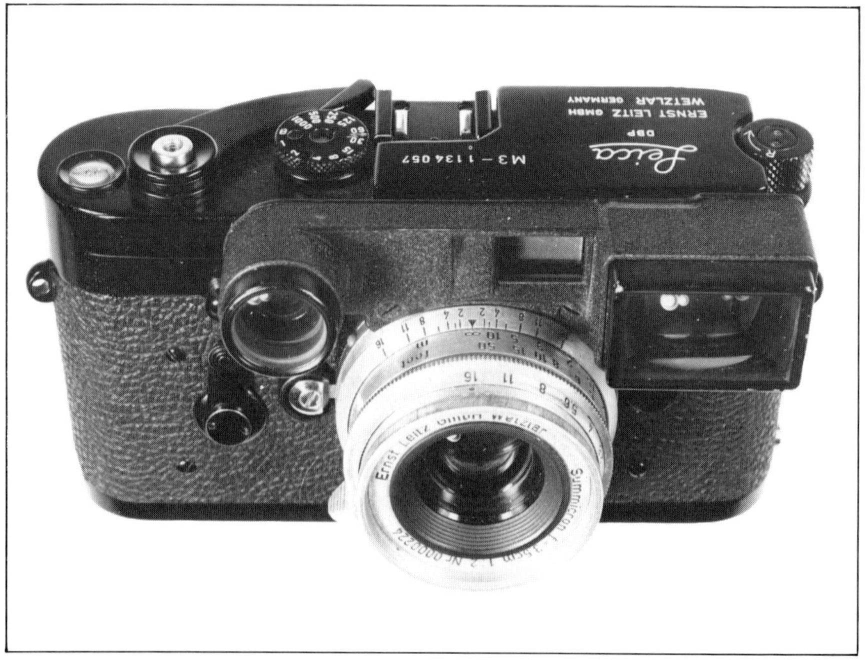

The camera was subjected to several changes and improvements during its lifetime; first the frame selector lever (or previewer) was added, which allowed the frame in the viewfinder to be changed manually, no matter what lens was inserted; this was done, starting from camera No. 785,801, in 1955. From 1957 (from camera No. 844,001) the pressure plate, which was previously made of glass, was made of metal. The advance movement was changed in 1958 from the original two strokes to a single stroke, starting from camera No. 915,251 and in 1956 the sequence of shutter speeds also changed.

The first M3 had the following sequence: B-1-2-5-10-25-50-100-200-500-1000; this changed to B-1-2-4-8-15-30-60-125-250-500-1000 and it is evident that the second scale is more equally spaced and there is also one additional speed. Electronic flash synchronisation in both cases was at 1/50 second. This happened in March 1957, when other changes were made, namely a new hinged back and an improved rangefinder.

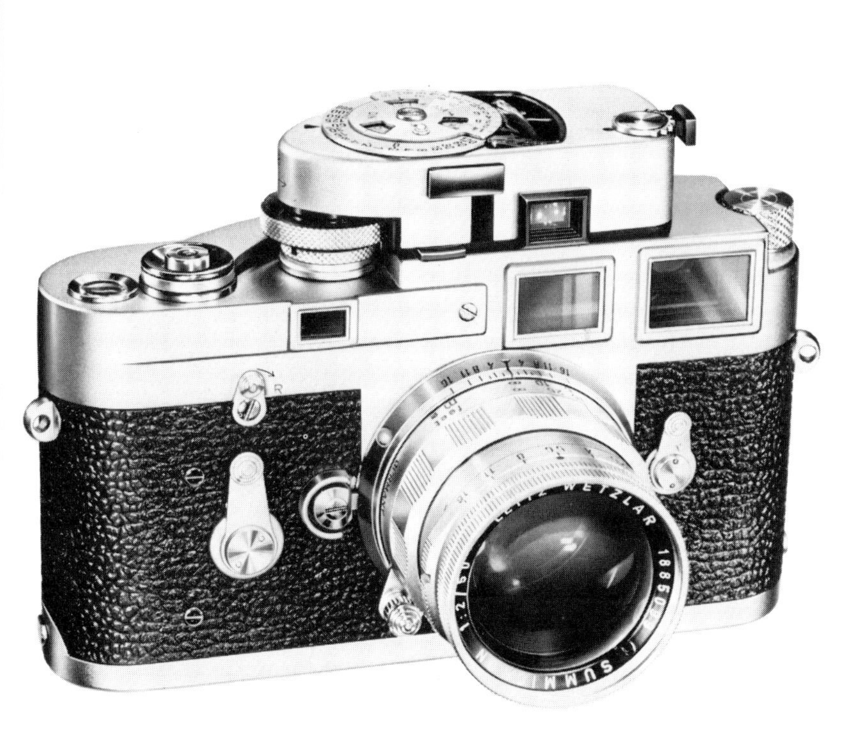

LEICA M3, late series, with early form of MR meter with projecting switch

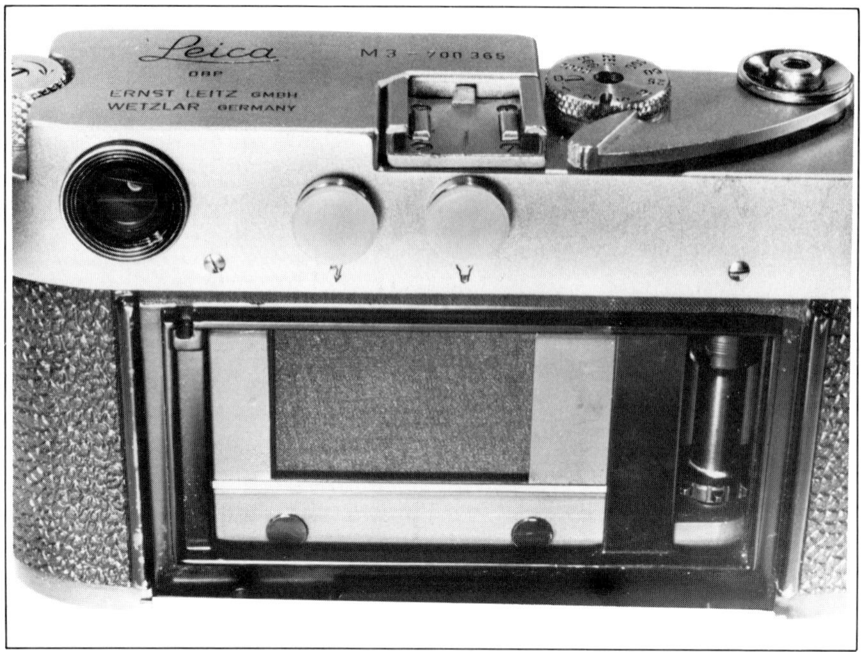

Back view of early model LEICA M3, No. 700,365

Smaller changes occurred: the body lugs which were previously triangular became round; the rewind knobs which had, at first, one red slot, then one red dot, finally had two red dots to indicate that it was moving and that the film was unwinding regularly; the screws which were on the back of the top cover later disappeared; the hinged back cover at first had pressure locks which were later discarded; when the M2 (which had two notches for the depth of field indicator visible in rangefinder) was introduced, they were also added to the M3.

At first the M3 was finished in chrome, and for a long period the only exception was the small series of about 150 MP's in black. Then a series of 100 black M3's was made in 1959, beginning with serial No. 959,401; several more small batches of about 200 cameras were made in 1960 and 1961, followed by a large series of 2,000 in 1962 (Nos. 1,044,001 to 1,046,000). After this series, more small batches were made, so that it is unlikely that more than 4,000 black M3's were manufactured altogether. Many of the series were allotted to Ernst Leitz, Canada, and in fact the M3 model was produced in large quantities over there. Also special models, with different finishes, were made for military use.

The code name for the bare camera was IGEMO and with lenses was IMARO with ELMAR f3.5 and IMOLO with ELMAR f2.8. Names changed during the years with the SUMMICRON: with earlier types of SUMMICRON f2 it was ISUMO, but later it became ISOUN with non-collapsible lens and ISMON with the dual range lens. With SUMMARIT f1.5 it was ISAIO and with SUMMILUX f1.4 IMOOT.

LEICA MP (Professional)

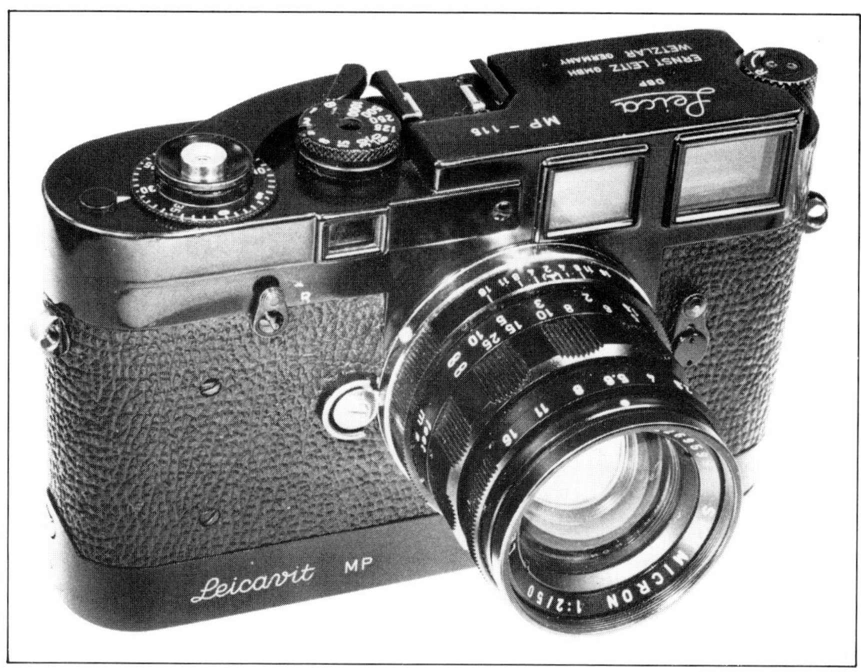

LEICA MP (Black)

A special variant of the model M3, the LEICA MP, made its brief appearance on the market in 1956; it was a camera suitable for the press reporter as it was, by noting their suggestions, that this camera was produced. There was an initial run in 1956 of eleven cameras marked MP1 to MP11, then the factory files indicate allocion for serial numbers of MP12 to MP500 for this camera; however actual production runs were from MP12 to MP150 in black finish, and from MP151 to MP450 in chrome finish. The ledger where deliveries were recorded lists the last number as 402, delivered on August 22nd, 1958.

The frame counter was of the external, manual reset type (later to be fitted to the M2) the range/viewfinder system was as that fitted to the M3. The advance mechanism was the two stroke type and no self timer was fitted. The rangefinder did not have the depth of field indicator notches as used on the later M3. Under the base cover with the drawing which illustrated how to insert the film, there was the number of the body and the letter P. Most important of all were the number and letters MP on top, and the fact that the camera was delivered equipped with the LEICAVIT MP rapid wind base; because of this the MP was also equipped with a winding shaft for the film take-up spool, which the M3 did not have and the M2 had later, so the M2 can also use the LEICAVIT (and so can the M1).

Other technical features were those of the M3, with speed sequence from B to one second, 1/2 – 1/4 – 1/8 – 1/15 – 1/30 – 1/60 – 1/125 – 1/250 – 1/500 and 1/1000; the viewfinder had frames for 50 – 90 and 135 lenses with preview lever, and the button for unlocking the lens had a collar around it as on the M3.

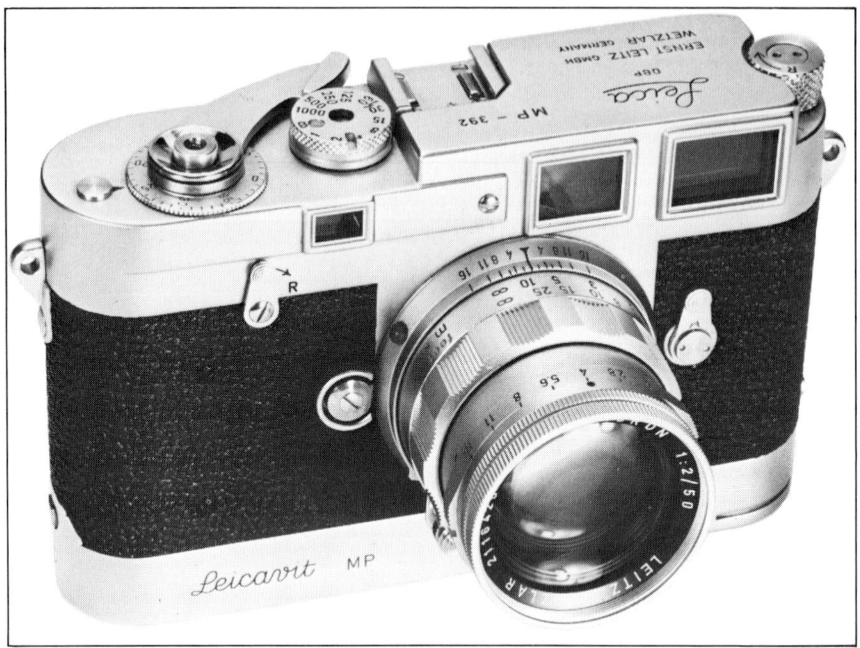

LEICA MP (Chrome)

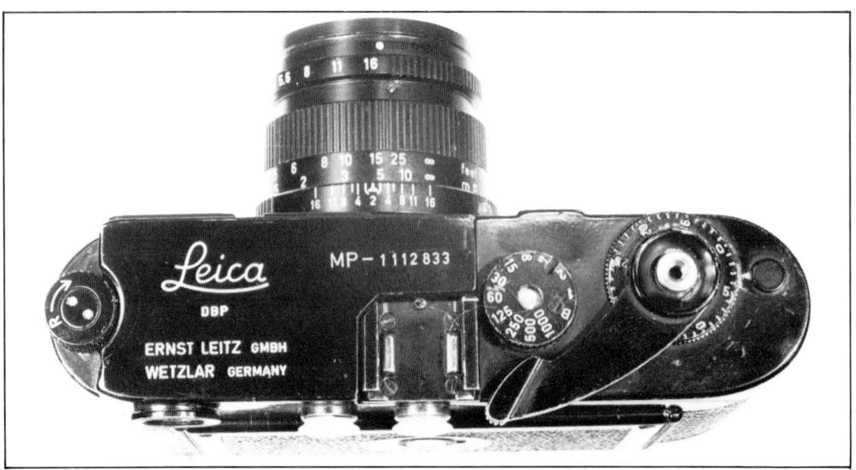

A LEICA MP believed to have been made to special order, utilising an M2 serial number but complying with the MP specification in all respects.

Chapter 8

Development of the
LEICA M

Following their tradition of making a simpler and less expensive model, Leitz introduced in 1958 the M2. It had most of the characteristics of the M3, except for the self-timer and the automatic resetting of the frame counter, but it had a viewfinder system that was quite different in both its construction and its facilities. Automatically changing frames were provided for 35, 50 and 90mm lenses, in place of the 50, 90 and 135mm frames of the M3. This was probably more useful for the general photographer, and also for press photographers who tended to favour wide-angle lenses. This viewfinder system became the basis for the viewfinders of all subsequent LEICA M models when additional frames were added to accommodate other focal lengths. Making provision for the 35mm

LEICA M2

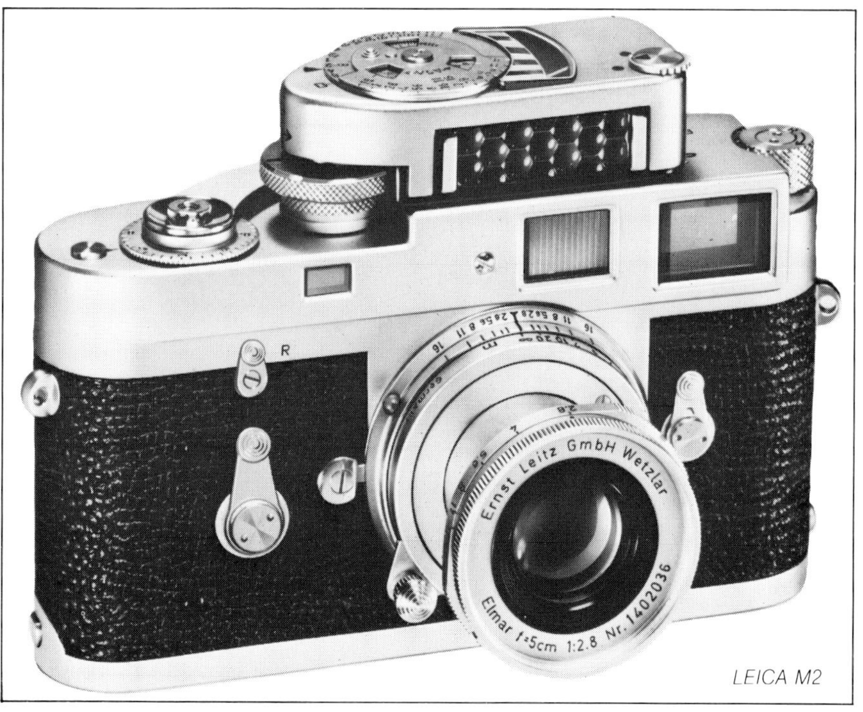

LEICA M2

frame meant that the viewfinder image was reduced in size compared to the near life size of the M3 image.

Production of the M2 started in 1958 with No. 926,600. A year later the self-timer was restored for the benefit of the amateur photographer when he wished to be included in the picture. In the first series of M2 a rewind button was provided instead of a lever as on the M3.

A trend was beginning to show that the black camera was again "in". The M2 was finished either in black or in chrome, black being always more expensive. The first batch of black M2's were 500 cameras, the first serial number being 948,601. The following bach of 400 cameras (starting with serial number 949,101) had the self timer and were chrome, later there were a few hundred more M2's produced finished in black (see page 101). Cameras with and without the self timer were produced in approximately the same quantities with also a few hundred serial numbers allocated to Ernst Leitz Canada.

The M2 type was the large production model that could use the LEICAVIT: it can therefore be considered as a simplification of the MP type. Consequently it was a very popular model, ranking in production only second to the M3. Compared with some 200,000 M3's there are on record some 75,000 M2's in chrome, plus 1,800 black, and 4,200 with delayed action release; Canada produced another 1,600 and there were 2,000 of the M2-R type.

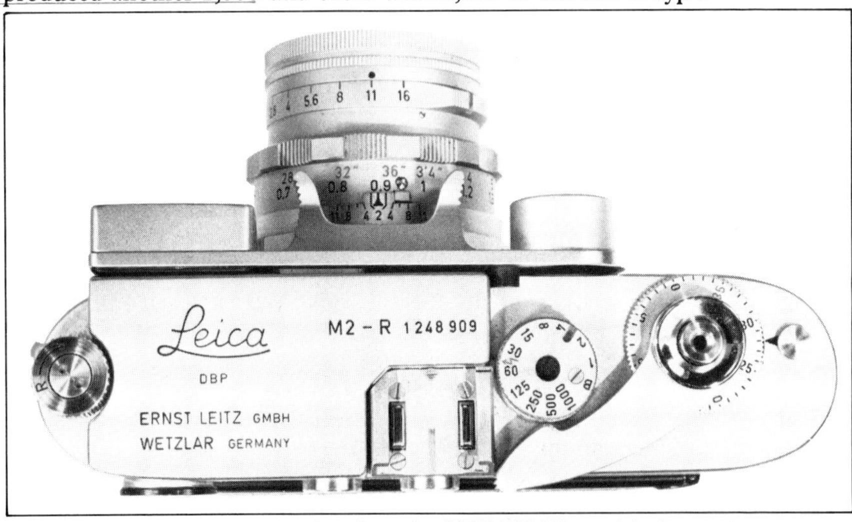

LEICA M2-R complete with 50mm close focussing SUMMICRON as originally supplied

The cameras equipped with self release were called M2-S in the USA, but this was never engraved on them.

The M2 was also a long lived model; it was in production until 1967 and proved very successful. It was the first M model that was adaptable for electric motor drive for sequence shots, the motors being made in the U.S.A. The cameras had to be modified there, and later in 1966, a batch of 276 cameras was made by Leitz and they bear the marking "M2M". The M2 had the full speed range from B to 1/1000th of a second in the new difinitive scale range, with full flash synchronisation. The camera mainly differed from the M3 in respect of the range/viewfinder system, 35/50/90, manual frame-set counter and other minor details.

An interesting feature of the M2 was the depth of field indicator visible in the viewfinder (later fitted to the M3), there were two tabs, or notches, in the rangefinder field, a wide one on top and a narrow one on the bottom. When the double image of an object, not exactly in focus, was within the width of the narrow notch, it indicated that the object was nonetheless sharp if the lens was stopped down to 5.6; the wider notch indicated sharpness of focus if the lens was stopped down to 16.

Code names were KOOHE for the bare camera, KIHOO for the camera with ELMAR f2.8 lens, KIOOL for the camera with the normal SUMMICRON f2 lens, KNOOG with the dual range SUMMICRON, and finally KSOOB with the SUMMILUX f1.4 lens.

M2-R cameras were manufactured in 1969-70, initially for the U.S. Army [KS-15(4),] but a number were sold by Leitz N.Y. These cameras had the M4 type of quick-load spool. Most were supplied with close focus 50mm SUMMICRON's.

LEICA MP2

Further examination of the files indicates the existence of the MP2 and that there should have been a run of 512 MP2's in 1958 starting from serial No. 952,000. These were however M2's supplied initially with LEICAVIT MP base and it would have avoided confusion if they had been known as M2-P. The essential difference is that the viewfinder system of the MP was based on that of the M3, and that of the MP2 on that of the M2.

The genuine MP2 is a rare item indeed: two specimens in black were made, belonging to a small series from No. 935,501 to 935,511; other cameras, all in chrome, were in the series from 952,001 to 952,015. The main difference between the MP and MP2 is that the latter is equipped with all the electrical circuitry to make it possible to use the electric motor drive, as an alternative to the LEICAVIT. Leitz even went so far as to experiment with their own electric motor, but the American-made one was also useable.

The German prototype for the electric motor was similar to the American one as far as the motor itself was concerned, but the battery case was made cylindrical and screwed on the bottom, so that it served as a handgrip.

Apart from the viewfinder, the other features were almost the same on both the MP and MP2. One noticeable difference, however, was that there was the rewind lever on the MP, whereas there was the button on the MP2, as on the early M2. The two small series of MP2 were made respectively in 1962 and 1963.

It is uncertain if the MP2 cameras were ever sold to customers or whether some of them were simply handed over to the professionals for evaluation. A few are now in private collections.

An illustration of the camera will be found in Chapter 17 where it is fitted with the Wetzlar motor.

LEICA M1

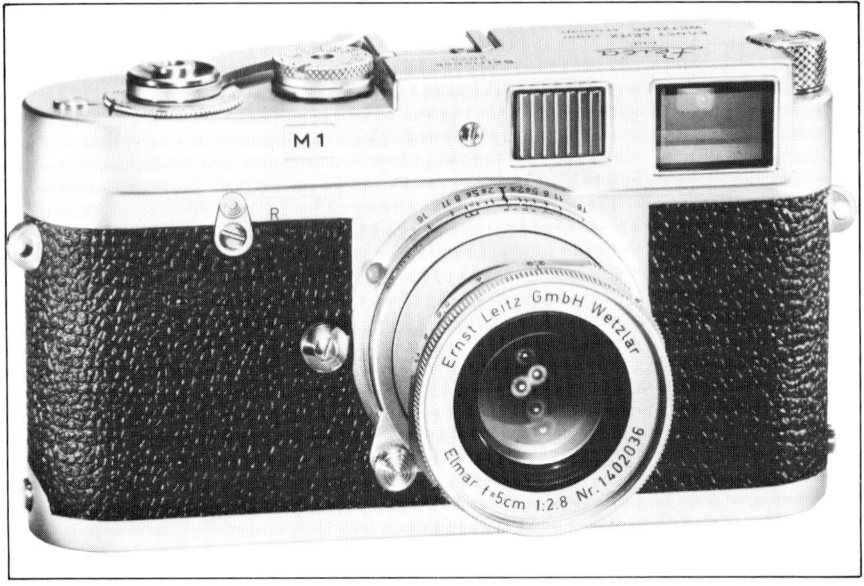

LEICA M1

The LEICA M1, introduced in 1959 with No. 950,001, is a simplified version of the M2. It was produced mainly for scientific applications, such as photomicrography, and as a wide-angle camera. Like the old LEICA Standard it had no rangefinder, but it did have a viewfinder with frames for 50mm and 35mm lenses. These frames had parallax correction, so although there was no rangefinder, there was an arm in the usual position to contact the lens focusing ring and give the parallax correction as the lens was focused by simple reckoning of the distance.

The camera had the same shutter speed range as the M3 and M2, and full flash synchronisation. The type number was not marked on top of the camera, but on the blanked off rangefinder window. The frame counter was of the manual resetting type, as on the M2, and the take-up spool spindle could accept the LEICAVIT. Least expensive of all LEICA M series, it was ideal for use as an ever-ready camera with a 35mm lens, or for using with the VISOFLEX with long focus lenses.

It was made until 1964 and was also the last LEICA to bear a code name, which was KOOCT for the camera without lens. With the ELMAR f3.5/50mm lens the code was KOOML and with the more usual (by then) ELMAR f2.8/50mm the code was KOOEU.

The M1 could be converted to the M2 by Leitz by the addition of a rangefinder system. It is quite possible, therefore, to find a M2 with a M1 number and without "M2" engraved on the top-plate. The original "M1" engraved on the blanked off rangefinder window would, of course, have been lost in the conversion.

LEICA MD

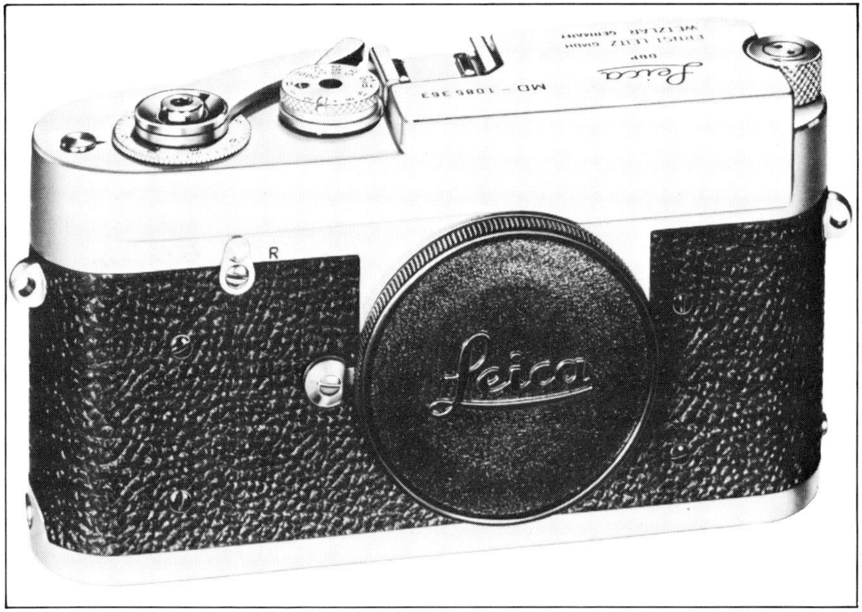

LEICA MD

In 1965 the MD had been introduced to replace the M1. As it was intended for scientific use, no viewfinder or rangefinder was fitted.

An interesting feature for scientific work was that the camera could be equipped with a special baseplate with a slot in it. This allowed insertion of index strips, about 4mm wide, that covered a small part of the negative. The opening for the strips was on the picture side nearer the rewind end of the camera. This permitted one to record any pertinent information directly on the negative by just writing it on a strip of clear plastic and inserting it into the camera through the light trap in the baseplate before making the exposure.

Shutter speeds were in the usual range from B to one second and all the way to 1/1000. The lens mount could take any M series lens, but obviously most of the work would be done with a reflex attachment or, in some cases, with lenses of fixed focus at fixed distances. However, the MD could be used as a normal camera by fitting an appropriate viewfinder.

It remained in production for only two years (1965-66) as it was soon

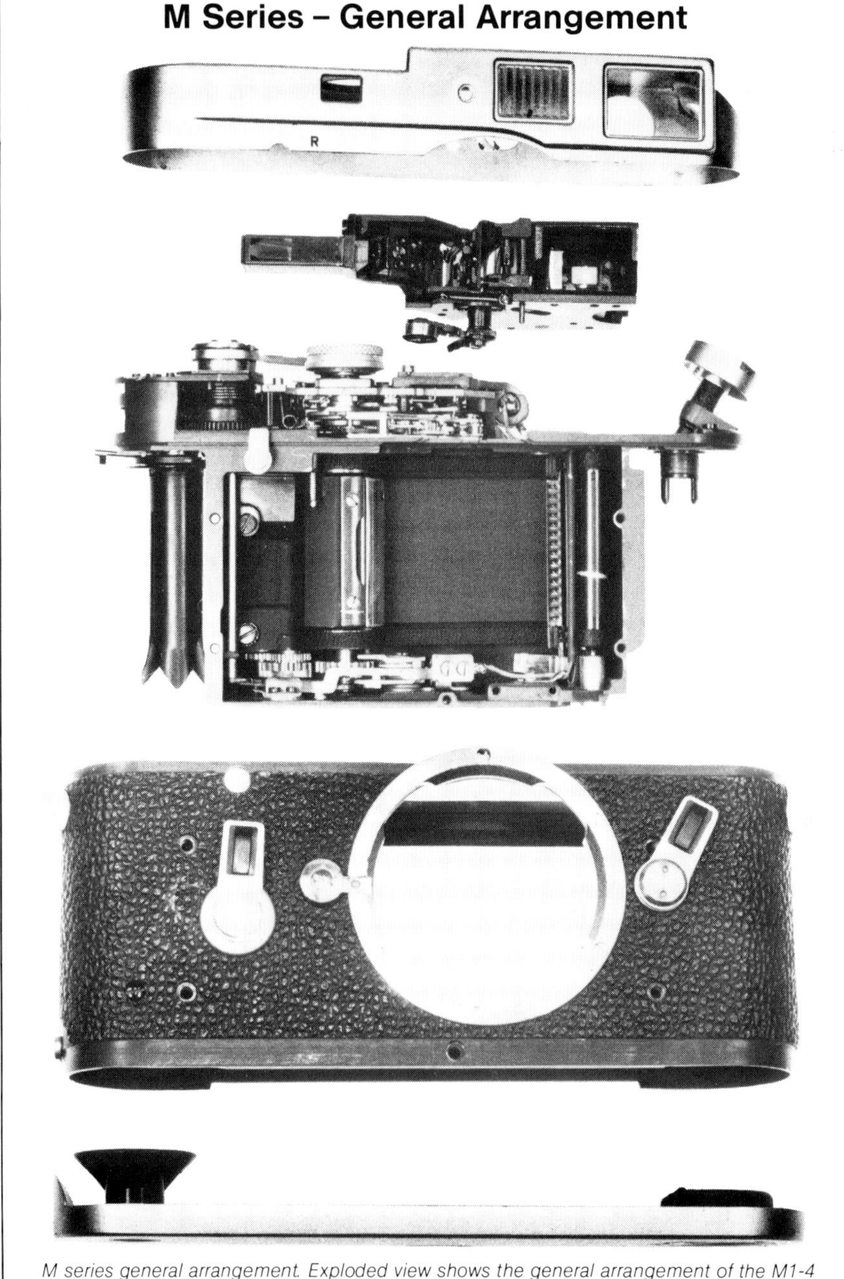

M series general arrangement. Exploded view shows the general arrangement of the M1-4 cameras; top plate, rangefinder unit, main shutter crate, body shell and base plate

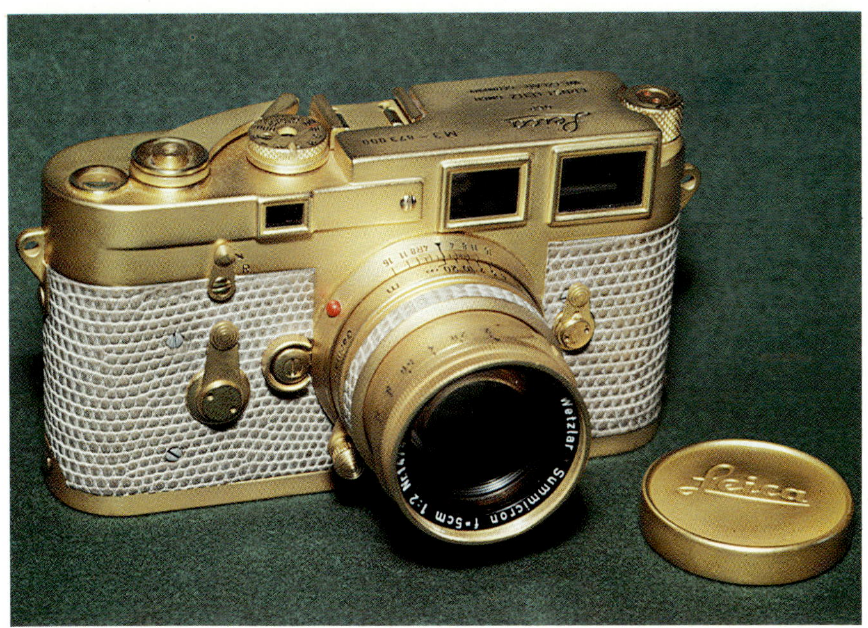

Two unusual gold plated cameras. The M3 at the top was sold at auction in Italy and is said to have belonged to the Tiranty family, the Leitz distributors in France. It is not the M3 presented to Philippe Tiranty by Leitz in 1957. The gold M5 is retained at Wetzlar: it was apparently a special order that was never taken up.

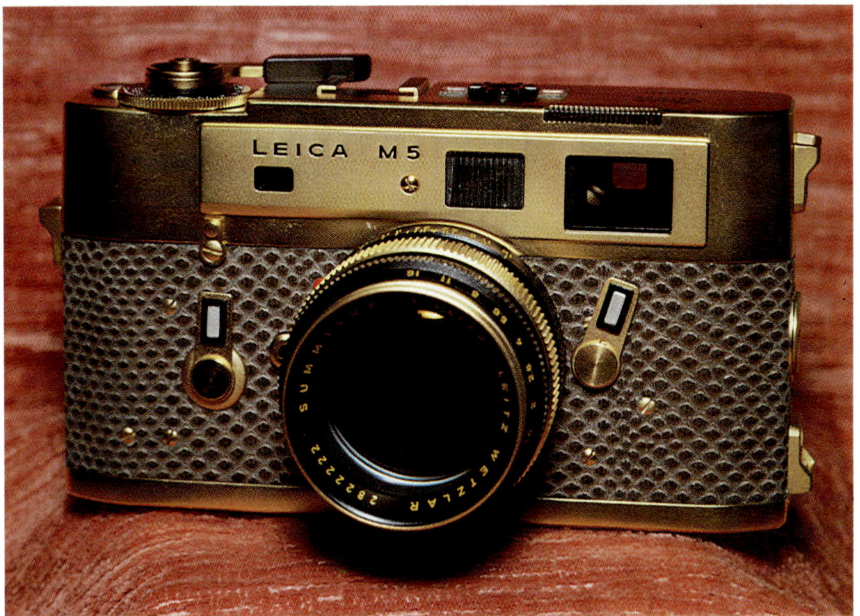

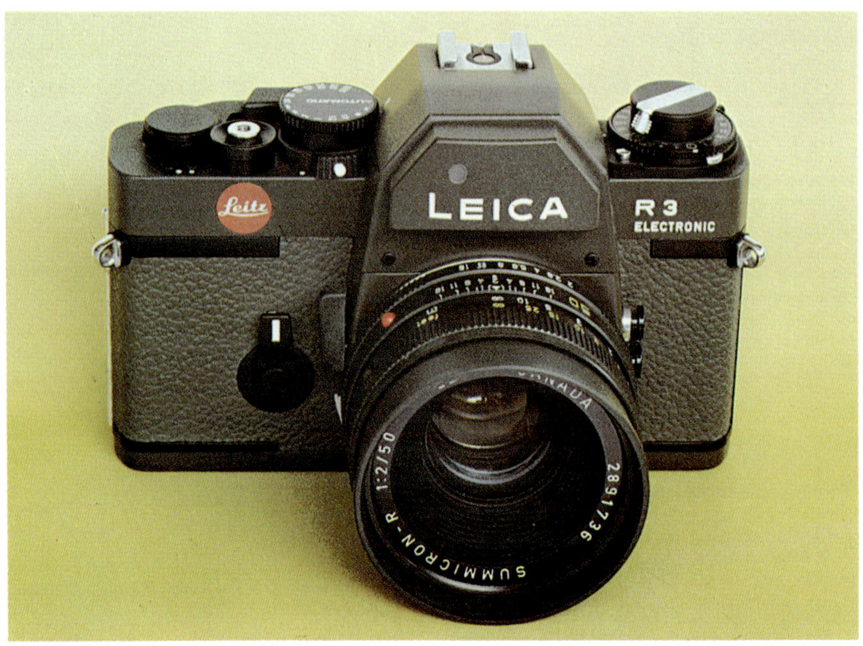

Leitz have adopted the practice in recent years of offering their cameras in special finishes in limited editions. At the top is the so-called "Safari" R3 and below the R4 in gold.

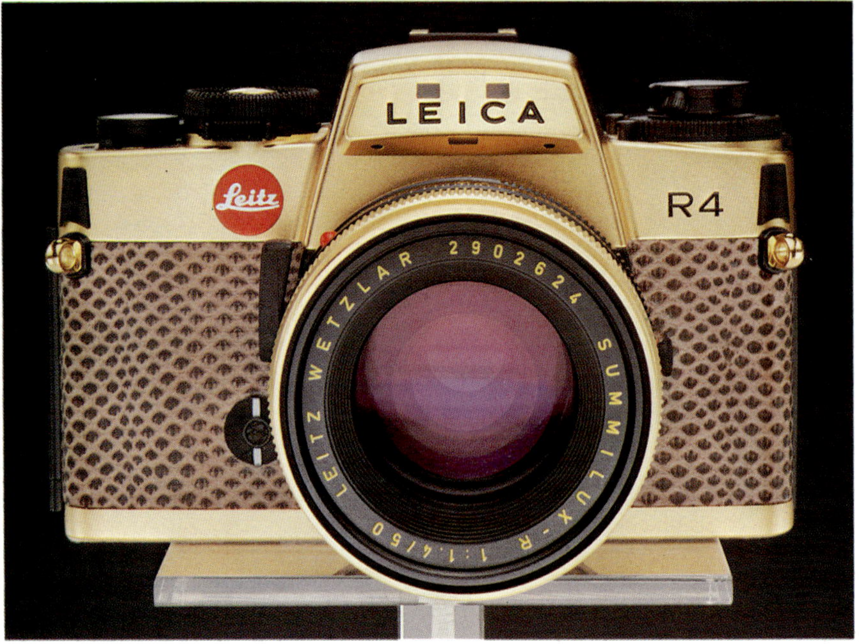

superseded by an improved model, the MDa. About 3,500 cameras were made and the last serial number was, 1,160,820.

The known variants of this model are those named "Post Cameras" that are described in Chapter 14. These were made specially for the postal services of some countries; they were never sold to the general public.

LEICA M4

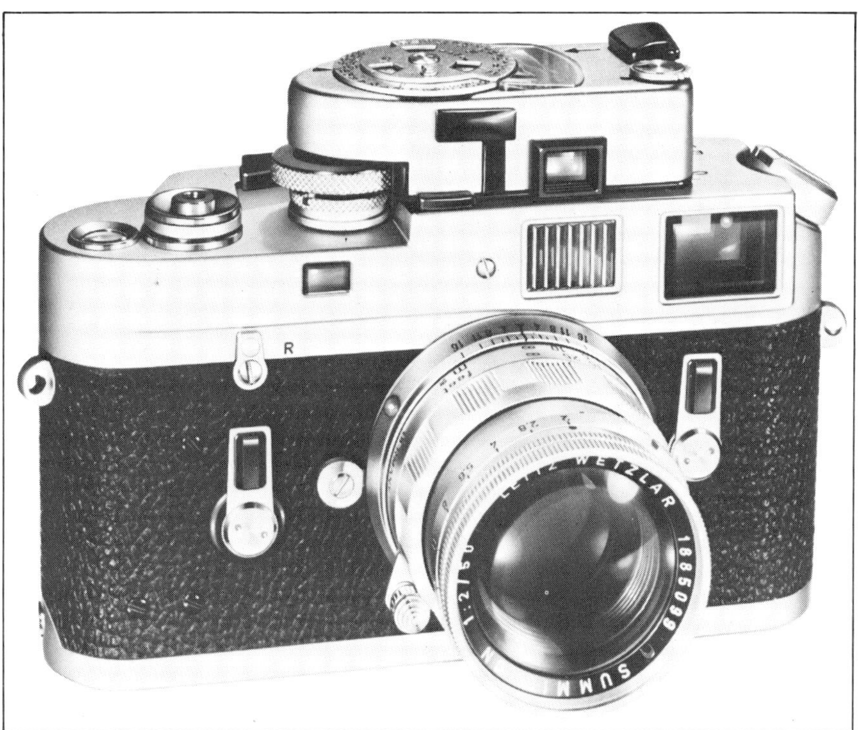

LEICA M4 with Leicameter MR4 with switch on top to avoid fouling rewind crank

Following the policy of constant improvement of the LEICA without any planned obsolescence of the existing models, the LEICA M4 was introduced in 1967, starting with serial number 1,175,001.

It had the best features of the M3 and M2 combined, with further added refinements. The body was only slightly altered by the presence of a new rewind crank in place of the extendable knob, slanted outward to ease operation; the lever folded when not in use. The viewfinder had the frames for 35, 50 and 90mm lenses, as on the M2, plus a 135mm frame. The 35mm and 135mm frames appeared together.

The preview lever, the self-timer and the rewind lever were all in their usual positions, as in the M3 model. use of the camera was made easier by an improved loading system, which did not require inserting the free end of the film into a separate take up spool. The frame counter was self-resetting to minus two when the camera was opened. The film advance lever was of improved design, with a hinged tip for easier use. The self timer, frame selector and rewind lever were also of new design. Indicating a departure from the classical shapes in favour of a new look, more modern and perhaps with a wider appeal.

Initially the M4 was produced in the standard chrome finish, and later the black enamelled M4 was manufactured. After that black and chrome models were produced.

The M4 was also specially made by Leitz, in small batches, for direct use with the American-made electric motors and duly marked M4 MOT or in some cases M4M; these were always black cameras.

Some numbers were allotted to Ernst Leitz Canada and production officially stopped in 1971 with serial number 1,286,700; however late in 1973 it was decided to make another small number of black M4's, finished in the new black chrome, which had been developed for the M5's from both Canada and Wetzlar. Late production Canadian M4's in black chrome were actually engraved with Leitz Canada wording, whereas earlier cameras assembled in Canada carried "Wetzlar" engraved top-plates.

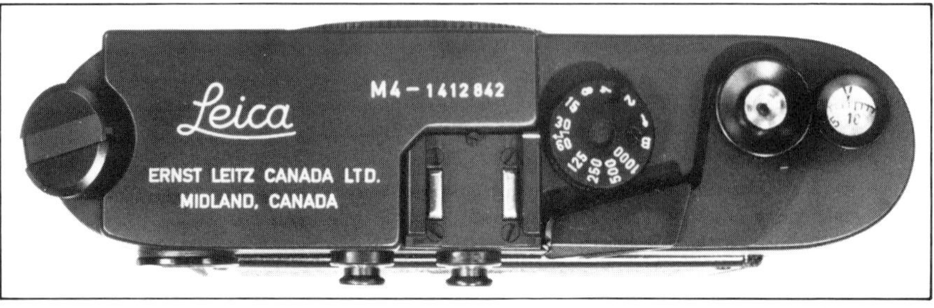

Top plate detail of black/chrome LEICA M4, (E. Leitz Canada)

LEICA M4 detail of rewind lever extended

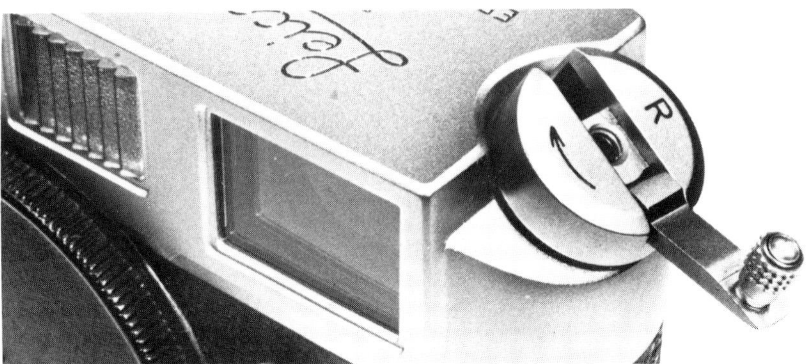

The last M4 occurs in 1975 with numbers from 1,443,000 to 1,443,170.

The shutter speed dial had the standard sequence: B-1-2-4-8-15-30-60-125-250-500-1000. The flash synchronisation was the same as in the M3, but with standard 3mm coaxial socket which did not require a special cable.

For the M4 the new LEICAMETER MR4 was very suitable, its field of measurement being the same as the 90mm lens field so readings could be taken using the 90mm frame in the viewfinder as a guide.

The film type indicator was still on the back cover as in the M3, and markings on top of the camera were also of the same style. A curious detail of the black enamelled M4 was that the strap eyelets were chromed, but on the final black chrome series they are black.

LEICA MDa

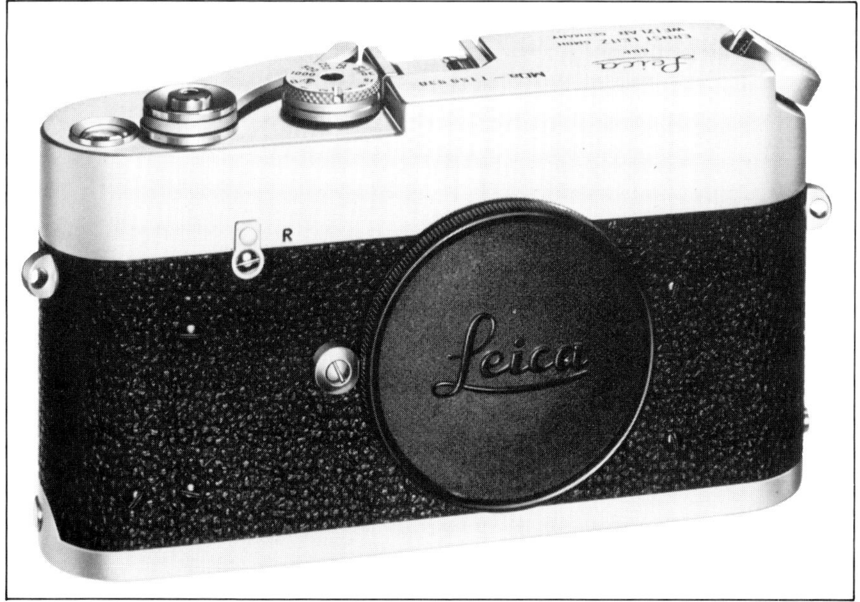

LEICA MDa

The change from the M3 model to the M4 model brought about the consequential change from the MD to the MDa. The latter possessed some of the distinctive features of the M4, most prominent of which was the new rewind crank instead of the now out-of-date knob. This was placed at an angle which made it more convenient in operation.

The speed range of the shutter was, as usual, from B and one second to 1/1000 through the scale of 1-2-4-8-15-30-60-125-250-500-1000.

There was neither self-timer nor preview lever. The inside of the body also differed in several details; it had no viewfinder-rangefinder, but it had the special groove to receive the index strips used to write on the film. The camera was sold with the standard baseplate, but one could purchase the special baseplate with the slot as an accessory.

Full flash synchronisation was provided, as on all M series LEICA's with two 3mm coaxial sockets for contact of the bulb and electronic flash. Production started with serial number 1,159,001 and ended with 1,412,550; the scientific camera was then replaced with the new model MD-2.

A feature of the MDa was the exposure counter with automatic resetting when the camera back was opened, as on the M4. All known cameras of this type are bright chromed, a practice that would completely change with the new types.

LEICA M4-2

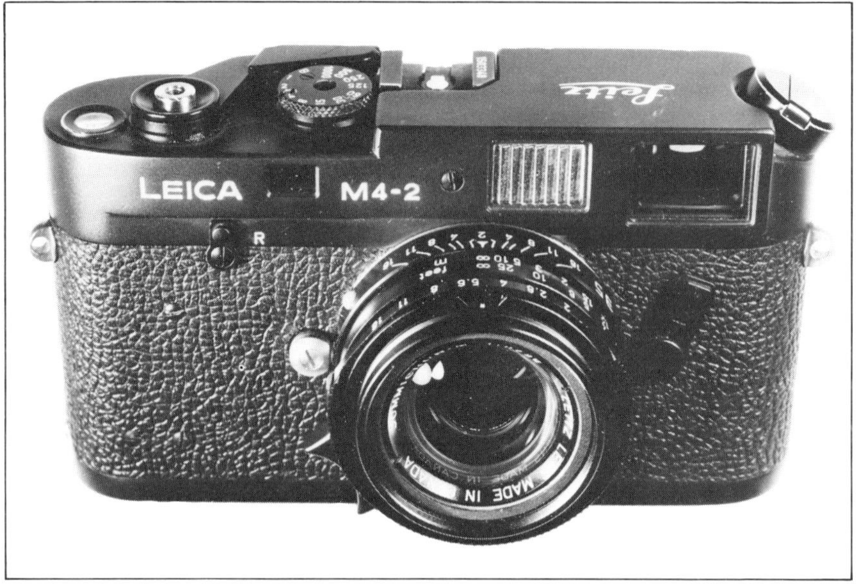

LEICA M4-2

The next model in the M series of cameras was the LEICA M5 which had through-lens metering, but this is dealt with in the next chapter.

The M4-2 was introduced in 1977 as a replacement for the M4 for which there was continuing demand. It did not differ greatly from the preceding type, only in refinements and the addition of more useful features, as in the tradition of Leitz. Production started with No. 1,480,001 and lasted through 1980 to end at No. 1,533,350.

The cameras of this series were all black, with the notable exception of those made in 1979 to celebrate the centenary of the birth of Oskar Barnack. These were gold-plated and had special numbers. Initially the total of "gold" M4-2 cameras should have been 500 (serial numbers 1,527,201-1,527,700), but on seeing the demand the factory decided that another series of 500 should be delivered which were numbers 1,528,151-1,528,650. Mechanically the camera was similar to the M4: only the self-timer had been dispensed with, but every camera was equipped with the electrical wiring and power shaft necessary for use with an electric motor. This motor was somewhat similar to the American one previously used with M2 and M4 cameras, but had been redesigned by Leitz and was powered by four instead of eight batteries.

Another important addition was the hot-shoe for flash in the accessory clip, but both contacts for bulb and electronic flash were retained on the back of the rangefinder cover.

Code No. 10,410 for black and 10,420 for gold type. The script on the front of the camera was similar to that used for the M5 (q.v.). The script on the top was new and was a replica of the classic LEICA logo. All this model was manufactured in Canada.

Of some interest for the collectors is the fact that about 95 cameras were delivered with a red disc in front bearing the name "Leitz"; these cameras are numbered from 1,468,001 to 1,468,091 plus a possible further 5 or 6. Any other camera with different numbers bearing the red disc is to be taken with the knowledge that the red shield has been added by someone other than the factory. This is the official information on the subject and is important because of the higher price the red shield cameras command.

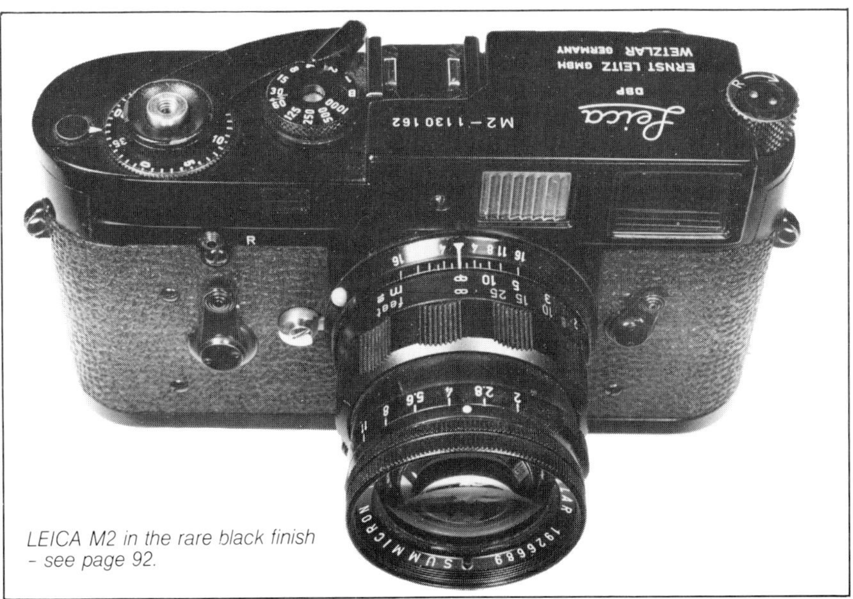

LEICA M2 in the rare black finish – see page 92.

LEICA MD-2

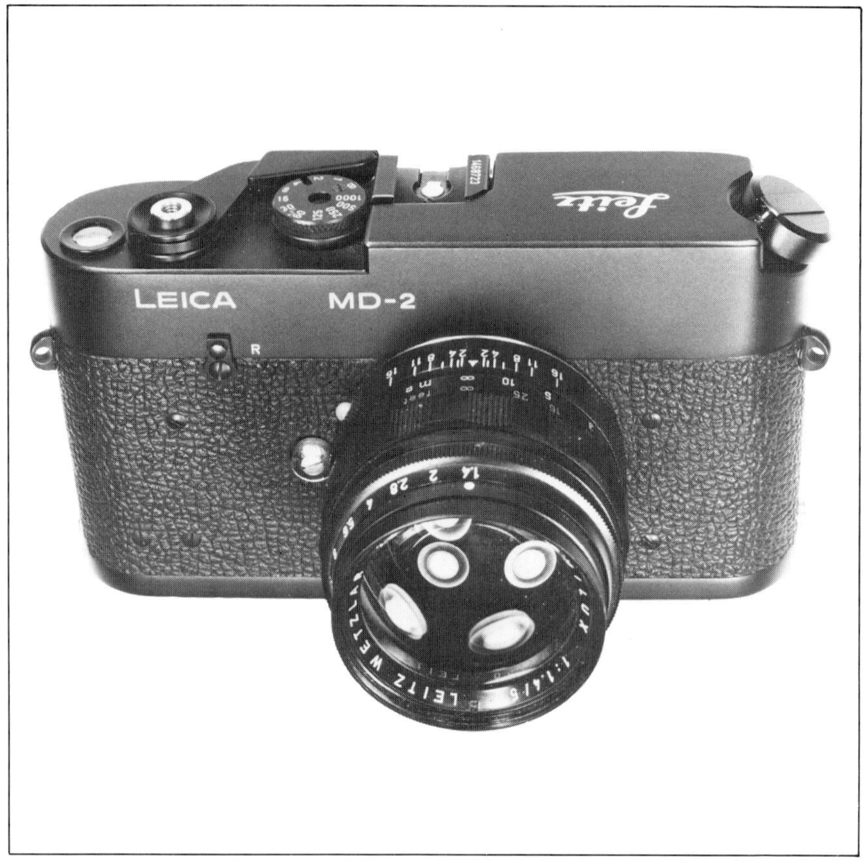

LEICA MD-2

When production of the main model of the rangefinder camera switched from the M4 to the M4-2, so the "scientific type" MDa changed into the MD-2. The first number in the factory list occurs in 1980, so it is possible that in the years after 1976, when there is a last mention of the MDa, the remaining cameras of this type were being sold.

The MD-2 has the hot-shoe contact in the accessory slide, and is prepared to take a motor drive, as all cameras are equipped with wiring and power shaft.

The script "Leica" and "MD-2" is on the camera front and the classic Leitz logo on top. Code No. is 10,105. All the cameras of this type are black.

A novel type of film reminder is on the hinged back: it consists of an aluminium disk on which it is possible to write with a pencil the type and speed of the film inside the camera.

LEICA M4-P

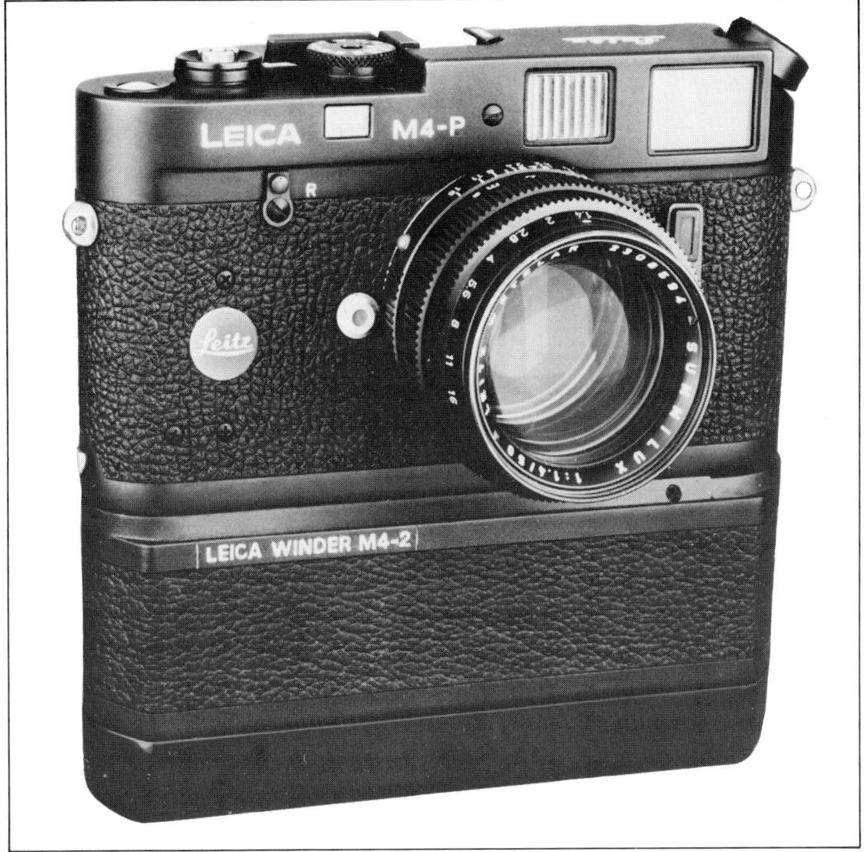

LEICA M4-P with M4-2 Winder

The LEICA M4-P is yet another step in the constant development of the rangefinder camera by Leitz: needless to say that in general appearance and main characteristics the M4-P is very similar to the M4-2. It was announced in 1980 and has been produced since that year.

The most important addition is in the number of frames that are present in the viewfinder, six instead of four, appearing two at a time when the appropriate lens is inserted. The two extra frames are for the 28mm lens (thus increasing the possibilities of the camera without having to insert an accessory viewfinder) and for the then newly-developed 75mm f1.4 SUMMILUX lens.

This system of having two frames at a time is very clever, because it is compatible with all existing lenses: the 28mm appears with the 90mm; the 35mm with 135mm as before, and the new 75mm with the 50mm. All are parallax corrected down to the minimum focusing distance.

All cameras of this type are equipped with the motor drive facility, and the previous type of motor is useable, although an improved one with electronic interlocking has also been produced.

There is no self-timer, but there are still three contacts for flash, one hot shoe and two on the camera back.

The script on the front is in the new fashion with a Leitz logo on top of camera. The cameras are produced in Canada and sport the red disc in front that was so popular with the M4-2. The code No. is 10,415.

All the M4-P cameras were supposed to have been produced in black chrome finish: however in 1983 a special series of 2,500 cameras were finished in bright chrome and marked to celebrate the anniversary of the first experiment with the miniature camera by Oskar Barnack in 1913.

These cameras have the usual special number from 1 to 500 in five series, each bearing one of the letters that comprise the word LEICA. Their code No. is 10,416.

It is interesting to note that several lenses were also engraved, and an undisclosed number of motors; also a special bag in light brown leather was prepared for the outfit. A light-meter was also delivered in bright chrome finish, although without engravings.

Another special batch, this time originating in Canada, comprised 200 cameras with the engraving "Everest" in a special logo, made to commemorate the use of these cameras by the Canadian Everest team. (Also an equal number of R4 were issued).

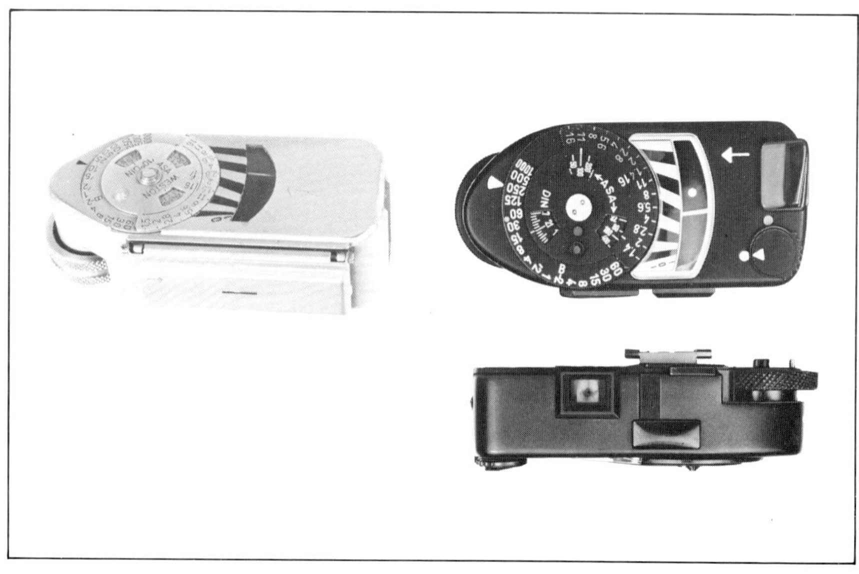

Chapter 9
Through-Lens Metering

The biggest shortcoming of the rangefinder LEICA compared with the 35mm SLR camera of the time was its lack of through-lens metering. What is more, the separate meter mounted on top ruined the lines of what otherwise was an extremely elegant instrument. Leitz had experimented with built-in meters before they went the whole way with through-lens metering. Two of these prototypes are illustrated.

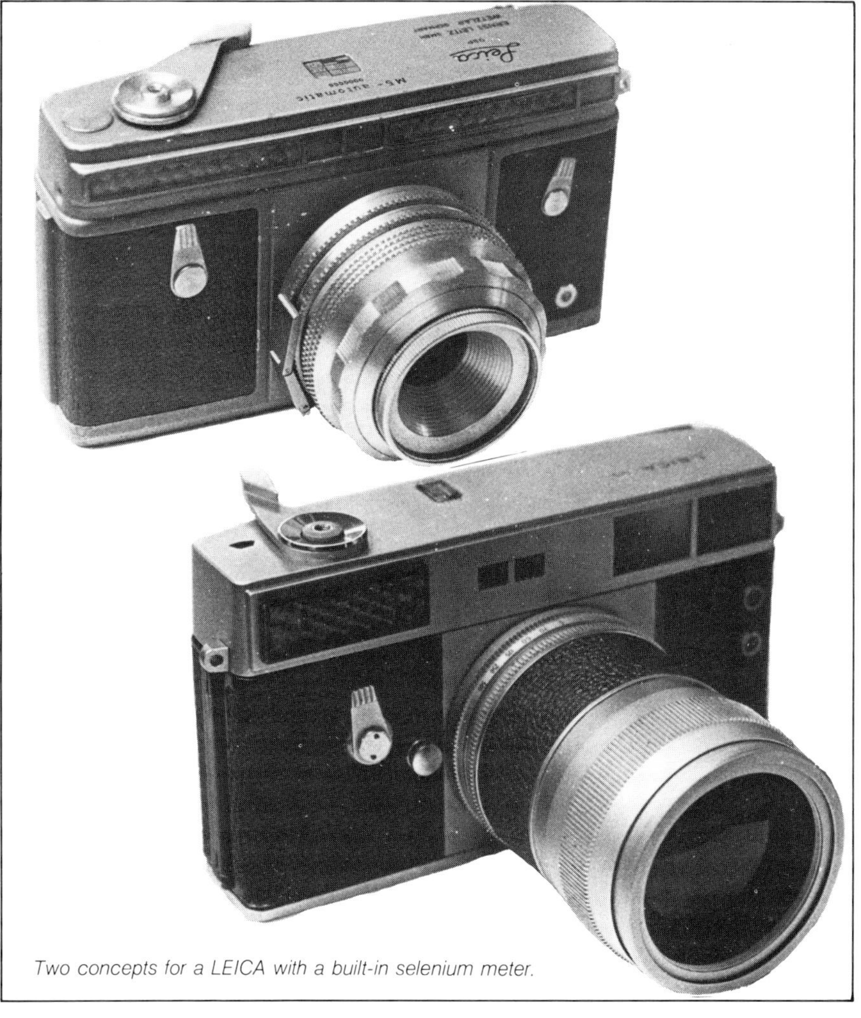

Two concepts for a LEICA with a built-in selenium meter.

LEICA M5

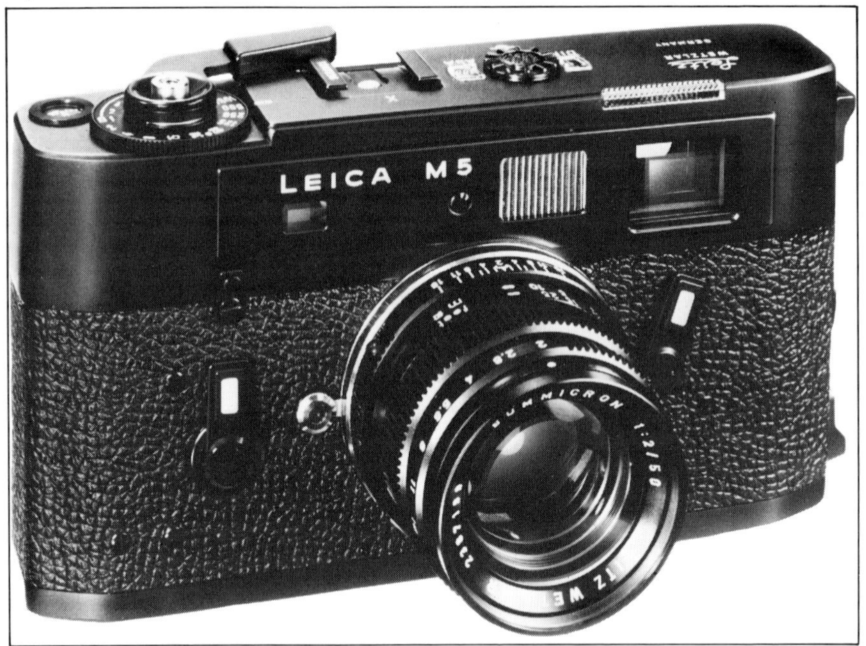

LEICA M5

A new camera was introduced in 1971, the M5. This was the first rangefinder camera to have T.T.L. metering. It started with serial number 1,287,001, although there was an initial run of 50 cameras, again called the "null" series, this in effect being the pre-production run.

The M5 model was completely different from all the other cameras; it was heavier and had a bigger body; body length was 150mm and the body tapered at each end. The overall height of the camera from base to the top of the release button was 87mm and body depth 35mm, including flange. But the dimensions were just one of the changes; the M5 had an integral light metering system with a CDS cell, carried by a moving arm which was suspended just in front of the focal plane shutter and swung out of the way before an exposure was made; so true through-the-lens metering had arrived. Correct exposure was obtained when the exposure meter needle coincided with shutter speed needle. This could be obtained either by altering the shutter speed or the lens aperture setting.

The range/viewfinder was of a modified M4 design. Apart from the standard 35/50/90/135mm viewfinder frames, a small barrel outline was also indicated, this being equal in area to the spot meter reading for the 50mm lens. Along the bottom of the viewfinder (also indicating the bottom of the 35mm lens frame) was situated the shutter speeds scale 1/2 to 1/1000, an index point for shutter speed in use and a moving needle for the meter reading. When both the index point and needle coincided, exposure was correctly set for the particular film being used.

With a 35mm lens in use, the spot meter reading for that lens was defined by the 35mm viewfinder frame, also indicated in the field of view. 28mm wide-angle lenses with serial No. 2,314,920 and above could be used directly on the camera with full metering facility, but lenses with numbers below that had to be modified in order to prevent the cell arm from being fouled, no meter reading was possible in this case, nor was it possible with either the 21mm or 15mm lenses. Early 21mm f4.0 and f3.4 versions required modification before being fitted into this camera in order to prevent damage to either the rear optics or the meter arm. Collapsible lenses, such as the 50mm ELMAR and the collapsible versions of the 50mm SUMMICRON and 90mm ELMAR, could not be collapsed on the M5 because they would damage the meter arm. The preview lever, when pushed to the extreme right (looking from the front) also served as a battery check switch.

The shutter speed dial was concentric with the advance lever, but under it, instead of on top as on the LEICAFLEX, and had markings for speeds from one half of a second upwards in the usual sequence of 2-4-8-15-30-60-125-500-1000. One second was omitted as this permitted more consistent intermediate slow shutter speeds from 1/2 to 1/30 of a second; the number coincided with B because the lightmeter was able to compute exposure speeds up to 30 seconds which were marked under an arc with B at both extremes; thus the long exposures were 1 second, 2-4-8-15-30 seconds, but they had to be manually set with cable release with shutter on B. This situation is noticed in the movement of the dial which had no click stops in the B range. On top of the camera there was also the self-resetting frame counter and the film speed dial, actuated by a knurled wheel and with two windows, one for DIN and one for ASA settings. In front of the camera there was the preview lever, the reverse release and the self timer. The folding rewind crank was on the base cover, at one end, the other end had the folding base locking catch with combined tripod socket. The 3mm coaxial flash contacts were at the back of the top plate and the fastest electronic flash speed was 1/50th, marked by a dot on the speed dial.

In addition there was also a hot-shoe contact in the accessory clip which allowed the use of a fixed flash on top of the camera, along with another via the standard contacts. The hinged back, like the one on the previous M types, opened and had a film-type reminder and a simple exposure calculator.

The camera had yet another improvement for easy loading; there was a removable take-up spool with three open-ended prongs, as in the M4. Finally, the shoulder strap was no longer fastened to eyelets on both sides of the camera, but passed through two flat retainers on the same side so that the camera hung vertically when carried in this way. The battery receptacle was located on the same side of the body as the shoulder strap.

In the course of the lifespan of the camera two practical changes were made. One was the addition of a third retainer for the shoulder strap so that the camera could be hung either vertically on its side, or in the conventional way with the base horizontal. A second improvement was made by stiffening the spring that held the shutter speed dial in position; on the first cameras the speed could be changed by accident.

The engraving was different with "LEICA M5" in capitals on the front of the camera; the name "Leitz" in script on the top in place of "LEICA", and then "Wetzlar Germany". The letters GMBH and DBP had disappeared; the serial number was engraved sideways on the accessory shoe.

The LEICA M5 was made in bright chrome or black chrome finish.

LEICA CL

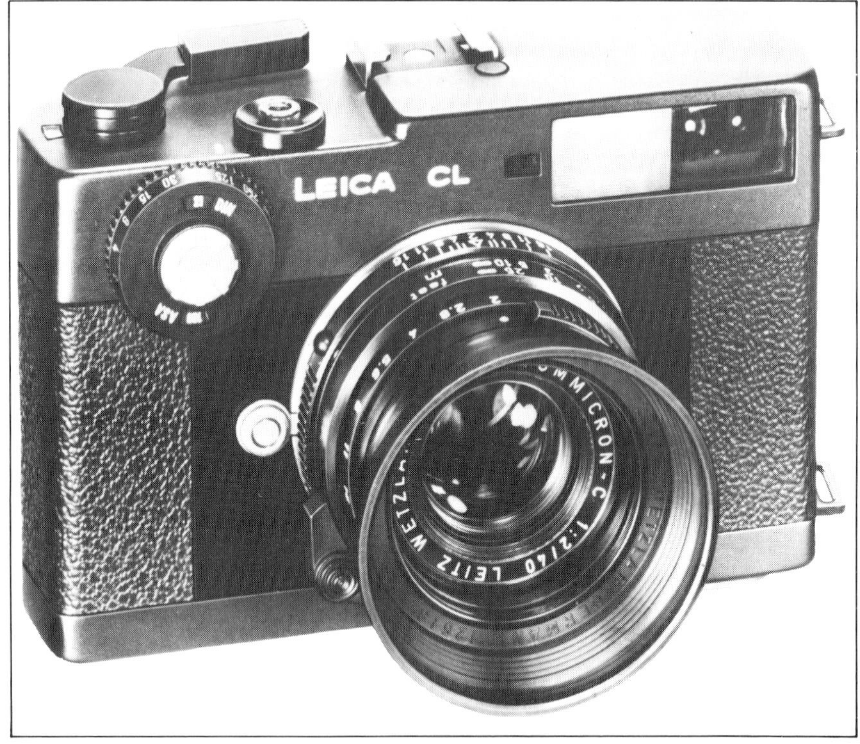

LEICA CL

The small or Compact LEICA, as the letters CL indicate, was the sensation of 1973. Not only because of its small size and its new lenses, but because the new camera, designed in Wetzlar by Leitz technicians, was made by Minolta in Japan under the agreement reached by the two companies. Production started from No. 1,300,001.

The LEICA CL was the most sophisticated camera of its size at the time because it had many features of the larger camera. It could be regarded as the first of the true compact 35mm cameras as we know them today, except that none of these popular instruments can take interchangeable lenses.

The body length was only 120mm, the height 75mm and the depth 32mm. The camera had the same lens flange as the M series, enabling it to use most of the M range lenses, although two special lenses were made for it; a 40mm SUMMICRON-C f2 and a 90mm ELMAR-C f4. Similar restrictions applied with respect to collapsible lenses as with the M5 because of the meter arm. The lenses coupled to a rangefinder of only 31.5mm base length, which was accurate enough for normal work. Most importantly, the camera had a similar type of through-the-lens metering system as the M5.

On top of the camera there was only the advance lever and the release button, plus the self resetting frame counter which no longer had marks but the series of even numbers 2-4-6-8 etc instead. Also on the top plate was the hot-shoe flash contact, which was the only one on this camera and served for electronic flash or bulb. On the front there was a large dial for the shutter speeds setting with a smaller knob concentric with it for the film speed adjustment. The speeds were 2-4-8-15-30-60-125-250-500-1000th of a second plus B. Also the intermediate speeds could be used (except between 1/30th and 1/60th seconds). Along the top of the viewfinder was the speed scale, and to the right an exposure meter indicator. Correct exposure was when the needle was in the central notch.

On turning a folding catch in the centre of the base by a quarter turn, the back and base of the camera came off in a single piece for film load and battery change. Due to the body opening in this way it also freed the hinged pressure plate.

"LEICA CL" was engraved on the front of the camera with "Leitz Wetzlar" in script on top; on the base of the camera "made in Japan for Leitz Wetzlar" and "DPB US PAT."

The serial number was on the accessory shoe which was fixed from the inside of the camera, making it difficult to remove. The camera did not have a self-timer, mainly due to the fact that there was not really space for it.

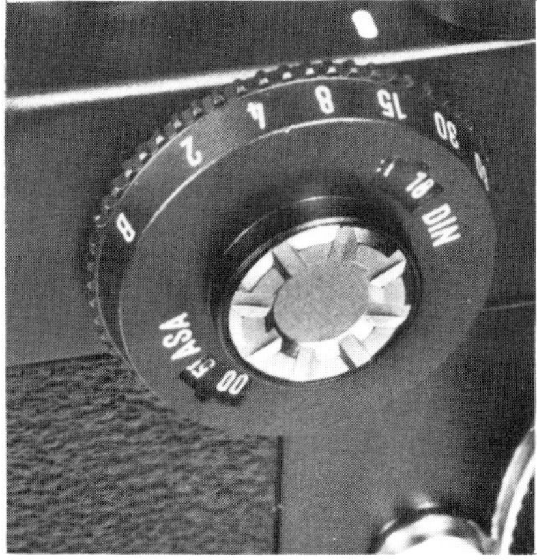

Detail of CL shutter speed dial.

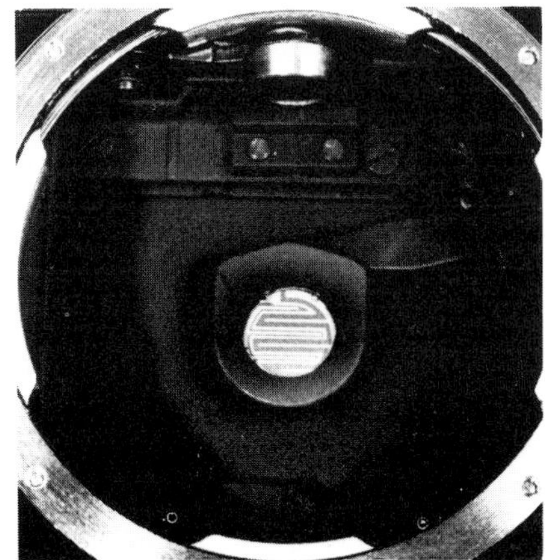

CL, detail of exposure meter.

By relocating the main mechanism and making the blinds run from top to bottom, the camera was effectively shortened therefore the designers achieved the compact size of the camera with all the above features. The viewfinder was also simplified and had the 40mm and 50mm frames appearing at the same time with the 90mm frame coming in with the insertion of the appropriate lens.

Contemporary lenses such as the 28mm ELMAR with numbers below 2,314,920; all 21mm lenses plus the 15mm HOLOGON, could not be fitted or modified for use on the CL, because of the meter arm assembly.

CL production ceased during 1975.

LEICA M6

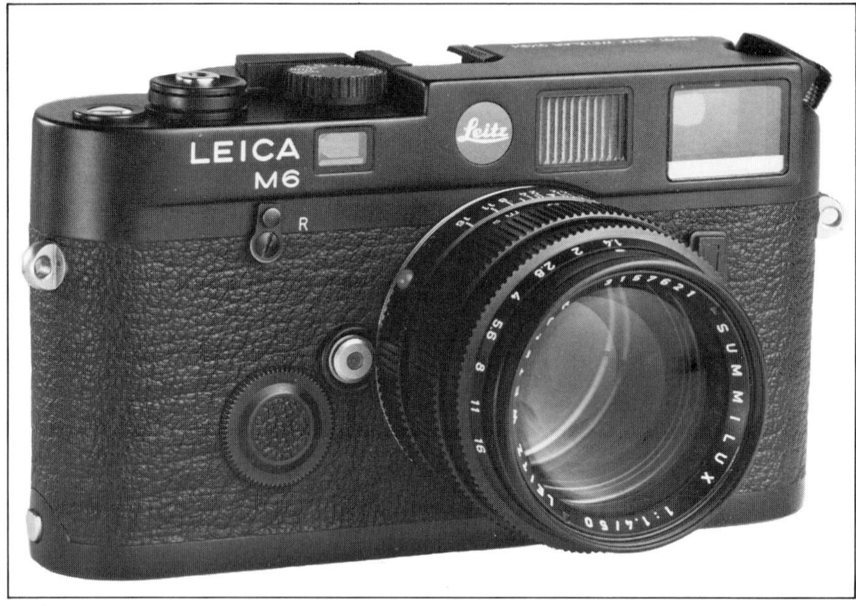

LEICA M6.

The most important improvement to the rangefinder camera was announced in the fall of 1984: a new model in the long list of the M types. The M6 is the camera with a fully electronic (no moving parts) exposure meter in the well known M4 body. Unlike the two previous models (M5 and CL) this new M6 has a silicon photodiode that is fixed in the top of the camera body and points to the centre of the image area. Here on the first blind there is a silvered spot of 12mm diameter, covering a 13% of the image area, that reflects the light passing through the lens.

That Leitz technicians have found space inside an already crammed mechanical camera for all the electronic components is no mean achievement.

Apart from the light-sensitive element, there is the battery box, located in front, a printed circuit with all the parts that make up the electronic circuitry, and a clever film-speed indicator that is located on the hinged back cover.

Using this camera is simplicity in itself. The film speed is adjusted with the disk on the back, and this information is transmitted to the computer by means of three gold-plated contacts when the back is closed. Light entering the lens is measured in real value, so lens aperture is automatically taken in. Shutter speed is also transmitted to the computer and everything is activated the moment a slight pressure is applied on the release button.

The results of the calculation done by the computer are shown in the viewfinder by means of two red triangles (two LEDs actually). If both are evenly lit the exposure is correct, if one is dim or totally off, then it is necessary to turn the lens diaphragm ring or the shutter speed dial in the direction indicated by the lighted diode to achieve the correct exposure. When pressure is removed from the release button the computer remains on for about ten seconds, then switches itself off to save the battery.

The sensitivity of the system goes from ASA 6 to ASA 6400. In practice this means that with a 100 ASA film the exposure is possible with a stopped-down lens at f32 in a speed range from one second to 1/1000 of a second; or again in technical term the sensitivity goes from 0,125 to 125,000 candela per square metre.

Since this is a spot metering TTL, it is necessary to know what part of the area in the viewfinder is measured. This is obtained in a clever way by using the different rangefinder and viewfinder frames combined.

Once the exposure meter is explained, the rest is easy. The camera has the same viewfinder as the M4-P, with six frames that are selectable with the preview lever as always.

There are only two flash contacts, one in the accessory shoe and the other on the camera back. Gone is the bulb contact, but modern flash lamps can be used up to 1/30 of a second. For the electronic flash the maximum speed is 1/50 and is indicated by the usual arrow on the speed dial.

The distance between the rangefinder objectives is 69.25mm, but the effective baselength is 49.9mm as with the M4-P. This is because the viewfinder optical system minifies the image 0.72x in order to accommodate the frame for the 28mm lens. In the same way the view- and rangefinder images of the M2, M4 and M4-2 and their derivatives are smaller than that of the M3 because they cater for the 35mm lens whereas the M3, which gives a nearly life-size image, does not have a frame for any lens wider than 50mm.

The camera can be motor driven. It can, of course, be used even if the light meter batteries are dead because all the operations are mechanical, except for light measurement. In this respect it represents the best marriage between electronic metering and a purely mechanical shutter.

Some minor changes are to be found in the engravings on the camera. "LEICA M6" is always on the front top cover, but there is also a red disc with the Leitz logo. On the camera top there is the full inscription "ERNST LEITZ WETZLAR GMBH".

Chapter 10

The LEICAFLEX – First LEICA Reflex Camera

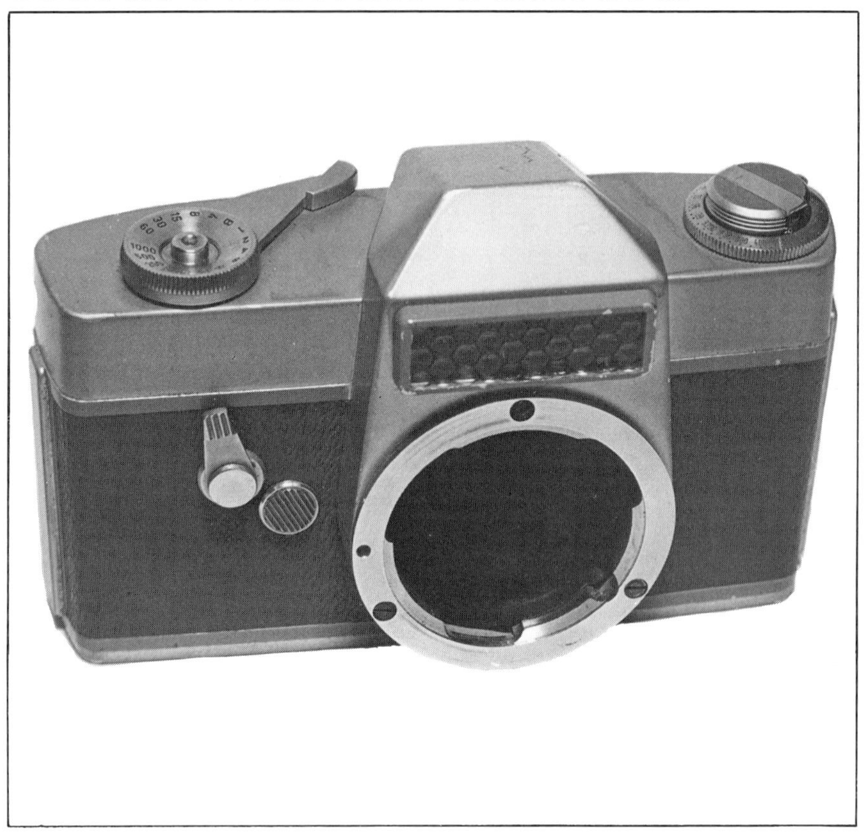

Early mock-up of a LEICA reflex camera.

For years Leitz had built the finest rangefinder cameras, supplying at the same time as series of reflex attachments (the VISOFLEX) which were used with lenses of long focal length. Pressure from the public pushed the company to introduce a reflex camera, which was being developed at the time.

In the Leitz museum at Wetzlar is an experimental LEICAFLEX with a removeable folding hood which suggests that the first Leitz reflex might have appeared with interchangeable finders. However, this was not to be and the first LEICAFLEX had a fixed finder, but with built-in metering, to be followed four years later with the through-lens metering SL.

LEICAFLEX

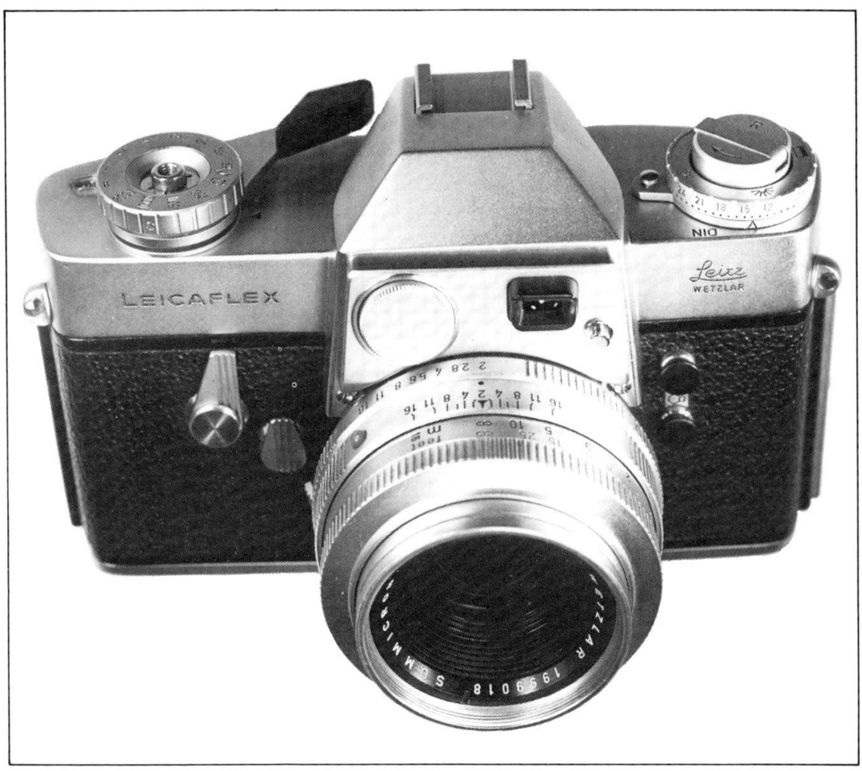

Early LEICAFLEX with chrome lens.

The LEICAFLEX appeared in 1964 with the serial numbers starting from 1,080,001 and was produced until 1968 at a rate of nearly 8,000 cameras, on average, per year. Production ended in 1968 (with the introduction of the LEICAFLEX SL model) with the number, 1,174,700.

As expected the LEICAFLEX was a refined camera of great reliability. It had a bayonet mount of its own, which of course necessitated a whole new series of lenses. The bayonet was of much larger diameter to accommodate the anticipated wide angle and wide aperture lenses. However, M lenses, and lens heads which could be used on the VISOFLEX, could also be used on the LEICAFLEX with the same adapters and focusing mounts as were necessary with the VISOFLEX by using an additional special adapter ring, 14127, to make up for the extra depth of the M camera-VISOFLEX combination compared with the LEICAFLEX body and to adapt to the LEICAFLEX bayonet. These lenses would have to be stopped down manually to the required aperture after focusing. Of course, the lenses made specially for the LEICAFLEX had the automatic diaphragm coupled so that focusing was at full aperture.

There was a CdS exposure meter that did not measure the light through the lens, but had its own tiny window just above the lens mount. The cover for the battery that powered it was alongside. The automatically resetting frame counter had marks for every frame and numbers every four frames, instead of every five as on all LEICA's before.

The shutter was an improvement over existing blind types because it ran at a speed of 1/100th of a second, which allowed for a higher electronic flash synchronisation and a very high top speed of 1/2000th of a second.

The speed scale was thus: B-1-2-4-8-15-30-60-125-250-500-1000-2000, with the dial on top of the advancing lever, and the release button in the centre. The mirror operation was similar to that of the VISOFLEX; a three position lever in the front of the camera allowed three modes of operation: normal, with instant return, with lever in the up position, no return with the lever in the horizontal position, and mirror locked up in the down position. This mirror lock-up ability means that the original LEICAFLEX is the only LEICA reflex camera that can be used with the early 21mm, f3.4 SUPER-ANGULON with its protruding rear element. Reflex viewing was impossible with this lens and one had to use a special 21mm viewfinder in the accessory shoe.

The bright screen had the shutter speed indicator on the bottom, and the lightmeter indicator at the right with matching needles – the centre spot with microprisms was for focusing. Film speed was set on a ring placed around the rewind crank. On the same ring there was a separate indicator for the film type. 3mm flash contacts were in front with appropriate symbols. The camera body was rather larger than the M types and it had a fully opening back for film insertion, the take up spool being fixed into the camera with three slits to take the film leader.

The camera body was exceptionally clean, with few screws visible. The accessory shoe was fastened from the inside. Leitz apparently did not utilise an

Mark 1 & Mark 2 Differences

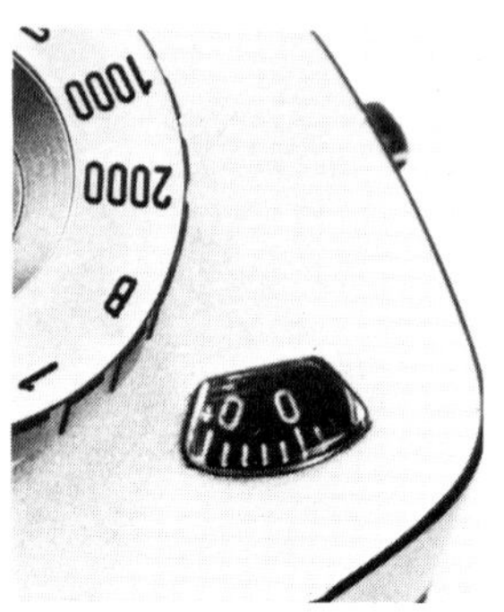

Film counter pie shaped on Mark I camera.

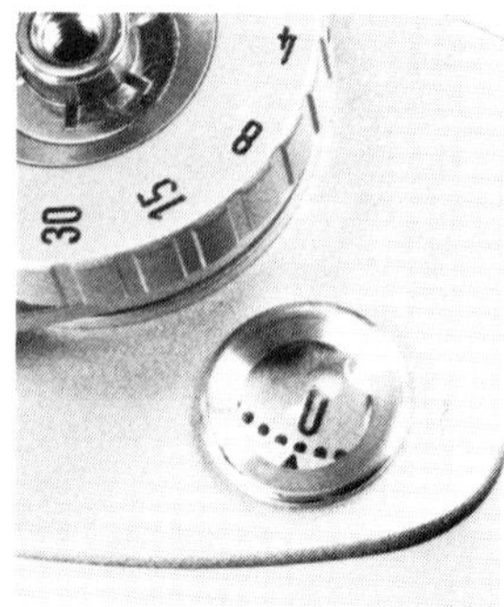

Film counter round framed on Mark 2

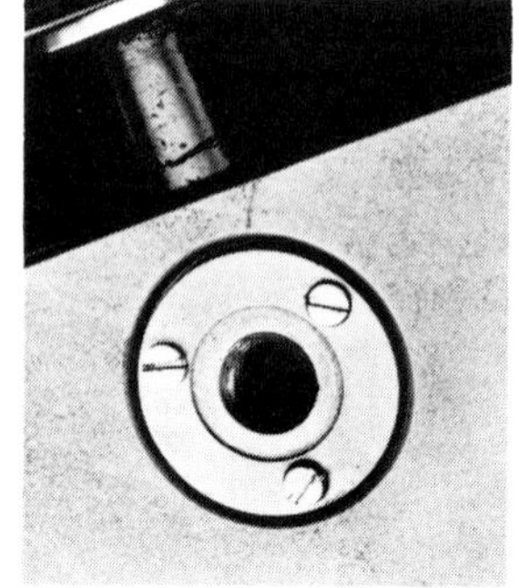

Tripod screw fitting on LEICAFLEX Mark I

interchangeable viewfinder system as this would have detracted from the compactness of the pentaprism housing. The engraving was different from earlier practice, the name "LEICAFLEX" in block capital letters on the front, with "Leitz" engraved in script. On the base was "LEITZ Wetzlar Germany" and the camera serial number, by the rewind release.

Early production cameras, which have been dubbed Mark I, had a pie-shaped frame counter. Later models, the Mark II, had a circular frame counter, and other changes were also made; a meter cut-off switch was incorporated in the film-advance mechanism and the tripod bush was made integral with the base-plate. A very few early cameras came with chrome 50mm SUMMICRON-R's.

LEICAFLEX SL

The logical development of the LEICAFLEX was the SL type, SL meaning "Selected Light" meter reading. Made from 1968 to 1974, production of the SL started from number 1,173,001. The most important feature was the through-the-lens metering system. The metering spot was the same diameter as the microprism zone in the viewfinder. The absence of the external cell gave the camera a more streamlined appearance.

Lenses made for the earlier type of LEICAFLEX would fit the SL but could not operate the full-aperture metering system. The new lenses had two cams and the earlier ones could be converted by Wetzlar.

In place of the three position mirror control there was a button which allowed a preview of the depth of focus by closing the diaphragm to the pre-set aperture, and for stop-down meter reading with the earlier lenses. Apart from this, the controls were similar to those of the LEICAFLEX, with the speed dial in black on top of the advance lever and with the release button in the centre. Speeds were the same as on the first model, with B, one second and then running up to 1/2000th of a second with the flash mark at 1/100. Speed sequence was 1-2-4-8-15-30-60-125-250-500-1000-2000.

There were two 3mm coaxial sockets on the front and the possibility of using both bulb and electronic flash.

Around the rewind crank there was the film speed indicator for setting the light meter and also a film type indicator with a separate ring. The camera had a self timer in the usual front position and the self-resetting frame counter. The battery for the CdS light meter was relocated to the bottom, and the rewind release button was also there, as on the original LEICAFLEX. The catch for unlocking the lens was red and was easily located.

The back of the camera opened completely and made insertion of the film simple. The take up spool was of the quick-load type with several notches which catch the free end of the film, and there were rollers on both sides of the film gate.

The camera was made in chrome with a limited number in black. From 1969 it was modified to take an electric motor drive. These LEICAFLEX SL MOT's

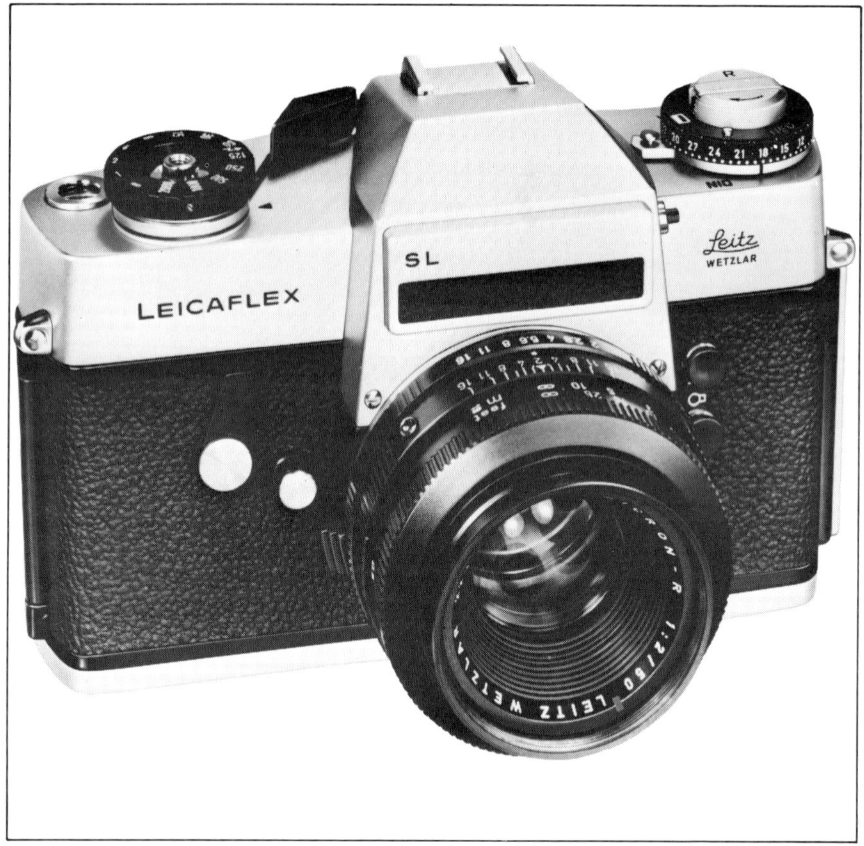

LEICAFLEX SL

were all black. They were fitted with a motor drive shaft, and had all contacts and associated controls on the bottom plate so that the motor could be connected and disconnected without disturbing the film inside the camera. The motorized cameras did not have a self-timer. A total of 980 LEICAFLEX SL2-MOT cameras were made.

An ample assortment of lenses and related accessories, such as near-focusing devices, bellows and rapid focusing lenses, made the LEICAFLEX system a most complete one. The LEICAFLEX SL could use any lens suitable for the VISOFLEX. These lenses in their VISOFLEX mounts were fitted via adaptor 14,167 (for early model LEICAFLEX 14,127) and would then focus over exactly the same range as on the VISOFLEX.

A limited number of LEICAFLEX SL's were available to order with a plain ground-glass screen (similar to the VISOFLEX screen), without focusing aids but having an engraved circle indicating the area of the meter.

LEICAFLEX SL2

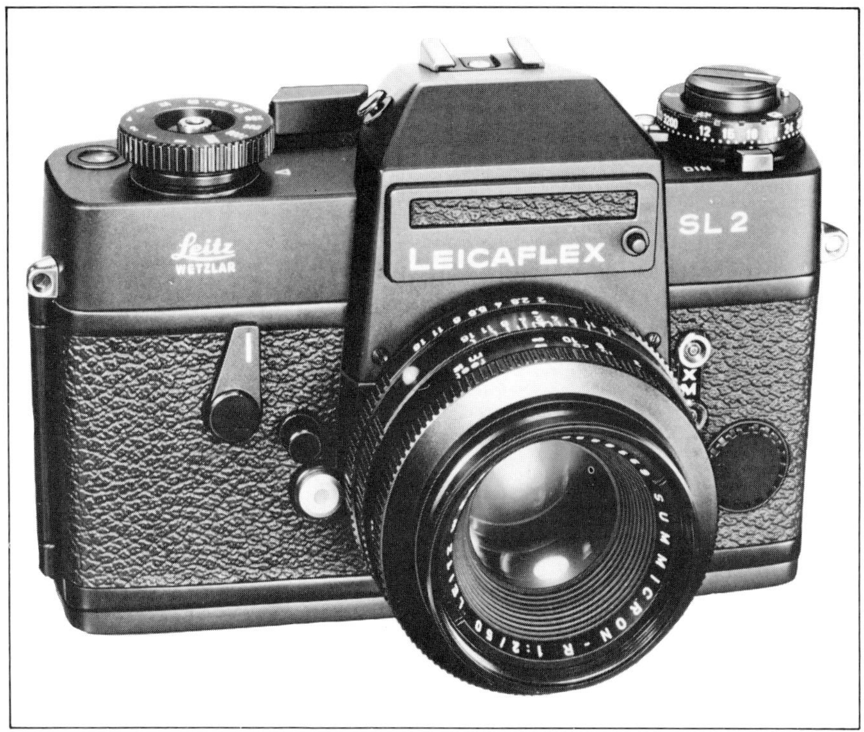

LEICAFLEX SL2

The last LEICAFLEX, and the last of the Leitz purely mechanical reflex cameras, was announced in Autumn 1974; it was similar in appearance to the LEICAFLEX SL, but was a redesigned camera with many extra features. Production started from No. 1,374,001.

Body shape and dimensions were the same, but the main additional features were:- a 3mm circle in the centre of the focusing screen incorporating a split-image rangefinder, a four-fold increase in sensitivity of the meter, a hot-shoe contact for flash.

By looking in the viewfinder other differences were seen: at the bottom there was an f-stop scale alongside the shutter speed scale and the exposure meter needle was matched by an elongated needle. Since the exposure sensitivity had been increased by four steps, an illuminator had been added to ease reading of the lower part of the scale. This light was operated by a separate battery and the switch for this was the button to be seen on the pentaprism housing. This battery also served as a spare for the light-meter battery, which was located in the camera base.

The way in which the camera opened to load the film was improved, it now opened in two steps: first a safety lock under the film speed indicator had to be moved, then the rewind crank was raised and this freed the back which then swung open. Film loading was similar to that of the SL, with the fixed take-up spool which had slots to take the end of the film.

The SL2 had a self-timer and was made in either silver-chrome finish or in black chrome. Later a motorized version, the LEICAFLEX SL2 MOT, was introduced, in black chrome and 1020 were made. Shutter speeds were traditional, with B, then 1-2-4-8-15-30-60-125-250-500-1000 and 2000 positions. The film speed indicator for the light meter was set by moving a ring around the rewind crank, as on the SL model. Rewind was actuated when a button on the camera base was depressed. Focusing could be done either by the split-image rangefinder, or by microprism, or on the outer area of the groundglass.

Markings on the camera were different from those of the LEICAFLEX SL: looking at the camera from the front, to the left hand side, where once the word "LEICA" had been, "Leitz" now appeared on the central part of the body, under the pentaprism, "LEICAFLEX" was written in capital letters; and on the right hand side of the camera body the letters "SL2" (with "MOT" if the camera was of this type) appear. The serial number was on the bottom edge of the base.

The SL2 was the last all-mechanical reflex camera made by Leitz, and also the last one to be made in Wetzlar: not surprisingly good used cameras of this type are still very much on demand, either as collector items or for actual use.

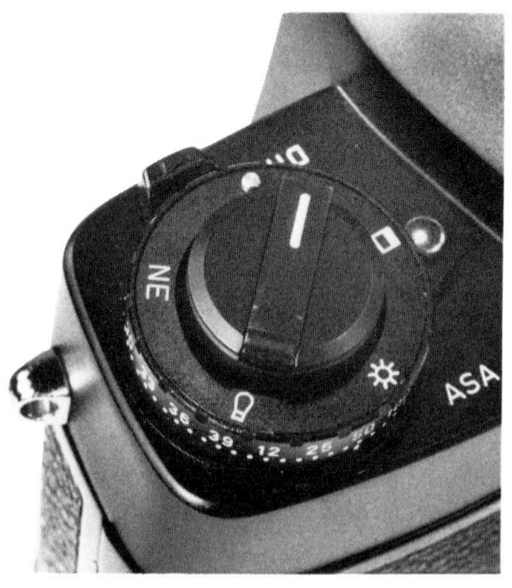

Detail showing rewind lever, A.S.A. setting dial, film indicator and back lock release on LEICAFLEX SL2

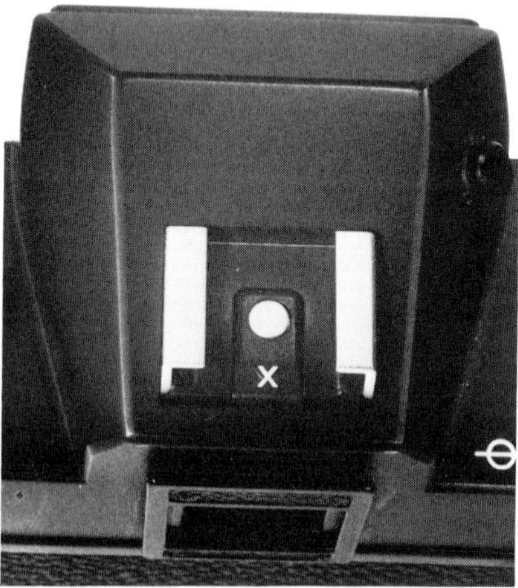

Hot flash shoe on pentaprism of LEICA SL2

Chapter 11

The Electronic LEICA Reflex Cameras

In 1976 Leitz introduced their first all electronic reflex camera. There were practical reasons for the change: commercially a camera with automatic exposure control was needed and the cost of producing the mechanical shutter was becoming too high in relation to the competition.

Of course, the technical department at Leitz had been looking into the matter from quite a time and the replacement for the LEICAFLEX SL2 arrived as expected.

LEICA R3

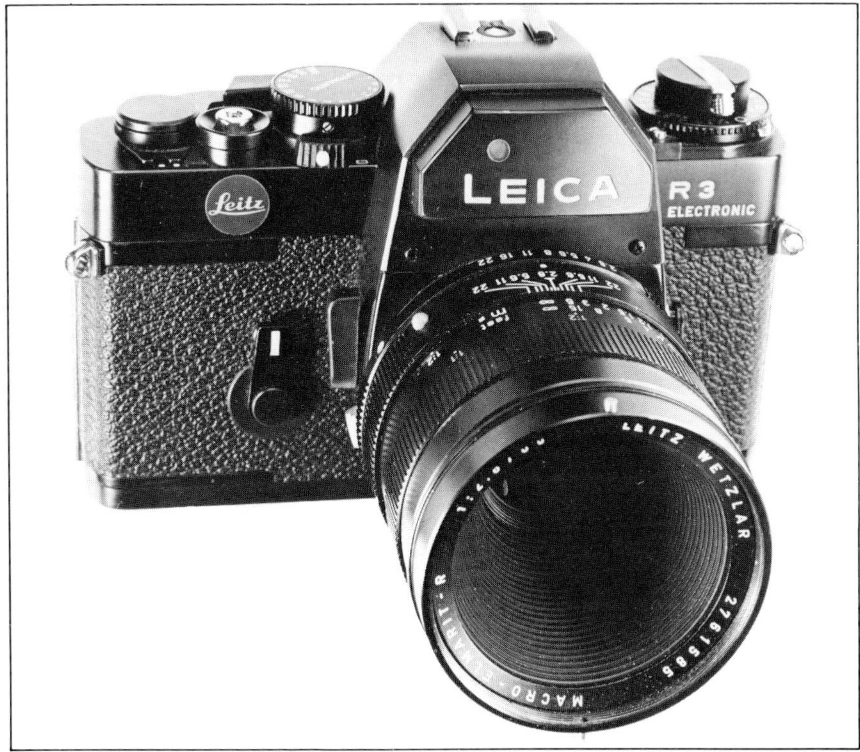

LEICA R3

The name "LEICAFLEX" was dropped in favour of "LEICA" because it was felt that it was the name with the greatest impact on the public. The new camera was called the LEICA R3, the R referring to the fact that it was the third major new camera of the reflex type, the first two being the original LEICAFLEX and the two SL models. It fitted in nicely too with the LEICA M cameras, M standing for "Messen" meaning measuring. It is also necessary to say that by the time the LEICA R4 appeared on the scene, during the few years that had passed since the Swiss firm of Wild took over the management of Leitz their interest toward the photographic side of the company had increased significantly.

The LEICA R3 was introduced in 1976 and stayed in production for only four years, up to 1979; however, it was produced in sizeable quantities (60 thousand cameras) thanks to the new manufacturing facilities in Portugal. Only the first 2,000 cameras were made in Wetzlar (and so engraved), the rest in Vilanova de Famalicao.

Leitz technicians moved with their usual safety factor in mind: the new camera was electronic but retained the possibility of still operating should the batteries go dead.

The camera body showed such a departure from the previous design that it obviously housed a totally different shutter. Gone were the blinds of rubberised cloth, and in their place there was a Leitz-designed Copal-built shutter. This was

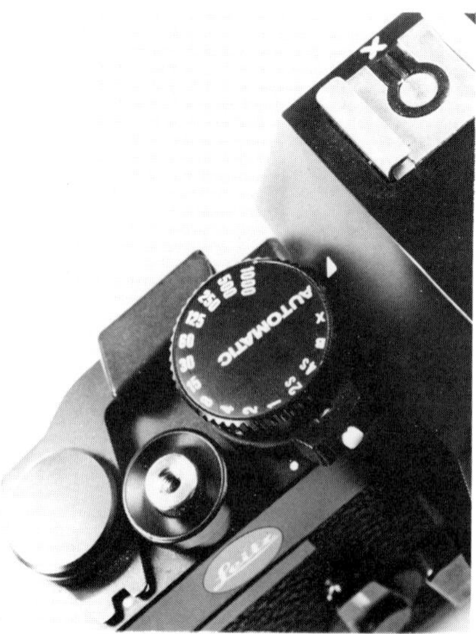

Switch under shutter speed dial for selecting spot or integral metering. The lever with the "V" notch attached to the film advance spindle was for selecting single or multiple exposures

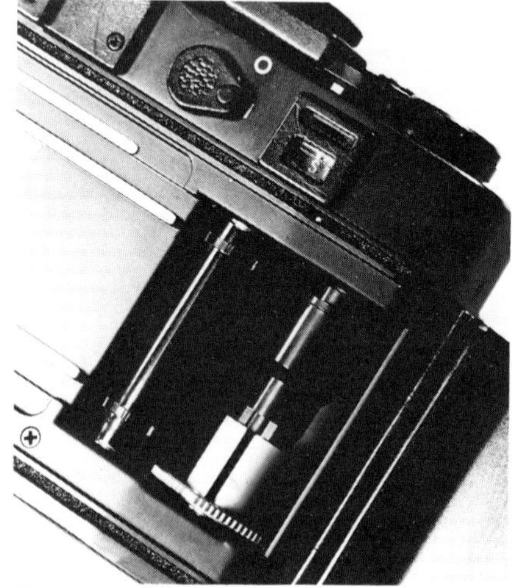

Rear of the R3 with the back open, showing the film take-up spool, the on/off switch, the film counter window and the small window above it for the indicator that showed whether the film was advancing properly. A small orange-coloured bar moves across this window as the film advances.

of the vertical movement type, with metal leaves operating under electronic control. Tiny electromagnets released first one set of leaves, then the other, with the time interval being calculated by an electronic computer which received information pertaining to the film speed and aperture of the diaphragm. The system was an aperture-priority one, and the shutter speed could be manually set, following the needle indication, or left to the camera if the shutter speed dial was set to "A". The new system required that lenses be fitted with the so-called third cam to operate.

As already mentioned, there were two mechanically regulated speeds, one was "B" and the other was marked "X" for flash, and corresponded to 1/100 of a second; also the self-timer was mechanical. Film speed was indicated via a ring around the rewind crank where there was also provision for +2,–2 steps in override of the exposure meter. Light metering took place through the lens in two ways: spot metering over the area covered by the microprisms at the centre of the screen, or integrated over the whole frame.

For the first case there was one photoresistor in the bottom of the camera; for the second two more resistors placed in the pentaprism were switched on. Hot-shoe and two contacts on the left-hand side of the lens mount (looking from above) provided flash synchronisation.

The camera had many unusual features: one was the lever to close the eyepiece opening to prevent light entering the measuring system when taking pictures with the self-timer; the other was a similar lever to switch the electronic system on and off.

A useful and simple device was a window in the back that showed if a film was in the camera and what type it was, thus dispensing with the memorising devices of the past. A small window on the back of the top plate showed if the film was really moving when winding took place, supplementing the normal exposure counter. A small lever coaxial with the winding lever released the shutter release/film-wind interlock to allow multiple exposures on the same frame.

Several variants of this camera were made. Apart from those produced in Germany; first there was the bright chrome model (code No. 10,031), then the black chrome version (code No. 10,032); and a motor driveable model R3-MOT (code No. 10,033). This last version could be fitted with an electric motor (or rather a winder) for a speed of two frames per second. An interesting separate electronic control for the motor allowed one to programme the camera for remote and fully automated picture-taking, with intervals from less than one second to ten minutes from frame to frame.

5,000 of the so-called "Safari" version in military green was made during 1977-78 with matching lenses (code No. 10,034). Finally a thousand copies of the Barnack anniversary gold-plated model with lizard skin covering were made in 1979 (code No. 10,050).

LEICA R4

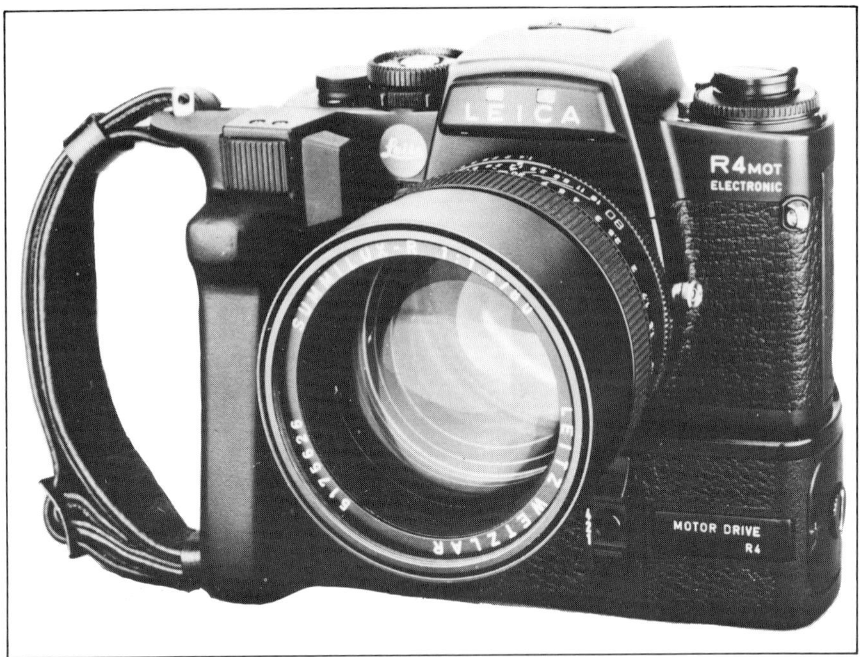

LEICA R4, black, showing earlier designation "R4 MOT Electronic" and with Motor Drive R4 and Handgrip. All R4's are capable of taking a motor drive or winder and the name of the camera was later changed to simply LEICA R4.

At the Photokina of 1980 Leitz introduced their most complex and sophisticated reflex camera, the LEICA R4.

The best of the available technology is incorporated into a small camera body. An electronic circuit was developed for Leitz by Ferranti of England. The steel-bladed shutter is controlled in five different ways by means of a selector providing five operating modes. These are:-

1) Aperture priority, integral exposure measurement.
2) Aperture priority, selective exposure measurement.
3) Shutter priority, integral exposure measurement.
4) Automatic programme, integral exposure measurement. In this mode the camera automatically selects an aperture/shutter speed combination depending on the brightness of the light.
5) Manual, selective exposure measurement. The automatic controls are disengaged and both aperture and shutter speed are set manually. The meter readings are still displayed.

Again as with the R3 there is provision for mechanical operation at the "X" speed of 1/100 of a second and "B"; therefore the speed dial carries the following scale: 100-B-X-1-2-4-8-15-30-60-125-250-500-1000. This scale appears in a vertical row on the right-hand side of the viewfinder when the manual,

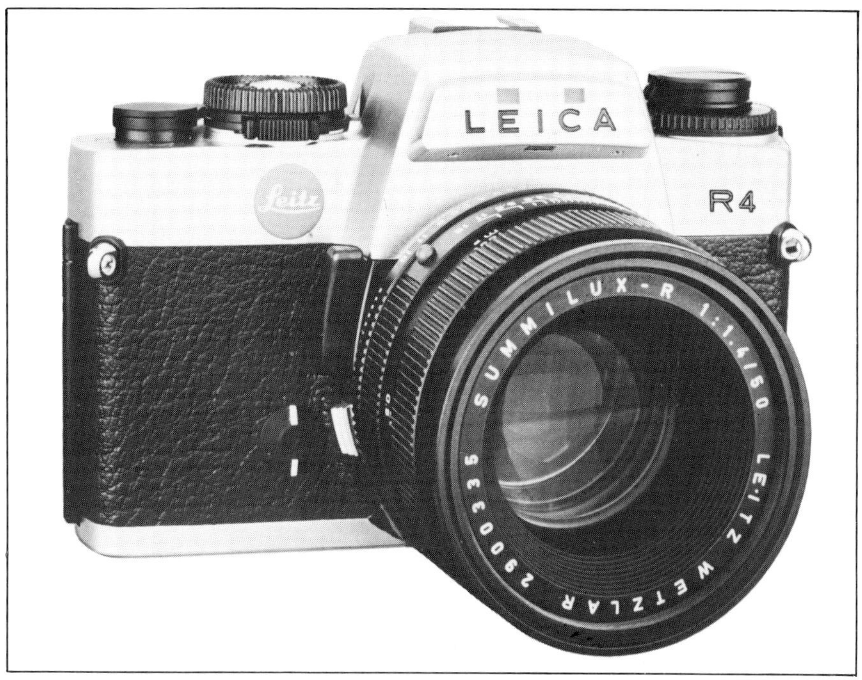

LEICA R4, chrome

automatic (indicated by a "P" for programme) and aperture-priority systems are in use; and an aperture scale from 1,4 to 32 is presented when the shutter-speeds-priority system is engaged.

The camera is remarkable for its uncluttered design. The controls are grouped in two sets: on the right there is a film transport lever and the speed dial, under which is a lockable lever to change programmes. There are three small windows: one displays what programme is engaged (the same indication is given by a LED in the viewfinder when the release button is lightly depressed to the first stop); another shows how many frames have been used; the third indicates if the film is moving regularly. On the left-hand side there is the rewind crank, that serves also as the lock for the opening back; the film-speed-setting ring, with indications in ASA and DIN; the range override (plus or minus two stops); the button that releases the film-speed ring which serves also for checking the battery – when fully depressed a LED lights up if the battery is good.

Near the viewfinder a rotatable button serves to close the opening and prevent light from entering when the camera is not used without the eye being at the viewfinder; a similar button in front engages the self-timer that is then operated by a slight pressure on the release button. Pressing the release fully down operates the shutter normally.

The camera has a hot-shoe plus another flash contact on the left side of the lens mount. It can be electrically driven by a winder (2 frames per second) or a motor drive (5 frames per second) and be operated by the remote control and programmable system.

Using the camera is extremely easy once the film speed is set on the dial. The shutter speed or the lens aperture, selected either automatically or manually, are indicated by the lighting of a LED alongside the proper value calculated by the computer.

Closing the diaphragm for depth of field preview is by means of a substantial lever on the right-hand side of the lens mount (looking from above). Rewinding the film is carried out after a button is pushed on the underside, where the power shaft and electrical contacts are also located. The underside of the camera can be protected by a plastic cover fastened in place by a screw that engages the tripod bush.

Possibly the greatest innovation of all is the facility for changing the viewfinder screen from the standard one (with split image rangefinder and microprisms) to a plain ground glass one, or one with microprisms over the whole centre circle, or one ruled with cross hairs, or a plain clear screen for use with optical instruments. Leitz devised a small set of tweezers, and a brush that are supplied with any new screen to make changing easy and ensure that this critical item is kept clean.

Any lens of the modern reflex series can be used (a few of the early types cannot operate because they protrude too much inside the camera). Of course the lenses not equipped with the so-called third cam cannot operate the automatic system, although the camera can be used with stop-down metering. Also offered for the first time by Leitz is the databack that permits the insertion of the date and other numerical information on the film.

The LEICA R4 is manufactured in black or bright chrome. In 1984 a series of 1,000 cameras were also offered finished in gold with lizard skin covering. This was not a commemorative issue but simply an extra special luxury item, in the same manner as the original "Luxus" of 55 years before.

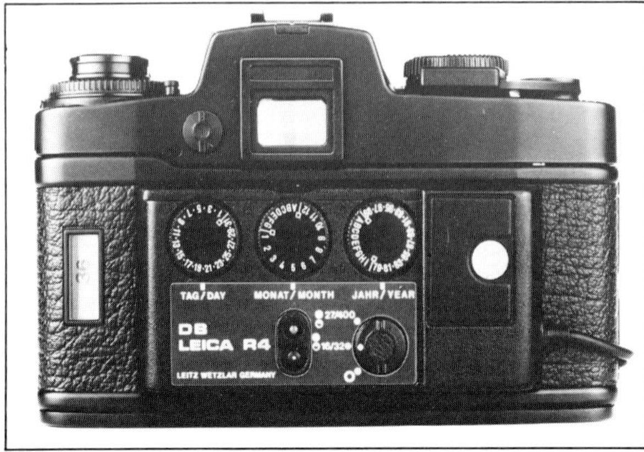

*LEICA R4 fitted with
Data Back*

LEICA R4-S

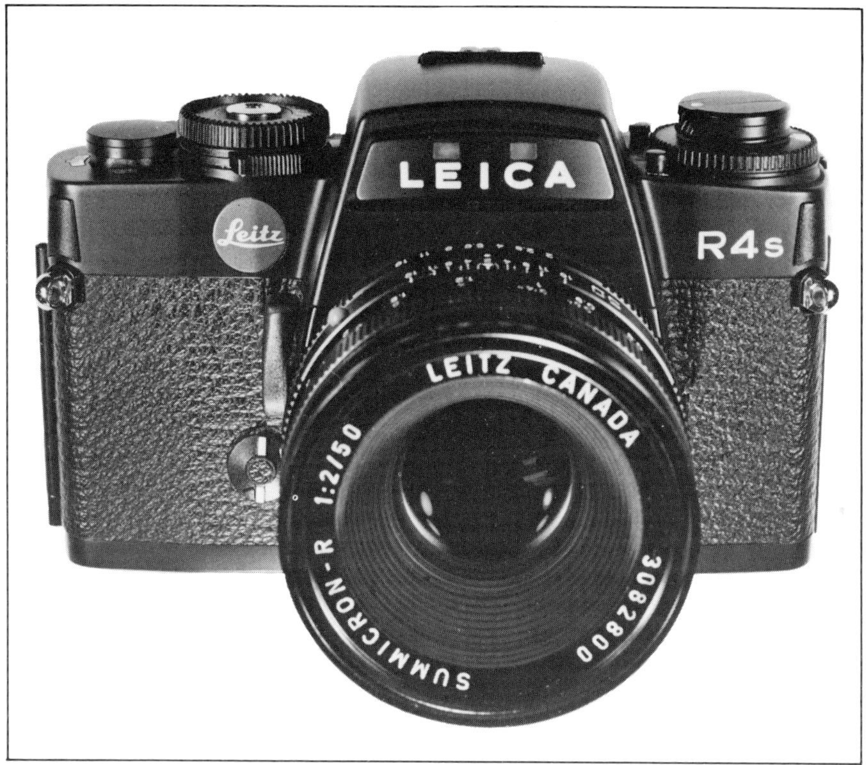

LEICA R4-S

Following the traditional Leitz policy of offering cameras of uncompromising quality at a lower cost than the top model, the LEICA R4-S was introduced in 1983.

Identical in every other respect to the R4, this camera features a simplified shutter control with three instead of five programmes. The user has a choice between manual control and two aperture-priority programmes, with spot metering or whole field metering. All the rest remains unchanged, including the motor drive system and interchangeability of the focusing screen.

It is worth saying that in the R4 and R4-S the switch over from spot metering to area metering is no longer accomplished by using different light-sensitive elements: instead there is a tiny optical system that slides over or back from the light photodiode, changing its field of view through the mirror system. This is a very sophisticated device, employing a multifaceted mirror to concentrate the light precisely on the photodiode. No less thant 1,345 concave mirrors are grouped on a surface of a rectangle 20 x 29mm that swings out of the way when the picture is taken.

Chapter 12

Limited Edition Anniversary and Commemorative Cameras

Leitz started their custom of issuing limited editions of certain cameras with special engraving and serial numbers in 1972 for the Olympic Games which were held in Munich that year. They then celebrated the LEICA's own half century in 1975 and following the success of that issue have extended the practice since.

1972 MUNICH OLYMPIAD

"Olympic" Model LEICAFLEX SL, limited issue of 1,000 engraved and numbered cameras. A further 200 were produced carrying the Olympic rings logo but without special serial numbers.

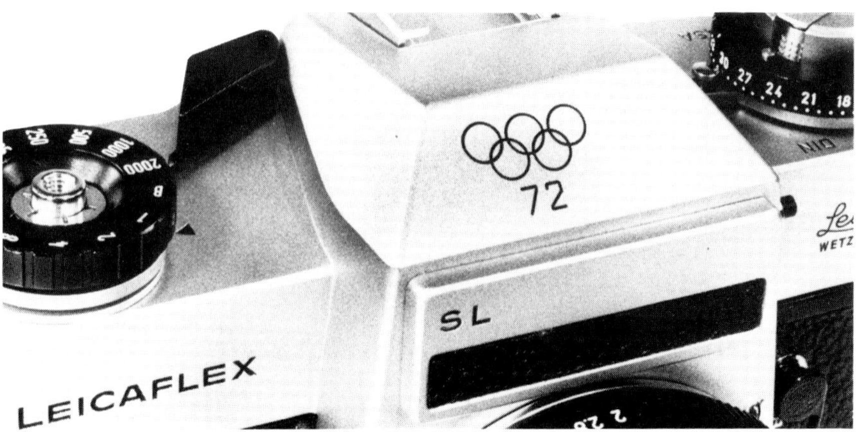

1975, 50th Anniversary of the LEICA

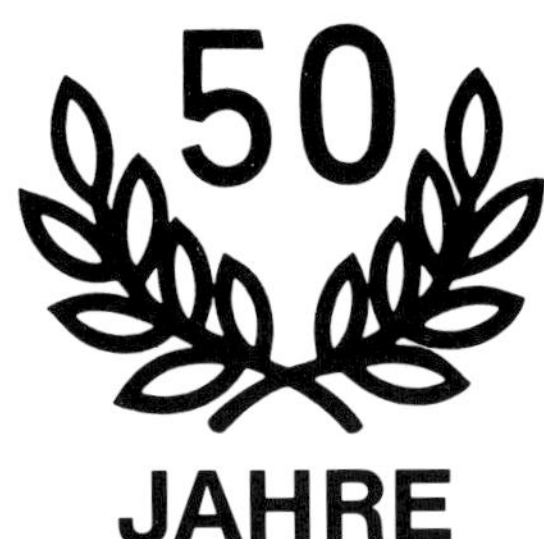

1975 marked the 50th Anniversary of the introduction of the LEICA to the photographic world. Leitz decided to celebrate the occasion by manufacturing a special series of the then current cameras, i.e. the M5, the M4, the CL and the SL2. These cameras all carried the 50th Anniversary Oak Leaves on the front, and a special three-digit serial number on the back prefaced with a single letter from the word LEICA. As far as can be ascertained, 1,750 were manufactured of each type except for the CL; in the case of the LEICA M4, 1,400 in Wetzlar and the remaining 350 at E. Leitz, Midland. 3,500 CL's were produced.

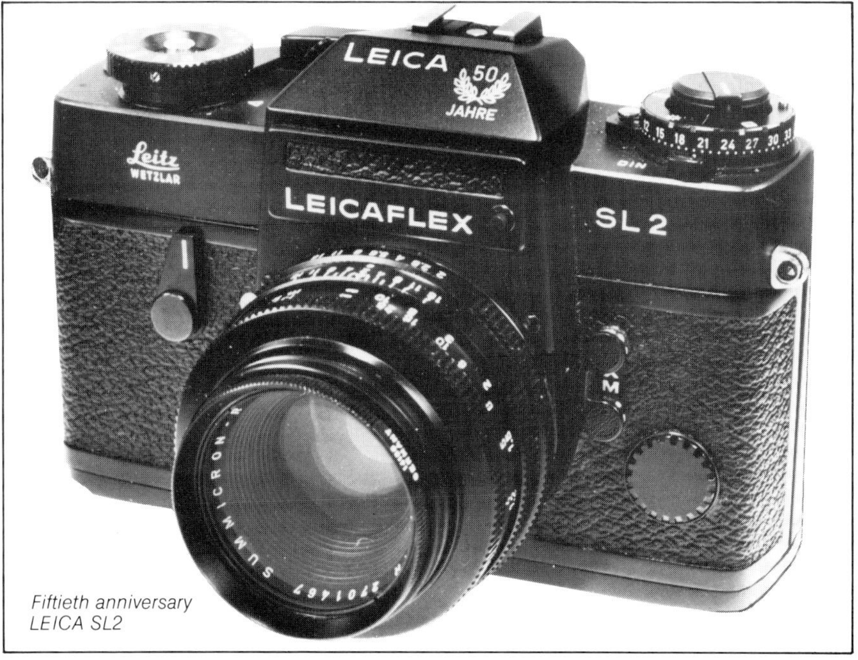

Fiftieth anniversary
LEICA SL2

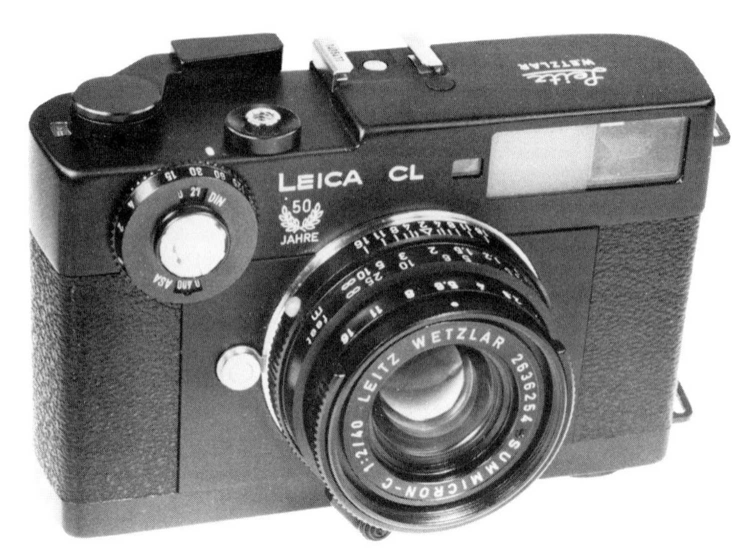

Fiftieth anniversary LEICA CL

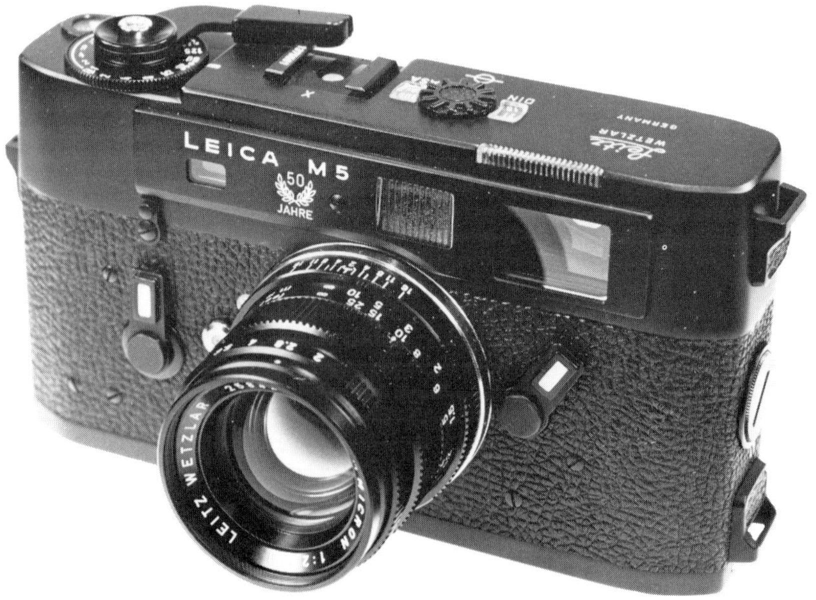

Fiftieth anniversary LEICA M5

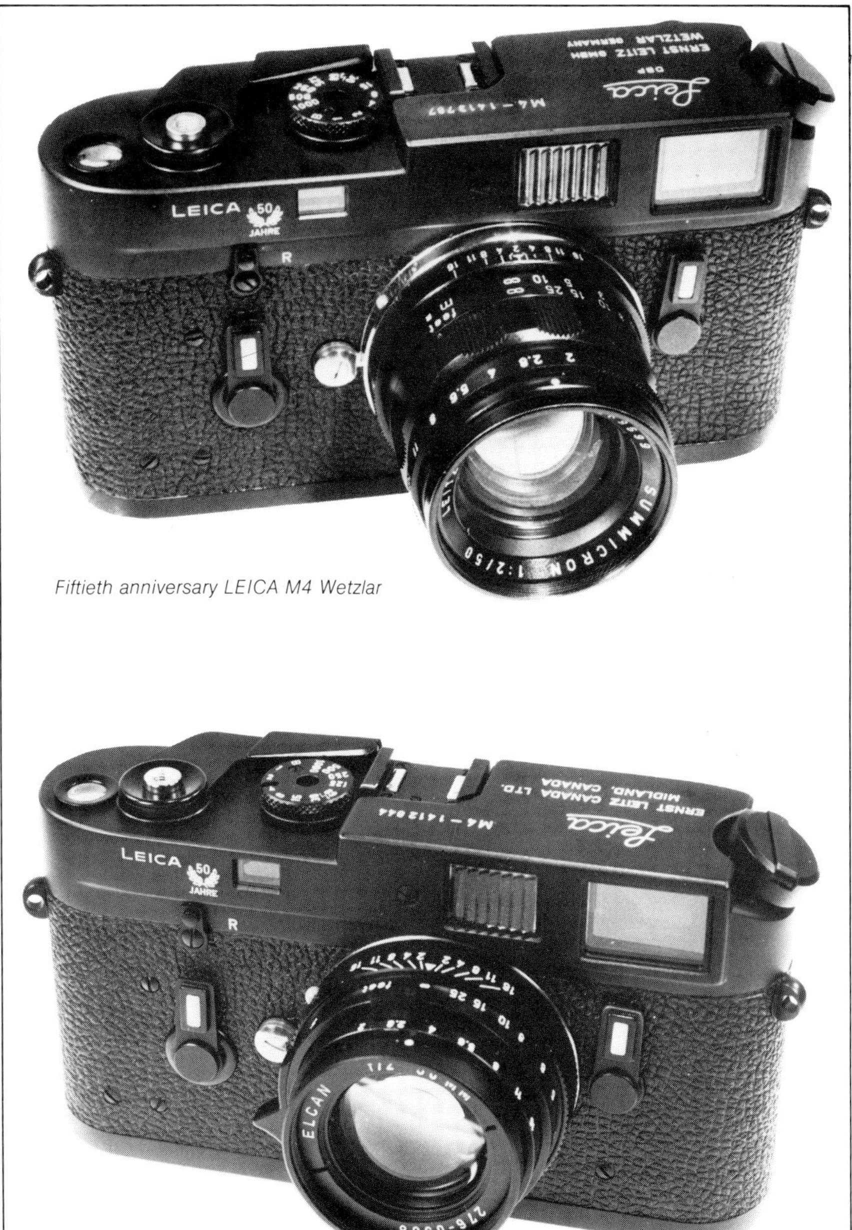

Fiftieth anniversary LEICA M4 Wetzlar

Fiftieth anniversary LEICA M4 Midland Canada fitted with 50mm F2 ELCAN Lens

1979 OSKAR BARNACK CENTENARY

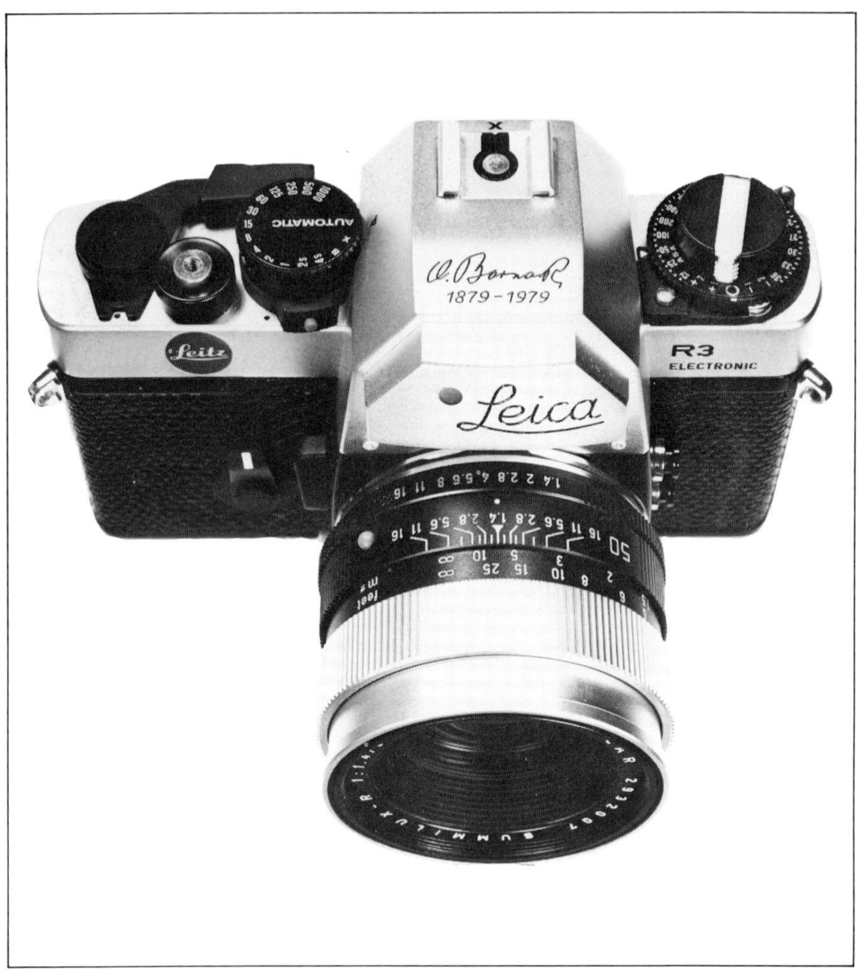

The 100th anniversary of the birth of Oskar Barnack on 1st November, 1879, was marked by the issue of 1,000 each of R3's and M4-2's in 24 carat gold plate. The cameras were covered in black reptile skin and came in a fitted mahogany case. They were engraved with the replica signature "O. Barnack" and the years "1879-1979" on the pentaprism housing of the R3 and the top plate of the M4-P.

1982 CANADIAN EVEREST EXPEDITION

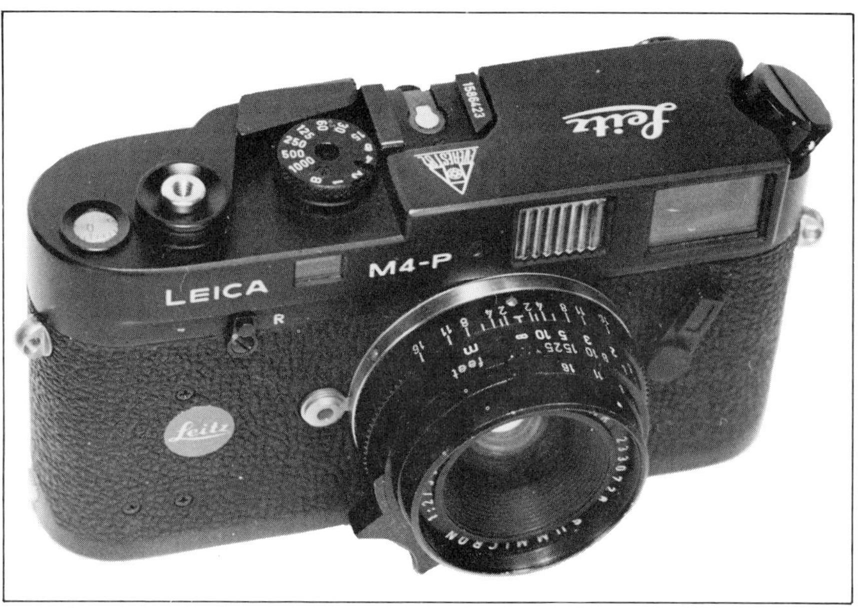

The successful scaling of Mount Everest by the Canadian expedition in 1982 was marked by a special issue of the R4 and M4-P engraved with the Expedition's logo. 200 of each model were issued in North America.

1983 LEICA PROTOTYPE – 70th ANNIVERSARY

A special edition of the M4-P in silver chrome was issued at the end of 1983 to commemorate the 70th anniversary of when Oskar Barnack completed the first prototype of the LEICA. The cameras had a special serial number and were engraved with the curved script logo and the years "1913-1983" on the back of the top plate and the front edge of the baseplate (which was black). The edition was limited to 2,500 only and supplied in some countries only in sets with lenses. The lenses were also engraved with the script logo and were the 35mm SUMMICRON-M, the 50mm SUMMICRON-M and the 90mm TELE-ELMARIT-M.

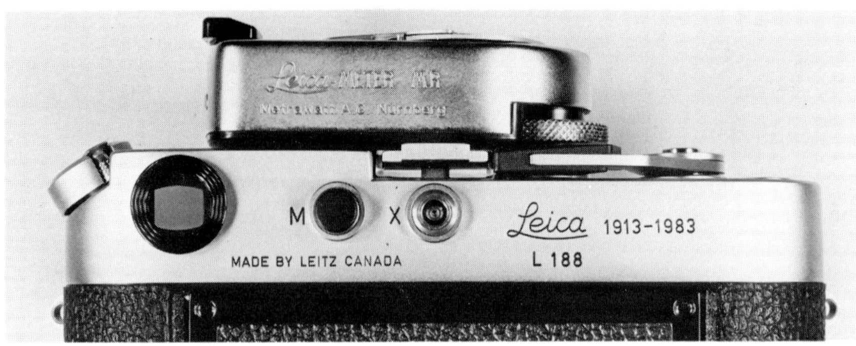

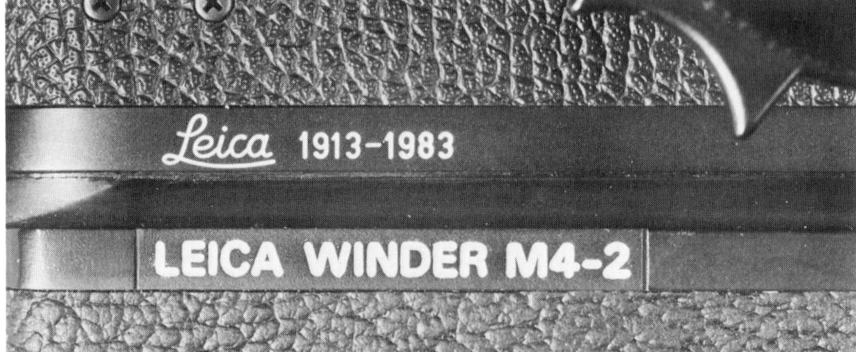

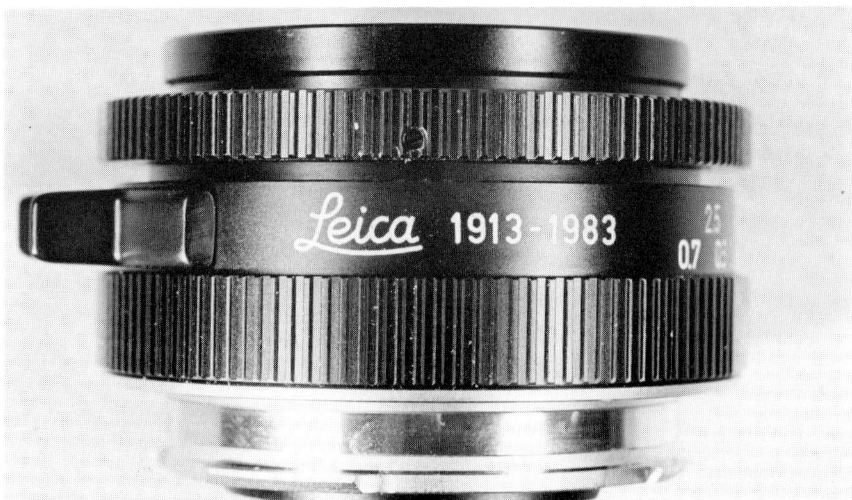

Prototype 70th Anniversary cameras:
Top, Inscription and special serial number on back of top-plate.
Middle, Inscription on front of black base-plate.
Bottom, Inscription on 35mm SUMMICRON-M.

LHSA 10th ANIVERSARY, 1978

This was not a Leitz issue but a privately commissioned special engraving by the LEICA Historical Society of America to commemorate the tenth anniversary of their founding in 1968. Leitz, Rockleigh, engraved 100 R3's on top of the prism housing with the Society's logo and the years 1968-1978. The cameras were sold by the Society to its members.

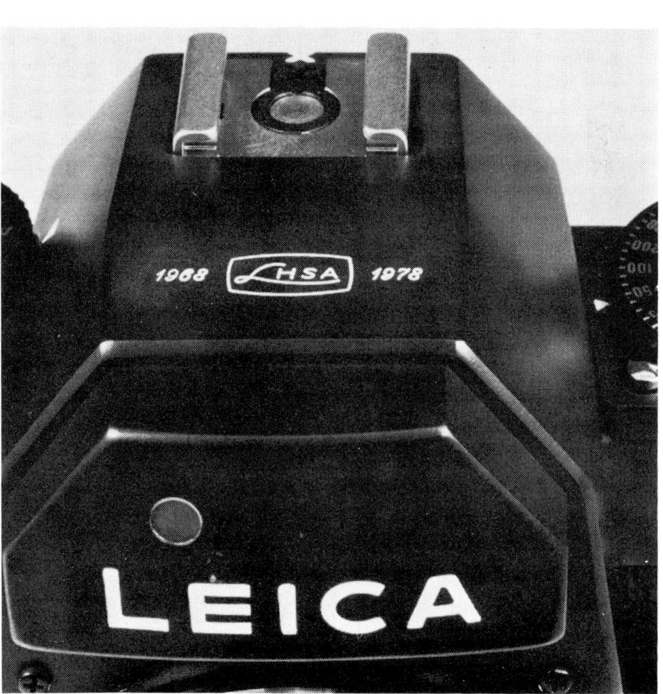

Picture reproduced from LHSA journal "Viewfinder" with permission.

Chapter 13

Wartime and Military LEICA Cameras

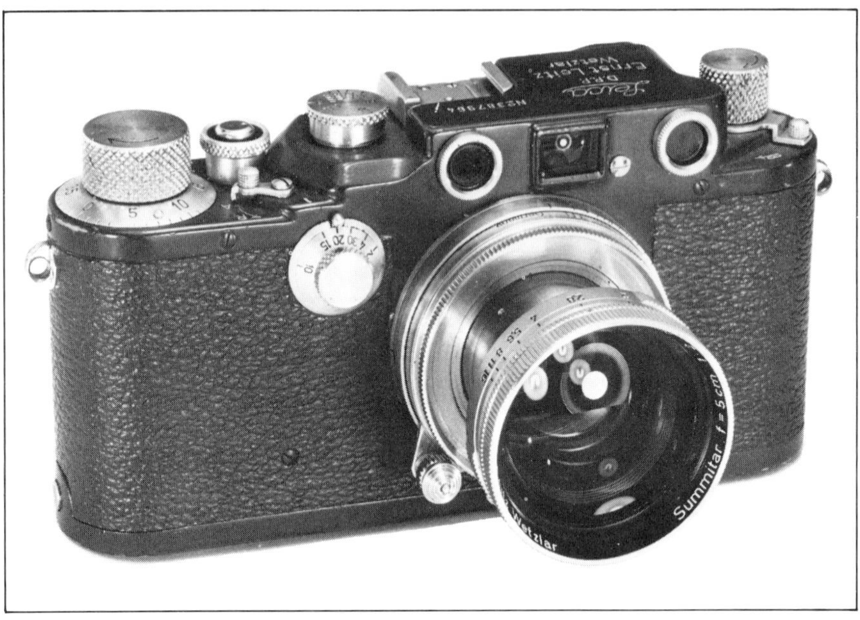

LEICA IIIc (grey).

LEICA camera production during the period of the Second World War, 1939-45, embraced a surprising variety of models. The following figures are derived from Leitz official production records. Throughout this chapter, production figures marked with an asterisk (*) are approximate only and are based on allocated serial numbers: the actual production figures in these cases are believed to be well below the quoted figures. The wartime model range comprised the following:-

LEICA I, Model B, Rim-set Compur	16
LEICA II, chrome	797
LEICA Standard	1,179
LEICA 250 (Reporter)	403
LEICA 250 (Reporter), Motor drive	28
LEICA IIIb, chrome	13,400
LEICA IIIc, chrome or grey	30,000*
LEICA IIId, chrome	427

Of all the cameras listed above we shall never know the actual number used by the various armed services. However, research in recent years had made the situation much clearer and reduced the scope for speculation and wishful thinking. The vast majority of these cameras were not marked as military equipment. The service which made the greatest use of the LEICA was the more technologically advanced air force, the Luftwaffe.

As far as can be determined the majority of cameras destined for official use were sent by Leitz to a central government purchasing office in Berlin. Either this organisation, or the service concerned, then carried out any additional identification engraving and marking. The only exception to this was the Luftwaffe: according to Leitz records some 1,800* LEICA IIIc's were destined for the Luftwaffe and it is now thought that the "Fl" number was engraved before delivery. The "L" in the Leitz records against the serial numbers of these cameras could indicate the Luftwaffe also bought direct or that the cameras had been ordered ready engraved. A small number of IIIb's were also recorded in this way.

The German wartime military engraving did not follow a consistent pattern but fell generally into the following groups:-

    1) Engraving on top-plate of camera
    2) Engraving on back rim of top-plate
    3) Impression on vulcanite at back of body
    4) Painted on vulcanite at back of body – a method which appears to have
       been confined to the early war period.

The Luftwaffe engraving on the top-plate was normally only "FL No. 38079". This was presumably either a stores reference number or possibly a military

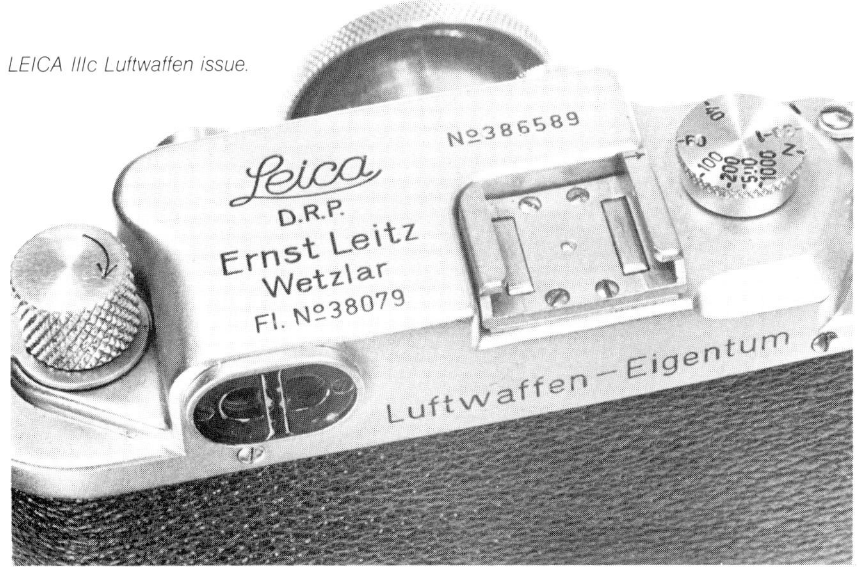

LEICA IIIc Luftwaffen issue.

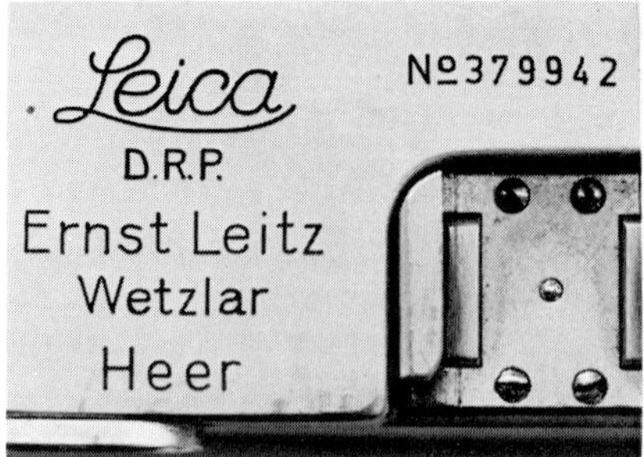

Engraving on Army issue IIIc

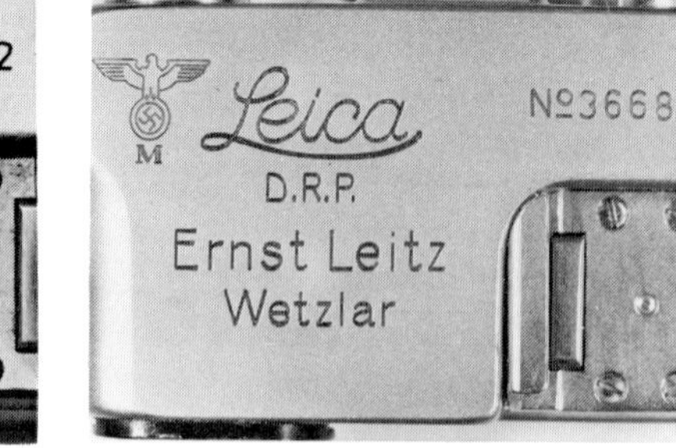

Engraving on Navy issue IIIc. This one has the "Reichsadler"

contract number. Some cameras carried the additional engraving "Luftwaffen Eigentum", meaning Luftwaffe property. This was on the back rim of the top-plate. It is interesting that in an article in the British "Miniature Camera Magazine" for May, 1941, in which the Editor is reporting on his examination of a captured IIIc, the first he had seen, he comments that captured German aircraft had revealed that many pilots carried LEICA's and that "The standard Luftwaffe Leica is a IIIb , not the new model, and is finished not in black but in Luftwaffe grey, with the name 'Luftwaffe' prominently lettered in silver across the back." This must have referred to the grey-painted vulcanite as grey top-plates were not made until later in the war.

Other services nearly always used the top of the top-plate for engraving. Army LEICA's were either marked "Heer" (Army) just under the name "Wetzlar" on the top-plate, or "W.H." for (Wermacht Heer) in the same position. Naval LEICA's were usually limited to an "M" (for Marine) followed by a number located above the commencement of the serial number. Naval LEICA's are the only type that may have had the Reichsadler (a swastika surmounted by an eagle) engraved on the top left hand corner of the top-plate. Other engravings have come to light over the years, some of these may well be genuine, others may not.

Marking on the vulcanite on the back of the body is known to exist on a few of the early army cameras as "Heer-Eigentum" (Army property), but is more usually seen on the earlier Luftwaffe cameras as "Luftwaffe Eingentum" and is presumably what the Editor of the "Miniature Camera Magazine" was referring to.

The colour of wartime cameras is the next area of interest. In general:-

1) The main bulk had a normal chrome top-plate and black body.
2) Some are know to exist with a normal chrome top-plate but with the black vulcanite painted over grey.
3) In the later war years, when the raw materials for chrome plating became difficult to obtain, approximately 3,400* cameras were produced with top and bottom plates and vulcanite all in grey paint, but with chrome trim.

Only a minority of grey cameras were engraved with any additional markings;

also grey cameras were supplied to all three services, they were not exclusive to the Luftwaffe.

Next comes the usage of the letter "K". It used to be assumed that this referred to a winterised camera for use in low temperature climates and stood for "Kaltfest" (coldproof). In fact it designates a LEICA with a shutter mounted in ball bearings – "Kugellager". Ball bearings would of course make the shutter much more efficient at low temperatures than one with normal bearings. The "K" was engraved on the top-plate immediately after the serial number and/or stamped in white on the shutter blind. It is understood that all cameras after No. 388926 had ball bearing shutters.

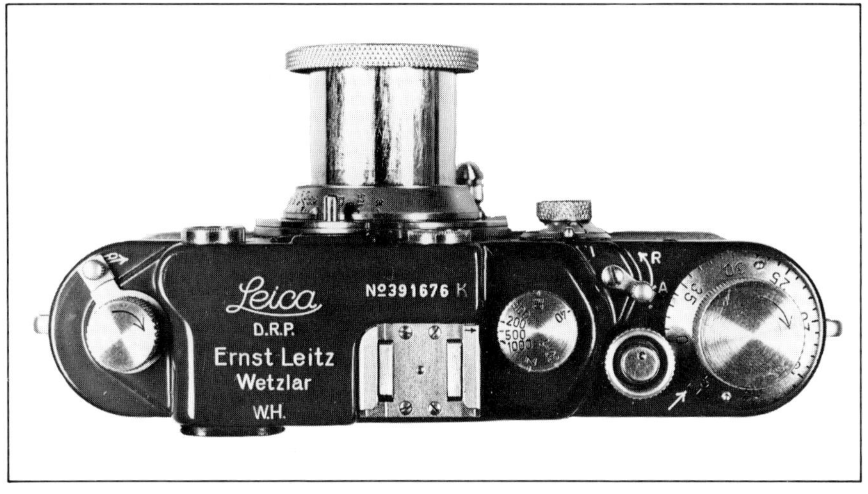

LEICA IIIc with ball-bearing shutter. Note the letter "K" after the serial number. This one was Army issue and has the "W.H." marking

Red shutter blinds have also caused confusion. Leitz experimented during the development of the camera with different blind materials, including some cloth from Kodak in the late twenties or early thirties and, no doubt, from other suppliers as well. In 1937 a small batch of LEICA III's, destined for the Far East, were fitted with blind material that was red on one side. This was apparently to prevent the intense tropical light penetrating the blind and effecting panchromatic film. During the war years Leitz were hard pressed to find suitable materials and at one time used up the remaining red stock. Hence a number of cameras appear with blinds red on one side.

Lenses and other accessories of course were also used by the services and these were also engraved accordingly. An interesting accessory produced for the Luftwaffe during the war was a special combined holder and sun-shade for the LEICA equipped with a SUMMITAR lens. It was meant for hand-holding by an airman with gloved hands. It was an aluminium casting with engraving on top

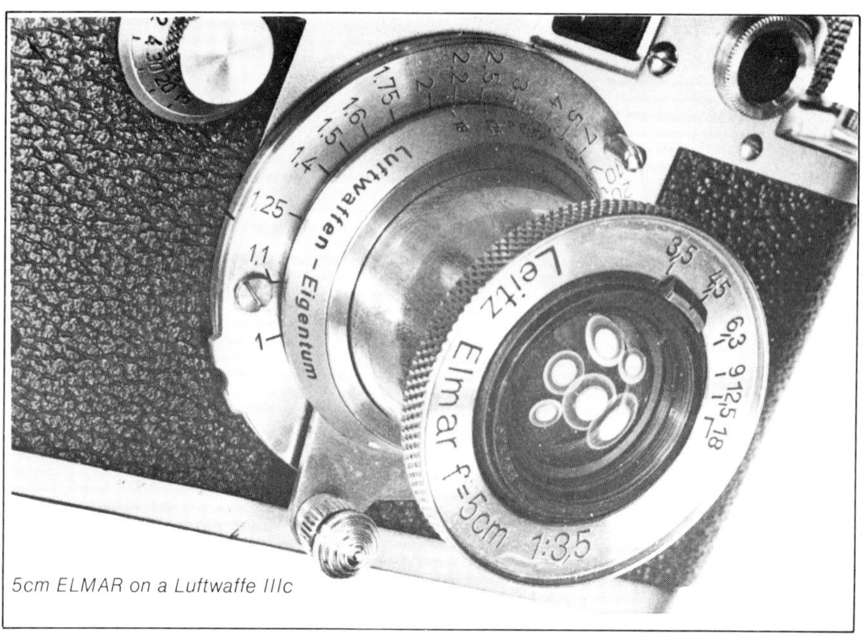

5cm ELMAR on a Luftwaffe IIIc

Special Luftwaffen combined lens hood and camera mount designed for LEICA IIIc with rapid winder SNCOO.

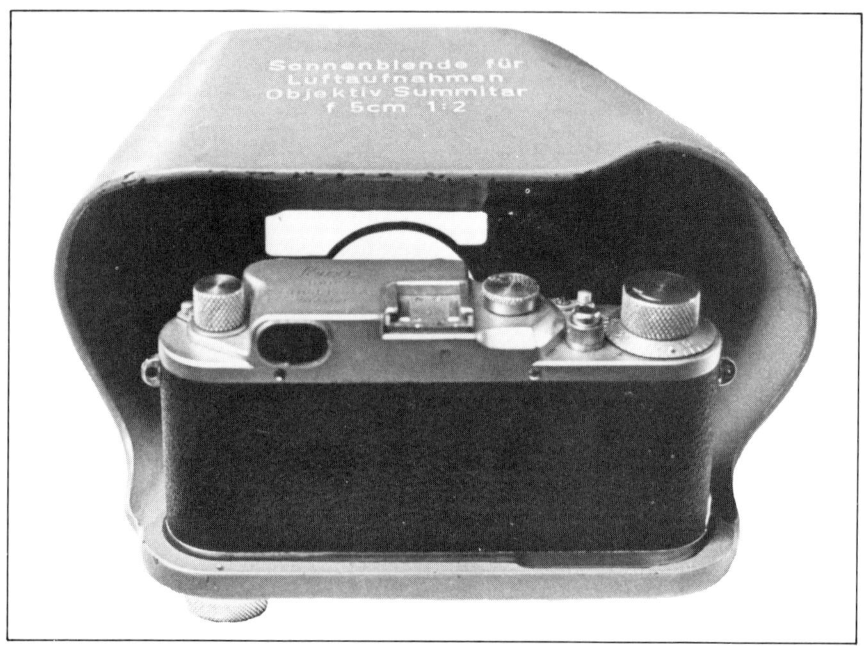

that clearly indicated its purpose, and slots in the bottom so that the rapid wind device, SCNOO, could be used.

Much has been written about German wartime LEICA's and much confusion exists. Recent research is slowly clearing the air and the myths are being dispelled. No doubt in the course of time cameras will turn up with unusual engravings and some may be authentic and some may not.

The Germans were not alone in using LEICA's during the war. The Italian armed forces also used them. Some pre-war IIIb's were issued to the Air Force with the engraving "R. Aeronautica" where the "R" stood for "Regia" (Royal). A rather unusual motorised 250 in brand new condition materialised at an auction during 1983 bearing the engraving "E. Aeronautica" and nobody can work out the meaning of the "E". Several IIIc's in a single batch were bought after the war by the Air Force and engraved "Aeronautica Militare" in red above the serial number. Many of these cameras are now in private collections after having been disposed of by the military.

The British services also used LEICA cameras during the last war. A certain number were requisitioned at the beginning of the war, either from the stock of E. Leitz, London, or from retailers. Also at the beginning of the war the British government requested the temporary loan of cameras, and in many cases these were actually returned to their owners after the end of hostilities. The most curious story though is illustrated by the camera shown here. It is a wartime manufactured camera with the Royal Navy engraving "Patt 8665" (Pattern 8665). According to the story, which cannot be verified, these cameras were supplied to Sweden during the war and then flown to England in the same Mosquito aircraft that collected Swedish ball bearings. This was during the middle period of the war. The cameras were then engraved with the naval marking.

LEICA IIIc Royal Naval issue.

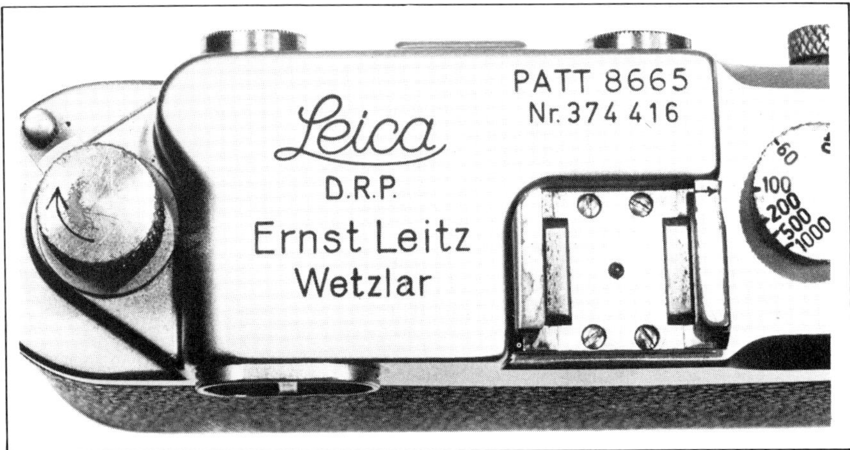

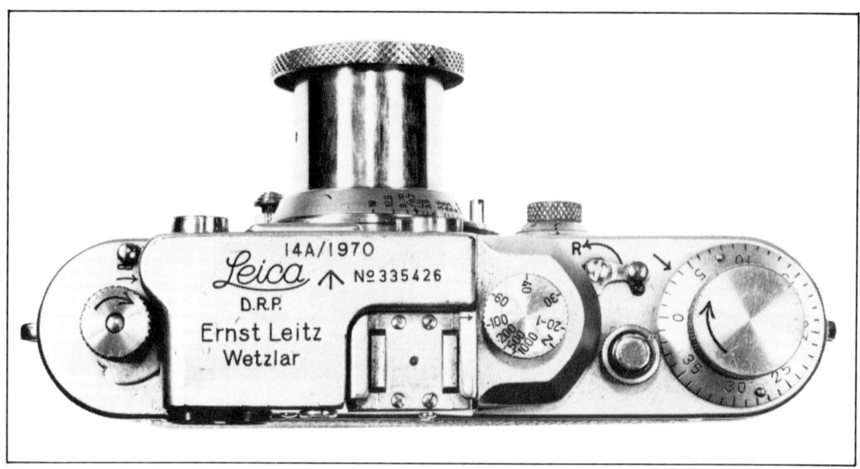

LEICA IIIb Royal Air Force issue.

After the war there was a continued interest in the LEICA by several countries' armed forces. To cite a few examples: The American army bought the IIIf, then the M2 (known by the army code KS-15), followed by the M4 in a special version (known as KE-7A). The Swedish army had a small series of IIIg's specially made in black. These had the three Swedish crowns engraved on the

American Army LEICA M4 KE-7A manufactured by Leitz Midland.

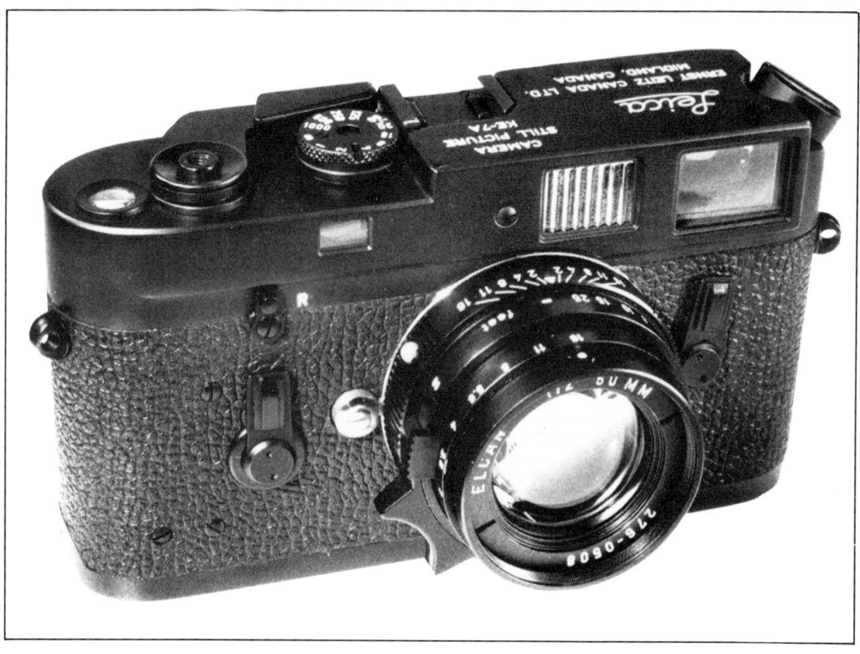

back of the camera and also on the barrel of the 5mm, f2.8 ELMAR lenses with which they were fitted. The German army used the M1 in a dark green finish. These cameras had the numbers "5 + 13.5" engraved on the top-plate under the "WETZLAR Germany" wording. This clearly related to the lenses to be used with the camera, whose viewfinder had frames for these focal lengths. They also used the M3, also in olive paint. The example illustrated is engraved "Bundeseigentum" (Federal property). Apart from these known destinations,

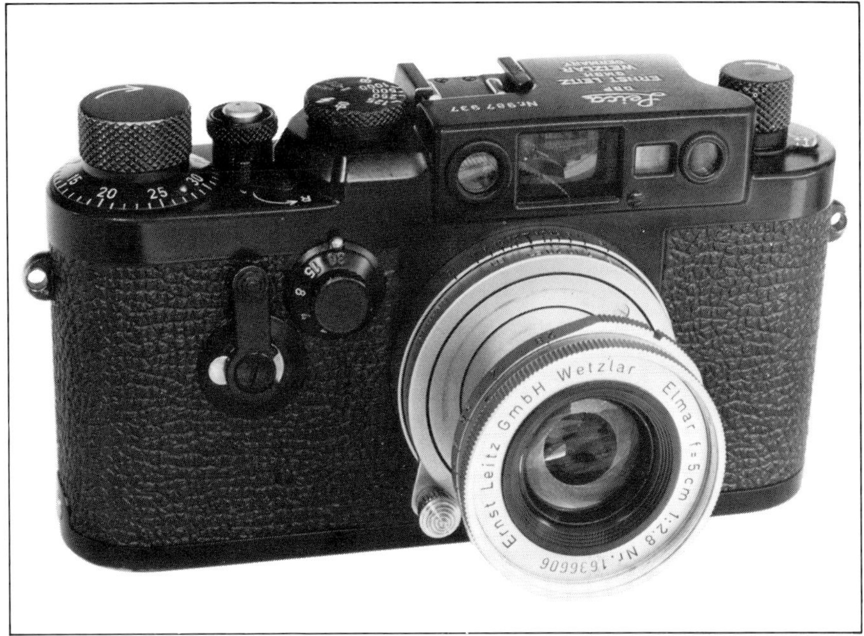

LEICA IIIg Swedish Air Force issue
left: engraving on lens
right: engraving on back of camera

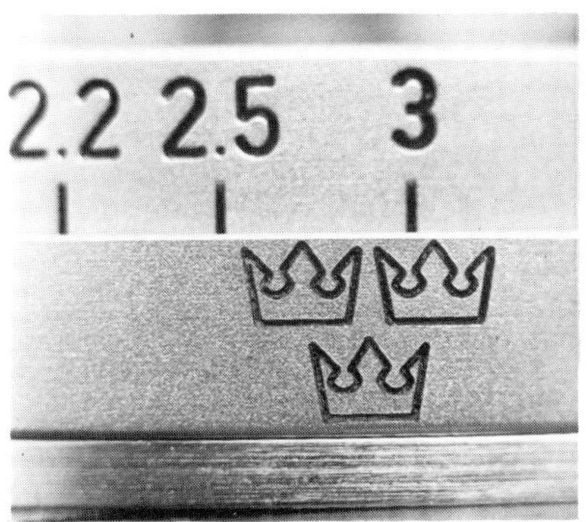

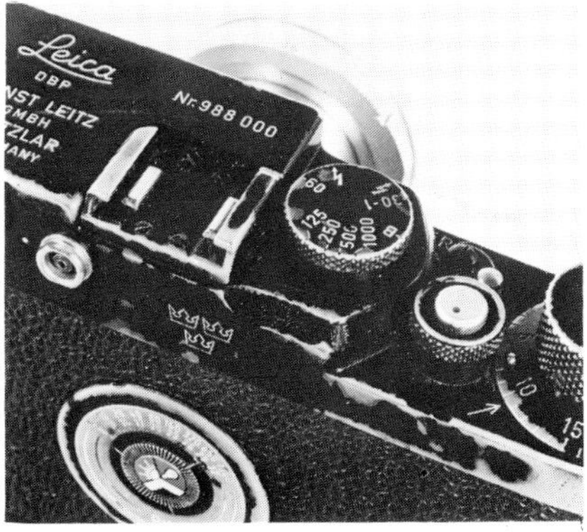

the factory records show that the M1, M2 and M4 were also produced in dark green and the M2 in grey.

The M4's for the American army, mentioned above, were manufactured in Canada. The detailed instruction manual for the camera's use and repair, which was produced by the U.S. Armed Forces Technical Services, is very comprehensive and makes fascinating reading. There is one part that should horrify any LEICA enthusiast. It gives precise instructions on how to destroy the camera to prevent its falling into enemy hands. It says that the camera body and lenses should be thoroughly smashed with a hammer or hatchet, or if necessary with explosives!

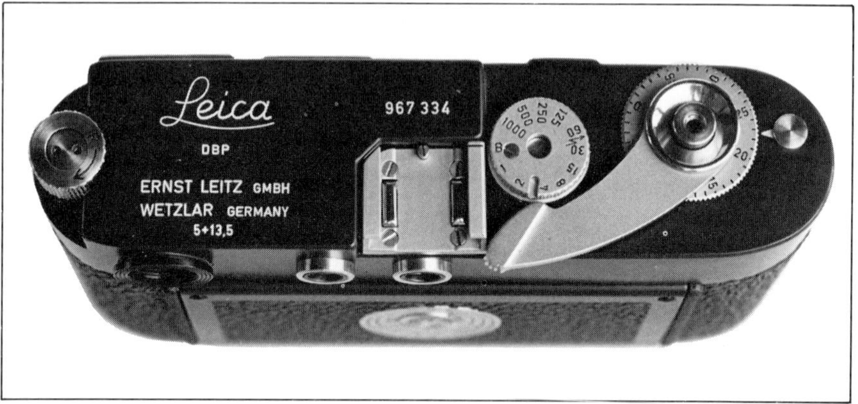

Military LEICA M1 dark green with special markings 5 × 13.5 on top plate (Leitz collection).

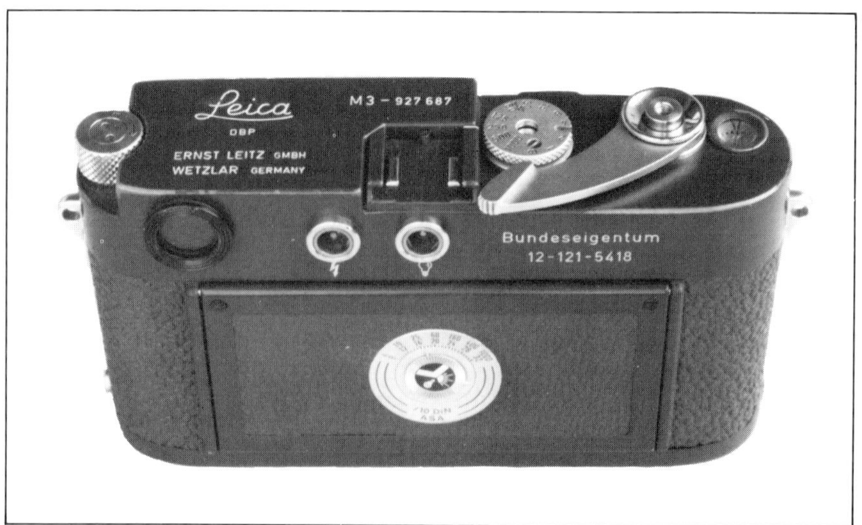

Military M3 in olive paint.

Chapter 14

Special Purpose LEICA Models

There are many LEICA models which the general public has never seen, of which only the specialist or the real LEICA enthusiast knows to exist.

"MIFILMCA"

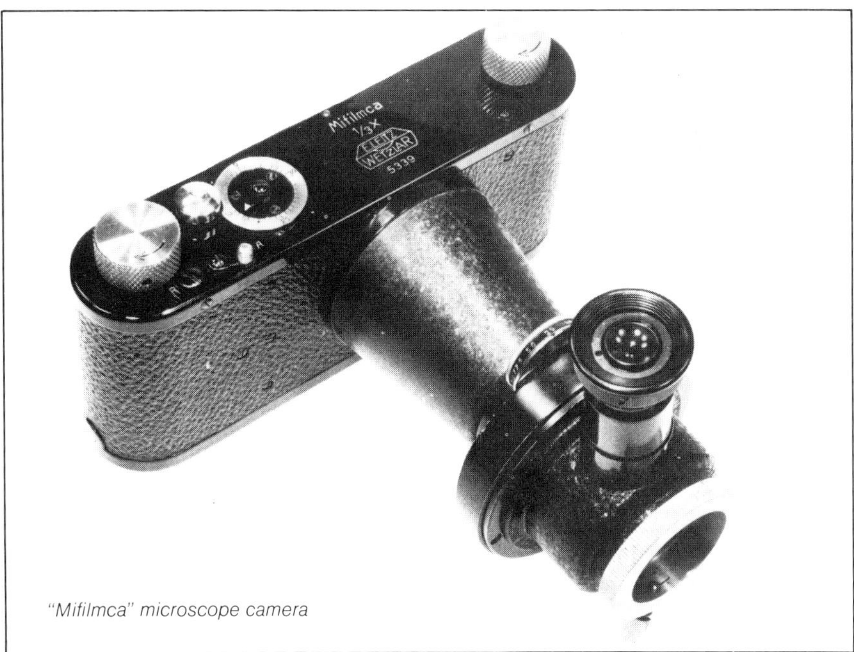

"Mifilmca" microscope camera

The 'Mifilmca" was a specialised camera which was made in extremely limited quantities in the 1920's before the introduction of interchangeable lenses enabled any LEICA camera to be used with the separate MIKAS attachment. This camera was for microscopic use and was supplied complete with a fixed MIKAS-type attachment for direct connection onto the tube of the microscope. The camera body was basically the Compur-B body, (i.e. with no shutter and no viewfinder). The camera body was engraved Mifilmca X1/3. Very few examples of these are known to exist and they occur in two forms. The earlier type had a fixed, MIKAS-type attachment with black crackle paint on the tube. The later form took a screw-in MIKAS.

X-RAY CAMERAS

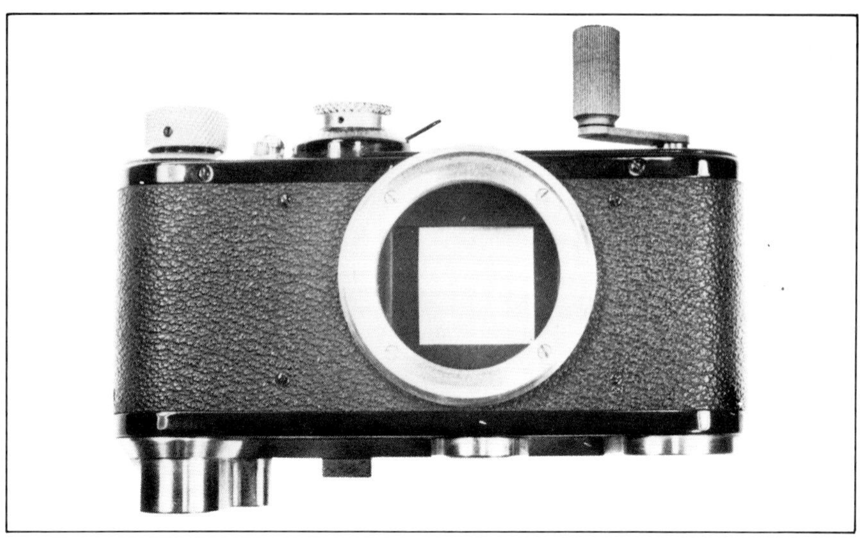

Wetzlar "X-Ray" camera

A most unusual camera is the X-ray type made just before the war by order of the German Ministry of Health, but sold also to hospitals abroad; it was advertised in special leaflets destined for medical suppliers. This camera differed from any other type. The main feature was the square format, 24 x 24mm, to cope with X-ray screens. The camera body was rather like a Standard, but without the

New York "X-Ray" camera

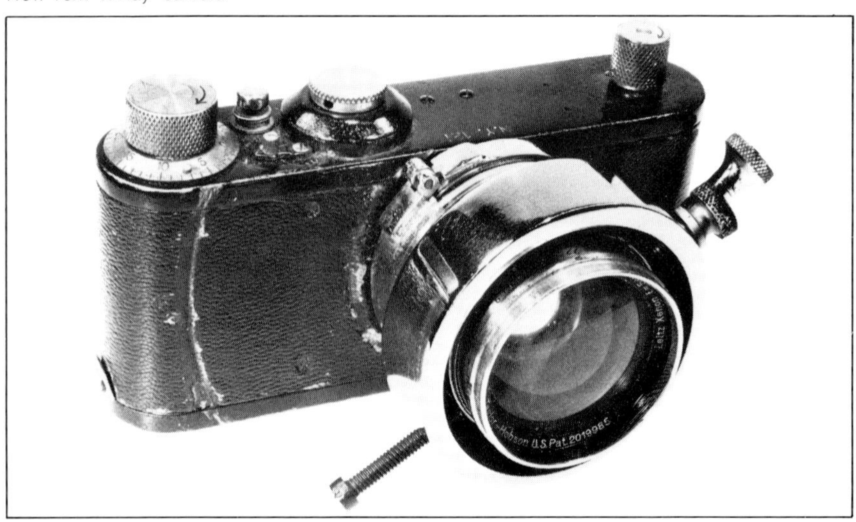

viewfinder. The lens was a fixed-focus XENON f1.5 mounted in a conical adaptor which had a plate with four screws by which the camera was mounted onto the X-ray machine. The camera also had a breach mount actuated by a large lever. Camera bodies could be easily changed in this fashion when the film cartridge was fully exposed with the 50 frames that were possible on a single roll. The code name of the device, complete with lens and accessories, was RYOOK.

In the early part of World War II Leitz, New York, converted LEICA Standards into X-ray cameras for the Westinghouse Corporation. They differed from the Wetzlar X-ray cameras in being normal 24 x 36mm format instead of 24mm square. When stocks of Standards were exhausted other models and second-hand cameras were converted.

POST CAMERAS

Another interesting camera of odd format is the Post camera, so called because it is used by the postal authorities to record the telephone meter readings. It is a camera of unusual design based on the simpler non-rangefinder bodies. Some cameras of this type were made with the standard picture size of 24 x 36mm but most of them had a 24 x 27mm picture size.

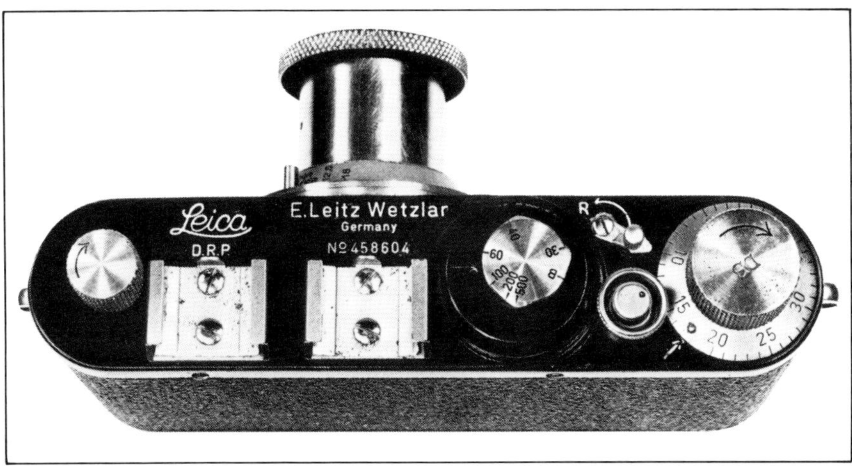

LEICA Ic "Post" 24mm x 36mm

The LEICA Ic is an early post-war example of a "post" camera in black paint finish and engraved DB on the wind-on knob.

There are really four different models of the real "post camera" of postwar vintage, and even a couple more if the special Ig is also considered along with some 200 units of a type called "Blitzspecial" derived from the last "post" type. The first model was derived from the M1, modified to accept a format of 24 x 27mm: this camera was required by the German Fernmeldetechnisches

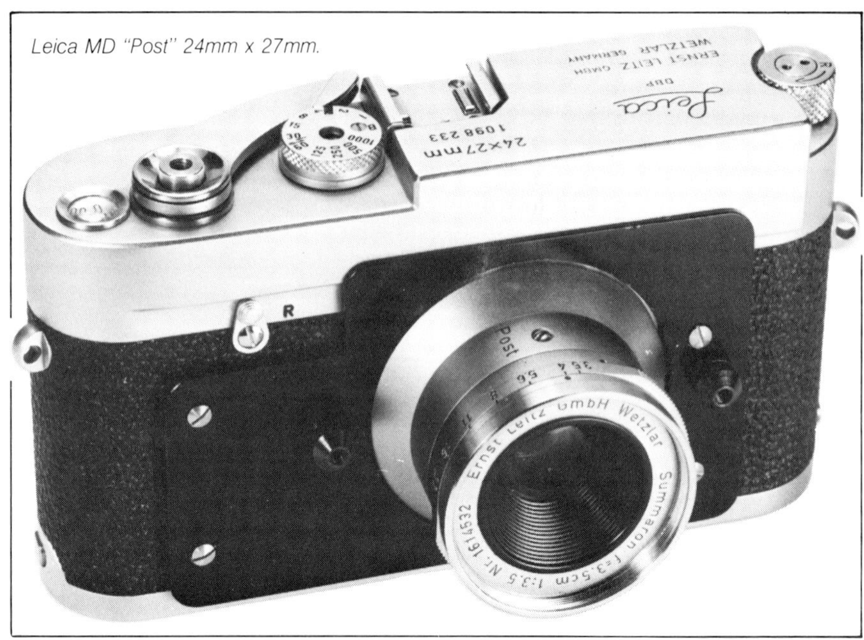

Zentralamt and was equipped with a fixed-focus SUMMARON 35mm set to a ratio of 1:12,7: on earlier cameras it had an aperture of f3.5 and on later ones f2.8. The camera was equipped with a front plate that allowed it to be snapped in and

LEICA MDa Post camera, 24mm x 27mm.

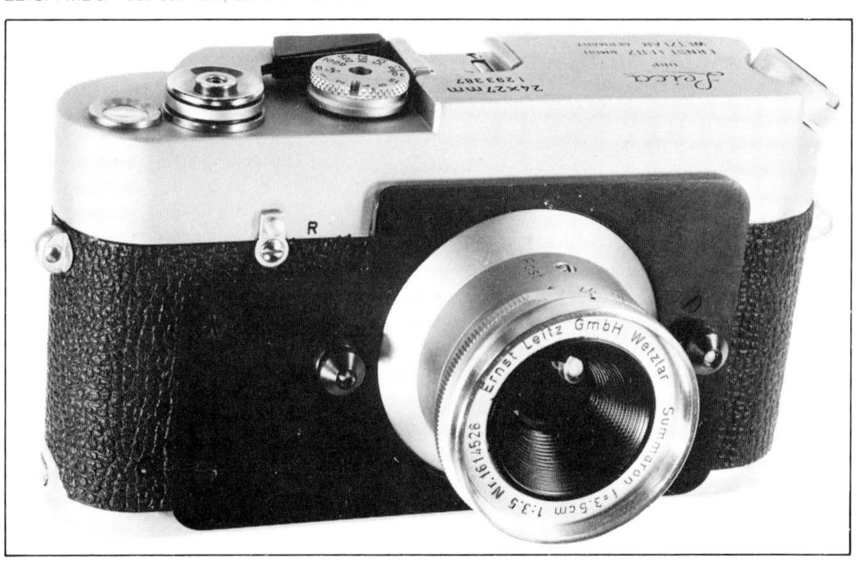

out of place in a device used to photograph telephone meters. Lighting was provided by a flash outfit made by the Swiss firm of Alos. 32 of these cameras were delivered, followed by a second series of 300 MD's with standard picture size of 24 x 36 mm but in "post" configuration that included a locked shutter knob on the flash speed.

In 1968 the camera model changed to MDa and 220 "post" cameras with 24 x 27 format were delivered, followed by another 200 cameras with the normal format of 24 x 36.

DISPLAY DUMMIES

Specials of a different kind are the various display cameras made by Leitz. First are the empty cameras, known as "Atrappe". They look like genuine LEICA or LEICAFLEX cameras because they are made with genuine parts, but they cost only a fraction of the price of a real camera because there is nothing inside. They are made for showcases, and to minimise the risk of theft. There are known Atrappe versions of all the main models since the LEICA III. At the beginning they wore no special number, then a five figure number with the letter "A" was used; lately, on the R3 and R4 cameras, the serial number is just blanked.

There are dummy lenses as well to go with Atrappe cameras: the engravings on the front ring is somewhat different from the real thing.

Pre-war dummies are rare because they were a source of scarce spare parts.

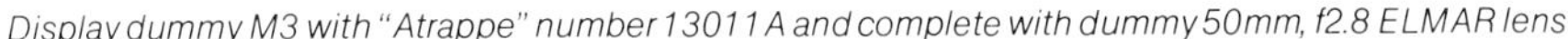

Display dummy M3 with "Atrappe" number 13011A and complete with dummy 50mm, f2.8 ELMAR lens

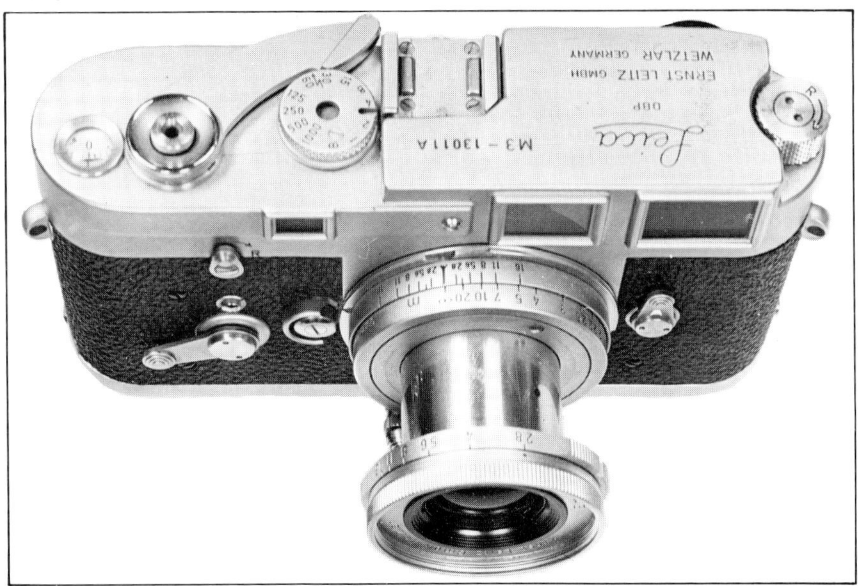

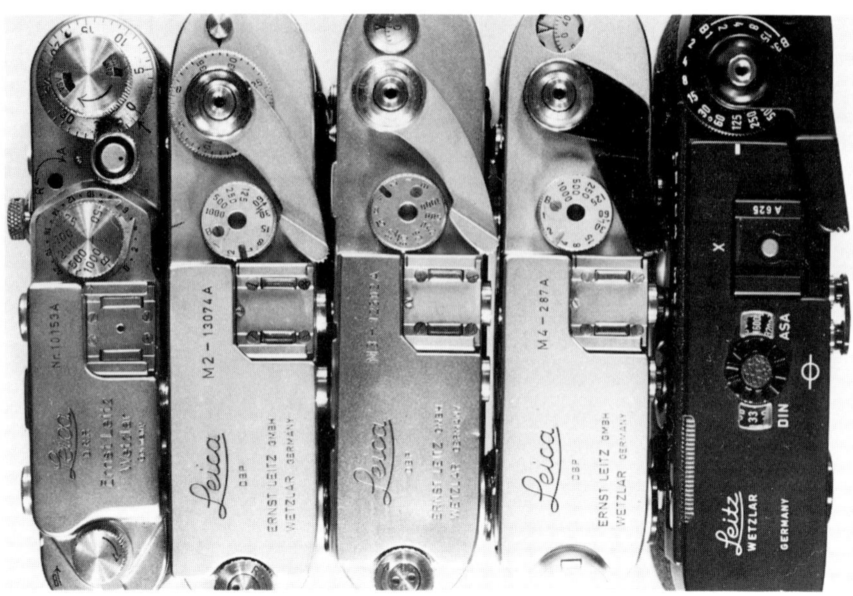

A royal flush of "Atrappe" dummies; IIIf, M2, M3, M4, M5.

Leitz also made cut-away models with working shutters for demonstration and exhibition purposes. These are known as "schnitt" cameras. They were much more costly to produce than the standard camera and so very few were made.

Finally there are the very large display models. These were made in even

Cut-away M3 to demonstrate mechanism

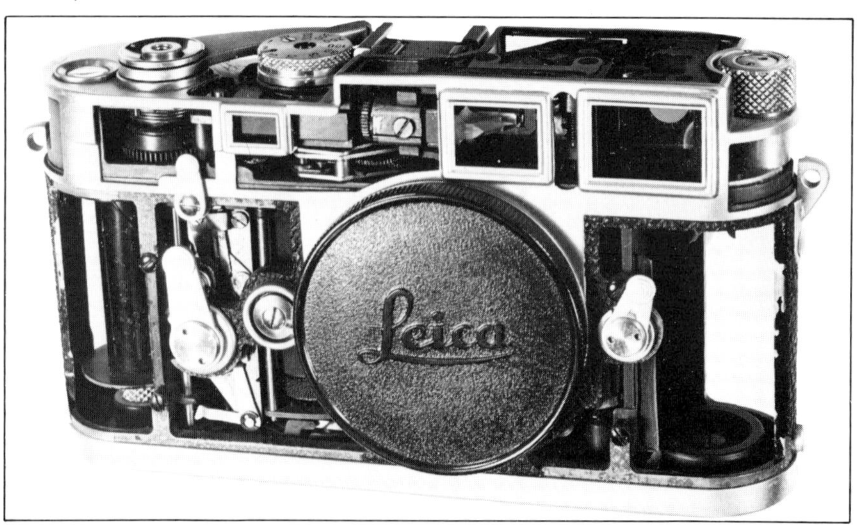

smaller quantities for exhibition and dealers' displays. Pre-war models of the IIIa are known as well as the post-war models of the IIIf and M3. As far as is known, no more were made after that. These models are the ultimate collectors' items.

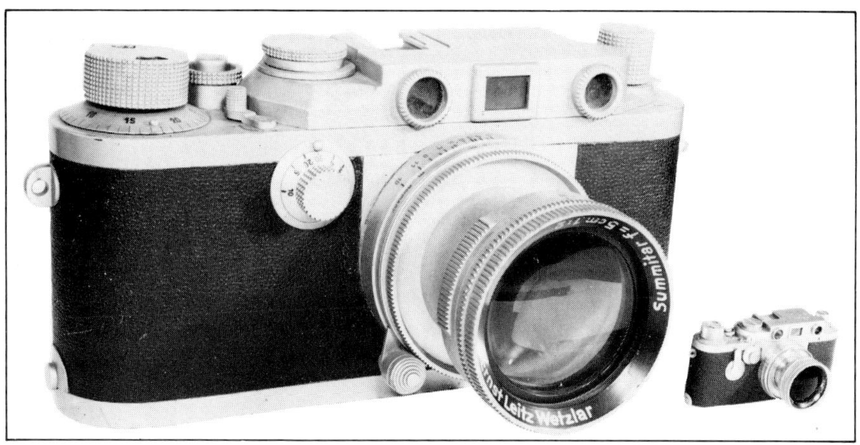

Large display models with the real cameras for comparison.
Top, IIIf; Bottom, M3.

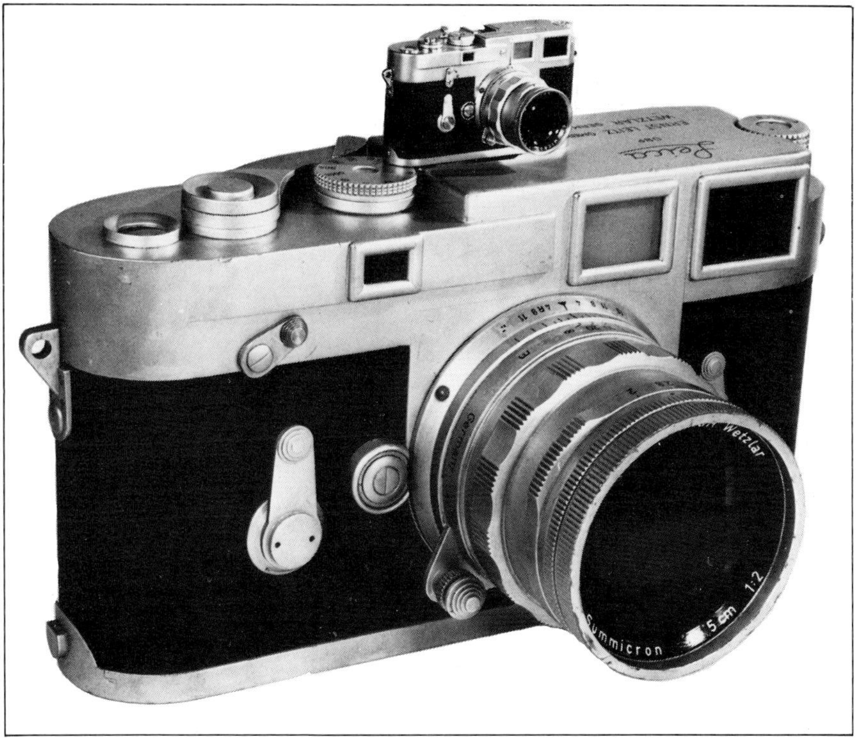

NON-LEITZ CONVERSIONS

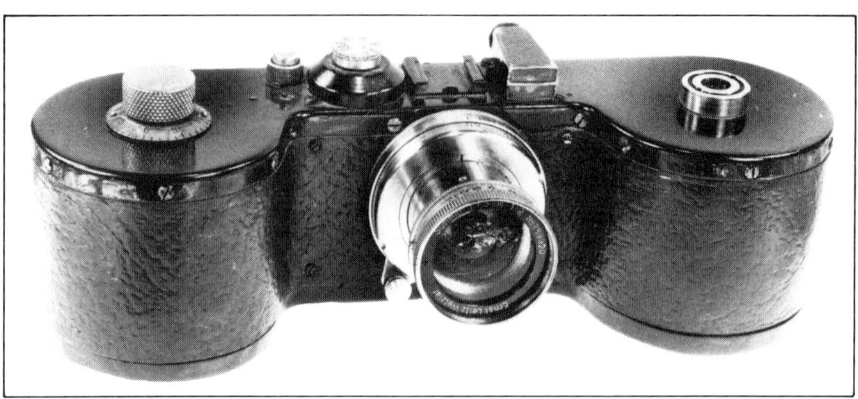

"British" LEICA 250

This is a most unusual "LEICA". It is a British manufactured 250 model, made from an original LEICA pre-war Standard with the wind-on gears extended outwards and using open spool-to-spool operation. It can be assumed that these models were made during the war for special uses.

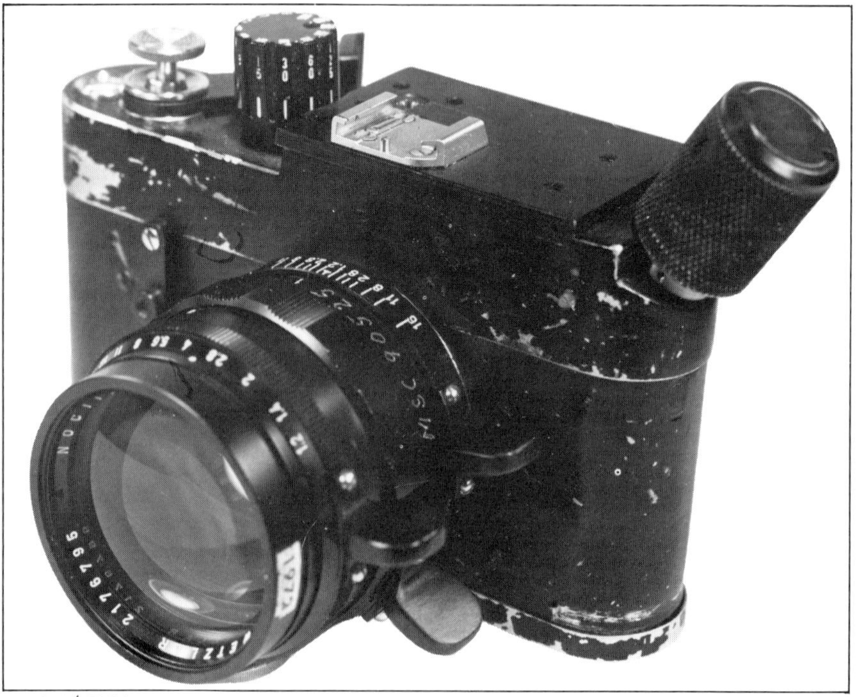

"NASA" LEICA

NASA LEICA M4. The Space Administration in the USA modified a number of cameras for Lunar use by entending the controls for use with heavily gloved hands. As far as is known, LEICA's were not used on the Moon.

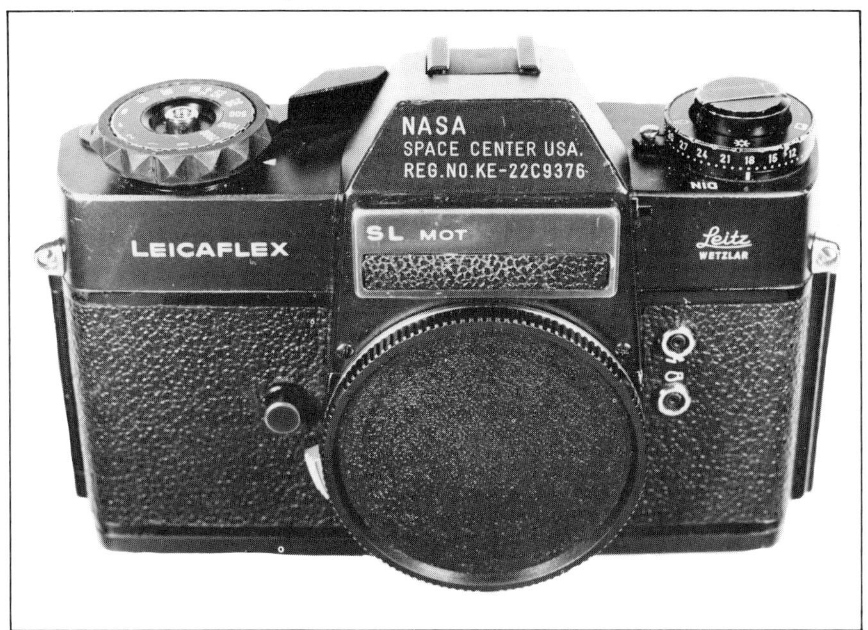

Another NASA modification was of the LEICAFLEX SL MOT with a studded speed dial to make it easier to use with gloves.

In all its sixty years history it is surprising that so few non-Leitz conversions of the LEICA have survived, or are indeed known. No doubt many cameras were modified for special purposes in military, medical or scientific use. Some of these may well be languishing in university, hospital and industrial laboratories. Any information, and illustrations, that would help to complete the LEICA story would be most welcome! A "LEICA 750", converted from a Ic, with enormous spool chambers has come to light and is believed to be a British conversion, like the "British 250" described above, but for what purpose is unknown. (Lager, Leica Illustrated Guide, Vol.2, p207).

Accessories for the LEICA were designed and made by other manufacturers to extend the facilities of the camera, usually Leitz incorporated them themselves. These accessories were often adopted and sold by Leitz agencies, especially Leitz New York. Examples are the "Direkt" delayed action release, "Rapido" rapid winder (which replaced the camera's wind-on knob, and "Vacub", the first flash gun to synchronise with the LEICA shutter, all from the early 1930's. The item described on the next page did involve a modification to the camera.

Leitz experimented with lens turrets on LEICA's from the early days. An example exists at Wetzlar. (See illustration page 157). The first available cameras with this facility were modifications carried out by Haber & Fink in the U.S.A. after the war. The camera was modified by removing the flange and adapting the front to carry the turret. Leitz also brought out a lens turret accessory, code OROLF, which enabled screw lenses to be used on bayonet models, without any modifications.

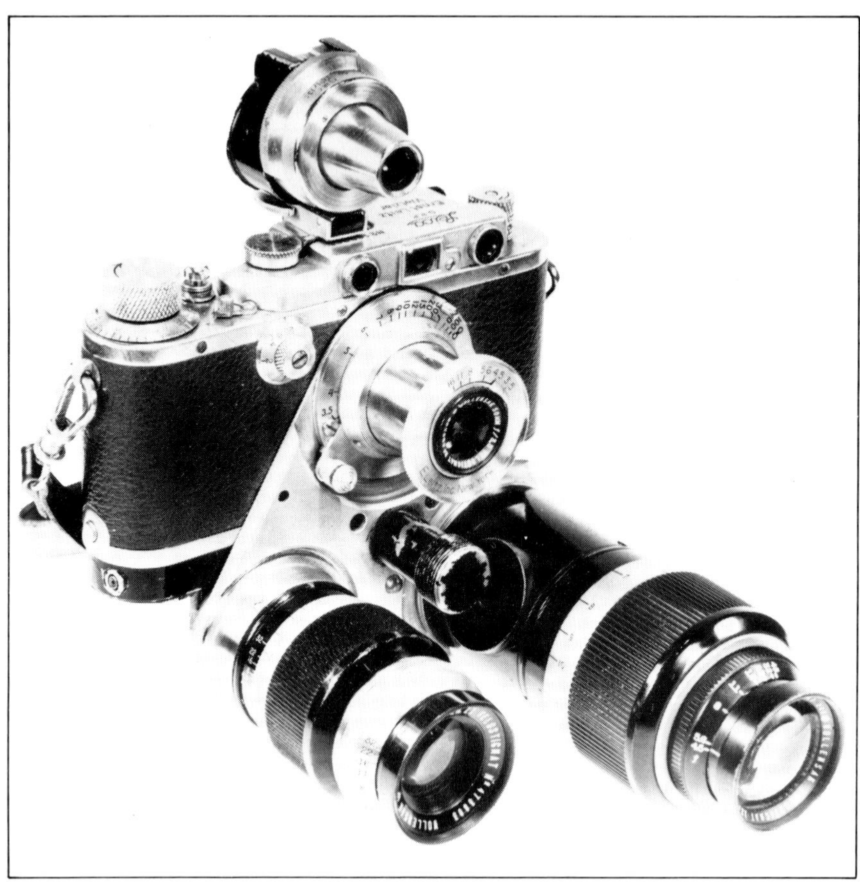

Haber and Fink turret on modified camera

Chapter 15

Experimental Models

At Wetzlar there is a fascinating section where prototypes are kept; of course not all of them can be found here as many have been lost! However the experimental models which were never commercially produced are sometimes just as interesting as the well-known ones.

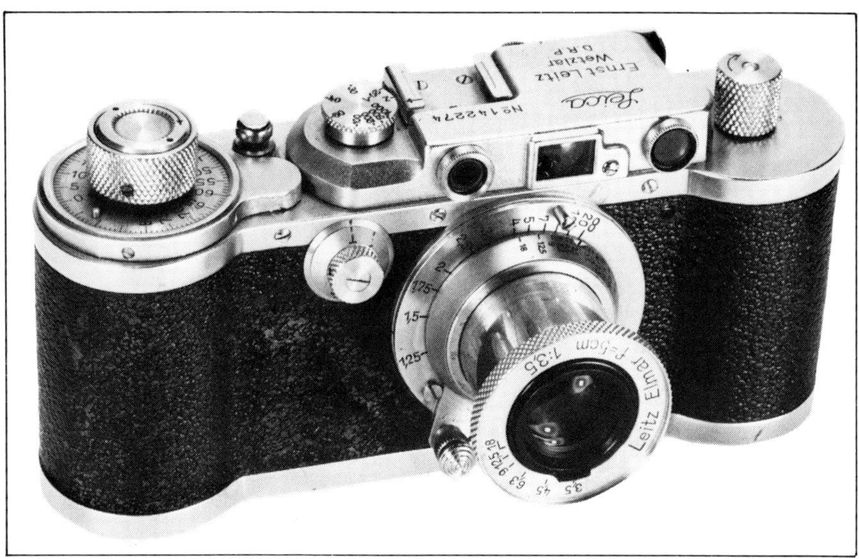

LEICA Type 75

For example, there is the LEICA 75 type (slightly larger than the normal one and smaller than the "250") that was built to investigate the marketability of a camera with an extended length of film. It was made in 1934. It has the mechanical characteristics of the model IIIa and is chrome finished; the rangefinder cover bears the number 142,274. This was the only LEICA other than the 250 to have cassette-to-cassette film loading.

Another very interesting prototype is the stereo LEICA ("Doppel") made personally by Oskar Barnack, probably in 1935. It is actually two cameras in one, with a double shutter. The body of the stereo LEICA is 193mm long, but height and depth are the same as on the standard camera. The elongated body allowed the placing of two lens flanges whose centres were 71.5mm apart; this separation is more or less equivalent to the distance between the eyes. The stereo frame size was 24 x 22.5mm. After each exposure the film was advanced the equivalent space of two frames and the pictures were taken with 35mm lenses. The single viewfinder was centred exactly between the lenses.

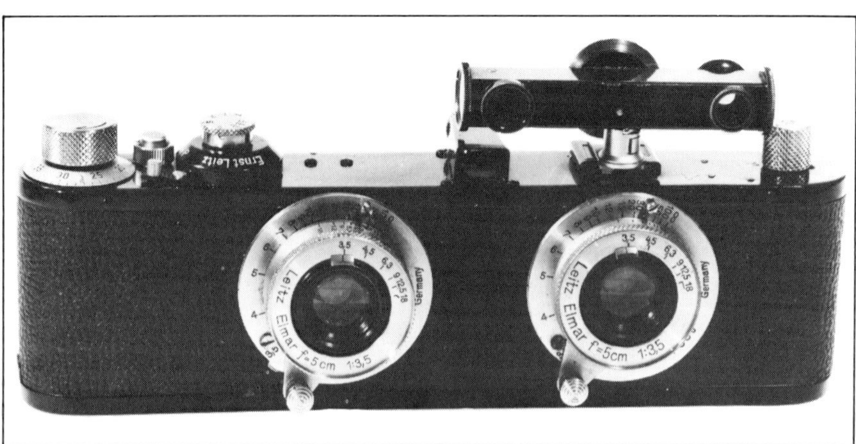

LEICA "DOPPEL"

The reason for making this camera was that with the stereo attachment that Leitz made at the time, the stereo pair were satisfactory if the scene was stationary, but if the subject was moving, the result would be that one picture differed from the other because the single curtain shutter would make first one exposure and then the other. With the stereo camera both curtains were actuated at the same time, since they were mechanically inter-connected and therefore both pictures of the stereo pair would be taken exactly at the same time.

Another very interesting prototype is the LEICA-H, which was a possible successor to the G. This was a project, from about 1959, for a half-frame (18 x 24)

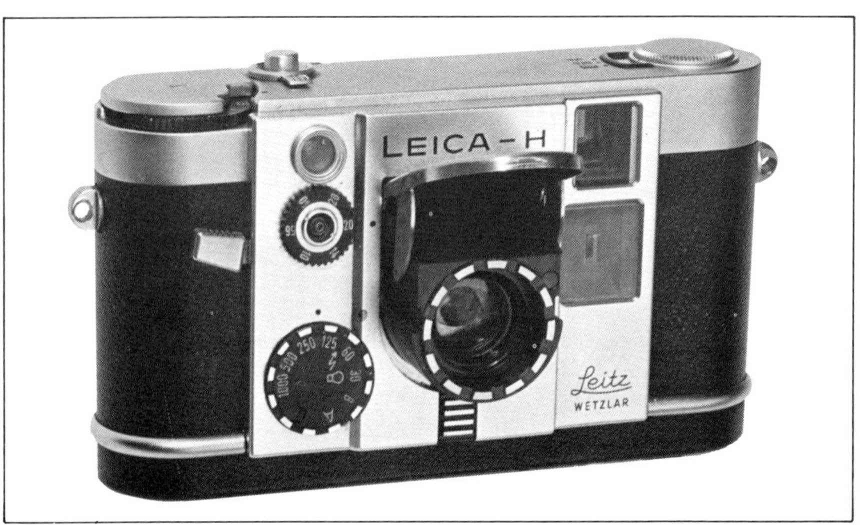

LEICA H camera (Leitz collection)

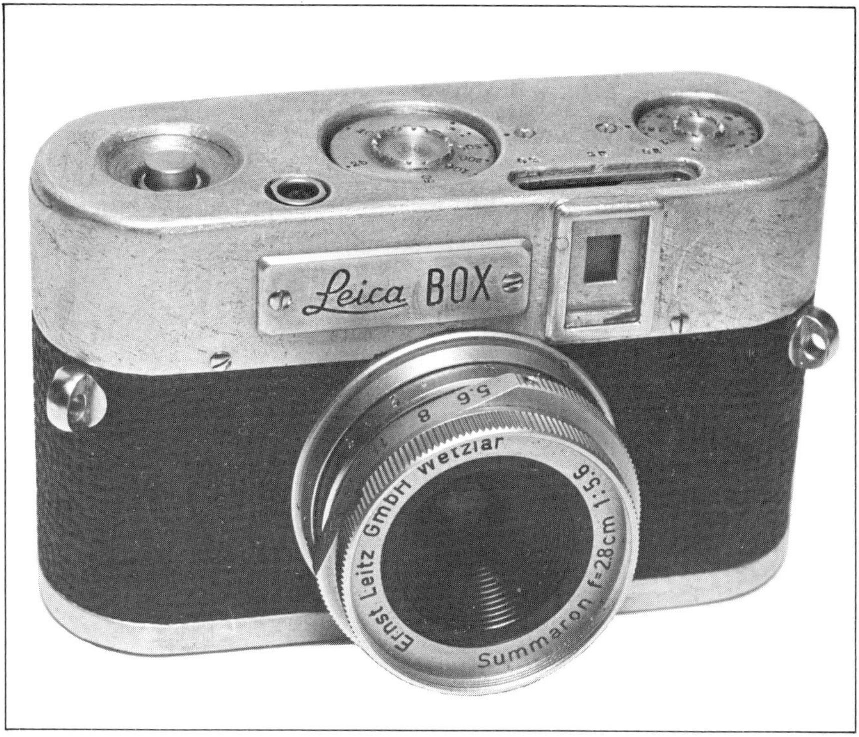

The LEICA Box, a prototype half-frame compact camera.

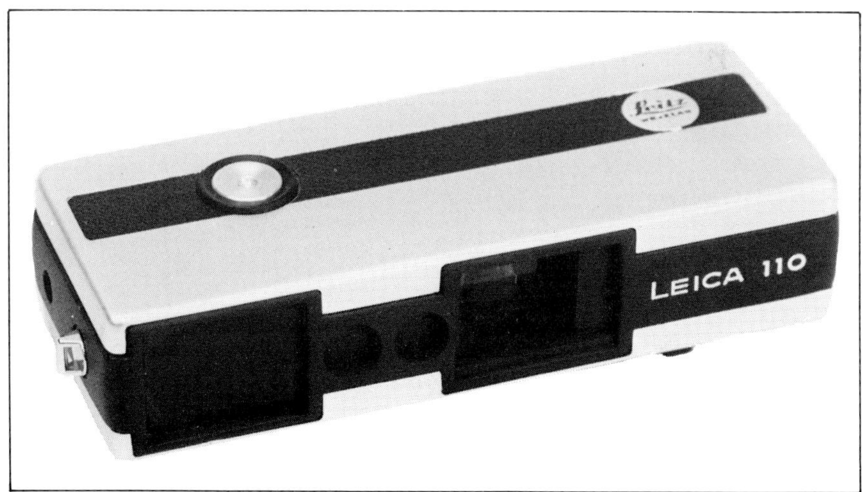

The LEICA 110, which nearly went into full scale production.

pocket camera with exposure meter, speeds to 1/1000 of a second and an f2.8 lens that has aperture settings on the back of the camera, near the release button. Amongst the notable features are the compact size, the streamlined film transport lever and retractable lens mount and the under-hinged cover that is released with the button at the bottom of the flap. This camera is completely finished and is retained by the Leitz family. Two other interesting prototypes are also illustrated here. The LEICA Box was a half-frame camera of the early fifties when this format looked as if it might become a popular size. The LEICA 110 almost reached full scale production and was to have been shown at Photokina 1974, but a re-appraisal of the market showed that it was an inappropriate product for Leitz.

Many other experimental cameras were manufactured at Wetzlar in the search for perfection; in years to come further research will give us information on many more fascinating models. Some have already been mentioned and illustrated in the appropriate chapters, such as the prototype LEICA 72 with a special cylindrical-shaped optical viewfinder and the LEICA IV which can be regarded as a very early prototype of the M3. A few more examples are given here.

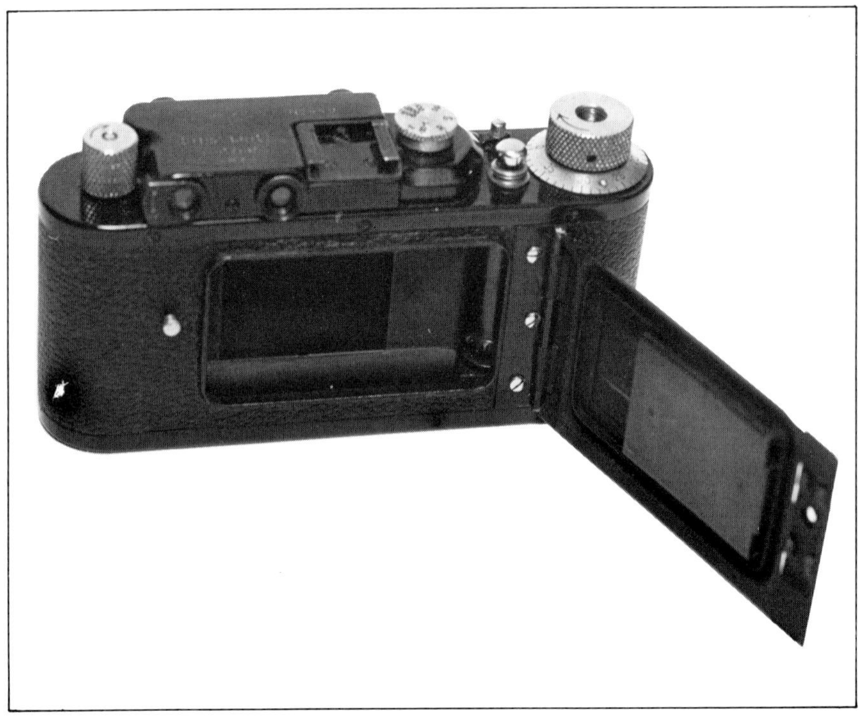

Experimental Model II with opening back (Leitz collection) ·

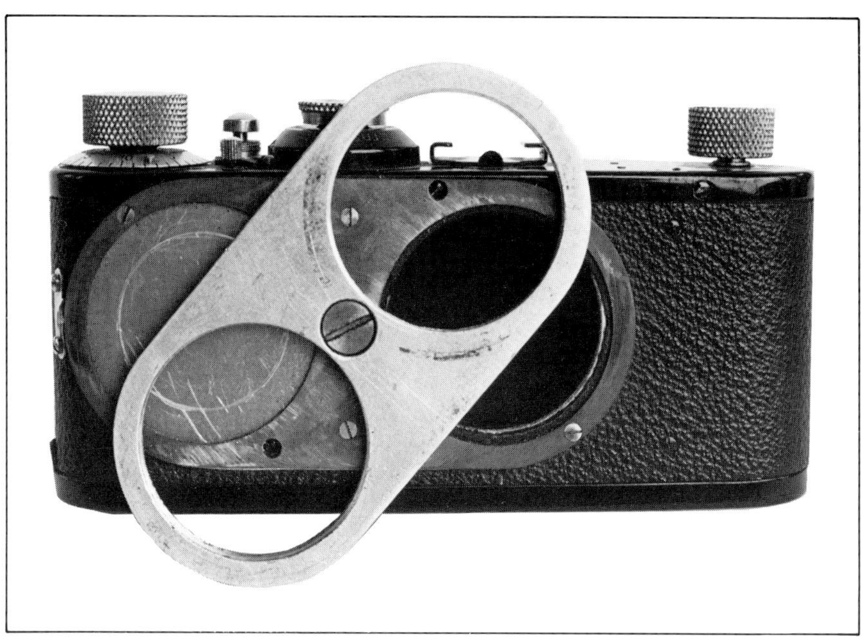

Experimental factory turret camera (Leitz collection)

Experimental LEICA 250 showing tall bodied camera

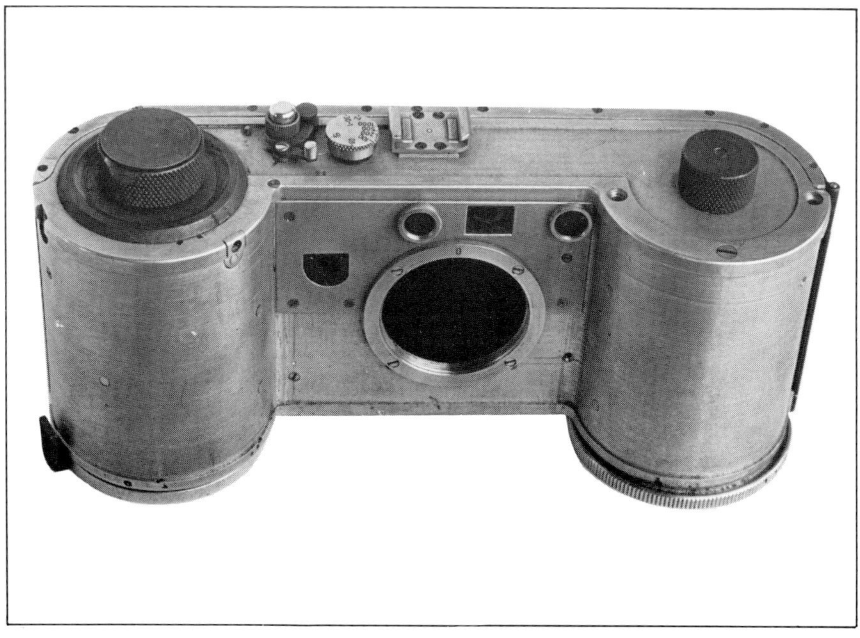

Finally, an example exists at Wetzlar of a Special 35 mm Panoramic Camera designed by Oskar Barnack during the 30's. The lens pivots about its axis and is controlled by a clockwork escapement.

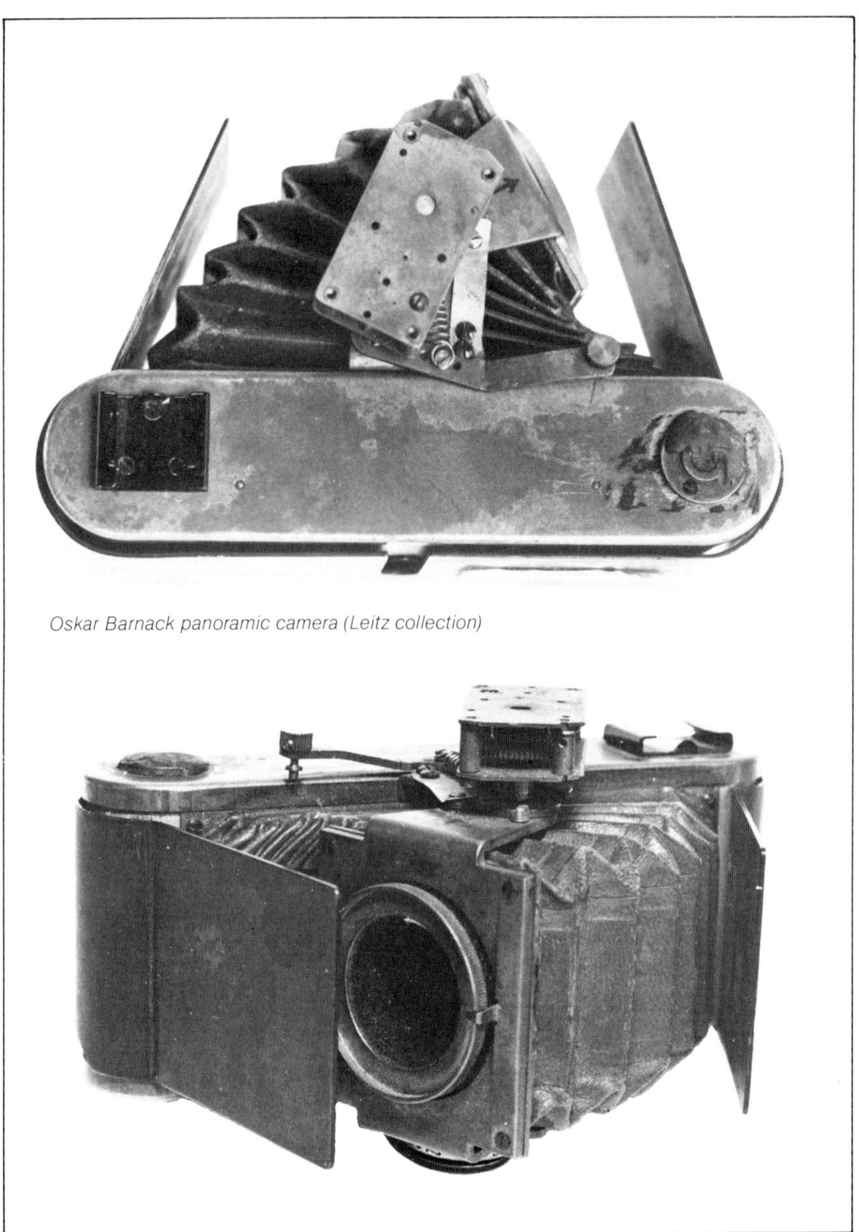

Oskar Barnack panoramic camera (Leitz collection)

Chapter 16

Factory Cameras

Under this general heading come all the cameras that Leitz retained for their own use. None of these should have "escaped" into private collections, although it is believed that sometimes when a particular model had been superseded unmodified examples might have been sold to staff. A few factory cameras have shown up over the years.

"Null Serie" cameras comprised the pre-production run. They were built to evaluate a new design and to get the details of the final production design worked out. Potential production problems would also be identified at this stage. Some cameras from the "Null Serie" production might be lent to professional photographers for evaluation. They often carried special serial numbers outside the normal sequence: for example, four digits of which the first two were zeros in the case of the M3 (see illustration in Chapter 7), or four digits followed by an asterisk in the case of the MP pre-production models.

"Betriebs" cameras were used internally in the factory either for photographic or test purposes. They were engraved on the top-plate with "Betriebsk.", for "Betriebskamera" or "works camera". They also had a non-standard three or four digit serial number.

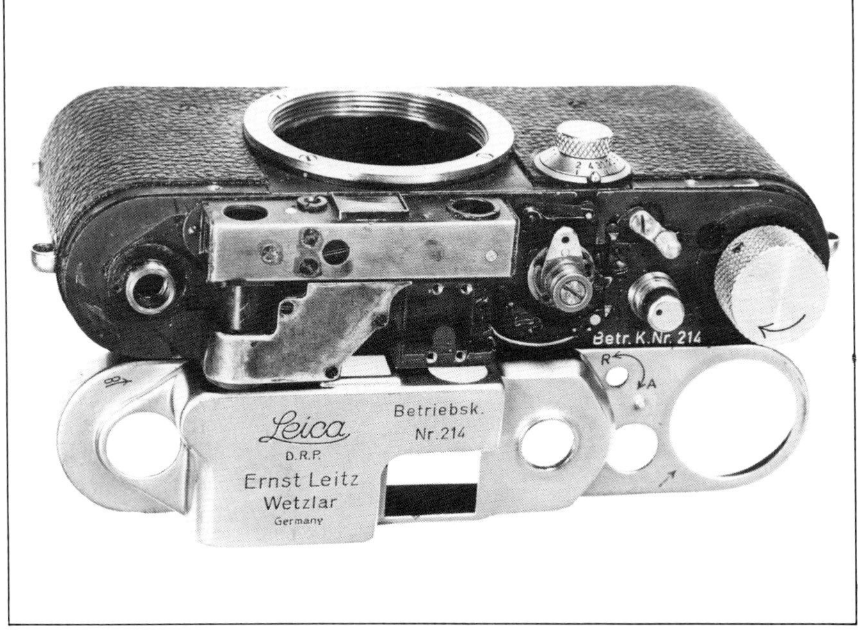

"Betriesk." IIIc engraved on top-plate and on housing under top-plate

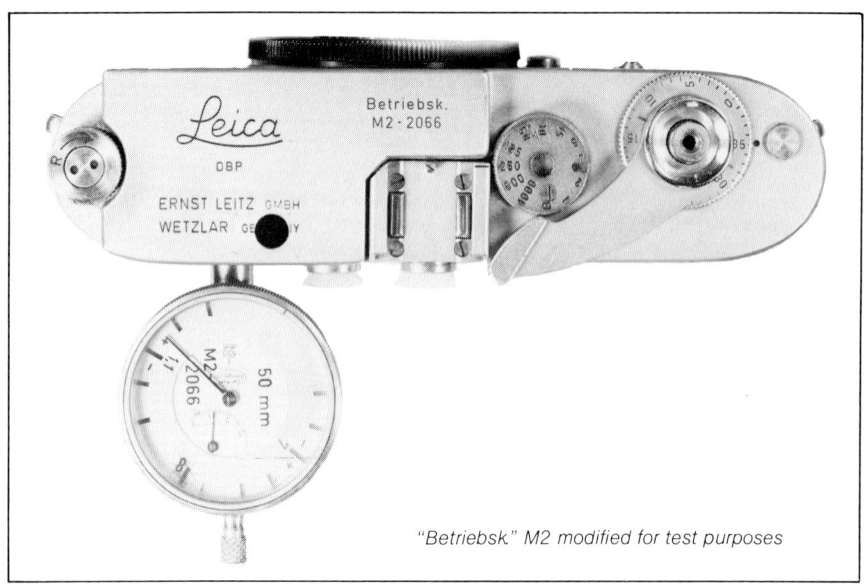

"Betriebsk." M2 modified for test purposes

Yet other cameras were engraved "Leitz Eigentum" (Leitz property) on the back rim of the top-plate. These cameras presumably went outside the factory for photography in the field by staff or by outsiders, perhaps to evaluate lenses or films. They may also have been loaned out for demonstration purposes or to replace a customer's camera when his own was being repaired.

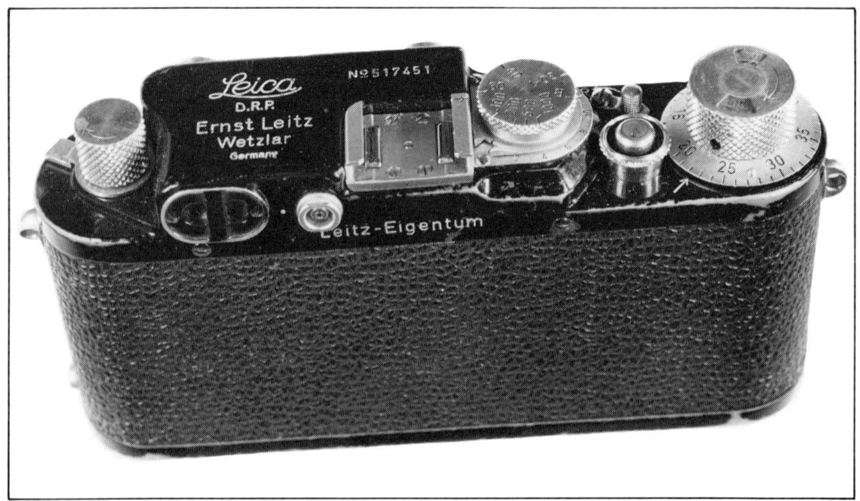

"Leitz Eigentum" IIIf, probably a prototype with a number coming as it does in the middle of the IIIc production run in 1949/50

Finally, there were also cameras specifically reserved for loan. These were engraved "Leih-Kamera" (loan camera) on the back rim of the top-plate. Leitz agencies also had loan cameras engraved as such.

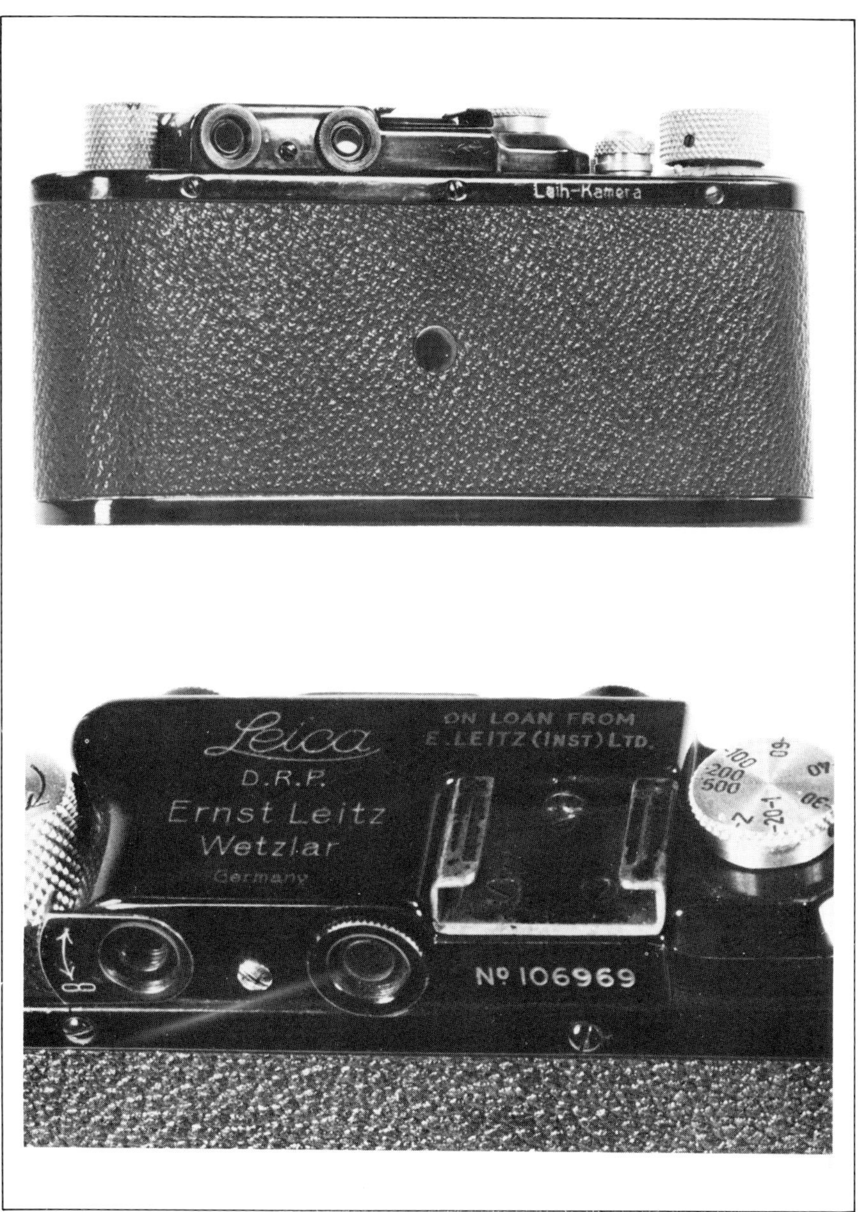

Two loan cameras, above a Wetzlar "Leih-Kamera" and below a Leitz agency loan LEICA II

Chapter 17

Motors and Winding Aids

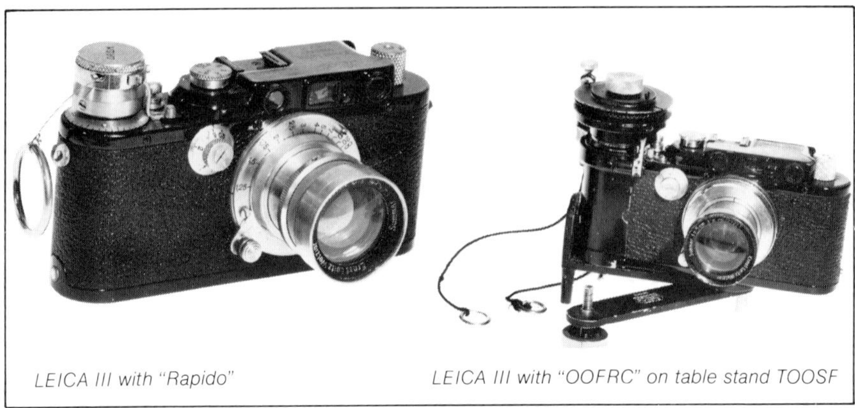

LEICA III with "Rapido"   LEICA III with "OOFRC" on table stand TOOSF

There were, before and after the LEICA was produced, several tries at motorised cameras using 35mm film: it was, however, only the success of the LEICA as a normal camera, but with a relatively large supply of film and quickness of operation, that prompted research into the possibility of making the film advance and shutter cocking more rapid and automatic. For a brief period there was a device made by another manufacturer known as the "Rapido". This fitted in place of the winding knob and contained a recoiling steel wire with a draw ring for rapid winding, but it was quickly rendered obsolete by Leitz who introduced a special baseplate which replaced the normal camera base. It contained a spring-loaded spindle that could be actuated by a trigger to advance one frame of film with a single stroke. Operating the trigger with the left index finger, and the release with the right one, the camera could be used with ease and far greater speed. Code name of this device was SCNOO. A later version for the LEICA IIIc was also made of this type.

A different idea was behind the introduction of the accessory called OOFRC; this was, in effect, a remote release and winder conveniently operated by strings which could be actuated at a distance; one string actuated the winding mechanism, much like an outboard motor starter, and the second actuated the release by a lever, (This accessory was designed for using a camera in a location unsuitable for hand operation, such as industrial processes or certain wildlife applications). When using this device, depending on the dexterity of the operator, the camera could take several pictures in a very short time. Automation did not arrive until the production of the MOOLY clockwork motor which was made (in small quantities) from 1938 until after the war. This motor was an accurate and strong clockwork mechanism capable of taking up to 12 pictures on one full winding of its spring in approximately 9 seconds. It had a counter and an external connecting arm to release the shutter.

Some motors were made with a selector button in front to give them a two speed operation, while the later series for the IIIc utilised an internal shutter release connection.

Motors were first made for the short bodied III, IIIa and IIIb cameras, but later they were also made in a longer case suited for the IIIc type. While in production they were made in chrome finish, for the early cameras, and black paint finish mainly for the later IIIc series. So altogether there are many detail variants.

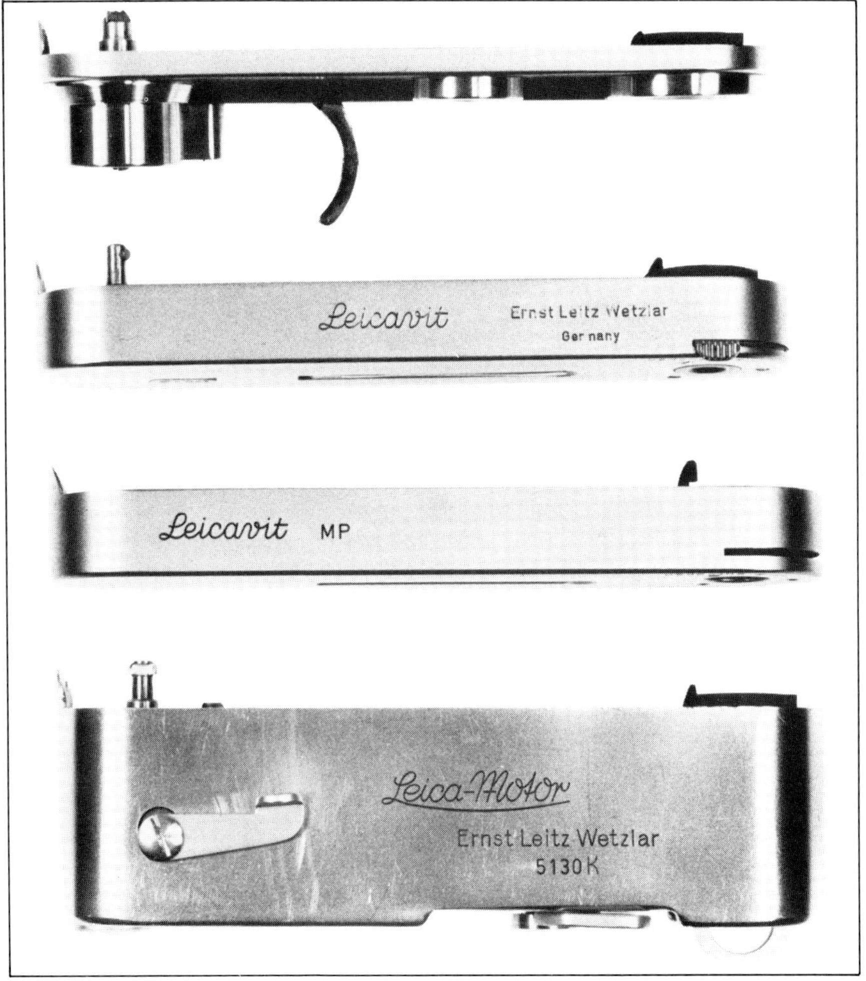

From top to bottom: rapid wind bases "SCNOO" for models IIIa and IIIb; "LEICAVIT" for models IIIc to IIIg inclusive; "LEICAVIT MP" for MP, M1 and M2; LEICA-motor "MOOLY" for models IIIc illustrated.

The rapid wind device LEICAVIT produced after the war was similar to the pre-war SCNOO. It was made to fit all cameras with the long body of the IIIc No. 400,000 and above and had the code name SYOOM. It was more streamlined than its earlier predecessor, and the trigger folded neatly inside the base. A new type of LEICAVIT MP was then made for the LEICA MP model. Later it was also marketed as an accessory to be used on the M2 and M1 cameras and had the code name SMYOM.

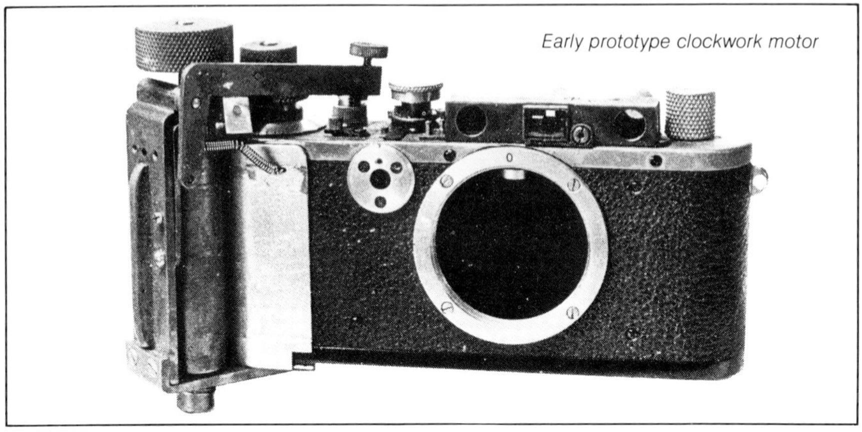

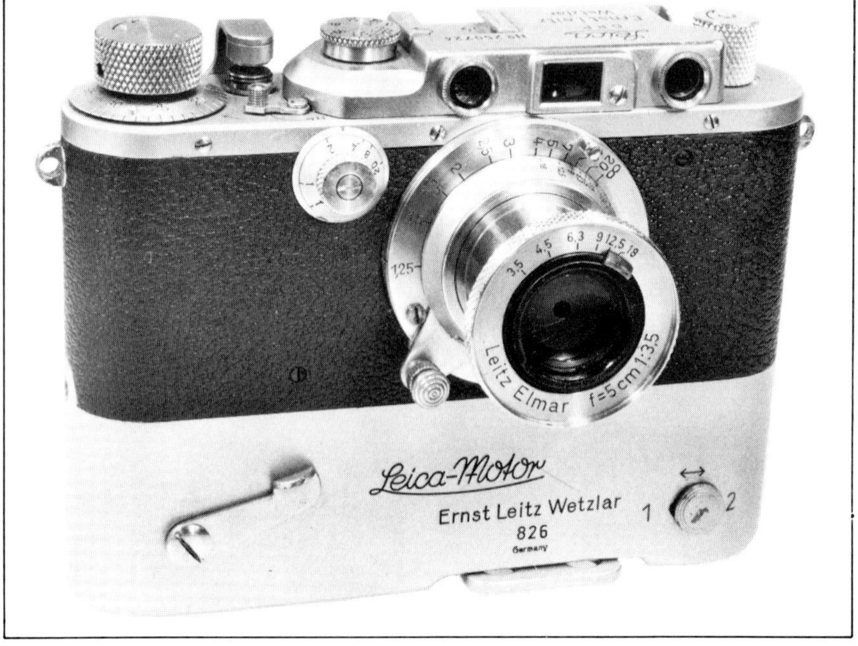

"MOOLY" two-speed

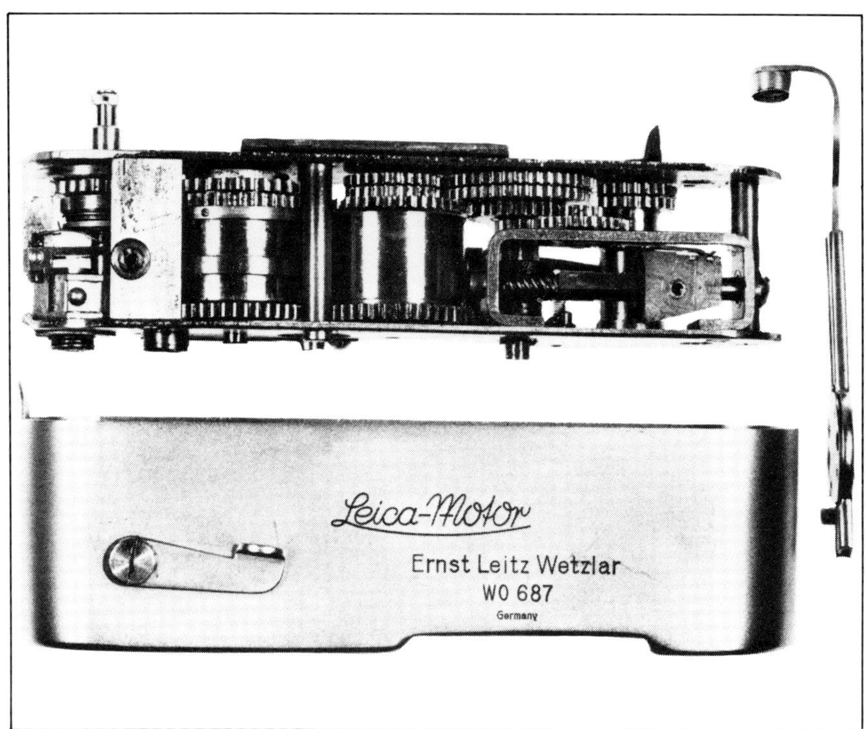

"MOOLY" showing motor case removed

The electric motor drive for LEICA cameras is an old story: as usual Leitz were amongst the first to experiment with electric motor drives and they had the right camera to work with, the 250 model. Just before and during the war they produced a massive motor drive which replaced the base of the camera, and had to be fed with electricity from an external source; motors were made in several different types, for 6 volts, 12 and 24 volts drive, the 6 volts types were made mostly for the army, as surveillance cameras and could be operated from a motorcycle battery. In this case modified cameras were used. These had a drive coupling shaft and internal release mechanism.

Other electric drive 250 cameras could have been used as aircraft cameras, either automatically or manually operated. On the motor drive was a switch for continuous operation or single shots.

The electric motors for the 250 were made at first with an external release, like the MOOLY, then with internal release like the clockwork motor driven IIIc. The cameras adapted for motor drive also had a roller to ensure better contact of film with the sprocket. It was normal for the motor to have the number of the camera to which it was originally coupled noted on the connecting cover plate in addition to its own number.

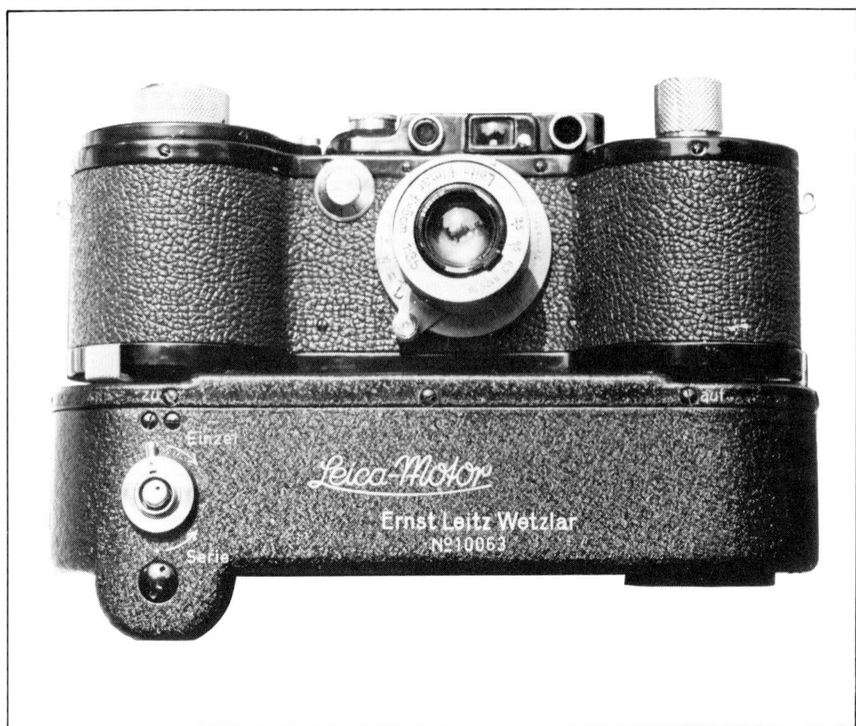

LEICA 250 with electric motor

After the war there was a demand from journalists and other groups, for Leitz to make a motor drive suitable for their cameras. Leitz were not enthusiastic in the beginning, however a practical solution came from America; the cameras were specially adapted, firstly to the M2 and later to the M4. When it became evident that the motor was a welcome accessory to the LEICA system, production was undertaken by Leitz of New York and the cameras were specially made in Wetzlar; being mostly M4 but some M2 models have also been made by Leitz and are duly marked M2-M, M4-M or M4-MOT. The American motor is a very compact unit which fits beneath the camera and has a detachable battery pack and a two speed operation.

As mentioned regarding the MP2, this camera was devised for the possible use of an electric motor apart from the LEICAVIT; some prototypes were made in Wetzlar with motors with a battery case that worked as a handle (see photo).

Meanwhile Leitz technicians were busy working on their own version of an electric motor drive for the LEICAFLEX; a prototype was built for this camera but did not reach the stage of manufacture because the camera body itself was being modified at the time in anticipation of the next model. So in actual fact the first Leitz motor-drive reflex was the LEICAFLEX SL.

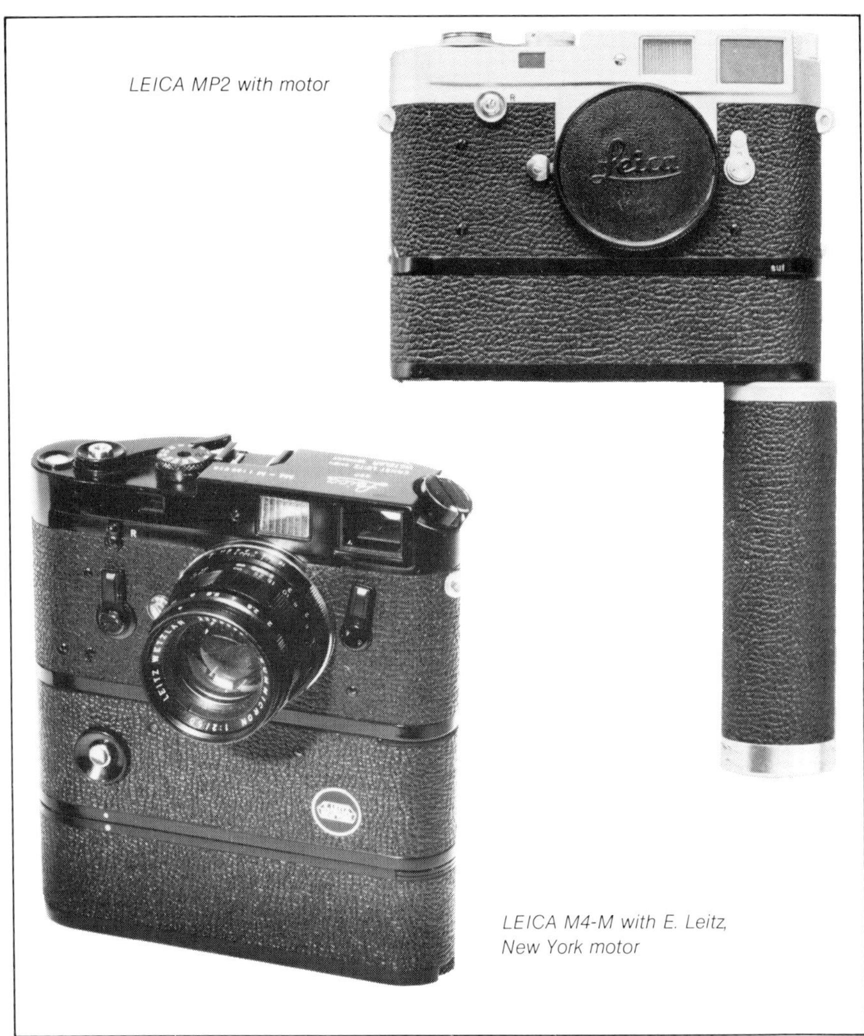

LEICA M4-M with E. Leitz,
New York motor

The main advantage of the SL MOT was the fact that it could be added to or taken off the camera without disturbing the film, and vice versa the film could be changed without removing the motor.

The battery pack could be changed as quickly as a machine gun magazine, and there were various types of battery packs, ranging from the standard AA batteries to nickel-cadmium rechargeable type, or to a plug connecting a bigger external battery. The motor-drive of the LEICAFLEX was very rugged and also very fast because extra power was needed to drive the mirror reflex mechanism. The manufacturer did guarantee at least 4 frames per second, but 5 were possible with

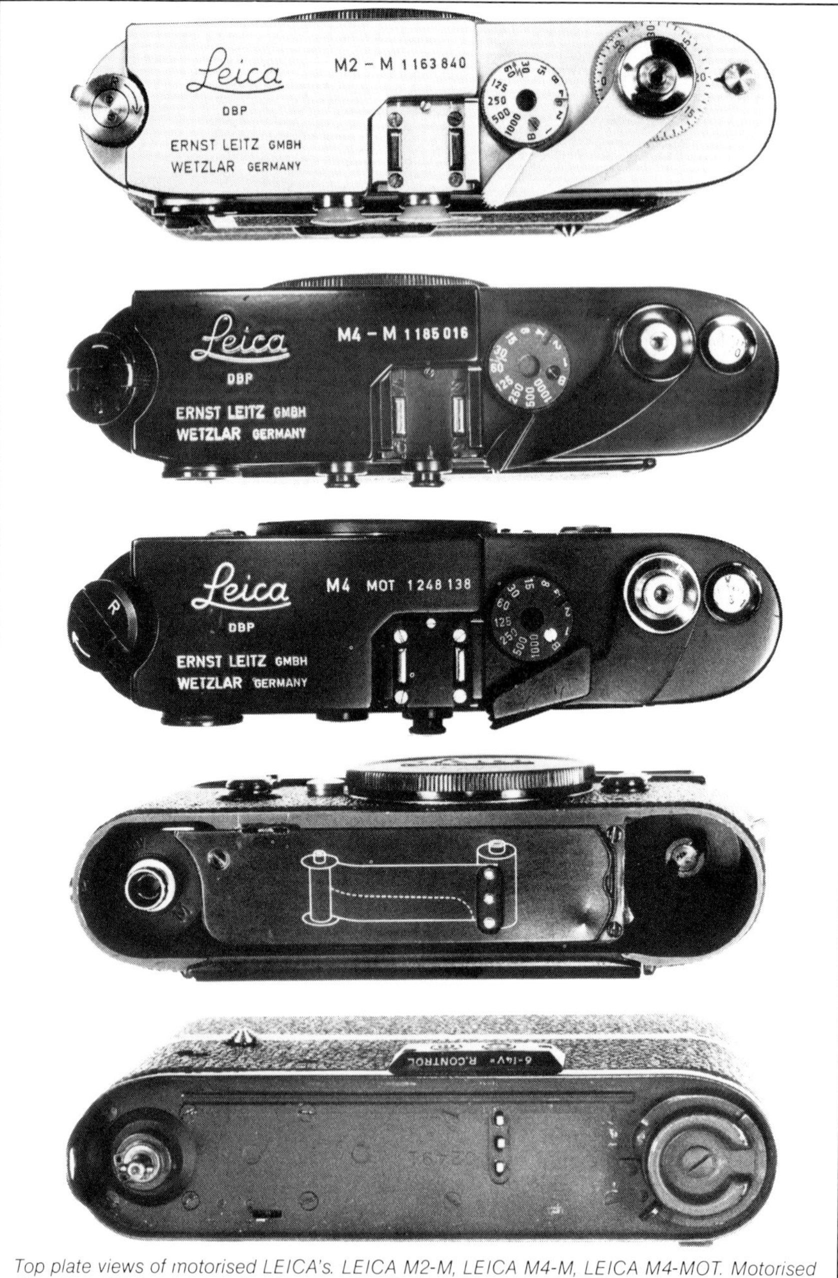

Top plate views of motorised LEICA's. LEICA M2-M, LEICA M4-M, LEICA M4-MOT. Motorised M model, with base upwards, showing electrical motor connections. Motor, top upwards, showing drive and electrical connections.

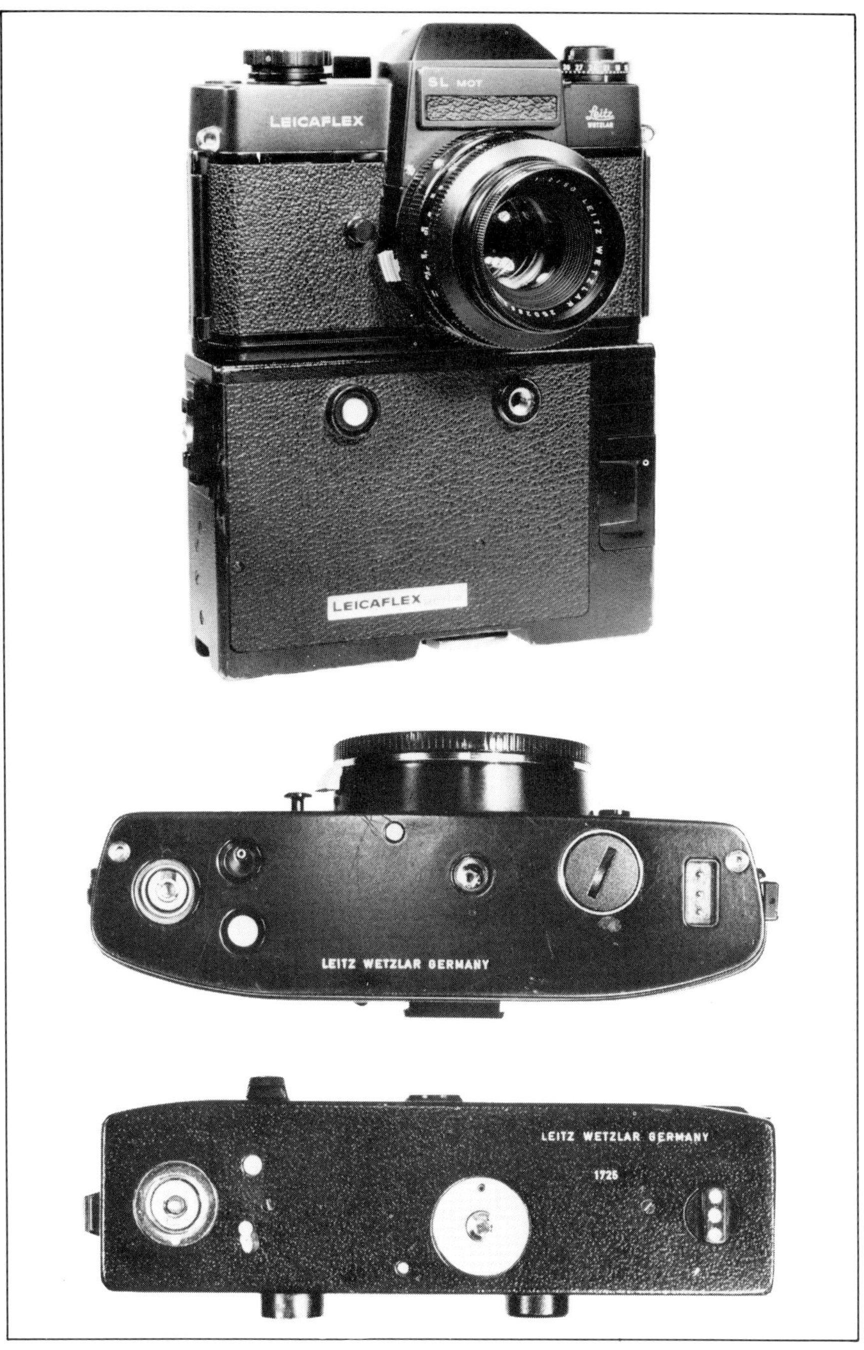

a well charged battery. LEICA motors were made in two types, first with no provision for the single shot and then with a switch that enabled one to choose the operating system.

The camera became invaluable for sport and technical work, such as photographing crash simulation tests of motor cars. Remote control also became feasible with motor drive, by automatic release of the shutter or by using radio controls from any distance. This system had greatly progressed since the early remote release mechanism one, where it was necessary to use "strings of different colours" in order to be sure of the operation.

A special tandem coupling device was produced so that two LEICAFLEX SL MOT cameras could be used side-by-side with their shutters firing alternately for picture sequences of 6-7 frames per second.

The LEICAFLEX SL2 MOT could also be used with the same motor and tandem coupling.

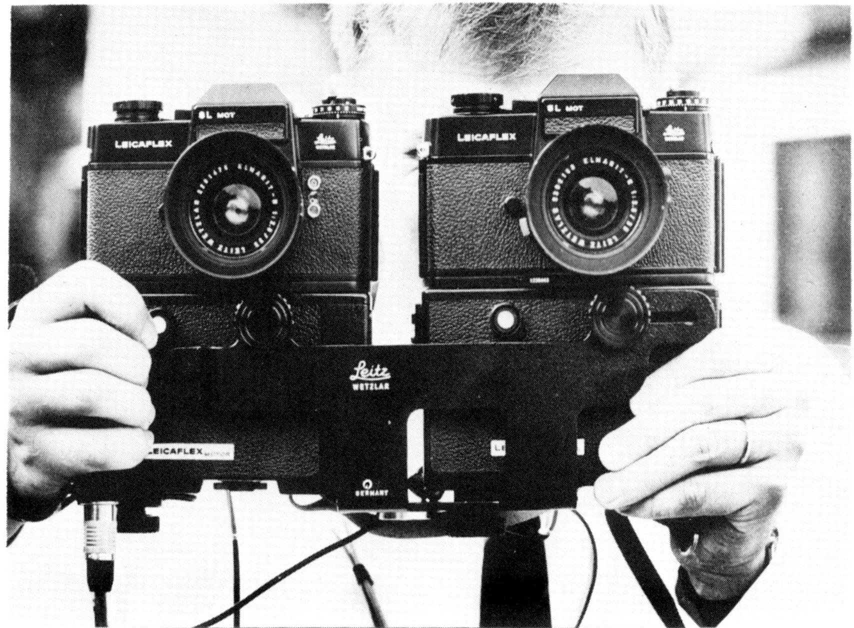

Tandem LEICAFLEX

In the late seventies and with the advent of new models, the possibility of motorising the cameras was always present: the rangefinder models from M4-2 onwards were all equipped to take a winder, by means of an internal coupling and release; the motor, code number 14214 was driven by four AA cells either disposable or rechargeable; following the first model a second motor was

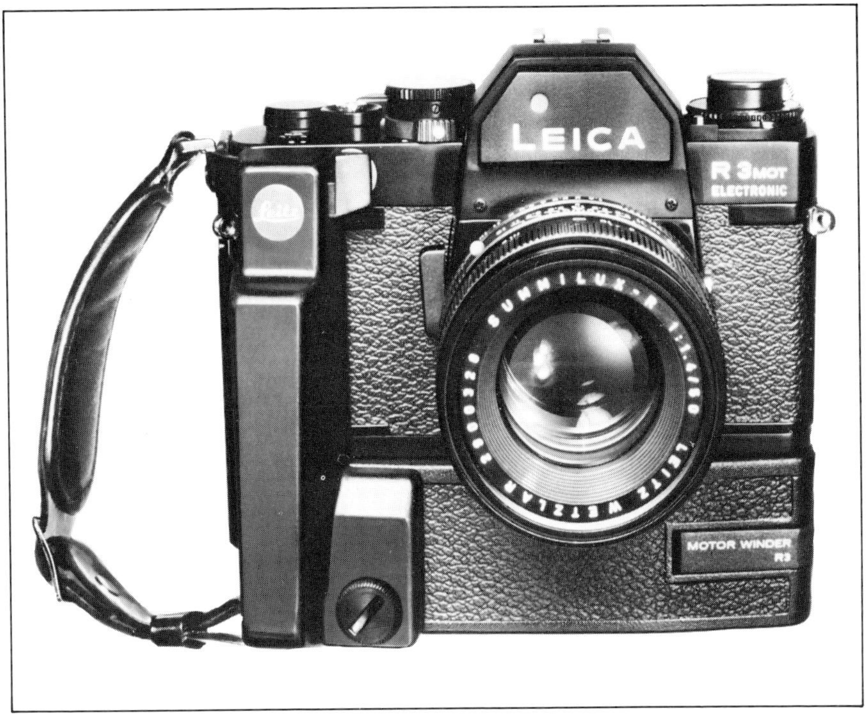

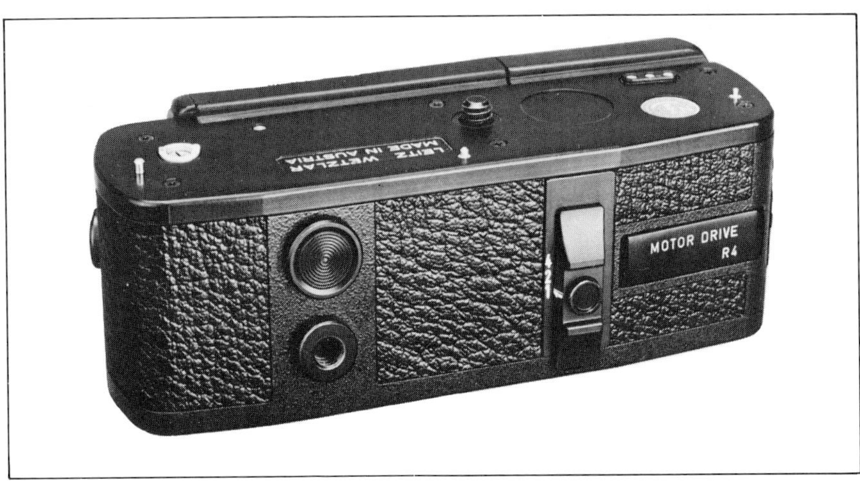

Later motors are lighter and more compact and fit the camera snugly; fitted with a handgrip the whole outfit can be handled more securely and comfortably in the confusion and turmoil of a news event.
Top: R3 MOT with winder and handgrip
Bottom: R4 Motor Drive

developed, similar in appearance and interchangeable, but with an electronic control inside that enabled a better operation and continuous operation (the first type had to be triggered for each shot). Finally along with the M6 an improved version was produced that has the standard tripod bush with ¼ in thread.

The reflex cameras also got their motors: the R3 was built in a special MOT version that could use a motor allowing up to two frames per second, and driven by six AA cells. Among the accessories a practical handgrip and tripod support; also a remote control with frame counter and programmable delay between shots were provided.

All R4 and R4-S cameras are prepared to take either the motor winder or motor drive. Electrical connection between camera and motors (all gold plated) appear simpler on the R4, with three contacts, than on the R3 with four contacts. The winder is smaller and lighter, uses six AA cells and can go up to two frames per second; the motor drive uses ten AA cells and has a selector which enables single shots to be taken, or two frames per second or continuous running at up to 4-5 frames per second. The electronic control is also available. An interesting detail is that when the motor is engaged to the camera, the batteries of the latter are not used and therefore there is a greater safety in the operation of electronic circuitry, for example when it is very cold and the camera batteries can become too weak.

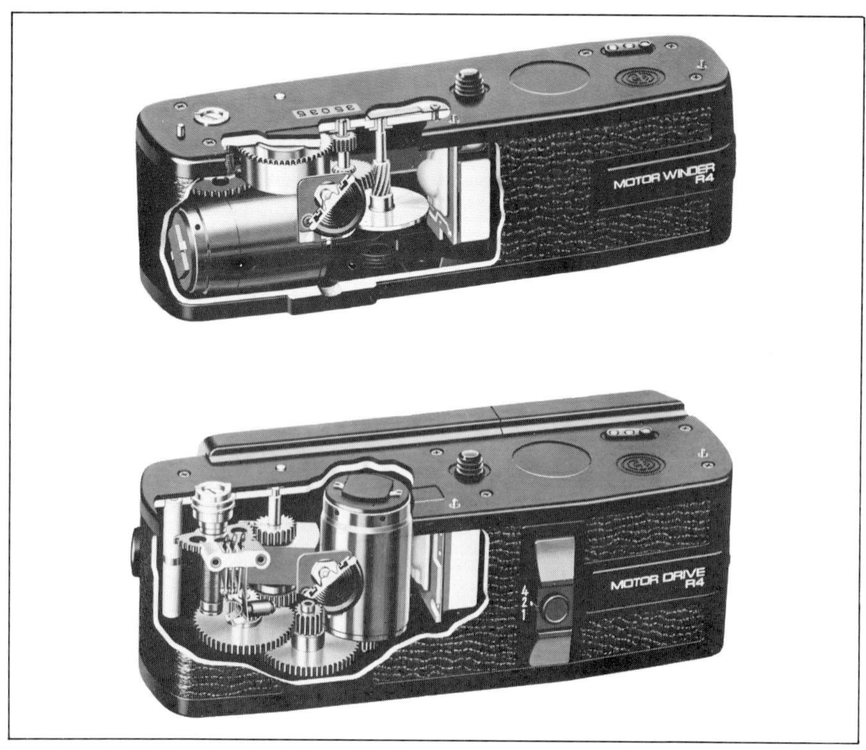

Chapter 18

Stereophotography

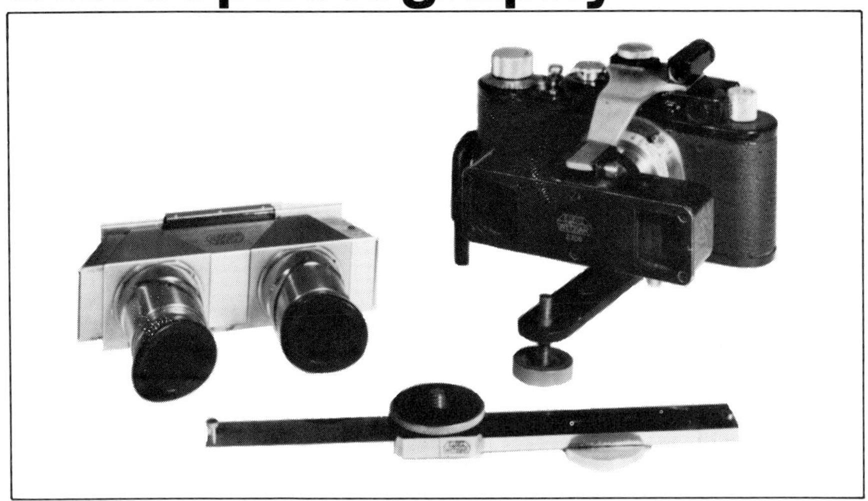

LEICA stereo equipment, viewer "VOTRA", stereo slide "FIATE", taking attachment "VORSA"

Photographic systems for illustrating things in three dimensional aspect have been very popular at times, and Leitz has produced quite a few accessories for this purpose. Simplest of them all was the stereo slide bar, code name FIATE made in 1929; it was a bar 150mm long which could be fixed to a tripod, and carried a sliding shoe onto which was fastened the camera; it was therefore possible to take a picture and move the camera along 70-75mm and take a second picture of the same subject. When viewed together with a binocular viewer the pair of pictures would give a true three dimensional effect because they were taken from points as far apart as the eyes; of course the operation, although simple, required some time so that this accessory could be used only for still pictures, such as landscapes.

The stereo "Doppel" camera, illustrated in Chapter 15 would have overcome this problem but it was never produced. Its prototype, however, still remains and is indeed a very interesting piece of equipment.

For snapshots in stereo the Stereoly attachment was also made: it consisted of a twin prism system that was placed in front of the standard 50mm lens and produced two images approximately 18 x 24mm side-by-side on the normal 24 x 36mm frame; the pair was then viewed with a special viewer. The code name of the Stereoly was VORSA and of the viewer VOTRA.

Many years later, in Canada, a completely new stereo device was produced with a more sophisticated design. This followed a revival of interest in stereo photography, assisted by the popular use of colour film and the possibility of projecting the pictures onto the screen through polarizing filters, to be viewed with polarizing glasses.

The new device was called the Stemar and it was in reality not an accessory but a lens (so much so that there were two lenses in a single mount). The first examples were made in Germany before the war; there were types with 3.5 cm focus and f2.5 or f3.5 aperture, other types with 3.3 cm focus and f3.5 aperture. All these were obviously screw mount types. Only when production was undertaken in Canada were both the screw mount and bayonet mount types offered, and they were all of the 3.3 cm focal length.

The device could be used alone for short range photography or with an additional prism system (not unlike the Stereoly) that increased the stereo base to give more depth to pictures taken at the distance of ten feet or more.

The equipment was completed by a viewfinder of the right vertical size and a special pair of HEKTOR projection lenses with polarizing glasses for viewing the projected image.

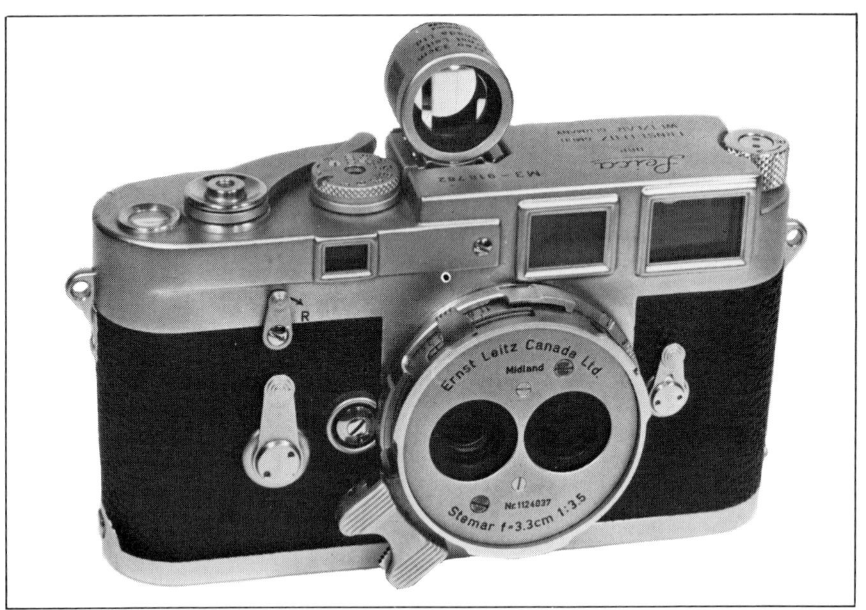

"STEMAR" for model M series camera

The Canadian Stemar outfit was housed in a fine box containing the twin lenses, the prism group to enlarge the stereo base for long distance shots, the special viewfinder and the lens shade. Also available was a stereo viewer made of black plastic and with battery box for illumination.

A prototype twin 9 cm lens was also made but never reached production. A copy still exists at the Leitz works and it operates perfectly.

Chapter 19

LEICA Lenses

The story of the LEICA is also about its lenses and the never ending search for perfection, because a camera is only as good as its lens. This fact was very clear to Oskar Barnack, who asked that the job of designing the lenses for his new camera be entrusted to Max Berek, a scientist and a professor of physics, with a vast knowledge of optics.

It is well known that the first lens for the LEICA was the 50mm ELMAR f3.5: this was a lens design, based on the Cooke triplet of 1894 by H. Dennis Taylor, that Professor Berek adapted to suit the LEICA. At first the lens was called Leitz Anastigmat and had five elements in three groups, the rear-most group being made of three elements cemented together. This combination of elements (of different kinds of glass) was the result of research into reducing the aberrations which are the unavoidable defects of any single lens.

There were patent problems that forced Leitz to call that lens Anastigmat, but once they were overcome the name was changed to ELMAX, which contains the initials of **E**rnst **L**eitz and the name of Professor **Max** Berek. It so happens that very few LEICA I's have the Anastigmat lens, and few more the ELMAX.

Meanwhile the Leitz glass laboratory had developed new glasses with better refracting power, which enabled Professor Berek to design an improved type of lens with only four elements, of which two were cemented to form the rear group, and thus the ELMAR was born, in 1925.

SCREW-MOUNT LENSES TO 1954

NOTE: All quantities referred to in this chapter refer to screw fitting lenses only, unless stated otherwise

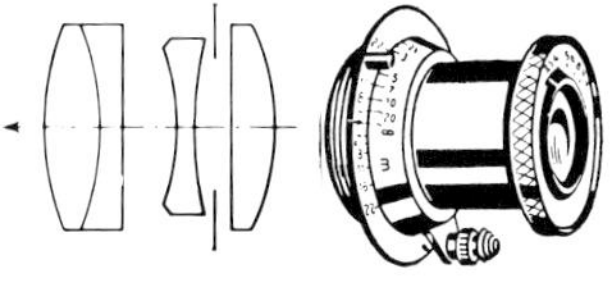

The 50mm ELMAR f3.5 lens is, by far, the longest lived and most abundantly produced lens in the LEICA family: it was manufactured in several versions (nickel and chrome plated) from 1925 to 1959 in both the fixed camera mount and in the screw mount, totalling some 360,000 units. Some thirteen thousand more were made from 1954 to 1961 in bayonet mount for the M types. Code name of the lens in screw mount was obviously ELMAR and in bayonet mount ELMAM.

The angle of view (angle covering the diagonal of the 24 x 36mm frame) was

46° and the minimum aperture f18 or 22 depending on the type, the nearest focusing distance was normally set at one metre, but there were examples of lenses that focused to 0,5 metre. The ELMAR f3.5 was later superseded by a faster f2.8 type. Lenses produced after April 1946 were coated.

When the LEICA with interchangeable lenses was introduced in 1931 a variety of lenses was needed to go with it. Three new focal lengths were offered, based on the ELMAR triplet design with four elements and cemented rear pair; also a faster 50mm lens based on a different design. The three new ELMAR's were:

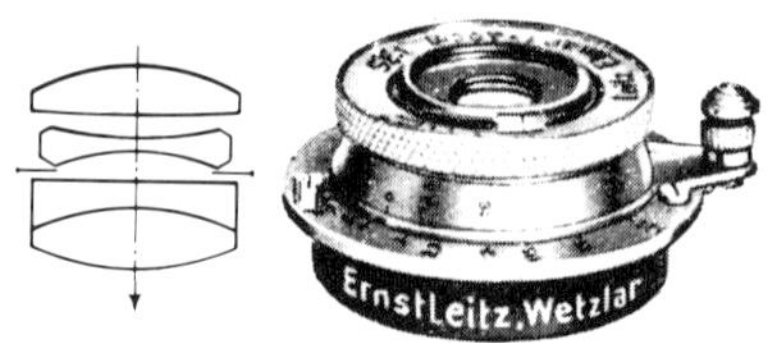

A wide-angle 35mm, f3.5 ELMAR code name EKURZ. Manufactured from 1931 to 1950 in great quantities, it became the traveller's companion. Its angle of view was 64°, minimum aperture f18 and nearest focusing distance one metre. Quantity 42,500 approximately.

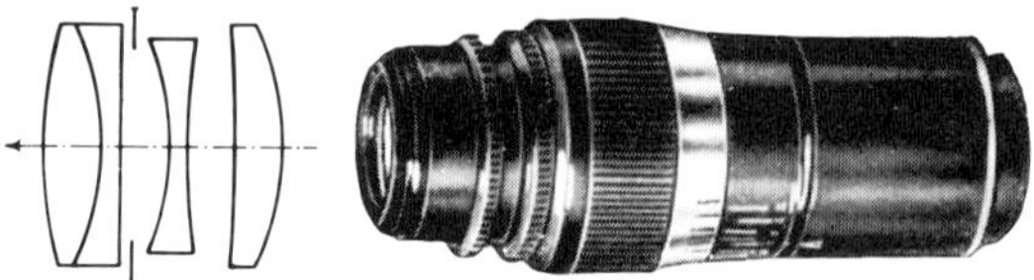

A long focal length lens was also introduced in 1931, the 135mm f4.5 ELMAR with a black painted barrel. Only a few thousands were built from 1931 to 1936 because it was soon superseded by the HEKTOR of the same focal length. Its angle of view was 18°, minimum aperture f36 and nearest focusing distance 1.5 metres. Code EFERN. Quantity 5,200 approximately.

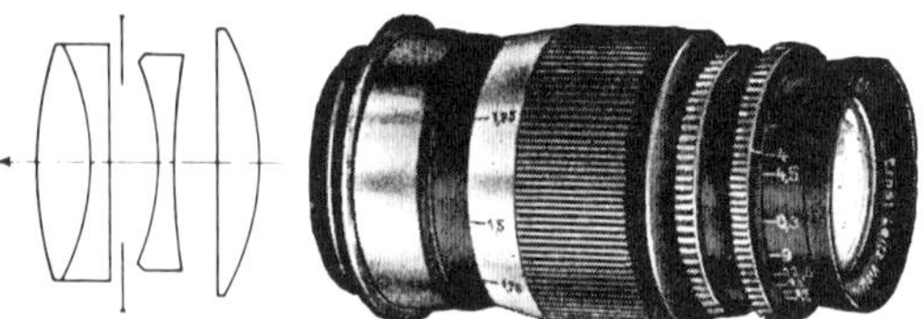

The third lens was the 90mm, f4 ELMAR, brought on the market in 1932, although production had started in 1931. The lens continued to be made until 1964, putting it close second to the 50mm type but longer lived if we consider that in bayonet mount it was made until 1968). Its angle of view was 27°, minimum aperture f32 and on late types f36 and nearest focusing distance one metre. Code name ELANG. Quantity 114,000 approximately.

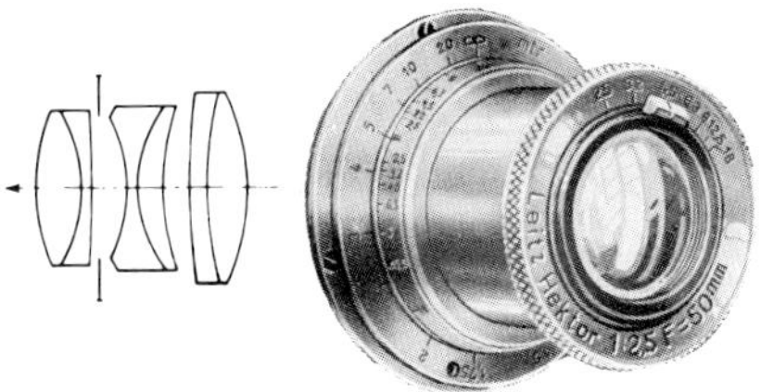

A faster option in the normal focal length of 50mm was offered at the same time with the 50mm f2.5 HEKTOR. This was a completely different design using six elements in three cemented pairs. As for the name, at Leitz they are positive; Hektor was Professor Berek's dog, so was Rex, a name that we'll find later. The 50mm HEKTOR lens was built from 1931 to 1937 and some of these lenses were also installed on fixed-lens LEICA I's. Its angle of view was 46°, minimum aperture f18, and nearest focusing distance one metre. Code HEKTOR. Quantity 10,300 approximately.

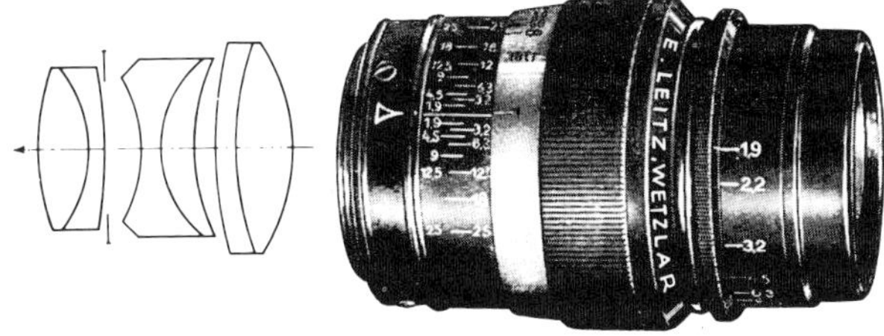

Another, faster Hektor design followed in 1932. This was the very fast 73mm, f1.9 HEKTOR, ideal for work in poor light. Its angle of view was 33°, minimum aperture f25 and nearest focusing distance 1.5 metres; Code name HEKON at first and later HEGRA. This lens was made in two different focusing mounts, the first one with helical movement and the other with parallel movement, which meant that the lens-head did not rotate. This latter lens was to take the special red and green striped filters for the new Agfacolor process, which had to retain their correct orientation during focusing. The last few were built in 1942. Quantity 7,000 approximately.

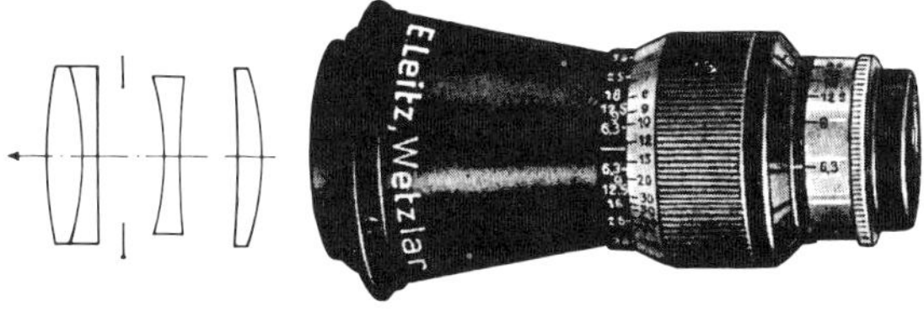

The last addition to the family in 1932 was the 105mm, f6.3 ELMAR also called "mountain" ELMAR because of its small size and light weight. Production lasted until 1937, all lenses were set in black painted barrel, with angle of view of 23°, minimum aperture f36 and nearest focusing distance about 2 metres, with the last marked point on the scale at 3 metres. Code name ELZEN. Quantity 4,000 approximately.

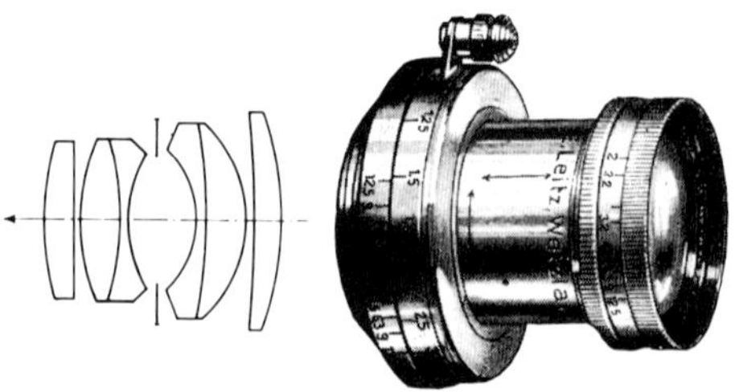

A new fast lens was introduced in 1933, the 50mm, f2 SUMMAR: this was an old name for a patented Leitz design for a six-element symmetrical lens made in 1902. The new SUMMAR was a modified Gauss type lens, also with six elements. It was produced from 1933 to 1940. At first the lenses were set in a nickel plated rigid mount; later the mount was made collapsible, and finally chrome plated. The angle of view was the usual 46°, minimum aperture f12.5, minimum focusing distance one metre, code name SUMUS. Quantity 123,000 approximately.

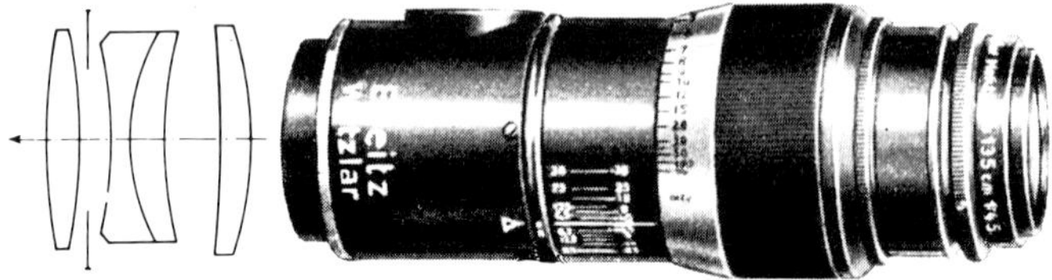

A variation of the Hektor design was used in 1933 for the replacement for the 135mm ELMAR. This was the 135mm, f4.5 HEKTOR. It had four elements of which the middle pair were cemented. It was produced in screw mount until 1960 and from 1954 in bayonet mount as well. Some 70,000 were made with screw mount and 30,000 more with bayonet. Angle of view was 18°, minimum aperture f32, later f36 with the new f scale, shortest focusing distance 1.5 metres. Code word HEFAR.

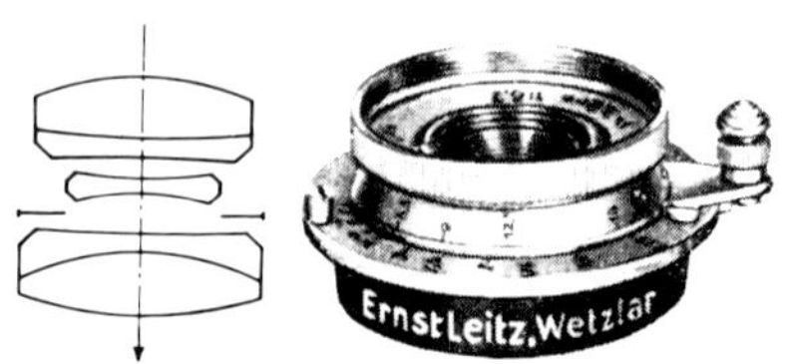

A further variation of the Hektor design produced the very wide-angle 28mm, f6.3 HEKTOR in 1935. This time the centre group was a single element whilst the two outside ones were cemented pairs. Production continued over a period of 20 years. Set in a chrome mount, the lens had a 75° angle of view, a minimum aperture of f25 and focused down to one metre. Code HOOPY. Quantity 10,000 approximately.

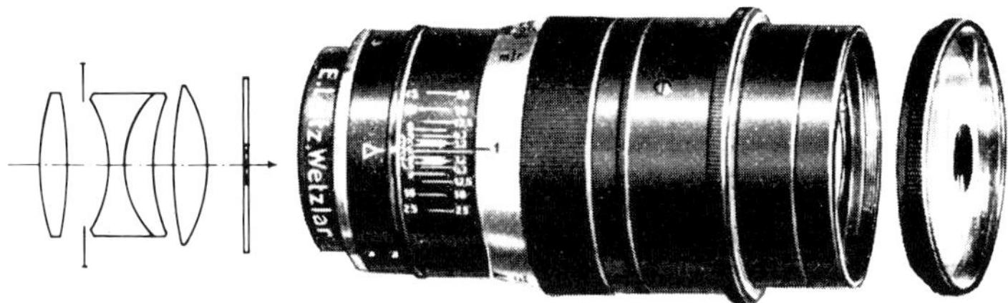

1935 also brought two more interesting lenses, the Thambar and the first TELYT. The THAMBAR is the most collectable of all Leitz lenses. It was a simplified Hektor design with a cemented pair in the middle and single elements on the outsides. It also had a detachable glass disc with a silvered central spot. This was to produce a soft focus effect for portraits and other applications. The spot cut off the light rays passing through the centre of the lens and allowed only the rays from the periphery to pass where some aberrations had been left on purpose, so the characteristic halo effect was obtained. The degree of softness could be controlled by stopping down. The THAMBAR was made until 1942; also in a short mount for the PLOOT reflex housing. Barrel was black, angle of view 27°, minimum aperture f18, nearest focusing distance one metre. Code TOODY. Quantity 3,000 approximately.

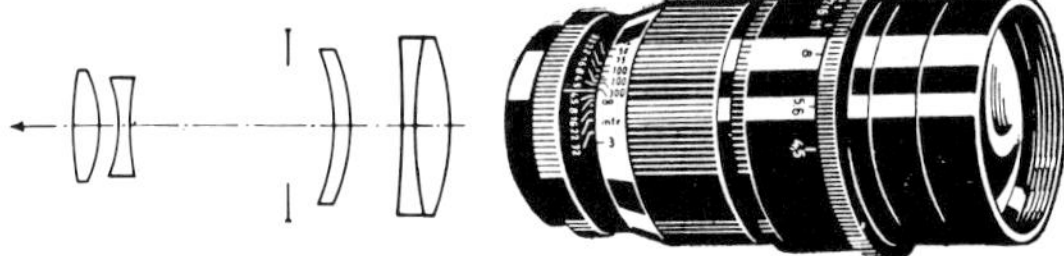

A telephoto lens (that is a lens whose physical length is shorter than its focal length) was introduced in 1935, along with a reflex housing that also increased the usefulness of the camera. The lens was the 200mm, f4.5 TELYT to be used with the reflex housing. It was a five element design in four groups, with an angle of view of 12° with minimum aperture f36 and closest focusing distance to 3 metres; code OTPLO for the lens alone and TOOLP if complete with the reflex housing whose own code name was PLOOT. It was built until 1960 when a new f4 type was introduced. Quantity 11,500 approximately. The PLOOT reflex housing later became the VISOFLEX I.

Another TELYT of twice the focal length was made in 1937: a 400mm f5 lens, this one also had five elements in four groups, and was manufactured until 1966 in two different shapes of black mount and naturally had to be used with the PLOOT reflex housing. Angle of view 6°, minimum aperture f32, shortest focusing distance 8 metres and code name TLCOO for the lens alone and TLOOB with the PLOOT. The new lens was actually designed in 1934 and some

had been supplied to press photographers for the Berlin Olympics of 1936.
Quantity 4,000 approximately.

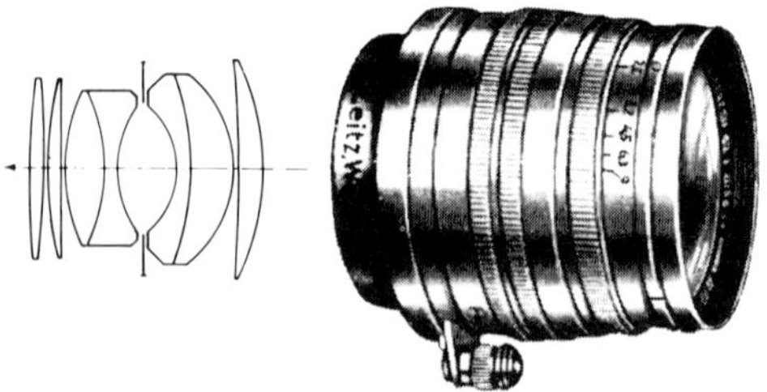

The fastest lens of the prewar era was introduced in 1936: it was the XENON
50mm f1.5 made under a TTH patent, further developed by Leitz technicians.
Built until 1950, this lens had seven elements in five groups. Its full potential
became more evident when coating was available. Angle of view 46°, minimum
aperture f9, nearest focusing distance one metre; code name XEMOO. Quantity,
6,000 approximately.

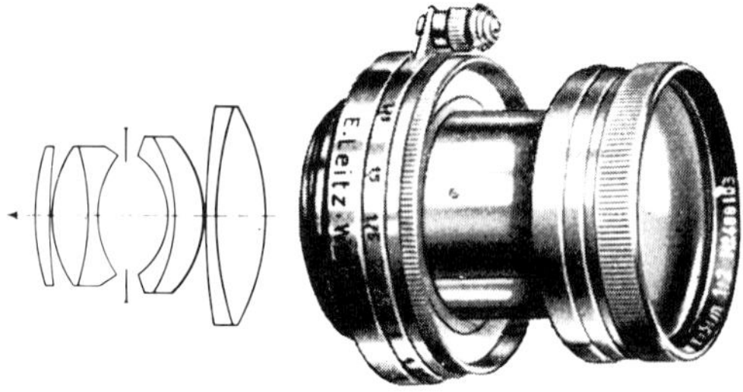

In 1939 the 50mm, f2 SUMMITAR replaced the SUMMAR as the normal fast
lens for the LEICA. It was an advanced design of the Gauss family, with seven
elements in four groups, in a collapsible non-rotating mount. This mount
allowed the use of the typical folding lens hood, made first for the XENON. Angle
of view 46°, minimum aperture f12.5 in the pre-war types and f16 in the later
models, nearest focusing distance one metre. Quantity 170,000 approximately.

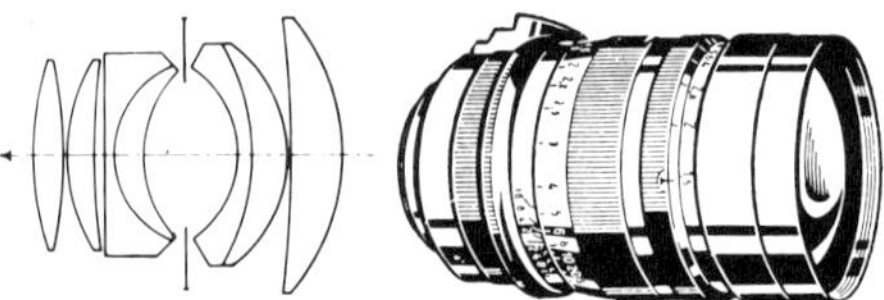

It seems that during the war only one new design was originated for general
use. This was the SUMMAREX, a seven-element, five-group lens not very
dissimilar to the XENON. Also built during the war was the 75mm, f0.85

SUMMAR, an extremely fast lens for infra red units. There is a sample left at Wetzlar which shows the rearmost lens element made of deep red glass, thus acting as a filter; in any case this special lens is not listed among the regular LEICA lenses in the factory records.

The SUMMAREX was built until 1960, at first in black painted mount, and in chromed mount after the war. Angle of view 28°, minimum aperture f16, nearest focusing distance one metre; code name SOOCX. Quantity 4,000 approximately.

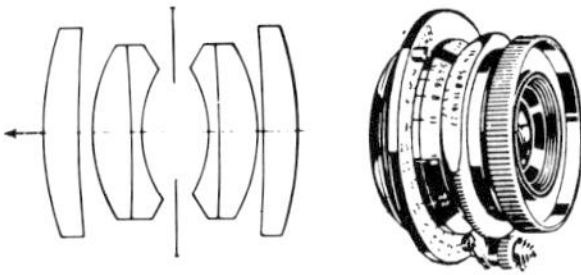

After the war the first new lens to appear was the wide-angle 35mm, f3.5 SUMMARON four-group symmetrical Gauss lens. It was an improvement over the venerable ELMAR design which was on its way to being phased out. Angle of view 54°, minimum aperture f22 and nearest focusing distance one metre. Code name SOONC. This lens was also made in bayonet mount after 1954. Quantity 80,000 approximately.

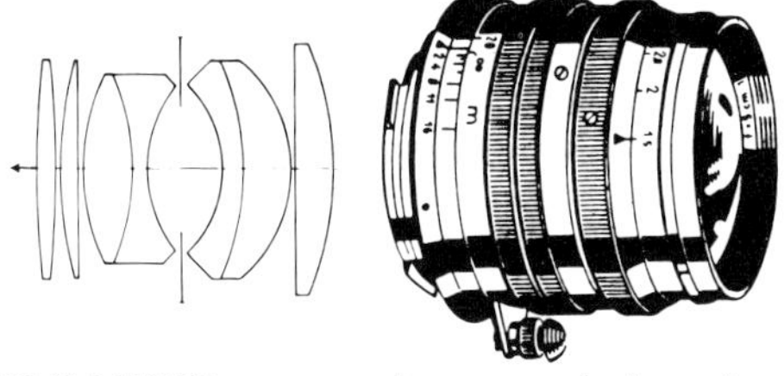

In 1949 the SUMMARIT appeared as an obvious improvement on the XENON, with the same basic design, but better correction and better performance at full aperture. Further improvements of this design eventually led to the 50mm f1.4 SUMMILUX and the second type of 50mm, f1 NOCTILUX. The SUMMARIT had an angle of view of 46°, stopped down to f16 and focused to one metre; its code name in screw mount was SOOIA and it was made in bayonet mount. Code name SOOIA. Quantity 39,000 approximately.

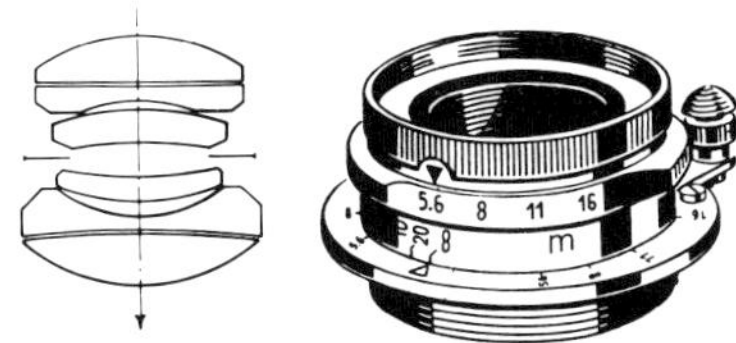

The last screw mount-only lens to be made was the 28mm, f5.6 SUMMARON which did not actually appear until 1955 and was made until 1963. It was typical of a symmetrical design with six elements in four groups. A notable feature was the large rear element which helped to reduce vignetting. Angle of view was 75° and about 6,200 were made.

LENSES FROM 1954 FOR SCREW AND M-CAMERAS

With the advent of the LEICA M3 in 1954 it required lenses with the new bayonet mount. Some of the lenses previously made in screw mount became available in bayonet mount as well. At the time code words were still being used so the M-series lenses simply had an M added to the original code-word. These were the 35mm, f3.5 SUMMARON, code SOONC-M; the 50mm, f3.5 ELMAR-M; or ELMAM; the 50mm, f1.5 SUMMARIT, code SOOIA-M; the 90mm, f4 ELMAR, code LEANG-M, or ELGAM, which was also later offered in a collapsible mount in bayonet fitting only so that it could be kept on the camera in the ever-ready case, code ILNOO; the 135mm, f4.5 HEKTOR, code HEFAR-M, or HEFAM.

The optical construction of the bayonet lenses was identical to that of their screw counterparts, so was their general appearance. Notable exceptions were the 35mm lenses which were available in a version with a special viewfinder attachment to make it possible to use them on the M3, which lacked a 35mm frame, without a separate viewfinder.

This period from the mid-fifties also was the beginning of the rapid advances in Leitz lens design, which have continued ever since, brought about by new optical glasses from their glass research laboratory and the application of computers. Optical designs, and mounts, have been continuously improved since this time, often without a change in lens name or even any formal announcement. This makes a detailed treatment of later lenses in a book of this size impossible* The classic designs become unrecognisable and the familiar names have come to refer to a particular maximum aperture; thus SUMMILUX is always f1.4, SUMMICRON f2, ELMARIT f2.8 and ELMAR f3.5 or f4. (after the 50mm, f2.8 ELMAR went out of production).

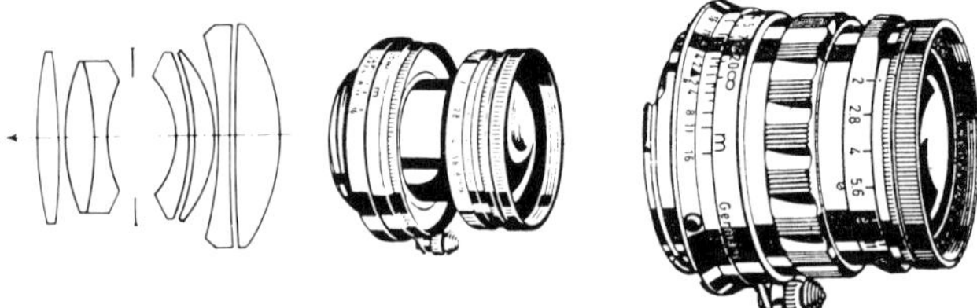

Although the LEICA M3 did not appear until 1954, the lens always associated with it is the 50mm, f2 SUMMICRON which was first launched in screw mount in 1953. Its name stands today for all the high quality f2 lenses of the LEICA. With seven elements in four groups, this lens had the characteristic that the front two pairs were not cemented, but had tiny "air lenses" between the glass

---

*For a complete description of all LEICA lenses from the beginning to the current range in 1985 see "LEICA and LEICAFLEX LENSES", also by Gianni Rogliatti, 2nd Edition, Second Printing with additions, Hove Foto Books, 1984. (Ed.)

elements. This design was to last until 1968 when it was superseded by a new design with only six elements, with one pair cemented, made of new glasses. A further improvement came in 1979 with a new design of six elements with two cemented pairs and a further reduction in weight. The SUMMICRON is second only to the 50mm ELMAR as far as production is concerned, being made in screw and bayonet mounts, both in collapsible and rigid forms. Additionally, a close-focusing version was available for bayonet mount cameras. All these were chromed. The new type was in a black rigid mount. Angle of view 46°, minimum aperture f16 and nearest focusing distance (normal) one metre. Code name SOOIC. Quantities, collapsible screw 61,000 approximately, rigid screw 1,100 approximately.

A few SUMMICRON's were set in a peculiar screw mount which had a Compur shutter built in for the purpose of flash synchronisation at all speeds. The focusing scale in feet indicates they were intended for the American market.

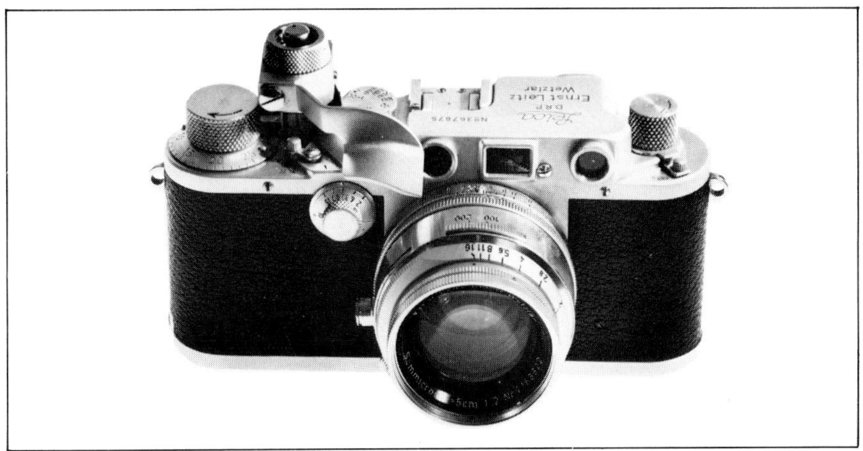

Compur SUMMICRON 50mm Lens (for flash synch at all speeds). Never commercially produced. (Operating lever missing).

The code for the first bayonet version in collapsible mount was SOOIC-M but the rigid mount came in 1956, code SOSIC. The close focusing version was SOMNI. After being improved several times, the lens is still in production.

A new, faster 50mm, f2.8 ELMAR came out in 1957, taking advantage of the new glasses. Code name for screw version ELMOO and for bayonet ELMOM.

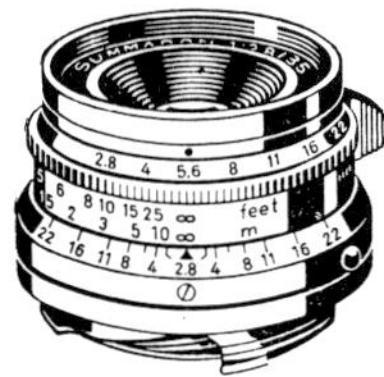

1958 was a vintage year for new lenses. The 35mm, f2.8 SUMMARON was one. It had six elements in four groups and was similar, but not identical to the f3.5 SUMMARON. It was made in screw mount until 1963 and in bayonet form until 1974. Angle of view was 64°, minimum aperture f22, nearest focusing distance one metre. Code, screw model SIMOO, approximately 5,200 were produced. The bayonet lenses had a shorter near focusing distance of 0.7 m. Code SIMOM, approximately 20,300 were produced. Code M3 type SIMWO, approximately 10,100 produced.

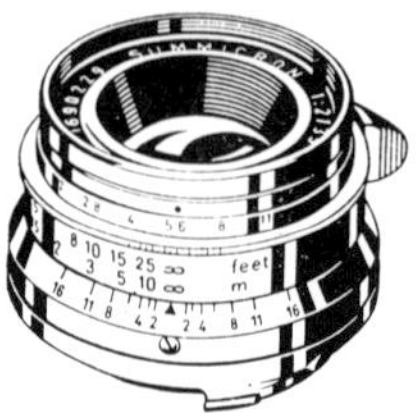

The 35mm, f2 SUMMICRON was faster and had eight elements in six groups symmetrically placed on both sides of the iris diaphragm. Built from 1958 to 1963 the screw mounted lenses are rather few nevertheless. The angle of view was 64°, the minimum aperture f16 and the nearest focusing distance 0.7 metre. Code name SAWOO. Quantity 500 approximately. The first bayonet-mount codes were SAWOM and SAMWO for the M3 version. The lens has had several redesigns since and is still in production.

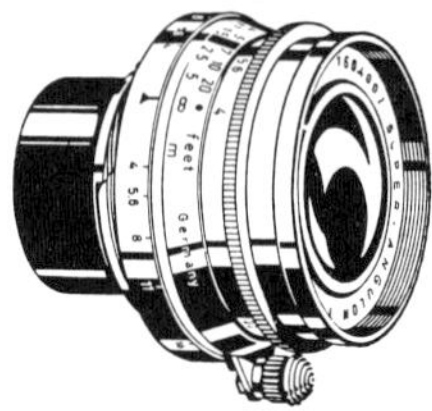

Still in 1958 an extremely wide-angle lens was introduced: the 21mm, f4 SUPER ANGULON; this lens design was very complex to achieve good results, there being nine elements in four groups. It was built until 1963; angle of view 92°, minimum aperture f22, nearest focusing distance 0.4 metre. Code name of screw version SUUON. Quantity 1,400 approximately. The bayonet version was SUMON. An improved, faster version at f3.4 was made from 1963-1980.

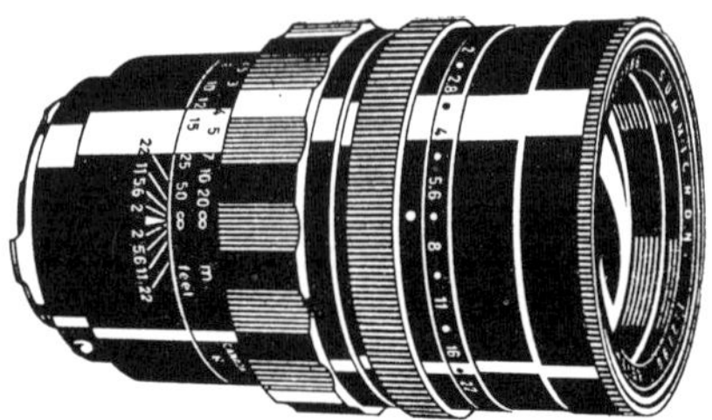

The final new lens in 1958 was the 90mm, f2 SUMMICRON. It had six elements in five groups. Angle of view 27°, minimum aperture f16, nearest focusing distance one metre. Code name screw version was SEOFF. Quantity 600 approximately. The bayonet model was SEOOM. The lens was redesigned in 1980.

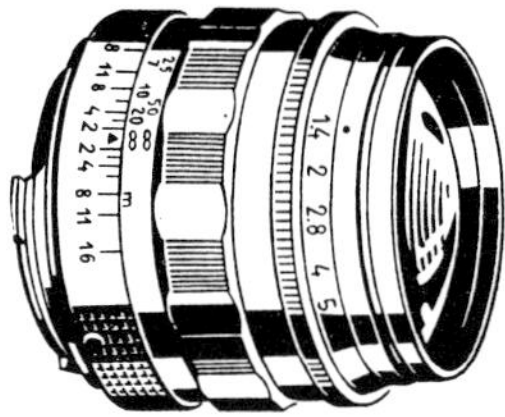

The 50mm f1.4 SUMMILUX was an improvement on the SUMMARIT and was built from 1959 to 1968, mostly in bayonet mount, but a limited production was also made in screw mount from 1960 to 1963 and duly advertised and coded. The seven elements five groups design resembled the XENON; angle of view 46°, minimum aperture f16, nearest focusing distance one metre. Code name for screw version was SOWGE. Quantity 550 approximately. The bayonet version was SOOME. A new design appeared in 1966 without further change of name, and is still in production.

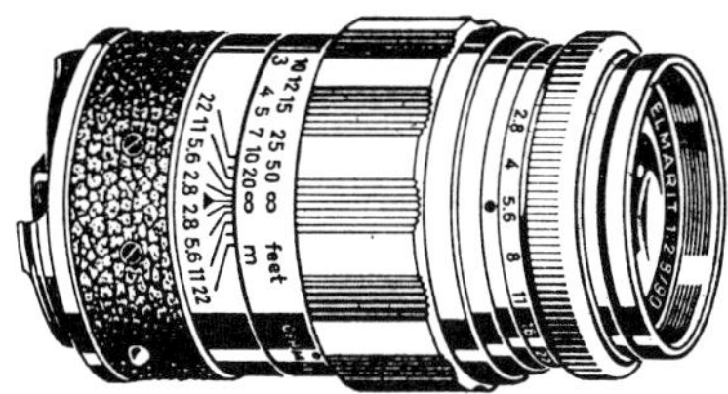

A new 90mm lens was introduced in 1959, the f2.8 ELMARIT. The new name was to indicate all f2.8 lenses thereafter. In screw mount it was produced until 1963, had five elements in three groups, angle of view 27°, minimum aperture f22 and nearest focusing distance one metre; code name ELRIT. Quantity 2,000 approximately. Bayonet version ELRIT-M. The 90mm, f4 ELMAR was redesigned in 1964 with only three elements, taking advantage of the new optical glasses, and a parallel focusing mount. Its code number was 11830. The lens head was available separately, code 11128, and the lens was also offered in screw mount, code 11730. The collapsible version continued to be made in the old optical design. Quantities were approximately 540 screw and 5950 bayonet.

Last of the lenses made for the screw mount cameras was the new 135mm, f4 ELMAR. It was introduced in 1960 and only a few thousand of the more than 23,000 were made with the screw mount, the rest being bayonet. Although the name ELMAR was used the design was quite different, with four elements, all independent, three of them being in front of the iris diaphragm. Angle of view was 18°, minimum aperture f22, nearest focusing distance 1.5 metres; also noticeable the fact that, in spite of being a screw mount lens, this one had no code name, only the number in the new code system: screw 11,750, quantity approximately 3,200, bayonet 11,850, quantity 20,400 approximately.

VISOFLEX LENSES

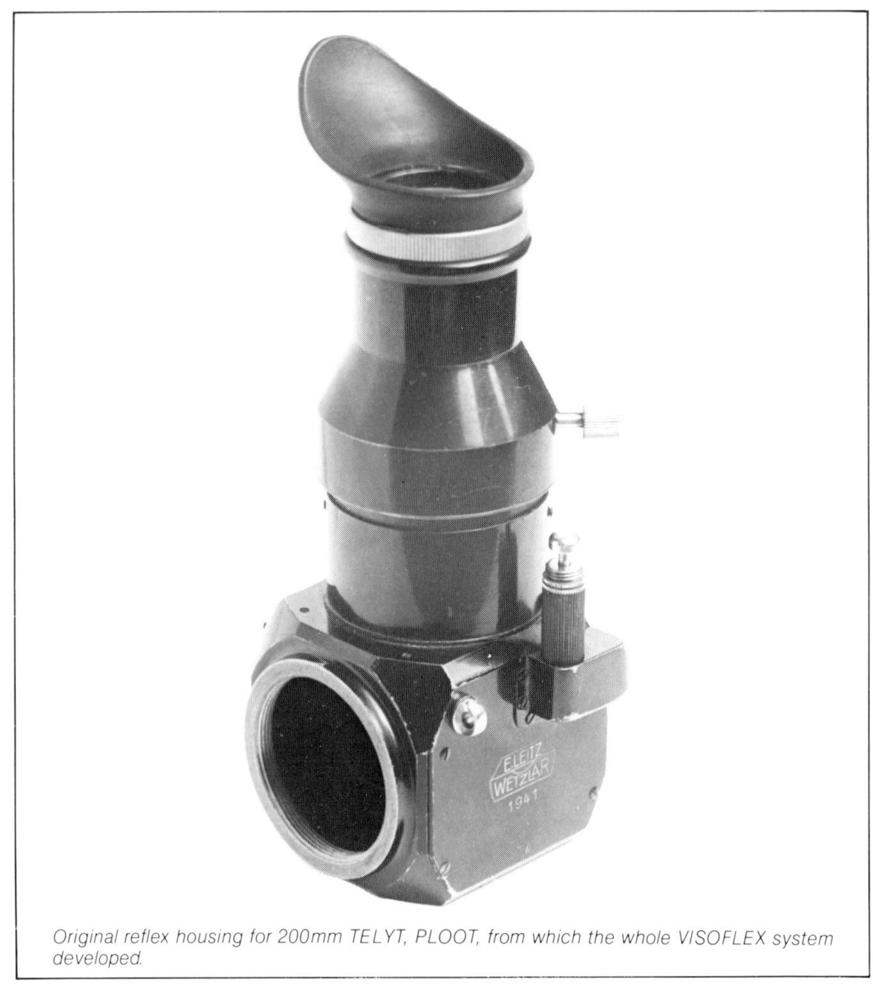

Original reflex housing for 200mm TELYT, PLOOT, from which the whole VISOFLEX system developed.

The original mirror-reflex housing, PLOOT, was introduced for the 200mm TELYT in 1935 because the rangefinder was not accurate for longer lenses. Over the years it was modified, it acquired a cylindrical shape instead of a cubical one, and came to be known as the VISOFLEX and there were two versions, one for screw and the other for bayonet cameras. Further lenses joined the original 200 and 400mm TELYT's, some of shorter focal length to take advantage of the reflex viewing. The lens heads of the 90 and 135mm lenses could be detached and used in special short focusing mounts, or some of the lenses could be supplied in short mounts.

A lighter and more compact reflex housing, the VISOFLEX II, with optical thickness reduced to 40mm, to allow lenses of 65mm and longer to be focused to infinity, was introduced in 1959. It was designed to allow the whole assembly to be used hand-held and in Leitz's view at the time gave the LEICA all the advantages of both rangefinder and SLR cameras until the advent of through-lens metering in the latter showed otherwise. An improved version, the VISOFLEX III was introduced in 1963.

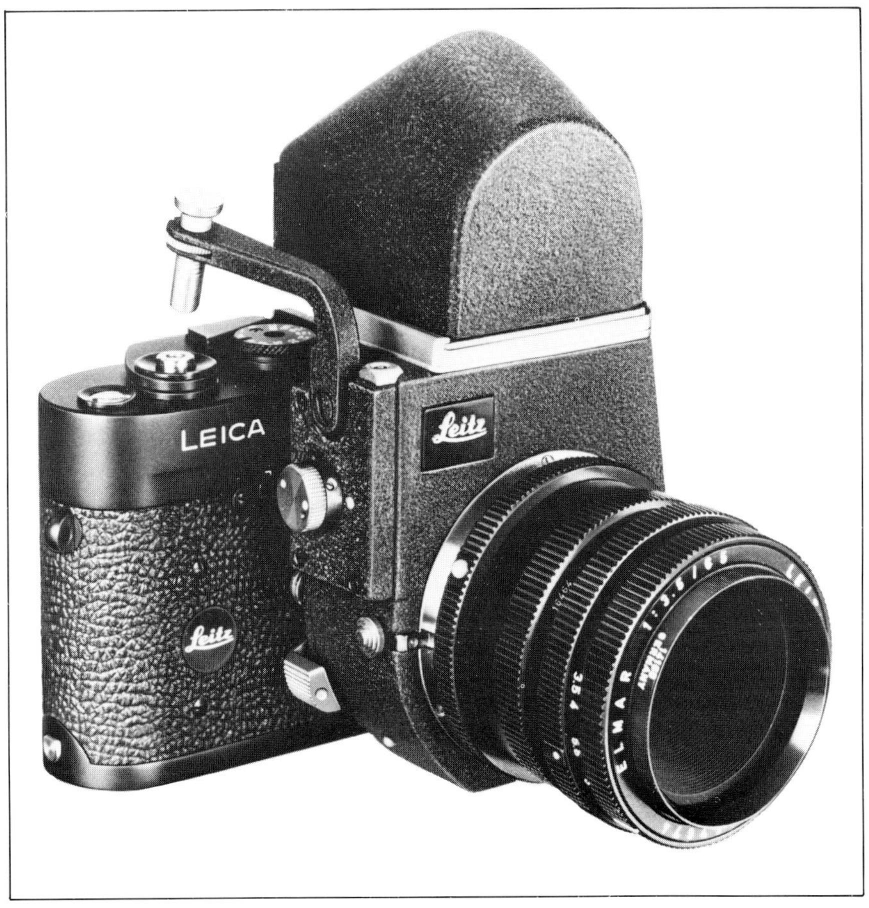

VISOFLEX III on M4-P with 65mm, f3.5 ELMAR and filter retaining ring 16160.

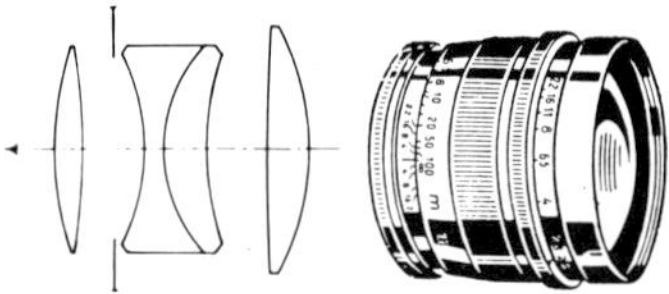

The HEKTOR f2.5/125mm was designed for use with the VISOFLEX and therefore sold only in short mount (but it was possible to use the tube TZFOO and a viewfinder as for the 200 and 400mm TELYT's and avoid the VISOFLEX). The HEKTOR was made from 1954 to 1963 in Wetzlar, and later units in Canada. Angle of view 19°, minimum aperture f22, nearest focusing distance 1.2 metres, code name HIKOO. Quantity 3,300 Approx.

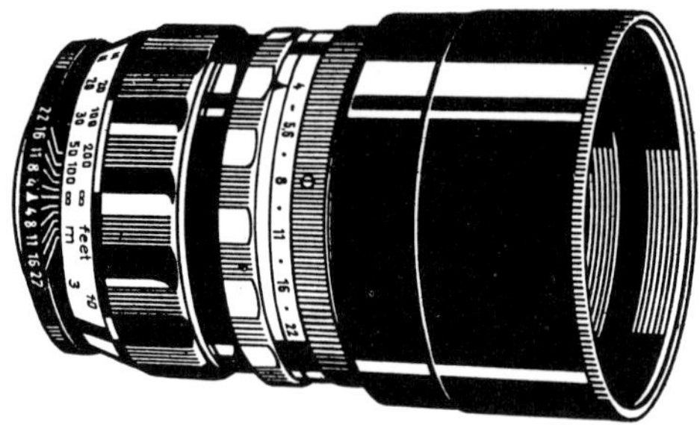

A new 200mm, f4 TELYT slightly faster than its predecessor and also heavier came in 1959. It had four elements all separated. Angle of view 12°, minimum aperture f22, nearest focusing distance 3 metres, code name TELOO. The 400mm f5 TELYT had been recomputed in 1955 with no increase in speed and no change in code, but it had a stepped shape mount instead of a conical one.

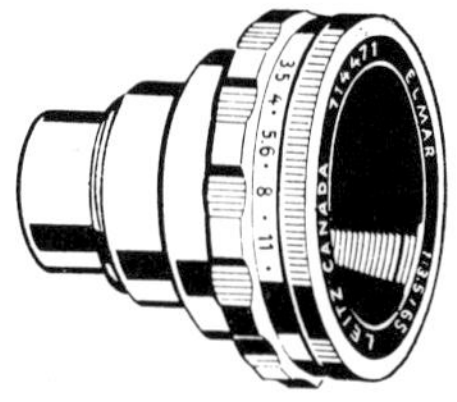

The 65mm, f3.5 ELMAR for the VISOFLEX was introduced in 1960; it was built at first in Wetzlar until 1968 and then in Canada. A classic ELMAR design with four elements in three groups, this lens had an angle of field of 37°, minimum aperture f22 and could be focused all the way to 1:1 ratio with the aid of the bellows. Code name OCMOR.

In 1961 the 280mm, f4.8 TELYT was introduced, for use on the new VISOFLEX II (and on its successor VISOFLEX III) angle of view of slightly less than 9°, minimum aperture of f22, focused to 6 metres.

Two TELYT type lenses with the same aperature f5.6 and focal lengths of 400 and 560mm were made in 1967 for use in conjunction with the VISOFLEX and the TELEVIT rapid focusing device. They were two-element achromats, very light in weight for their focal length. Both lenses shared the same detachable diaphragm system that stopped down to f32. The 400mm lens had an angle of view of 6° and focused to 3.6 metres; the 560mm lens had an angle of view of 4.4° and focused to 6.6 metres. In 1970 a completely new design was made for both lenses, retaining the same focal lengths, but with a different aperture of f6.8, and built-in diaphragm that still stopped down to f32.

The sliding focusing movement was now part of the lens mount. Still produced for LEICA reflex cameras.

The VISOFLEX is now discontinued, together with the lenses for it.

LATER M LENSES

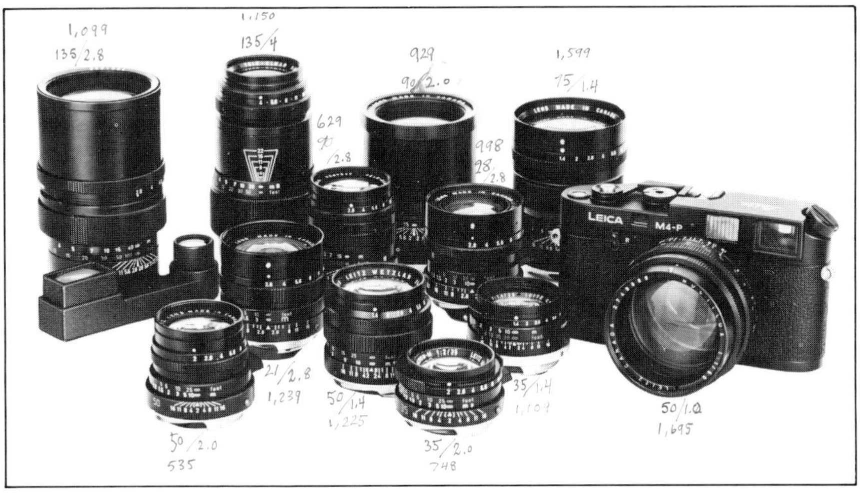

Modern LEICA M Lenses

The 35mm, f1.4 SUMMILUX appeared in 1961 as a really fast wide-angle lens. It is the longest lived of current designs, although the mount has been changed over its lifetime. Made in Canada, originally in M3 form with viewfinder attachment as well as normal form. Angle of view 64°, minimum aperture f16, focuses down to one metre.

1963 brought a faster 135mm lens, the f2.8 ELMARIT. This lens has a viewfinder attachment similar to that of the M3 35mm lenses, but the purpose is to magnify the image for more accurate focusing and easier viewing. It utilises the 90mm frame in the camera to show the 135mm field. This means it can be used on all M-series cameras. Angle of view 18°, minimum aperture f32, minimum focusing distance 1.5m.

Two lenses of telephoto construction were introduced in 1965. These were the 90mm, f2.8 TELE-ELMARIT, angle of view 27°, minimum aperture f16, focusing down to one metre, reformulated in 1974; and the 135mm, f4 TELE-ELMAR, angle of view 18°, minimum aperture f22, nearest focusing distance 1.5m.

Also in 1965 the 28mm, f2.8 ELMARIT became the lens of this focal length for M cameras. It has been reformulated twice since, in 1972 and 1979. The original version was made in Wetzlar and the later ones in Canada. Angle of view 76°, minimum aperture f22, nearest focusing distance 0.7m.

All the above lenses, together with the 35, 50, and 90mm SUMMICRON's and the 50mm SUMMILUX, are all still current.

In 1966 the fantastic 50mm, f1.2 NOCTILUX lens was announced. A Gauss type lens with aspherical elements to correct spherical aberrations without too many air-glass surfaces, this lens was the combined effort of the Leitz glass laboratory, the optical staff and the engineering specialist who devised practical ways to grind aspherical lenses for series production.

The NOCTILUX had an angle of view of 45°, minimum aperture f16, nearest focusing distance one metre. It was built until 1976 when a sensational new NOCTILUX f1 replaced the f1.2. A demonstration of progress is that the new faster type no longer needs an aspheric element to correct aberrations.

The appearance of the LEICA CL in 1973 brought along two lenses specially made for that camera. The 40mm, f2 SUMMICRON-C placed between the so-called normal length of 50mm and the moderate wide angle of 35mm. Its angle of view was 57°, minimum aperture f16 and it focused to 0.8 metre.

The 90mm, f4 ELMAR-C had an angle of view of 27°, minimum aperture f22 and nearest focusing distance one metre. Both lenses could also be used on LEICA M cameras.

The only other non-Leitz lens besides the SUPER-ANGULON made for the M-type camera was the 15mm, f8 HOLOGON, made by Zeiss. It was an extreme wide-angle lens of fixed aperture with an angle of view of 110° and focusing down to 20cm. Both lens and its special viewfinder have been long discontinued, but command a very high price on the collectors' market.

In the decade since the fiftieth anniversary a renewed interest by the company has brought out an ample series of new lenses for the M system. Continuing progress in glass research, and better facilities for calculations with bigger computers, has enabled the lens specialists at Leitz to offer new lenses that are better corrected, faster and sometimes lighter than before. It should be noted that when a Leitz lens is lighter this doesn't mean that something has been sacrificed, only that the new glasses allow for making a lens with with less elements but with equal or better performance.

As already noted, a new 50mm SUMMICRON was introduced in 1979, along with its 35mm namesake, a new 28mm ELMARIT also appeared in 1979. In 1980 the 21mm SUPER-ANGULON was replaced by the 21mm, f2.8

ELMARIT and in the same year the new lighter weight 90mm SUMMICRON came out as well as the very fast 75mm, f1.4 SUMMILUX.

The LEICA M system now comprises twelve lenses with focal lengths from 21 to 135mm and all except the 21mm can be accommodated in the camera's viewfinder. Longer and shorter focal lengths are now confined to the LEICA reflex system and the rangefinder cameras operate in the region for which they are best suited.

LEICA REFLEX LENSES

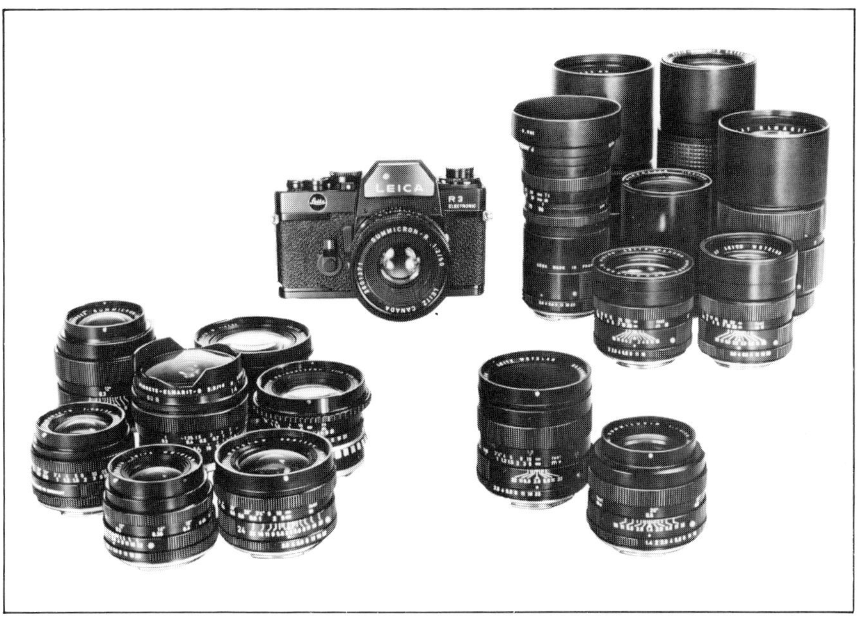

A group of reflex lenses contemporary with the LEICA R3.

The first LEICAFLEX had a complement of six lenses and these were indicated by well known names followed by the letter R.

The "standard" lens of the first batch of reflex lenses, made in 1964, was the 50mm, f2 SUMMICRON-R; it stopped down to f16, had an angle of view of 45° and focused to 0.5 metres. It was built until the end of 1976 to be superseded in 1977 by a new type.

There were four lenses of the ELMARIT family, all with f2.8 aperture and focal lengths from 35mm, to 90mm, 135mm and 180mm. Finally there was an ultrawide-angle lens, the 21mm, f3.4 SUPER ANGULON-R from Schneider. This lens was not a retrofocus, so it protruded into the camera necessitating the lift-up mirror mechanism and a special finder (the same as used for M cameras).

A new SUPER ANGULON of 1969 could be used normally with full reflex viewing. It was much more complicated, with ten elements in eight groups, its maximum aperture was f4 and minimum f22; angle of view was the same at 92° and so was the nearest focusing distance of 0.2 metres.

The 35mm, f2.8 ELMARIT-R had an angle of view of 64°, minimum aperture f22 and minimum focusing distance of 0.3 metres. With the advent of the LEICAFLEX SL in 1968 all the lenses were modified in the diaphragm control system, with the addition of a second cam to operate the exposure meter control.

The 90mm, f2.8 ELMARIT-R was a five-element four-group lens; its angle of view was 27°, the minimum aperture f22 and the nearest focusing distance 0.7 metres.

The 135mm, f2.8 ELMARIT-R had an angle of view of 18°, the minimum aperture f22 and the nearest focusing distance 1.5 metres.

And finally the 180mm, f2.8 ELMARIT-R had an angle of field of 14°, stopped down to f16 and focused to 2 metres. In 1969 both TELYT models with 400 and 560mm focal lengths were made also with LEICAFLEX bayonet mount; diaphragm stop down was not automatic as on lenses up to 180mm. Later the design of these TELYT lenses was changed into the f6.8 type and these, too, were made for the LEICAFLEX and are still in production.

A spate of new lenses was made available for the LEICAFLEX SL: The 28mm, f2.8 ELMARIT-R, angle of view 76°, minimum aperture f22 and nearest focusing distance 0.3 metres. The 50mm, f1.4 SUMMILUX-R, 45° angle of view, minimum aperture f16 and nearest focusing distance 0.5 metres. The 90mm f2 SUMMICRON-R was also introduced in 1970, angle of view of 27°, minimum aperture f16 and nearest focusing distance 0.7 metres. In that same year there were two lenses made for the LEICAFLEX by outside suppliers: one was the 35mm, f4 PA CURTAGON with perspective control; the minimum aperture was f22 and the minimum focusing distance 0.3 metres; the second was the zoom 45-90mm, f2.8 ANGENIEUX: the angle of view could change from 51° to 27°, its minimum aperture being f22 and the nearest focusing distance one metre.

In 1972 came the 60mm, f2.8 ELMARIT-R macro lens; with minimum aperture f22 and angle of view 39°. A Macro lens did in fact exist since 1970, this being the 100mm, f4 MACRO-ELMAR used with the focusing bellows; angle of field of this lens was 24.5°, its minimum aperture f22.

The 1973 catalogue carried three new lenses, a 35mm f2 SUMMICRON-R and a 250mm, f4 TELYT-R, made in Canada. The SUMMICRON had an angle of view of 64°, a minimum aperture f16 and a nearest focusing distance of 0.3 metres. The TELYT had an angle of view of 10°, minimum aperture f22 and nearest focusing distance 4.5 metres. Also listed was a mammoth 800mm, f6.3 TELYT-S; this bazooka-like lens is surely the largest in the whole Leitz production. The angle of view is 3°, the minimum aperture f32 and the nearest focusing distance 12.5 metres. The weight is 6.86 kilos or some 15 pounds!

In 1975 several new lenses were introduced: The 16mm, f2.8 Fisheye-ELMARIT-R incorporated a four-filter system that could be brought into the light path by rotation of a ring; the angle of view for the diagonal was 180°. Unlike cheaper fisheyes the ELMARIT covered the full 24 x 36mm frame. Smallest angle of view was f16 and closest focusing distance 0.3 metres.

The 24mm, f2.8 ELMARIT-R was the first lens in the LEICAFLEX range to use the floating elements principle for correct focusing down to near distance, and focusing goes to 0.3 metres. Minimum angle of view f22.

The 80-200mm, f4.5 VARIO-ELMAR was a zoom lens made by Minolta and adapted to the LEICAFLEX bayonet: a single movable barrel controlled both focusing (by rotation) and focal length (by sliding). Angle of view varied from 30° to 12° the minimum aperture f22 and nearest focusing distance 1.8 metres.

These three new lenses could only be used with the LEICAFLEX SL2 and LEICA R3 and R4 because of the different space taken inside the camera by the mirror mechanism.

The 19mm, f2.8 ELMARIT-R had an angle of view of 96°, minimum aperture f16 and nearest focusing distance 0.5 metres; the 180mm, f3.4 APO-TELYT-R had an angle of view of 14°, minimum aperture f22 and focused to 2.5 metres.

New in 1976 were the new 50mm, f2 SUMMICRON-R from Canada and a compact 180mm f4 ELMAR-R.

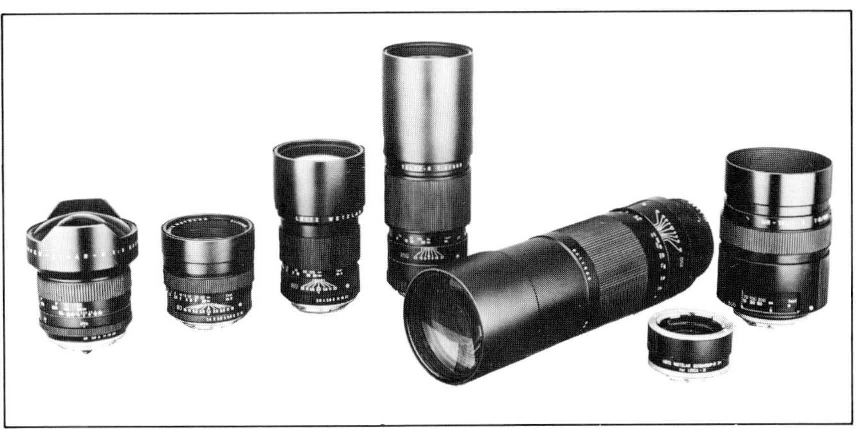

Some later reflex lenses, all introduced in 1980. From left to right:- 3.5/15mm, 1.4/80mm, new light-weight 2.8/180mm, improved 4/250mm, 4.8/350mm, 2xExtender-R, 8/500mm mirror lens.

Of all these lenses the following are still in production in 1985:
16mm Fisheye-ELMARIT-R, 19mm ELMARIT-R, 21mm SUPER-ANGULON-R, 24mm ELMARIT-R, 28mm ELMARIT-R, 35mm SUMMICRON-R, 35mm PA-CURTAGON-R, 50mm SUMMILUX-R (but with a new compact mount) 50mm SUMMICRON-R, 60mm MACRO-ELMARIT-R, 90mm SUMMICRON-R, 180mm ELMAR-R and APO-TELYT-R, and the 400mm, 560mm and 800mm TELYT-R lenses.

The Leitz reflex camera system has been the recipient of much attention in the seventies and eighties. Proof is in the number of fine lenses that have been offered. In some cases Leitz has resorted to other well known manufacturers to complete its own complement when it was the case of special types of no great production.

A good example is the SUPER-ELMAR-R an extremely wide-angle lens, but no fisheye; with only 15mm focus and f3.5 this lens has an angle of 110°. It is produced by Zeiss for the LEICA, and has the feature of a built-in filter turret with four filters, for it would be impossible to fit regular filters on such a wide angle lens.

In 1984 a brand new 35mm, f1.4 SUMMILUX was offered along with a sensational 280mm, f2.8 APO-TELYT; such a fast and long lens enables the user (specially the sports photographer) to have two lenses at his disposal if he carries along a 2x Extender; the resulting 560mm f5.6 lens is still very competitive in terms of speed, and no bigger than a 300mm. The 2x Extender-R itself was introduced in 1980.

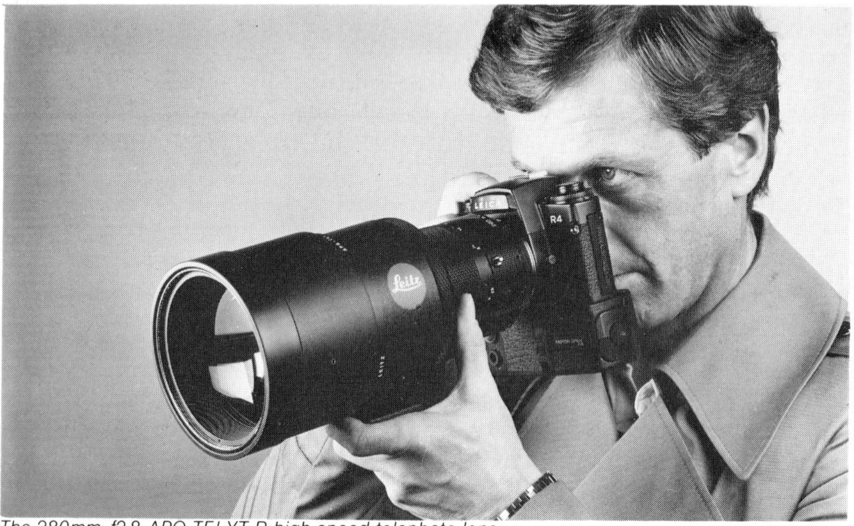

The 280mm, f2.8 APO-TELYT-R high speed telephoto lens

Also new in a series of fast lenses is the SUMMILUX-R with 80mm focus and f1.4, introduced in 1980. A new 90mm f2.8 ELMARIT was introduced in 1983. The 100mm MACRO-ELMAR-R was improved in 1978 and the 35mm ELMARIT-R in 1979. A totally new 180mm, f2.8 ELMARIT-R was among the many new lenses of 1980, a year which also saw the new 250mm f4 TELYT-R and 350mm f4 TELYT-R.

In the same year a mirror (catadioptric) lens of 500mm, f8 was put in the catalogue, coming from Minolta, and in 1983 a very compact zoom lens, the 35/70mm, f3.5 VARIO-ELMAR-R was introduced.

As for the other zoom lens, it first got its range broadened from 80/200 to 75/200, then again to 70/210, thus achieving a 1 to 3 ratio, while at the same time obtaining a slight increase in lens speed from the former f4.5 to f4.

The LEICA R system now comprises thirty lenses, with focal lengths from 15mm to 800mm, plus the 2xExtender.

Chapter 20

LEICA as the Universal Camera – Accessories for Every Purpose

The LEICA, as a camera, has a most successful life story, but the range of its accessories is almost unbelievable. It was not only the large range of accessories such as interchangeable lenses, motor drives and near focusing accessories that made it so special, but the small and inconspicuous pieces show the extreme care that has been taken to make photography with a LEICA an art where nothing has been left to chance. Leafing through the catalogues issued over the years we find some of the most fascinating objects. The code word list at the end of the book briefly describes the varied accessories manufactured between 1925 and the end of the code word era in 1960, making the LEICA the most comprehensive "system" camera.*

EARLY ACCESSORIES

Right from its beginning the LEICA was equipped with a number of accessories which greatly increased its scope and usefulness. First accessory for the early LEICA was obviously the rangefinder FODIS, which actually antedated the camera by a year. It soon became FOFER, with a bigger scale wheel for greater accuracy, and was followed by the angular viewfinder WINKO which allowed the already small camera to be used in an unobtrusive manner by the photographer looking at right angles with respect to where the camera was really aimed.

Landscape pictures could be taken with the panoramic head FIAMA, first making sure that the camera was horizontal with the spirit level FIBLA, later DOOLU, which fitted in the accessory shoe. The lens hood FISON and a comprehensive range of filters gave the LEICA man the same control as with the best cameras of the day. With the introduction of successive new lenses the range of filters grew so that it is now a fascinating study in itself.

From the earliest years a system for stereophotography was offered, which we have already seen, and Leitz were also developing ways for making the LEICA suitable for close-up and technical work.

---

*For a complete guide to all LEICA accessories from the beginning to the present day see the "LEICA ACCESSORY GUIDE" by Dennis Laney, Hove Foto Books, 1984.

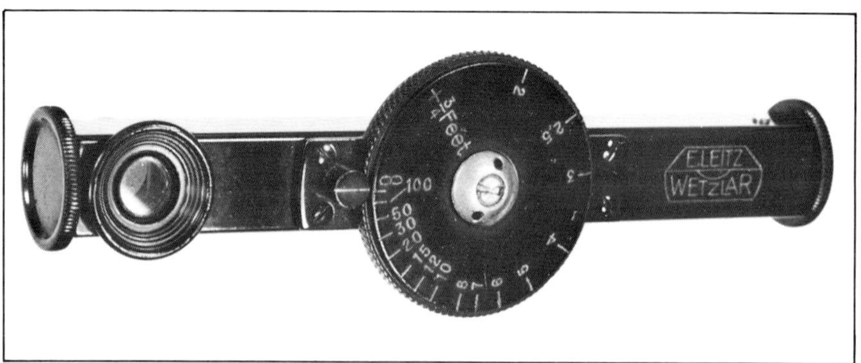

Rangefinder FOFER and angular viewfinder WINKO

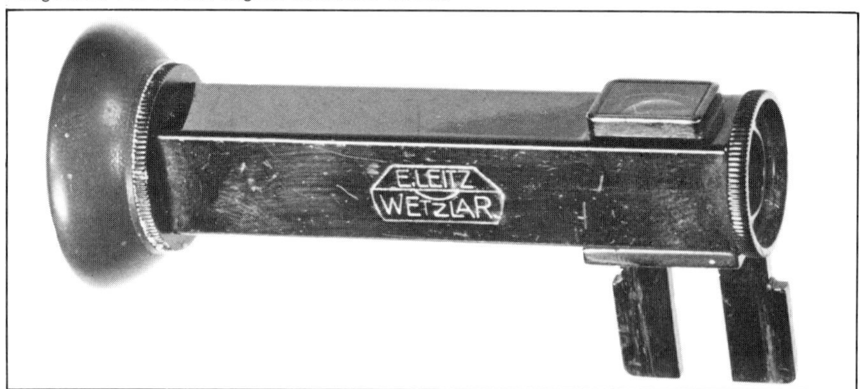

VIEW FINDING

A selection of viewfinders

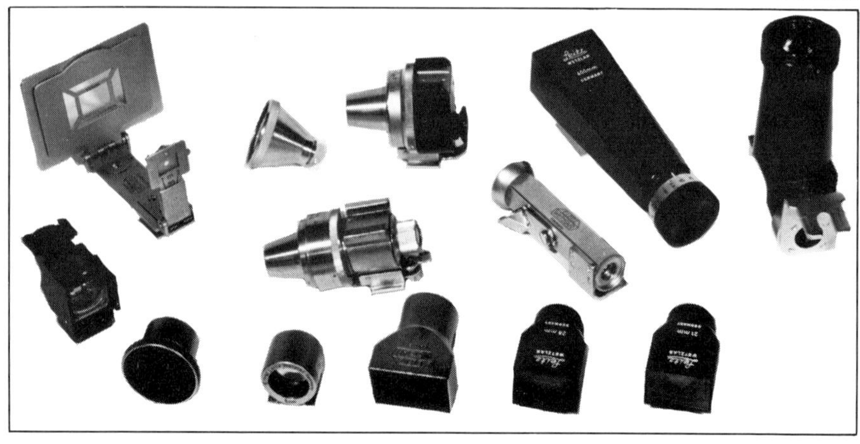

As the range lenses of different focal length grew, so did the variety of viewfinders to go with them. There were simple ones, for a single lens each, and universal ones for a number of focal lengths. These might have the various fields marked on a screen inside, such as the "torpedo" finder VISOR, or have masks for a variable image size, as in the VIDOM and VIOOH finders, or there were the frame finders for sports. Every lens for the rangefinder cameras from 21mm to 400mm had its own viewfinder that could be fitted into an accessory shoe.

CLOSE-UP AND COPYING

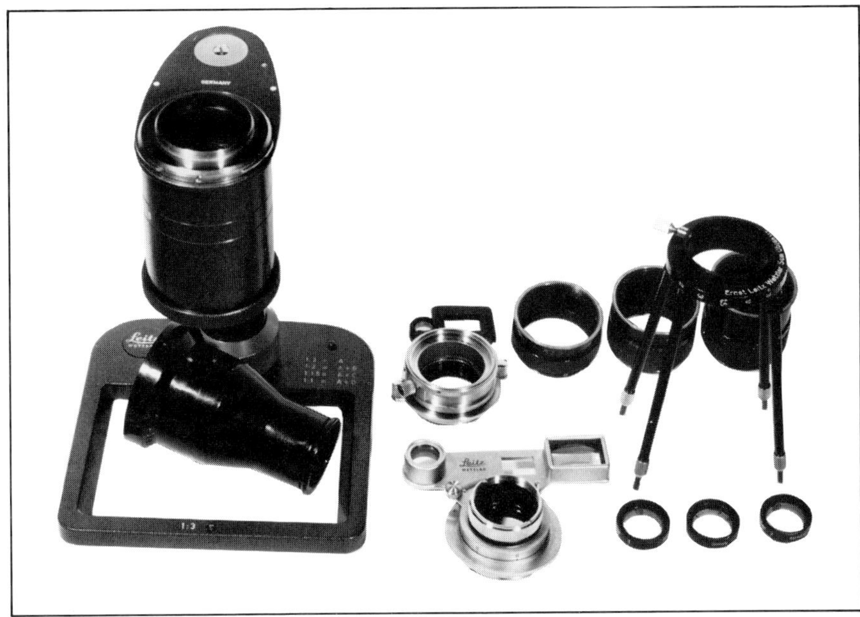

Selection of near focusing devices

Near focusing and reproduction devices were always important accessories for the LEICA, making it a specialised camera for scientific work. There are two distinct methods of near focusing; one with supplementary front lenses, such as the device BEOOY, and the other with extension tubes between the lens and the camera body.

The first system was used mostly on fixed lens models, the second on all interchangeable lens models; the devices were the BELUN for 1:1 reproduction ratio, BEHOO for up to 1:3 reduction ratio or the NOOKY, a continuous focusing device, first made for the 5cm, f3.5 ELMAR lens and later, with slight changes in code, for the other 5cm lenses. For larger formats the BOOWU device with extendable legs, made the copying of pictures and documents much easier.

Specialised accessories for scientific, medical and copying work, such as the rotating and sliding stages for fine focusing were also available. These grew into complete assemblies with lights and stands and adapters and extension tubes for all manner of specialised purposes, including microphotography. The VISOFLEX reflex housings were also used in this way.

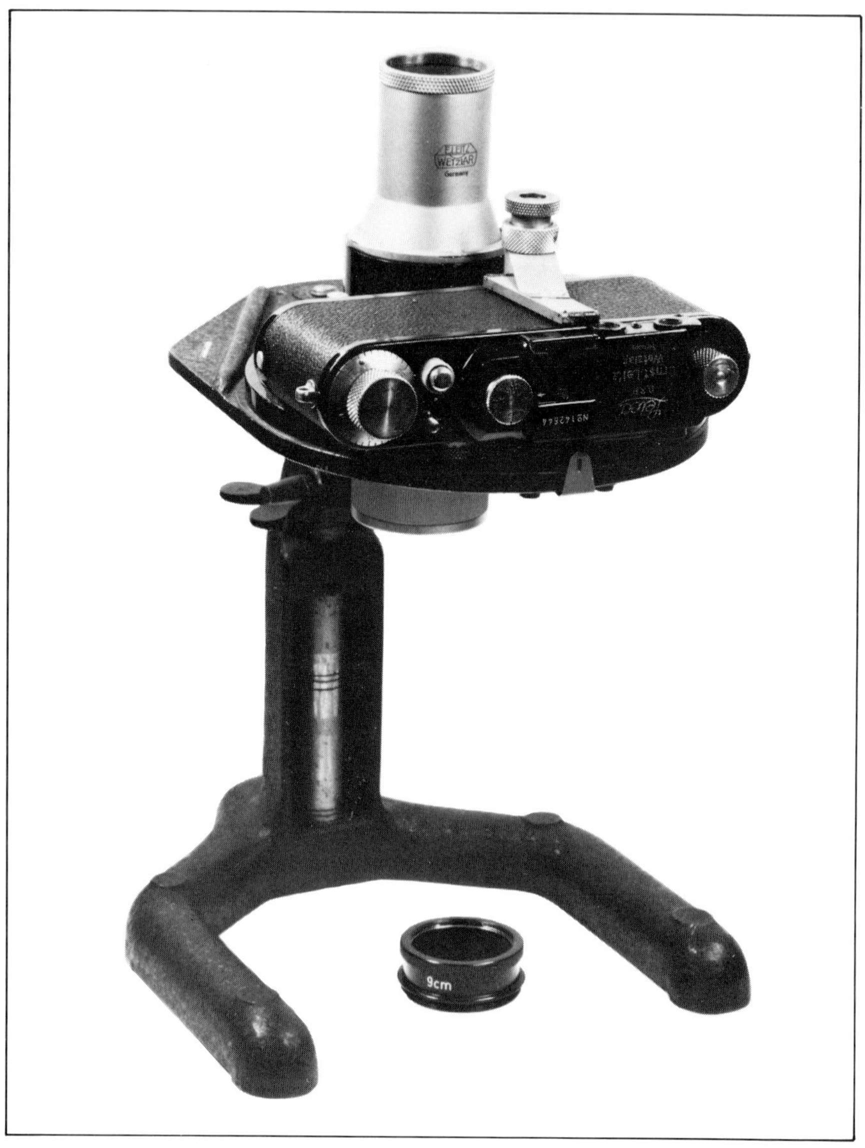

Rotating Focusing Stage OORES with 5x Magnifier LOOCG on Special Tripod Foot SPOOV.

AND EVERYTHING ELSE

Other interesting accessories were the leather cases. Apart from simple ever-ready cases, there were the well fitted ones which contained one camera and a complement of lenses and related accessories. The flat leather cases of the pre-war series remain unsurpassed; the shoulder strap acted as a safety hold in the lid, so that it could not open even if the lock was not properly fastened. There was a full series of cases ranging from the small ETRIN for the camera with rangefinder and two cassettes, to the ETTWO for camera and two lenses, the ETTRE for camera and three lenses, the ETNEU for camera and four lenses, the ETGUS for camera and five lenses and finally the majestic ETMAX for the LEICA with seven lenses, universal viewfinder, angular finder, supplementary lenses, filters and spare cassettes.

There was a vast array of adaptor rings which allowed one to use nearly any lens on any camera: the rings for screw mount lenses used on M cameras were IRZOO, ISBOO and ISOOZ, depending on what frame appears in the viewfinder. OUBIO corrected the difference of length between VISOFLEX I and II or III. OUAGO was a focusing ring for the 90mm, f4 ELMAR and OTRPO adapted the 135mm HEKTOR. The tubes TXBOO for bayonet cameras and the similar TZOON, allowed one to use the TELYT lenses without reflex housing and with a simple sports finder SFTOO for 200mm lens and SQTOO FOR 400mm lens.

One may also count among the unusual accessories, the film holder for single pictures which was inserted into the camera, code name FCKOO for "c" and "f"

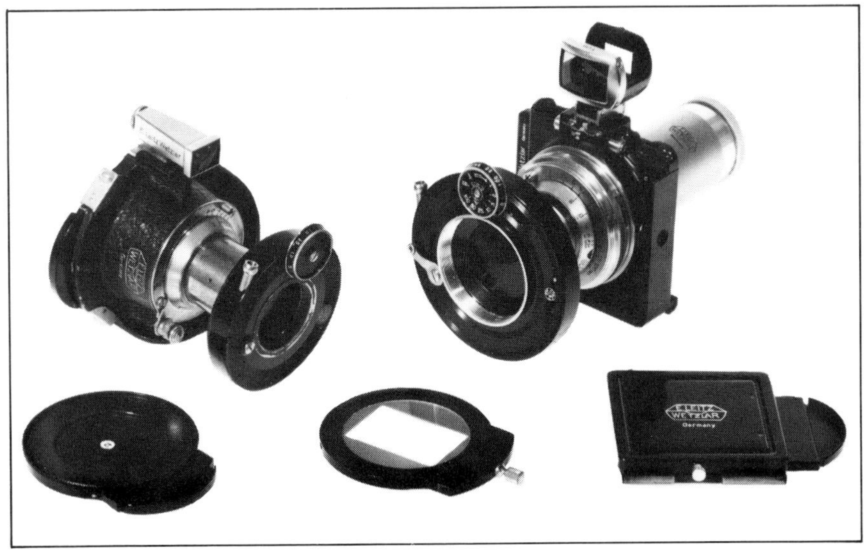

Single exposure housings, (left) early model "OLIGO" (right) post war version not commercially produced.

series models and FHKOO for previous models; or the ocular lens OSBLO which transforms any screw mount LEICA lens 50mm to 90mm into a medium power telescope.

There were even single exposure housings for using one's LEICA lenses for single pictures on a piece of film in a little dark slide. The Ibsor shutters of these could also be used for other purposes. Code name OLEYO and OLIGO depending on the shutter size; these shutters could be used in front of the lenses by holding the camera shutter open, and as they were also self cocking, allowed the rapid taking of many exposures.

Flash lighting was also considered by Leitz in the early days. There was a flash gun available as early as 1935 for use with one or two bulbs at the same time, it had a suitable synchronising device that was activated by a speed dial; code was BTLOO for the rangefinder cameras and BTOOK for the Standard camera. A special type of the above mentioned flash gun had a rotating head with three lamps which could be brought into position at one's will and therefore allowed quick action (what can be termed the basic idea of the flash cube).

After the war new types of flash unit were made, a bigger gun, the CEYOO, was first made with a standard battery pack, with the possibility of using both the small and big base bulbs. Later it was made with a condenser discharge pack which ensured a positive firing; the smaller flash was the Chico, code name DEOOC fitted in a small case and equipped like the CEYOO, with a reflector that folded like a fan.

The plastic cap for the flash contact is probably the smallest item in the Leitz catalogue and is followed in size by the M series release button adaptor which enables one to use a cable release. This adaptor is useful as it may also be used when wearing gloves as it raises the point of contact with the finger considerably.

The list of accessories is endless as the numbers run into many hundreds. Two later, and at the same time unusual, were the Tri-lens turret, made for the M series camera and which used screw-mount lenses to allow a quick change from one focal length to another (very few of these were made), and the Canadian Leitz filter turret for three filters, which could be used in place of an intermediate ring OUBIO between the lens and VISOFLEX II.

Finally, there are the well known Leicameter exposure meters, fitted first with selenium cells and later with CdS, and made or Leitz by Metrawatt.

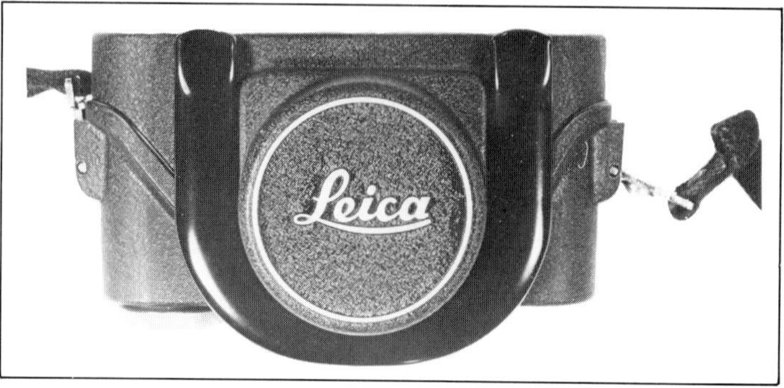

The ultimate in protection – the all-metal ever-ready case MBROO for any LEICA up to the IIIf

Chapter 21

LEICA – The Total System

The LEICA system was effective and successful because, from the beginning, Leitz made all the necessary apparatus to ensure consistent high quality throughout the photographic process. None of the equipment for handling 35 mm film that we now take for granted was available to the general public when the LEICA appeared on the market. Therefore right from the start Leitz had to design and manufacture apparatus for handling and processing the film, for enlarging and for projection.

FILM PROCESSING

In 1925 35 mm film was not available in cassettes but had to be bought in bulk and the photographer loaded his film into the LEICA cassette FILKA using the film winder AGRIF, or the mechanical ASPUL if he had a permanent darkroom and could fix it to the bench. The end of the film had to be trimmed to shape using the hinged template ABLON.

After the film was exposed he developed it in a dish using the developing drum FIMAN in the darkroom or in the Correx tank CORUN in daylight. He might then make contact prints with the printer ELDIA.

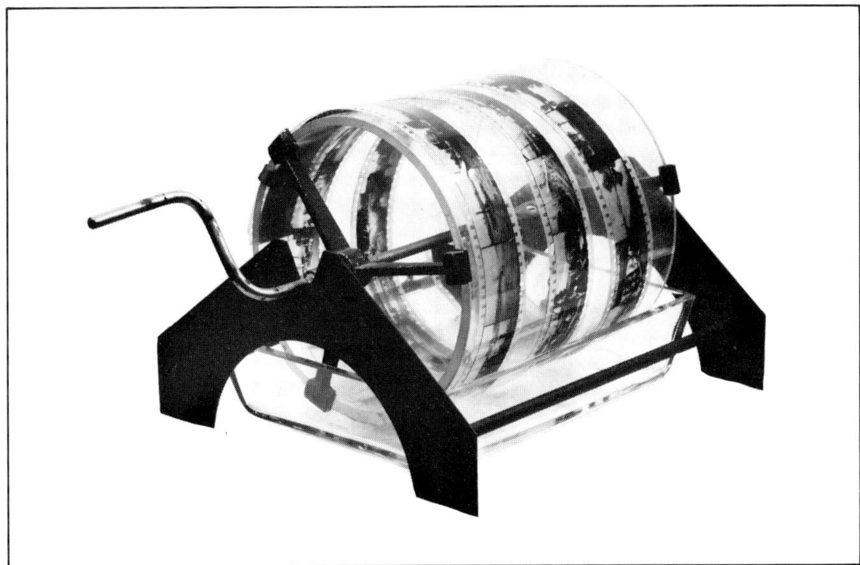

Developing drum FIMAN

ENLARGEMENT

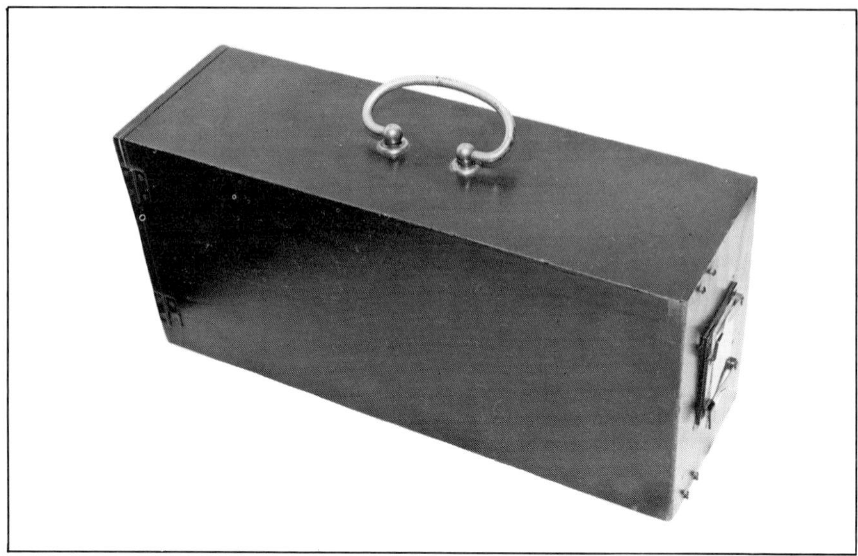

Enlarger FLEIN.

In the beginning there were two very simple enlarging devices, capable of producing prints of a fixed size. One was known by the code name of FLEIN and made copies of 3½ x 2½in. and the other was FILAR and made copies of 5½ x 3½in. They were simple boxes into which the sensitive paper was inserted at one end and the negative at the other; exposure was then made by daylight. However both devices could be equipped with an electric light accessory, transforming them into FLEOS and FILIX respectively.

More advanced types of enlarger were also made and the first big catalogue of 1931 listed four different types; the FILES which was a fixed lens of f3.5 aperture and 50mm focus, for negatives 24 x 36mm; the FILOY model was fairly similar but the lens had a variable iris diaphragm. The FILYT had a longer column which allowed it to make bigger prints and accept negatives up to the 4.5 x 6cm size and had a lens of 70mm focus and f3.5 aperture with diaphragm. Finally the VITOY was the largest of them all (for 24 x 36mm negatives), capable of making enlargements up to 15 x 18in. and was supplied with a series of special printing boards.

A couple of years passed and the 1933 catalogue illustrated at least six new enlargers: the VALOY was the first enlarger designed to take all Leitz screw mount lenses but in particular that fundamental lens the 50mm, f3.5 ELMAR. Normally it was used for 24 x 36mm negatives but it could take up to 3 x 4cm negatives.

The VALUX was similar to the VALOY but it had a more powerful illumination making for shorter exposures on the big enlargements; the VALFA was used for negatives of sizes up to 4 x 6cm and the VAKUT was similar except for the brighter illuminating system, and both were equipped with a Leitz enlarging 75mm, f4.5 lens.

The VARYL enlarger had a 90mm, f4 lens and could cope with large negative size. Finally the VAMAX was the largest of them all with a very tall column 4ft. (1.2m) long, several negative carriers and 50mm, f3.5 lens.

In 1933 the FOCOMAT I (followed by model II for larger negatives) with fully automatic focusing was introduced. An interesting picture viewing box or "reading desk" was also made under the code name VOPUL which enabled one to look at the images projected from the enlarger onto an inclined ground glass. A series of printing frames, FELIS and its bigger brothers, was also available.

After the war improved models appeared; the manual VALOY II, the automatic focusing FOCOMAT Ic and the professional FOCOMAT IIc. This latter led to the rapid FOCOMATOR for the commercial darkroom.

The latest Leitz enlarger, the FOCOMAT V35 Autofocus sets new standards in enlarging technology with its use of dichroic filters in its interchangeable modules for colour, black and white, and multigrade black and white papers.

PROJECTION

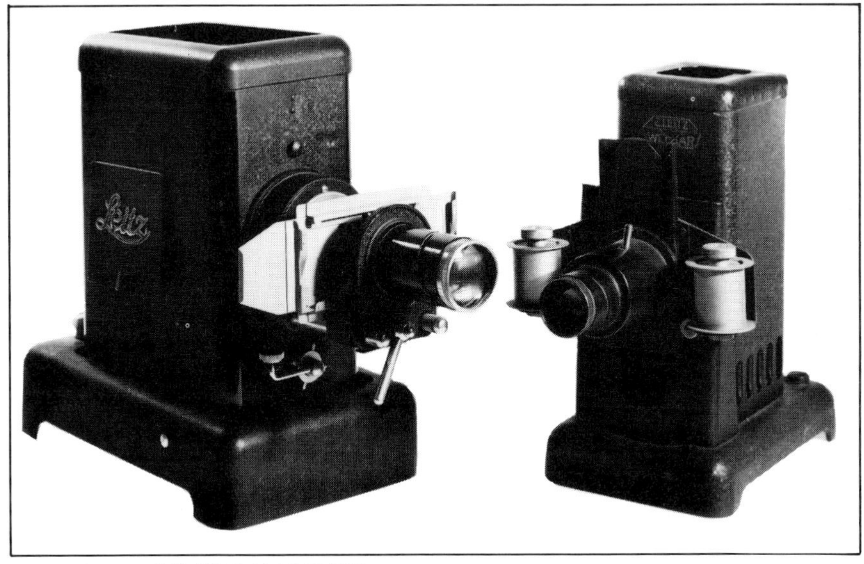

Early projectors, (left) VIII S, (right) ULEJA

Projectors also had to be provided for the 35mm format: the simplest was called the Standard type, code name ULKON and was essentially a lamp housing for a 100 watt lamp, and a film carrier with a lens flange into which screws the perennial 50mm, f3.5 ELMAR lens; the UBELA was more elaborate and could use either the 50mm, f3.5 ELMAR or the 73mm, f1.9 HEKTOR or 90mm, f4 ELMAR, and 105mm, f6.3 and 135mm, f4.5 ELMAR; it had a film magazine with semi-automatic film transport and 100 watt lamp.

The UDANO type was similar to the UDELA but projected glass transparencies and the UKABY was also similar but was supplied with 80 or 120mm fixed lenses; one should also note that Leitz advertised a semi-automatic slide changer WEDYA as early as 1933.

In 1939 a compact projector called GNOM (later PARVO) was introduced which could be contained in a suitcase 4 x 8 x 12in; it was also available in several versions with fixed 85mm, f2.5 or 100mm f2.5 HEKTOR lenses and for film (code words SIUUB and SOUUW depending on lens) and glass slides (same code with GLAS added). The type which could use any LEICA lens was SPUUV and SMUUY and an economy type was SUUEY and SNUUX.

When the lamp power was increased from 100 to 150 watts (along with other improvements) the small projector's name was changed to PRADO and code words were DUUOI for lenseless projector, DUUYO with 85mm, f2.5 HEKTOR lens and DUUXA with 100mm, f2.8 lens. There were also bigger PRADO's with 250 and 500 watt lamps and a host of lenses.

In the 1950's the PRADO design grew into a whole family of projectors with lenses colour corrected for colour slides and with models covering everything from a small room to a large auditorium. At the same period the first projector in the now familiar box shape and remote-control slide change and focusing, the PRADOVIT, appeared. This basic configuration has been developed over the years and can offer facilities such as automatic focusing, infra-red remote control, curved-field lenses for slides mounted without glass, elimination of the dark interval between slides which can produce eye strain, and lap dissolve with multiple projectors.

List of LEICA Camera Serial Numbers up to 1980

This information reproduced by the kind permission of Ernst Leitz Wetzlar

Leica-No.	Model	Year
100 – 130	I	1923
131 – 1000	I	1925
1001 – 2445	I	1926
2446 – 5433	I	1926/27
5434 – 5700	I	1928
5700 – 6300	Compur	1926-29
6301 – 13100	I	1928
13101 – 13300	Compur	1929
13301 – 21478	I	1929
21479 – 21810	Compur	1930
21811 – 34450	I	1930
34451 – 34802	Compur	1930
34803 – 34817	I(Luxus)	1930
34818 – 60000	I	1930
60001 – 71199	I	1931
71200 – 101000	II	1.2.32
101001 – 106000	Standard	21.10.32
106001 – 107600	II	1933
107601 – 107757	III	1934
107758 – 108650	II	1934
108651 – 108700	III	1933
108701 – 109000	II	1933
109001 – 111550	III	1933
111551 – 111580	II Chrom	1933
111581 – 112000	III	1933
112001 – 112500	II Chrom	1933
112501 – 114400	III	1934
114401 – 114050	St Chrom	1933
114051 – 114052	Reporter	1933
114053 – 114400	III	1934
114401 – 115300	II Chrom	1933
115301 – 115650	III	1934
115651 – 115900	II Chrom	1934
115901 – 116000	St Chrom	1934
116000 – 123000	III Chrom	1933
123001 – 123580	Standard	1934
123581 – 124800	III Chrom	1933
124801 – 126200	III Chrom	24.11.33
126201 – 126800	III	
126801 – 137400	III	1934
137401 – 137625	Standard	1934
137626 – 138700	III Chrom	1934
138701 – 138950	St Chrom	1934
138951 – 139900	III Chrom	1934
139901 – 139950	Standard	1934
139951 – 140000	II	1934
140001 – 141500	III Chrom	1934
141501 – 141850	Standard	1934
141851 – 141900	II	1934
141901 – 142250	III Chrom	1934
142251 – 142350	II	1934
142351 – 142500	III	1934
142501 – 142700	I Standard	1934
142701 – 143425	III	1934
143426 – 143750	II Chrom	1934
143751 – 143900	Standard	1934
143901 – 144200	III	1934
144201 – 144400	II	1934
144401 – 144500	Standard	1934
144501 – 145600	III	1934
145601 – 145800	Standard	1934
145801 – 146200	III	1934
146201 – 146375	II	1934
146376 – 146675	III	1934
146676 – 146775	II	1934
146776 – 147000	III	1934
147001 – 147075	Standard	1934
147076 – 147175	II	1934
147176 – 147875	St Chrom	1934
147876 – 148025	II Chrom	1934
148026 – 148850	III Chrom	1934
148851 – 148950	II Chrom	1934
148951 – 149350	III Chrom	1935
149351 – 149450	St Chrom	1934/35
149451 – 149550	II Chrom	1934/35
149551 – 150000	III Chrom	1935
150001 – 150200	Reporter	1934-36
from 150125 with 1/1000	Second	from 14.7.36

Leica-No.	Model	Year
150201 – 150850	III Chrom	1934/35
150851 – 151100	Standard	1935
151101 – 151225	III	1935
151226 – 151300	II	1935
151301 – 152500	III	1935
152501 – 152600	St Chrom	1935
152601 – 153175	III Chrom	1935
153176 – 153225	II	1935
153226 – 153550	III	1935
153551 – 153700	II	1935
153701 – 154150	III	1935
154151 – 154200	II	1935
154201 – 154800	III	1935
154801 – 154900	St Chrom	1935
154901 – 156200	III	1935
156201 – 156850	IIIa 1/1000	1935
156851 – 157250	III	1935
157251 – 157400	II	1935
157401 – 158300	IIIa	1935
158301 – 158350	Standard	1935
158351 – 158400	II	1935
158401 – 158650	IIIa	1935
158651 – 159000	III	1935
159001 – 159200	IIIa	1935
159201 – 159350	Standard	1935
159351 – 159950	III	1935
159551 – 159625	IIIa	1935
159626 – 159675	III	1935
159676 – 160325	IIIa	1935
160326 – 160375	III	1935
160376 – 160450	I	1935
160451 – 160700	II	1935
160701 – 161150	I Standard	1935
161151 – 161450	II	1935
161451 – 161550	IIIa	1935
161551 – 161600	III	1935
161601 – 161800	IIIa	1935
161801 – 161950	III Chrom	1935
161951 – 162100	IIIa	1935
162101 – 162175	III	1935
162176 – 162350	IIIa	1935
162351 – 162400	III	1935
162401 – 162500	IIIa	1935
162501 – 162625	III	1935
162626 – 162675	IIIa	1935
162676 – 162750	III	1935
162751 – 162800	IIIa	1935
162801 – 162825	III	1935
162826 – 162925	IIIa	1935
162926 – 162975	III	1935
162976 – 163050	IIIa	1935
163051 – 163100	III	1935
163101 – 163225	IIIa	1935
163226 – 163250	III	1935
163251 – 163400	IIIa	1935
163401 – 163450	Standard	1935
163451 – 163550	IIIa	1935
163551 – 163775	III	1935
163776 – 163950	IIIa	1935
163951 – 164150	Standard	1935
164151 – 164275	IIIa	1935
164276 – 164675	III	1935
164676 – 164900	IIIa	1935
164901 – 165000	II	1935
165001 – 165100	III	1935
165101 – 165300	II	1935
165301 – 165500	Standard	1935
165501 – 165975	III	1935
165976 – 166075	IIIa	1935
166076 – 166600	III	1935
166601 – 166750	IIIa	1935
166751 – 166900	III	1935
166901 – 167050	IIIa	1935
167051 – 167175	III	1935
167176 – 167200	IIIa	1935
167201 – 167225	III	1935
167226 – 167700	IIIa	1935
167701 – 167750	III	1935

Leica-No.	Model	Year
167751 – 168000	Standard	1935
168001 – 168200	II	1935
168201 – 168250	III	1935
168251 – 168325	IIIa	1935
168326 – 168400	III	1935
168401 – 168500	IIIa	1935
168501 – 168600	III	1935
168601 – 168725	IIIa	1935
168726 – 168750	III	1935
168751 – 168850	IIIa	1935
168851 – 169000	Standard	1935
169001 – 169200	III	1935
169201 – 169350	Standard	1935
169351 – 169450	II	1935
169451 – 169550	III	1935
169551 – 169650	II	1935
169651 – 170150	IIIa	1935
170151 – 170500	III	1935
170501 – 171300	IIIa	1935
171301 – 171550	II	1935
171551 – 171900	Standard	1935
171901 – 172250	IIIa	1935
172251 – 172300	III	1935
172301 – 172350	IIIa	1935
172351 – 172600	III	1935
172601 – 172800	II	1935
172801 – 173000	Standard	1935
173001 – 173125	IIIa	1935
173126 – 173176	III	1935
173177 – 173425	IIIa	1935
173426 – 173475	III	1935
173476 – 173500	IIIa	1935
173501 – 173650	Standard	1935
173651 – 173675	IIIa	1935
173676 – 173725	III	1935
173726 – 173825	IIIa	1935
173826 – 173900	III	1935
173901 – 174025	IIIa	1935
174026 – 174075	III	1935
174076 – 174100	IIIa	1935
174101 – 174125	III	1935
174126 – 174150	IIIa	1935
174151 – 174400	III	1935
174401 – 174650	II	1935
174651 – 174675	IIIa	1935
174676 – 174750	III	1935
174751 – 174950	IIIa	1935
174951 – 175125	III	1935
175126 – 175200	IIIa	1935
175201 – 175350	III	1935
175351 – 175450	IIIa	1935
175451 – 175500	III	1935
175501 – 175700	Standard	1935
175701 – 175750	III	1935
175751 – 175850	IIIa	1935
175851 – 175900	III	1935
175901 – 176100	IIIa	1935
176101 – 176150	III	1935
176151 – 176250	IIIa	1935
176251 – 176300	III	1935
176301 – 176600	IIIa	1935
176601 – 177000	III	1935
177001 – 177400	IIIa	1935
177401 – 177550	III	1935
177551 – 177600	IIIa	1935
177601 – 177700	III	1935
177701 – 177800	Standard	1935
177801 – 177900	IIIa	1935
177901 – 178000	III	1935
178001 – 178100	IIIa	1935
178101 – 178250	III	1935
178251 – 178550	IIIa	1935
178551 – 178600	III	1935
178601 – 179200	IIIa	1935
179201 – 179250	III	1935
179251 – 179500	IIIa	1935
179501 – 179575	II	1935
179576 – 179800	Standard	1935
179801 – 179900	II	1935

Leica-No.	Model	Year	Leica-No.	Model	Year	Leica-No.	Model	Year
179901 – 180100	IIIa	1935	196751 – 197400	IIIa	1936	218301 – 218700	II	1936
180101 – 180400	III	1935	197401 – 197500	Standard	1936	218701 – 218800	III	1936
180401 – 180475	IIIa	1935	197501 – 197550	IIIa	1936	218801 – 219600	IIIa	1936
180476 – 180700	III	1935	197551 – 197800	III	1936	219601 – 219800	II	1936
180701 – 180800	Standard	1935	197801 – 198200	IIIa	1936	219801 – 219900	IIIa	1936
180801 – 181000	II	1935	198201 – 198400	III	1936	219101 – 220000	III	1936
181001 – 181450	IIIa	1935	198401 – 198800	IIIa	1936	220001 – 220300	IIIa	1936
181451 – 181550	III	1935	198801 – 198900	III	1936	220301 – 220500	II	1937
181551 – 181600	IIIa	1935	198901 – 199200	IIIa	1936	220501 – 220600	IIIa	1936
181601 – 181700	III	1935	199201 – 199300	III	1936	220601 – 220700	III	1936
181701 – 182000	IIIa	1935	199301 – 199500	IIIa	1936	220701 – 220900	IIIa	1936
182001 – 182050	III	1935	199501 – 199600	III	1936	220901 – 221000	III	1936
182051 – 182300	IIIa	1935	199601 – 199800	II	1936	221001 – 221300	IIIa	1936
182301 – 182350	III	1935	199801 – 200100	IIIa	1936	221301 – 221400	III	1936
182351 – 182500	IIIa	1935	200101 – 200200	III	1936	221401 – 222150	IIIa	1936
182501 – 182700	Standard	1935	200201 – 200500	IIIa	1936	222151 – 222200	III	1936
182701 – 182850	II	1935	200501 – 200650	II	1936	222201 – 222300	IIIa	1936
182851 – 183500	IIIa	1935	200651 – 200750	Standard	1936	222301 – 222700	Standard	1937
183501 – 183600	II	1935	200751 – 201100	III	1936	222701 – 223000	II	1937
183601 – 183750	Standard	1935/36	201101 – 201200	III	1936	223001 – 223300	III	1937
183751 – 184400	IIIa	1936	201201 – 201300	IIIa	1936	223301 – 223600	IIIa	1936
184401 – 184450	III	1936	201301 – 201400	III	1936	223601 – 223700	III	1936
184451 – 184700	IIIa	1936	201401 – 201600	IIIa	1936	223701 – 224600	IIIa	1936/37
184701 – 184750	III	1936	201601 – 201700	Standard	1936	224601 – 224800	Standard	1936/37
184751 – 184800	IIIa	1936	201701 – 202300	IIIa	1936	224801 – 224900	IIIa	1936/37
184801 – 184950	III	1936	202301 – 202450	II	1936	224901 – 225000	III	1936/37
184951 – 185200	IIIa	1936	202451 – 202600	IIIa	1936	225001 – 225200	IIIa	1936/37
185201 – 185350	III	1936	202601 – 202700	III	1936	225201 – 225300	III	1936/37
185351 – 185500	II	1936	202701 – 202800	IIIa	1936	225301 – 225400	IIIa	1936/37
185501 – 185650	Standard	1936	202801 – 202900	II	1936	225401 – 225600	III	1936/37
185651 – 185700	III	1936	202901 – 203100	IIIa	1936	225601 – 226300	IIIa	1936/37
185701 – 185800	Standard	1936	203101 – 203300	III	1936	226301 – 226400	III	1936/37
185801 – 186100	IIIa	1936	203301 – 203400	Standard	1936	226401 – 227000	IIIa	1936/37
186101 – 186200	III	1936	203401 – 204100	IIIa	1936	227001 – 227050	III	1936/37
186201 – 186500	IIIa	1936	204101 – 204200	III	1936	227051 – 227600	IIIa	1936/37
186501 – 186550	III	1936	204201 – 204300	IIIa	1936	227601 – 227650	III	1936/37
186551 – 186800	IIIa	1936	204301 – 204500	II	1936	227651 – 231500	IIIa	1936/37
186801 – 186900	III	1936	204501 – 204600	III	1936	231501 – 231600	III	1936/37
186901 – 186950	IIIa	1936	204601 – 204800	IIIa	1936	231601 – 231800	IIIa	1936/37
186951 – 187000	III	1936	204801 – 205000	III	1936	231801 – 231900	III	1936/37
187001 – 187100	IIIa	1936	205001 – 205100	IIIa	1936	231901 – 232200	IIIa	1936/37
187101 – 187200	III	1936	205101 – 205300	III	1936	232201 – 232500	III	1936/37
187201 – 187400	IIIa	1936	205301 – 205400	IIIa	1936	232501 – 232800	IIIa	1936/37
187401 – 187500	III	1936	205401 – 205500	II	1936	232801 – 232900	III	1936/37
187501 – 187650	II	1936	205501 – 205700	Standard	1936	232901 – 233400	IIIa	1936/37
187651 – 187775	III	1936	205701 – 207300	IIIa	1936	233401 – 233500	III	1936/37
187776 – 187785	IIIa	1936	207301 – 207400	II	1936	233501 – 233700	Standard	1936/37
187786 – 187850	III	1936	207401 – 207600	Standard	1936	233701 – 233800	III	1936/37
187851 – 188100	IIIa	1936	207601 – 207800	III	1936	233801 – 234000	IIIa	1936/37
188101 – 188300	III	1936	207801 – 208000	IIIa	1936	234001 – 234100	II	1936/37
188301 – 188600	Standard	1936	208001 – 208300	III	1936	234101 – 234200	III	1936/37
188601 – 188750	II	1936	208301 – 208600	IIIa	1936	234201 – 234500	IIIa	1936/37
188751 – 189300	IIIa	1936	208601 – 208800	III	1936	234501 – 234600	III	1936/37
189301 – 189475	III	1936	208801 – 209000	IIIa	1936	234601 – 235100	IIIa	1937
189476 – 189800	IIIa	1936	209001 – 209600	III	1936	235101 – 235200	III	1937
189801 – 189900	III	1936	209601 – 209900	II	1936	235201 – 235800	IIIa	1937
189901 – 190200	IIIa	1936	209901 – 210100	IIIa	1936	235801 – 235875	III	1937
190201 – 190500	III	1936	210101 – 210200	III	1936	235876 – 236200	IIIa	1937
190501 – 190700	IIIa	1936	210201 – 210400	IIIa	1936	236201 – 236300	III	1937
190701 – 190900	III	1936	210401 – 210900	Standard	1936	236301 – 236500	IIIa	1937
190901 – 191100	IIIa	1936	210901 – 211000	III	1936	236501 – 236700	II	1937
191101 – 191200	III	1936	211001 – 211600	IIIa	1936	236701 – 236800	IIIa	1937
191201 – 191300	II	1936	211601 – 211700	III	1936	236801 – 236900	III	1937
191301 – 191350	IIIa	1936	211701 – 211800	IIIa	1936	236901 – 237000	IIIa	1937
191351 – 191500	III	1936	211801 – 211900	II	1936	237001 – 237200	III	1937
191501 – 191650	II	1936	211901 – 212400	IIIa	1936	237201 – 237500	IIIa	1937
191651 – 191750	Standard	1936	212401 – 212700	Standard	1936	237501 – 237600	III	1937
191751 – 191850	III	1936	212701 – 212800	IIIa	1936	237601 – 238000	IIIa	1937
191851 – 192100	IIIa	1936	212801 – 213200	III	1936	238001 – 238100	III	1937
192101 – 192400	III	1936	213201 – 213300	IIIa	1936	238101 – 238500	IIIa	1937
192401 – 192500	IIIa	1936	213301 – 213600	Standard	1936	238501 – 238600	III	1937
192501 – 192800	III	1936	213601 – 213700	II	1936	238601 – 238800	IIIa	1937
192801 – 192950	II	1936	213701 – 214400	IIIa	1936	238801 – 238825	III	1937
192951 – 193200	IIIa	1936	214401 – 214800	Standard	1936	238826 – 238900	IIIa	1937
193201 – 193450	Standard	1936	214801 – 215300	IIIa	1936	238901 – 239000	III	1937
193451 – 193500	IIIa	1936	215301 – 216000	III	1936	239001 – 239100	IIIa	1937
193501 – 193600	III	1936	216001 – 216300	IIIa	1936	239101 – 239300	III	1937
193601 – 194300	IIIa	1936	216301 – 216500	II	1936	239301 – 239400	IIIa	1937
194301 – 194650	III	1936	216501 – 216800	IIIa	1936	239401 – 239600	III	1937
194651 – 194850	II	1936	216801 – 217000	III	1936	239601 – 239700	IIIa	1937
194851 – 194950	Standard	1936	217001 – 217200	IIIa	1936	239701 – 239800	III	1937
194951 – 196200	IIIa	1936	217201 – 217300	III	1936	239801 – 240000	Standard	1937
196201 – 196300	III	1936	217301 – 217500	Standard	1936	240001 – 241000	IIIb	1937/38
196301 – 196400	IIIa	1936	217501 – 217700	III	1937	241001 – 241100	IIIa	1937/38
196401 – 196550	II	1936	217701 – 217900	II	1936/37	241101 – 241300	III	1937/38
196551 – 196750	Standard	1936	217901 – 218300	IIIa	1936/37	241301 – 241500	IIIa	1937/38

Leica-No.	Model	Year	Leica-No.	Model	Year	Leica-No.	Model	Year
241501 — 241700	II	1937/38	266001 — 266100	IIIa	1937	294901 — 295100	IIIa	1938
241701 — 241900	Standard	1937/38	266101 — 266200	III	1937	295101 — 295200	III	1938
241901 — 242000	II	1937/38	266201 — 266400	IIIa	1937	295201 — 295300	IIIa	1938
242001 — 243000	IIIb	1937/38	266401 — 266500	III	1937	295301 — 295400	Standard	1938
243001 — 243400	IIIa	1937/38	266501 — 266800	II	1937	295401 — 295500	III	1938
243401 — 243500	III	1937/38	266801 — 266900	IIIa	1937	295501 — 296000	IIIa	1938
243501 — 243800	II	1937/38	266901 — 267000	III	1937	296001 — 296200	II	1938
243801 — 244100	IIIa	1937/38	267001 — 267700	IIIa	1937	296201 — 296500	IIIa	1938
244101 — 244200	III	1937/38	267701 — 267800	III	1937	296501 — 296600	III	1938
244201 — 244400	Standard	1937/38	267801 — 267900	IIIa	1937	296691 — 296900	Standard	1938
244401 — 244600	III	1937/38	267901 — 268000	Standard		296901 — 297100	II	1938
244601 — 244800	IIIa	1937/38	268001 — 268100	IIIa	1937/38	297101 — 297200	IIIa	1938
244801 — 245000	Standard	1937/38	268101 — 268200	III	1938	297201 — 297400	III	1938
245001 — 245100	IIIa	1937/38	268201 — 268400	IIIa	1937	297401 — 297900	IIIa	1938
245101 — 245300	III	1937/38	268401 — 268500	III	1938	297901 — 298000	III	1938
245301 — 246200	IIIa	1937/38	268501 — 268700	IIIa	1938	298001 — 299000	IIIa	1938
246201 — 246300	III	1937/38	268701 — 268800	III	1938	299001 — 299200	III	1938
246301 — 246400	IIIa	1937/38	268801 — 269300	IIIa	1938	299201 — 299500	IIIa	1938
246401 — 246500	III	1937/38	269301 — 269400	III	1938	299501 — 299600	III	1938
246501 — 246700	II	1937/38	269401 — 269600	IIIa	1938	299601 — 299800	IIIa	1938
246701 — 247500	IIIa	1937/38	269601 — 269700	III	1938	299801 — 299900	III	1938
247501 — 247600	II	1937/38	269701 — 270100	IIIa	1938	299901 — 300000	Standard	1938
247601 — 248300	IIIa	1937/38	270101 — 270200	III	1938	300001 — 300100	Reporter	1938
248301 — 248400	II	1937/38	270201 — 270300	IIIa	1938	300101 — 300200	Standard	1938
248401 — 248600	Standard	1937/38	270301 — 270400	III	1938	300201 — 300300	II	1938
248601 — 248900	IIIa	1937	270401 — 271000	IIIa	1938	300301 — 300400	Standard	1938
248901 — 249000	III	1937	271001 — 271100	II	1938	300401 — 300700	IIIa	1938
249001 — 249200	IIIa	1937	271101 — 271600	Standard	1938	300701 — 300800	III	1938
249201 — 249400	II	1937	271601 — 271700	II	1938	300801 — 301000	IIIa	1938
249401 — 249500	III	1937	271701 — 271800	III	1938	301001 — 301100	III	1938
249501 — 249700	Standard	1937	271801 — 272300	IIIa	1938	301101 — 301400	IIIa	1938
249701 — 249800	IIIa	1937	272301 — 272400	II	1938	301401 — 301500	III	1938
249801 — 249900	III	1937	272401 — 274800	IIIa	1938	301501 — 301600	III	1938
249901 — 250300	IIIa	1937	274801 — 275200	III	1938	301601 — 201700	Standard	1938
250301 — 250400	III	1937	275201 — 275350	IIIa	1938	301701 — 301800	III	1938
250401 — 251200	IIIa	1937	275351 — 275650	II	1938	301801 — 301900	IIIa	1938
251201 — 251300	II	1937	275651 — 275675	IIIa	1938	301901 — 302000	III	1938
251301 — 251500	Standard	1937	275676 — 275700	III	1938	302001 — 302500	IIIa	1938
251501 — 251600	IIIa	1937	275701 — 275800	IIIa	1938	302501 — 302800	II	1938
251601 — 251800	II	1937	275801 — 276400	III	1938	302801 — 302900	III	1938
251801 — 252000	III	1937	276401 — 277000	IIIa	1938	302901 — 303200	IIIa	1938
252001 — 252200	II	1937	277001 — 277100	III	1938	303201 — 303300	III	1938
252201 — 252900	IIIa	1937	277101 — 277500	IIIa	1938	303301 — 303700	IIIa	1938
252901 — 253000	III	1937	277505 — 277900	Standard	1938	303701 — 303800	II	1938
253001 — 253200	IIIa	1937	277901 — 278100	II	1938	303801 — 303900	Standard	1938
253201 — 253400	III	1937	278101 — 278200	III	1938	303901 — 304400	IIIa	1938
253401 — 253500	IIIa	1937	278201 — 278500	IIIa	1938	304401 — 304500	III	1938
253501 — 253600	III	1937	278501 — 278525	III	1938	304501 — 304700	IIIa	1938
253601 — 253800	Standard	1937	278526 — 278550	IIIa	1938	304701 — 304800	III	1938
253801 — 254000	IIIa	1937	278551 — 278600	III	1938	304801 — 304900	IIIa	1938
254001 — 254200	III	1937	278601 — 278800	Standard	1938	304901 — 305000	III	1938
254201 — 254600	IIIa	1937	278801 — 279000	IIIa	1938	305001 — 305600	IIIa	1938
254601 — 254800	II	1937	279001 — 279200	III	1938	305601 — 305700	III	1938
254801 — 254900	III	1937	279201 — 279400	II	1938	305701 — 305800	Standard	1938
254901 — 256400	IIIa	1937	279401 — 280000	IIIa	1938	305801 — 306200	IIIa	1938
256401 — 256600	Standard	1937	280001 — 286500	IIIb	1938	306201 — 306300	III	1938
256601 — 256800	IIIa	1937	286501 — 286800	Standard	1938	306301 — 306500	II	1938
256801 — 256900	III	1937	286801 — 287000	III	1938	306501 — 306600	III	1938
256901 — 257400	IIIa	1937	287001 — 287200	IIIa	1938	306601 — 306800	IIIa	1938
257401 — 257525	III	1937	287201 — 287300	III	1938	306801 — 307000	III	1938
257526 — 257600	IIIa	1937	287307 — 287400	IIIa	1938	307001 — 307500	IIIa	1938
257601 — 257800	Standard	1937	287401 — 287600	II	1938	307501 — 308000	Standard	1938
257801 — 258200	III	1937	287601 — 288000	IIIa	1938	308001 — 308100	IIIa	1938
258201 — 259500	IIIa	1937	288001 — 290200	IIIb	1938/39	308101 — 308200	III	1938
259501 — 259800	II	1937	290201 — 290500	IIIa	1938	308201 — 308300	II	1938
259801 — 259900	Standard	1937	290501 — 290800	III	1938	308301 — 308500	Standard	1938
259901 — 260000	IIIa	1937	290801 — 291000	IIIa	1938	308501 — 308600	III	1938
260001 — 260100	Reporter	1937	291001 — 291200	Standard	1938	308601 — 308700	IIIa	1938
260101 — 260200	IIIa	1937	291201 — 291500	IIIa	1938	308701 — 308800	III	1938
260201 — 260600	III	1937	291501 — 291600	III	1938	308801 — 309000	IIIa	1938
260601 — 260800	IIIa	1937	291601 — 291800	IIIa	1938	309001 — 309200	Standard	1938
260801 — 260900	III	1937	291801 — 292000	Standard	1938	309201 — 309300	IIIa	1938
260901 — 261200	IIIa	1937	292001 — 292200	II	1938	309301 — 309400	III	1938
261201 — 261300	III	1937	291201 — 292400	Standard	1938	309401 — 309500	IIIa	1938
261301 — 261500	IIIa	1937	292401 — 292600	IIIa	1938	309501 — 309700	II	1938
261501 — 261600	III	1937	292601 — 292700	III	1938	309701 — 310000	IIIa	1938/39
261601 — 261800	IIIa	1937	292701 — 293000	IIIa	1938	310001 — 310200	III	1938/39
261801 — 262000	Standard	1937	293001 — 293100	III	1938	310201 — 310400	IIIa	1938/39
262001 — 262800	IIIa	1937	293101 — 293200	IIIa	1938	310401 — 310500	III	1938/39
262801 — 263000	III	1937	293201 — 293400	III	1938	310501 — 310600	IIIa	1939
263001 — 263600	IIIa	1937	293401 — 293500	II	1938	310601 — 311000	III	1938/39
263601 — 263900	II	1937	293501 — 293900	IIIa	1938	311001 — 311200	II	1938
263901 — 264000	III	1937	293901 — 294000	Standard	1938	311201 — 311400	IIIa	1939
264001 — 264800	IIIa	1937	294001 — 294600	IIIb	1939	311401 — 311700	III	1939
264801 — 265000	Standard	1937	294601 — 294800	II	1938	311701 — 311800	IIIa	1939
265001 — 266000	IIIb	1937	294801 — 294900	III	1938	311801 — 311900	III	1939

Leica-No.	Model	Year
311901 – 312000	IIIa	1939
312001 – 312200	Standard	1939
312201 – 312400	IIIa	1939
312401 – 312500	III	1939
312501 – 312800	Standard	1939
312801 – 313000	IIIa	1939
313001 – 313100	III	1939
313101 – 313200	IIIa	1939
313201 – 313300	III	1939
313301 – 313400	IIIa	1939
313401 – 313500	Standard	1939
313501 – 313600	III	1939
313601 – 314000	III	1939
314001 – 314100	III	1939
314101 – 314300	II	1939
314301 – 314500	Standard	1939
314501 – 314600	II	1939
314601 – 314700	III	1939
314701 – 314800	IIIa	1939
314801 – 314900	III	1939
314901 – 315000	IIIa	1939
315001 – 315100	II	1939
315101 – 315400	IIIa	1939
315401 – 315500	II	1939
315501 – 315700	IIIa	1939
315701 – 315800	III	1939
315801 – 316100	IIIa	1939
316101 – 316400	III	1939
316401 – 316700	IIIa	1939
316701 – 316900	Standard	1939
316901 – 317000	II	1939
317001 – 318000	IIIb	1939
318001 – 318200	IIIa	1939
318201 – 318300	II	1939
318301 – 318500	Standard	1939
318501 – 318800	II	1939
318801 – 318900	IIIa	1939
318901 – 319901	III	1939
319001 – 320000	IIIb	1939
320001 – 320200	II	1939
320201 – 320400	III	1939
320401 – 320600	IIIa	1939
320601 – 320700	II	1939
320701 – 321000	Standard	1939
321001 – 322000	IIIb	1939
322001 – 322200	II	1939
322201 – 322700	Standard	1939
322701 – 322800	IIIa	1939
322801 – 323000	III	1939
323001 – 324000	IIIb	1939
324001 – 324100	Reporter	1939
324101 – 324700	IIIa	1939
324701 – 324800	III	1939
324801 – 325000	II	1939
325001 – 325200	IIIa	1939
325201 – 325275	III	1939
325276 – 325300	IIIa	1939
325301 – 325400	I	1939
325401 – 325600	IIIa	1939
325601 – 325800	III	1939
325801 – 325900	IIIa	1939
325901 – 326000	II	1939
326001 – 327000	IIIb	1939
327001 – 327200	II	1939
327201 – 327400	III	1939
327401 – 327500	IIIa	1939
327501 – 327600	III	1939
327601 – 327800	IIIa	1939
327801 – 328000	Standard	1939
328001 – 329000	IIIb	1939
329001 – 329400	Standard	1939
329401 – 329600	II	1939
329601 – 329800	IIIa	1939
329801 – 329900	III	1939
329901 – 330000	IIIa	1939
330001 – 330200	III	1939
330201 – 330300	II	1939
330301 – 330500	Standard	1939
330501 – 330700	III	1939
330701 – 330800	IIIa	1939
330801 – 331000	Standard	1939
331001 – 332000	IIIb	1939
332001 – 332500	IIIa	1939
332501 – 332600	III	1939
332601 – 333000	IIIa	1939
333001 – 333100	III	1939
333101 – 333300	IIIa	1939
333301 – 333600	Standard	1939
333601 – 334000	IIIb	1939
334001 – 334200	III	1939
334201 – 334400	IIIa	1939
334401 – 334600	III	1939
334601 – 335000	IIIa	1939
335001 – 337000	IIIb	1939/40
337001 – 337200	II	1939
337201 – 337400	IIIa	1939
337401 – 337500	III	1939
337501 – 337900	IIIa	1939
337901 – 338100	II	1939
338101 – 338200	IIIa	1939
338201 – 338600	III	1939
338601 – 338900	IIIa	1939
338901 – 339000	III	1939
339001 – 340000	IIIb	1939/40
340001 – 340200	IIIa	1939
340201 – 340400	III	1939
340401 – 340600	IIIa	1939
340601 – 340700	III	1939
340701 – 341000	IIIa	1939
341001 – 341300	II	1939/40
341301 – 341500	Standard	1939
341501 – 341700	III	1939
341701 – 341900	IIIa	1939
341901 – 342000	III	1939
342001 – 342200	Standard	1939
342201 – 342300	III	1939
342301 – 342900	IIIa	1939
342901 – 343100	III	1939
343101 – 344000	IIIa	1939
344001 – 348500	IIIb	1939/40
348501 – 348600	Standard	1939/40
348601 – 349000	IIIb	1940
349001 – 349050	Reporter	1940
349051 – 349300	Standard	1940
349301 – 351100	IIIb	1940
351101 – 351150	II	1940
351151 – 352000	IIIb	1940
352001 – 352100	II	1940
352101 – 352150	Standard	1940
352151 – 352300	II	1940
352301 – 352500	Reporter	1940/41/42
352501 – 352900	II	1940/41/42
352901 – 353600	Standard	1940/41/42
353601 – 353800	Reporter	1942/43
353801 – 354000	Standard	1942/47
354001 – 354050	IIIa	1941/47
354051 – 354075	IIIa	1941/46
354076 – 354100	II	1947
354101 – 354200	IIIa	1947
354201 – 354400	II	1942/44
354401 – 355000	IIIb	1946
355001 – 355650	Standard	1947/48
355651 – 356500		
356501 – 356550	IIIa	1947/48
356651 – 356700	II	1947/48
356701 – 357200	IIIa	1948/50
357201 – 358500		
358501 – 358650	II	1948
358651 – 360000		
360001 – 360100	IIIa	1940/42
360101 – 367000	IIIc	1940
367001 – 367325	IIIc	1941/44
367326 – 367500	IIIc	1945
367501 – 368800	IIIc	1940/41
368801 – 368950	IIIc	1941
368951 – 369000	IIIc	1941
369001 – 369050	IIIc	1941
369051 – 369450	IIIc	1941
369451 – 390000	IIIc	1941/42
390001 – 397650	IIIc	1943/46
397651 – 399999		
400000 – 440000	IIIc	1946/47
440001 – 449999	IIc	1948/51
450000	IIIc	1949
450001 – 451000	IIc	1951
451001 – 455000	IIf	1951
455001 – 460000	Ic	1949/50
460001 – 465000	IIIc	1948/49
465001 – 480000	IIIc	1949
480001 – 495000	IIIc	1949/50
495001 – 520000	IIIc	1950
520001 – 524000	Ic	1950/51
524001 – 525000	IIIc	1950/51
525001 – 540000	IIIf	1950/51
540001 – 560000	IIIf	1951
560001 – 562800	Ic	1951
562801 – 565000	If	1951
565001 – 570000	IIIf	1951
570001 – 575000	IIf	1951/52
575001 – 580000	If*	1952/53
580001 – 610000	IIIf	1951/52
610001 – 611000	IIIf/ELC	1952
611001 – 615000	IIIf*	1952/53
Leica with light weight shutter		
615001 – 650000	IIIf	1952/53
650001 – 655000	IIf	1953
655001 – 673000	IIIf	1953
673001 – 674999	If	1953/54
675000	IIIf	1953
675001 – 680000	IIf	1953/54
680001 – 682000	IIf	1954
682001 – 684000	If	1955
684001 – 685000	IIIf/ELC	1953
685001 – 699999	IIIf Vorl.	1954
700000	M3	1954
700001 – 710000	M3	1954
710001 – 711000	IIIf Vorl. ELC	1954
711001 – 713000	IIf	1954
713001 – 729000	IIIf Vorl.	1954
729001 – 730000	IIIf Vorl. ELC	1954
730001 – 746450	M3	1955
746451 – 746500	M3 ELC	1955
746501 – 750000	M3	1955
750001 – 759700	M3	1955
759701 – 760000	M3 ELC	1955
760001 – 762000	If	1955
762001 – 765000	IIf	1955
765001 – 773000	IIIf Vorl.	1955
773001 – 774000	IIIf ELC	1955
774001 – 775000	IIIf	1955
775001 – 780000	M3	1955
780001 – 780090	M3 ELC	1955
780091 – 780100	If	1957
780101 – 787000	M3	1955
787001 – 789000	IIf	1955
789001 – 790000	If	1955
790001 – 799000	IIIf	1955
799001 – 799999	IIf	1956
800000 – 805000	M3	1955
805001 – 805100	M3 ELC	1955
805101 – 807500	M3	1955
807501 – 808500	If	1956
808501 – 810000	IIf	1956
810001 – 815000	IIIf	1956
815001 – 816000	If	1956
816001 – 816900	M3	1956
816901 – 817000	M3 ELC	1956
817001 – 820500	M3	1956
820501 – 821500	IIf	1956
821501 – 822000	IIf	1956
822001 – 822900	If	1956
822901 – 823000	IIIf kältef.	1956
823001 – 823500	IIIf	1956
823501 – 823867	IIIf ELC	1956
823868 – 825000	IIIf	1956
825001 – 826000	IIIg	1956
826001 – 829750	IIIg	1956
829751 – 829850	IIIf ELC	1956
829851 – 830000	M3 ELC	1956
830001 – 837500	M3	1956
837501 – 837620	M3 ELC	1956
837621 – 837720	IIIf ELC	1956
837721 – 839620	M3	1956
839621 – 839700	M3 ELC	1956
839701 – 840500	M3	1956
840501 – 840820	M3 ELC	1956
840821 – 844780	M3	1956
844781 – 845000	M3 ELC	1956
845001 – 845380	IIIg ELC	1956
845381 – 850900	IIIg	1956
850901 – 851000	If	1956
851001 – 854000	M3	1956
854001 – 858000	M3	1957
858001 – 861600	IIIg	1957
861601 – 862000	IIIg ELC	1957
MP- 1 – 11	MP	1956
862001 – 866620	M3	1957

Leica-No.	Model	Year
866621 – 867000	M3 ELC	1957
867001 – 871200	IIIg	1957
871201 – 872000	IIIg ELC	1957
872001 – 877000	M3	1957
877001 – 882000	IIIg	1957
882001 – 886700	M3	1957
MP- 13 – 150	MP schw. l.	1957
MP-151 – 450	MP chrom	1957
886701 – 887000	M3 ELC	1957
887001 – 888000	Ig	1957
888001 – 893000	IIIg	1957
893001 – 894000	M3	1957
894001 – 894570	M3 ELC	1957
894571 – 898000	M3	1957
898001 – 903000	M3	1957
903001 – 903300	M3 ELC	1957
903301 – 907000	IIIg	1957
907001 – 910000	Ig	1957
910001 – 910500	M3	1957
910501 – 910600	M3 oliv. l.	1957
910601 – 915000	M3	1957
915001 – 915200	M3	1957
915201 – 916000	M3	1957
916001 – 919250	M3	1958
919251 – 920500	M3	1958
920501 – 920520	M3	1958
920521 – 924400	M3	1958
924401 – 924500	M3 ELC	1958
924501 – 924568	Ig	1958
924569 – 924588	Ig	1958
924589 – 926000	Ig	1958
926001 – 926200	M2	1957
926201 – 926700	Ig	1958
926701 – 928922	M3	1959
928923 – 929000	Postk.	1958
929001 – 931000	M2	1958
931001 – 933000	M2	1958
933001 – 934000	IIIg	1958
934001 – 934200	IIIg ELC	1958
934201 – 935000	IIIg	1958
935001 – 935512	MP2	1958
935513 – 937500	M2	1958
937501 – 937620	M2	1958
937621 – 937650	M2 ELC	1958
937651 – 940000	M2	1958
940001 – 942900	M2	1958
942901 – 943000	M2 ELC	1958
943001 – 944000	IIIg	1958
944001 – 946000	M2	1958
946001 – 946300	M2	1958
946301 – 946400	M2 ELC	1958
946401 – 946900	M2	1958
946901 – 947000	M2 ELC	1958
947001 – 948000	M2	1958
948001 – 948500	IIIg	1958
948501 – 948600	M2 ELC	1958
948601 – 949100	M2 schw. l.	1958
949101 – 949400	M2 Vorl.	1958
949401 – 950000	M2	1959
950001 – 950300	M1	1959
950301 – 951900	M3	1959
951901 – 952000	M3 ELC	1959
952001 – 952015	MP2	1959
952016 – 952500	M1	1959
952501 – 954800	M3	1959
954801 – 954900	M3 ELC	1959
954901 – 955000	M3 ELC	1959
955001 – 956500	IIIg	1959
956501 – 957000	M1	1959
957001 – 959400	M3	1959
959401 – 959500	M3 schw. l.	1959
959501 – 960200	M2 Vorl.	1959
960201 – 960500	M2	1960
960501 – 961500	M2	1959
961501 – 961700	M3 ELC	1959
961701 – 966500	M3	1959
966501 – 967500	M1	1959
967501 – 968350	M2	1959
968351 – 968500	M3 ELC	1959
968501 – 970000	IIIg	1959
970001 – 971500	M2	1959
971501 – 972000	IIIg	1959
972001 – 974700	M3	1959
974701 – 975000	M3 ELC	1959
975001 – 975800	M2	1959
975801 – 976100	M2 Vorl.	1960

Leica-No.	Model	Year
976101 – 976500	M2	1959
976501 – 979500	M3	1959
979501 – 980450	M1	1959
980451 – 980500	M1 oliv. l.	1960
980501 – 982000	IIIg	1959
982001 – 982150	M2 Vorl.	1960
982151 – 982900	M2	1959
982901 – 983500	M2 Vorl.	1959
983501 – 984000	M2	1959
984001 – 984200	M3 ELC	1959
984201 – 987000	M3	1959
987001 – 987200	M3 ELC	1960
987201 – 987300	M2 ELC	1960
987301 – 987600	Ig	1960
987601 – 987900	IIIg	1960
987901 – 988025	IIIg schw. l.	1960
988026 – 988350	IIIg	1960
988351 – 988650	M2	1960
988651 – 989250	M2 Vorl.	1960
989251 – 989650	M2 Vorl.	1960
989651 – 989800	M2	1960
989801 – 990500	M2 Vorl.	1960
990501 – 990750	M2 schw. l.	1960
990751 – 993500	M3	1960
993501 – 993750	M3 schw. l.	1960
993751 – 995000	M2	1960
995001 – 995100	M2 ELC	1960
995101 – 995400	M2 Vorl.	1960
995401 – 996000	M2	1960
996001 – 998000	M3	1960
998001 – 998300	M3 ELC	1960
998301 – 1000000	M3	1960
1000001 – 1003700	M3	1960
1003701 – 1004000	M3 ELC	1960
1004001 – 1005100	M2 VW	1960
1005101 – 1005350	M2 VW	1960
1005351 – 1005450	M2 ELC	1960
1005451 – 1005750	M2	1960
1005771 – 1007000	M2	1960
1007001 – 1011000	M3	1960
1011001 – 1014000	M2	1960
1014001 – 1014300	M3 ELC	1960
1014301 – 1017000	M3	1960
1017001 – 1017500	M1	1961
1017501 – 1017900	M2	1961
1017901 – 1018000	M2 ELC	1961
1018001 – 1020100	M2	1961
1020101 – 1020200	M2 ELC	1961
1020201 – 1022000	M2	1961
1022001 – 1022700	M3	1961
1022701 – 1023000	M3 ELC	1961
1023001 – 1027800	M3	1961
1027801 – 1028000	M3 ELC	1961
1028001 – 1028600	M1	1961
1028601 – 1031800	M2	1961
1031801 – 1032000	M2 schw. l.	1961
1032001 – 1035400	M3	1961
1035401 – 1035925	M1	1961
1036001 – 1026050	M2 ELC	1961
1036051 – 1036350	M3 ELC	1961
1036351 – 1037950	M2	1961
1037951 – 1038000	M2 ELC	1962
1038001 – 1038800	M3	1961
1038801 – 1039000	M3 schw. l.	1961
1039001 – 1040000	M3	1961
1040001 – 1040066	M1	1962
1040067 – 1040068	M3	1962
1040069 – 1040070	M1	1961
1040071 –	M3	1961
1040072 – 1040094	M1	1961
1040095 – 1040096	M3	1962
1040097 – 1040600	M1	1961
1040601 – 1043000	M3	1961
1043001 – 1043800	M2	1962
1043801 – 1044000	M2 schw. l.	1962
1044001 – 1046000	M3 schw. l.	1962
1046001 – 1046500	M1	1962
1046501 – 1048000	M3	1962
1047801 – 1048000	M3 ELC	1962
1048001 – 1050000	M2	1962
1050001 – 1050500	M1	1962
1050501 – 1053100	M2	1962
1053101 – 1053250	M2 lack.	1962
1053251 – 1054900	M2	1962

Leica-No.	Model	Year
1054901 – 1055000	M2 ELC	1962
1055001 – 1059849	M3	1962
1059850 – 1059999	M3 lack.	1962
1060000 –	M3	1962
1060001 – 1060500	M1	1962
1060501 – 1061700	M2	1962
1061701 – 1061800	M2 ELC	1962
1061801 – 1063000	M2	1962
1063001 – 1065000	M3	1962
1065001 – 1065200	M3 ELC	1962
1065201 – 1067500	M3	1962
1067501 – 1067870	M1	1963
1067871 – 1068000	Postk.	1963
1068001 – 1070000	M2	1963
1070001 – 1074000	M3	1963
1074001 – 1074500	M1	1963
1074501 – 1077000	M2	1963
1077001 – 1080000	M3	1963
1080001 – 1085000	Leicaflex	1964/65
1085001 – 1085450	M1	1963
1085451 – 1085500	M1	1963
1085501 – 1088000	M2	1963
1088001 – 1091000	M3	1963
1091001 – 1091300	M1	1964
1091301 – 1093500	M2	1964
1093501 – 1093750	M2 lack.	1964
1093751 – 1093800	M2 ELC	1964
1093801 – 1097700	M3	1964
1097701 – 1097850	M3 lack	1964
1097851 – 1098000	M3 ELC	1964
1098001 – 1098100	M1	1964
1098184 – 1098300	M1	1964
1098301 – 1199800	M2	1964
1099801 – 1099900	M2 ELC	1964
1099901 – 1100000	M2	1964
1100001 – 1102000	M3	1964
1102001 – 1102500	M1	1964
1102501 – 1102800	MD	1964
1102801 – 1102900	M1	1964
1102901 – 1103000	M3	1965
1103001 – 1104900	M2	1965
1104901 – 1105000	M2 ELC	1965
1105001 – 1106900	M3	1965
1106901 – 1107000	M3 ELC	1965
1107001 – 1109000	M2	1965
1109001 – 1110500	M3	1965
1110501 – 1112000	M3	1965
1112001 – 1114975	M2	1965
1114976 – 1115000	Postk.	1965
1115001 – 1128000	Leicaflex	1965
1128001 – 1128400	MD	1965
1128401 – 1130000	M3	1965
1130001 – 1130300	M2 lack.	1965
1130301 – 1132900	M2	1965
1132901 – 1133000	M2 ELC	1965
1133001 – 1134000	M3	1965
1134001 – 1134150	M3 lack.	1965
1134151 – 1135000	M3	1965
1135001 – 1135100	M3 ELC	1965
1135101 – 1136000	M3	1965
1136001 – 1136500	MD	1965
1136501 – 1137000	MD	1966
1137001 – 1138900	M2	1966
1138901 – 1139000	M2 ELC	1966
1139001 – 1140900	M3	1966
1140901 – 1141000	M3 ELC	1966
1141001 – 1141896	MD	1966
1141897 – 1141968	Postk.	1966
1141969 – 1142000	Postk. 24 x 27	1966
1142001 – 1145000	M2	1966
1145001 – 1155000	Leicaflex	1966
1155001 – 1157590	M3	1966
1157591 – 1157600	M3 lack.	1966
1157601 – 1158995	M3	1966
1159001 – 1160200	MDa	1966
1160201 – 1160820	MD	1966
1160821 – 1161420	MDa	1966
1161421 – 1163770	M2	1966
1163771 – 1164046	M2 Motor	1966
1164047 – 1164845	M2	1966
1164846 – 1164865	M3	1966
1164866 – 1164940	Postk. 24 x 36	1967
1164941 – 1165000	M2	1967
1165001 – 1173000	Leicaflex	1967

Leica-No.	Model	Year
1173001 – 1173250	Leicaflex SL	1968
1173251 – 1174700	Leicaflex	1968
1174701 – 1175000	Leicaflex SL	1968
1175001 – 1178000	M4	1967
1178001 – 1178100	M4 ELC	1967
1178101 – 1185000	M4	1967
1185001 – 1185150	M4 Motor	1968
1185151 – 1185290	M4 lack.	1968
1185291 – 1185300	Postk. 24 x 27	1968
1185301 – 1195000	M4	1968/69
1195001 – 1205000	Leicaflex SL	1968
1205001 – 1206736	MDa	1968/69
1206737 – 1206891	M4 Motor	1969
1206892 – 1206941	Postk. 24 x 36	1969
1206942 – 1206961	Postk. 24 x 27	1969
1207000	M2 Lack.	1968
1207001 – 1207480	M4 lack.	1968/69
1207481 – 1215000	M4	1968/69
1215001 – 1225000	Leicaflex SL	1969
1225001 – 1225800	M4 lack.	1969
1225801 – 1235000	M4	1969
1235001 – 1245000	Leicaflex SL	1969/70
1245001 – 1246200	MDa	1969
1246201 – 1248100	M4 lack.	1969/70
1248101 – 1248200	M4 Motor	1969
1248201 – 1250200	M2R	1969/70
1250201 – 1254650	M4	1970
1254651 – 1255000	MDa	1970
1255001 – 1265000	Leicaflex SL	1970
1265001 – 1266000	MDa	1970
1266001 – 1266100	M4 lack.	1970/71
1266101 – 1266131	M4 olivegr.	1970
1266132 – 1267100	M4 lack.	1970
1267101 – 1267500	M4 Motor	1970
1267501 – 1273921	M4	1970/71
1273922 – 1273925	Postk.24x27	1971
1273926 – 1274000	Postk.24x36	1971
1274001 – 1274100	M4 Motor	1971
1274101 – 1275000	MD a	1971
1275001 – 1285000	LeicaflexSL	1971
1285001 – 1286200	MD a	1971
1286201 – 1286700	M4 lack.	1971
1286701 – 1286760	Postk.24x27	1972
1286761 – 1287000	unbelegt	
1287001 – 1287050	M5 Nullserie	1971
1287051 – 1287250	M5 hell	1971
1287251 – 1288000	M5 schwarz	1971
1288001 – 1289000	M5 hell	1971
1289001 – 1291400	M5 schwarz	1971/72
1291401 – 1293000	M5 hell	1971/72
1293001 – 1293672	MD a	1971/72
1293673 – 1293770	MDa Blitzsp.	1972
1293771 – 1293775	M4-KE 7	1972
1293776 – 1293877	MDa Blitzsp.	1972
1293878 – 1294000	Postk.24x27	1972
1294001 – 1294500	M5 hell	1972
1294501 – 1295000	M4-KE 7	1972
1295001 – 1296500	LeicaflexSL	1972
1296501 – 1300000	M5 schwarz	1972
1300001 – 1335000	CL	1973/74
1335001 – 1336990	LeicaflexSL	1972

Leica-No.	Model	Year
1336991 – 1337110	LeicaflexSLmot	1972
1337111 – 1338220	LeicaflexSL	1972
1338221 – 1338300	LeicaflexSL mot	1972
1338301 – 1339870	LeicaflexSL	1972
1339871 – 1339900	LeicaflexSL mot	1972
1339901 – 1341450	LeicaflexSL	1972
1341451 – 1341470	LeicaflexSL mot	1972
1341471 – 1342020	LeicaflexSL	1973
1342021 – 1342050	LeicaflexSL mot	1973
1342051 – 1342900	LeicaflexSL	1973
1342901 – 1343000	LeicaflexSL mot	1973
1343001 – 1344400	LeicaflexSL	
1344401 – 1344500	LeicaflexSL mot	1973
1344501 – 1345000	LeicaflexSL	1973
1345001 – 1347000	M5 hell	1972
1347001 – 1354000	M5 schwarz	1972
1354001 – 1355000	M5 hell	1972
1355001 – 1356500	M5 hell	1973
1356501 – 1360000	M5 schwarz	1973
1360001 – 1361500	MD a	1973/74
1361501 – 1363000	M5 hell	1973/74
1363001 – 1365000	M5 schwarz	1973
1365001 – 1365380	LeicaflexSL	1973
1365381 – 1365470	LeicaflexSL mot	1973
1365471 – 1366990	LeicaflexSL	1973
1366991 – 1367090	LeicaflexSL mot	1973
1367091 – 1367950	LeicaflexSL	1973
1367951 – 1368020	LeicaflexSL mot	1973
1368021 – 1368850	LeicaflexSL	1973
1368851 – 1368900	LeicaflexSL mot	1973
1368901 – 1369800	LeicaflexSL	1973
1369801 – 1369875	LeicaflexSL2 (Nullserie)	1974
1369876 – 1370700	LeicaflexSL	1973
1370701 – 1372440	LeicaflexSL	1974
1372441 – 1372630	LeicaflexSL mot	1974
1372631 – 1374000	LeicaflexSL	1974
1374001 – 1375000	LeicaflexSL	1974
1375001 – 1378000	M5 schwarz	1973/74
1378001 – 1379000	M5 hell	1973/74
1379001 – 1380000	MD a	1974
1380001 – 1381650	M4 schwarz	1974
1381651 – 1382600	M4 schwarz (Leitz Canada-Gravur)	1974
1382601 – 1383000	M5 hell	1974/75
1383001 – 1384000	M5 schwarz	1974/75
1384001 – 1384600	M4 schwarz	1974
1384601 – 1385000	MD a	1974/75
1385001 – 1386000	LeicaflexSL2	1974/75
1386001 – 1386100	LeicaflexSL2	1975
1386101 – 1386600	LeicaflexSL2	1974/75
1386601 – 1386700	LeicaflxSL2 mot	1975
1386701 – 1387450	LeicaflexSL2	1974/75
1387451 – 1387500	LeicaflxSL2 mot	1975
1387501 – 1391760	LeicaflexSL2	1974/75
1391761 – 1392000	LeicaflxSL2 mot	1975
1392001 – 1393420	LeicaflexSL2	1975
1393421 – 1393510	LeicaflxSL2 mot	1975
1393511 – 1394300	LeicaflexSL2	1975
1394301 – 1394600	LeicaflxSL2 mot	1975
1394601 – 1395000	LeicaflexSL2	1975

Leica-No.	Model	Year
1395001 – 1410000	CL	1974/75
1410001 – 1412550	MD a	1975/76
1412551 – 1413350	M4 schwarz (Leitz Canada-Gravur)	1975
1413351 – 1415000	M4 schwarz	1975
1415001 – 1415140	LeicaflexSL2	1975
1415141 – 1415230	LeicaflxSL2 mot	1975
1415231 – 1421000	LeicaflexSL2	1975
1421001 – 1421150	LeicaflxSL2 mot	1975
1421151 – 1425000	LeicaflexSL2	1975
1425001 – 1440000	CL	1975/76
1440001 – 1443000	LeicaflexSL2	1975/76
1443001 – 1443170	M4 schwarz	1975
1443501 – 1446000	LeicaflexSL2	1976
1446001 – 1446100	R3 hell LW	1976
1446101 – 1447100	R3 hell LP	1976
1447101 – 1449000	R3 schw. LP	1976/77
1449001 – 1450500	R3 schw. LW	1976
1450501 – 1450900	R3 hell LW	1977
1450901 – 1468000	R3 schw. LP	1977/78
1468001 – 1470000	R3 oliv LP	1977/78
1470001 – 1479000	R3 schw. LP	1977/78
1479001 – 1480000	R3 hell LP	1978
1480001 – 1482000	M4-2	1978
1482001 – 1485000	R3 oliv LP	1978
1485001 – 1491000	R3 schw. LP	1978
1491001 – 1492250	R3 hell LP	1978
1492251 – 1502000	R3 mot LP	1978
1502001 – 1508000	M4-2	1978/79
1508001 – 1523750	R3 mot LP	1979
1523751 – 1523850	R3 schw. LP	1979
1523851 – 1524850	R3 gold LP	1979
1524851 – 1525350	R3 hell LP	1979
1525351 – 1527200	M4-2	1979
1527201 – 1527700	M4-2 gold	1979/80
1527701 – 1528150	M4-2	1980
1528151 – 1528650	M4-2 gold	1980
1528651 – 1533350	M4-2	1980
1533351 – 1543350	R4 schw.	1980/81
1543351 – 1545350	M4-P	1980/81
1545351 – 1546350	MD-2	1980/81
1546351 – 1552350	M4-P	1981

KEY

Blitsp.	Motorised MDa
ELC	E. Leitz, Canada
Hell	Silver-chrome
Kaltef.	Winterised
Lack	Paint
LP	Leitz, Portugal
LW	Leitz, Wetzlar
Null Serie	Pre-Production model
Postk	Post camera
Schw'z	Black chrome
Schw. 1	Black paint
St.	Standard
Unbel't	Not issued
Vorl.	Delayed action

Note: Spaces in 'M' camera list relate to military camera production.

List of LEICA LENS NUMBERS

Year	From	To
1933	156 001	195 000
1934	195 001	236 000
1935	236 001	284 600
1936	284 601	345 000
1937	345 001	416 500
1938	416 501	490 000
1939	490 001	538 500
1940	538 501	565 000
1941	565 001	582 250
1942	582 295	593 000
1943	593 001	594 880
1944	594 881	595 000
1945	595 001	601 000
1946	601 001	633 000
1947	633 001	647 000
1948	647 001	682 000
1949	682 001	756 000

Year	From	To
1950	756 001	840 000
1951	840 001	950 000
1952	950 001	1 051 000
1953	1 051 001	1 124 000
1954	1 124 001	1 236 000
1955	1 236 001	1 333 000
1956	1 333 001	1 459 000
1957	1 459 001	1 548 000
1958	1 548 001	1 645 300
1959	1 645 301	1 717 000
1960	1 717 001	1 827 000
1961	1 827 001	1 913 000
1962	1 913 001	1 967 100
1963	1 967 101	2 015 700
1964	2 015 701	2 077 500
1965	2 077 501	2 156 300

Year	From	To
1966	2 156 301	2 236 500
1967	2 236 501	2 254 400
1968	2 254 401	2 312 750
1969	2 312 751	2 384 700
1970	2 384 701	2 468 500
1971	2 468 501	2 503 100
1972	2 503 101	2 556 500
1973	2 556 501	2 663 400
1974	2 663 401	2 731 900
1975	2 731 901	2 761 100
1976	2 761 101	2 809 400
1977	2 809 401	2 880 600
1978	2 880 601	2 967 200
1979	2 967 201	3 013 600
1980	3 013 601	3 087 000
1981	3 087 001	3 160 500
1982	3 160 501	3 249 100

Note: These numbers are allocated at the beginning of each year and this does not necessarily mean that they are all used in that year. Some may not be used until the next year or, even later.

GENERAL ALPHABETICAL CATALOGUE

Author's Notes:

The date that appears at the end of Code Descriptions is for reference only and cannot be taken as an absolute date of start of production for the item mentioned; it refers to the earliest catalogue or other Leitz literature where mention was found, and is for checking purposes.

Total number of items described over 2,000. Also included are the projectors and their accessories, enlargers and those parts of micro and macro equipment that relate closely to the camera, such as adaptors, focusing devices and so on.

When some items changed code word, both code words are indicated and a reference made in both cases. In a few instances it was found that the same code word has been used for two completely different items, separated by a long span of time, and this has also been indicated.

Code words listing is complete, as far as it was possible to ascertain, until 1960 when this system was dropped in favour of a numerical system. Some items that appear to have been marketed in the U.S.A. only by E. Leitz N.Y. have been indicated by the wording (USA catalogue).

In all cases where the same item was originally produced in black then later in chrome or nickel, the suffix CHROM or KUP was added to the code word, (i.e. EKURZ then EKURZ-CHROM or EKURZ-KUP, to indicate nickel finish.). These suffixes have been omitted for simplicity. The same comment applies to an item that was manufactured in screw fitting and then later in M fitting and the code was exactly the same with the suffix 'M', these have not been shown in every case. Although a tremendous amount of work has gone into the compilation of this over-all code word list, we do realise there may still be some missing code words and the author and publishers would appreciate hearing from any enthusiast with information relating to omitted code words. The only requirement is that the article must have been either manufactured or sold by E. Leitz.

A

ABCOO Film cutting knife for cutting film in the camera particularly useful for the 250 (1936-38).

ABCUU Epidiascope Vp 325 with two lenses, without lamp for distances between 3 and 5 metres (1960).

ABFOO Snapshot Leica with Elmar 3,5 cm 4,5 lens announced but not produced (1935).

ABLON Trimming template for Leica film (1935-38).

ABOOT Leica II black without spool chamber with Leitz Elmar 5 cm lens – until 1938 English catalogue only (1936).

ABUUZ Episcope Vp 325 without the Dia accessory (1960).

ACEDU Micro objective for projection No. 2 (1939).

ACHOO Leica III black without spool chamber with Leitz Summar 5 cm lens; until 1938 English catalogue only (1936).

ACOOS Leica III black with Leitz Elmar 5 cm lens until 1938 English catalogue only (1936).

ACUBE Micro objective for projection No. 1 (1939).

ADFIK Adjustable lens sunshade and combination filter holder in chrome finish (1949).

ADKOO Leica IIIa chromium plated without spool chamber with Leitz Summar 5 cm lens until 1938 English catalogue (1936).

ADOOR Leica IIIa chromium plated without spool chamber with Leitz Elmar 5 cm lens until 1938 English catalogue (1936).

ADSUM Adaptor for using the Summitar filters on the Hektor 28, Elmar 35, Hektor and Elmar 50,90 and 135 lenses (1949).

ADVOO Near focusing device for the Leica IIIg consisting of a supplementary viewfinder and lens (1960).

AFLOO Mechanical winder for winding film on to the spool chamber (1936-38).

AFLUU Lower plane glass plate with mask 18 x 24 mm for small projectors (1936).

AFOOV Leica III black without spool chamber without lens until 1938 English catalogue (1936).

AFUUV Film gate with semi-automatic film movement and film gate 18 x 24 mm for small projectors (1936).

AGIIU Clamping ring for draw tubes, with internal diameter 31,8 mm (Stand B) (1952).

AGNOO Leica IIIa chromium plated without spool chamber and without lens (1936).

AGNUU Slide changer with film gate 24 x 36 mm for Leica diapositives between glass plates measuring 3,5 x 12 cm (1936).

AGRIF Hand film winder for loading the spool chamber (1933-36-38).

AHOOT Reflecting viewfinder with front lens for 5 cm and 2,8 lenses for looking from above the camera (1936-38).

AHPOO Ahoot viewfinder in solid leather case (1936-38).

AIROO Leica II black without spool chamber without lens until 1938 English catalogue (1936).

AKTOO High power "Aktina" lamp for enlarging apparatus (1936-38).

AKTUU Film gate with semi-automatic film movement for small projectors (1936).

AKUUR Slide changer with circular opening of 43 mm diameter for 5 x 5 cm Leica glass slides (1936).

ALVOO Standard Leica black without spool chamber without lens until 1938 English catalogue (1936).

ALVUU Flex extension for projectors 12 ft long (1936-38).

AMXOO Leica model IIIb without spool chamber with Leitz Xenon 5 cm lens, chromium plated (1938).

AMXUU Press switch inserted in the flex of the projector (1938).

AMTOM Electromagnetic release to be used in connection with a timer, comprising flexible release (220 volt) bayonet (1960).

AMTOO Electromagnetic release to be used with timer, flexible release, for screw mount Leicas (220 volt) (1960).

AMUUP Electrical connecting cable with plug (1938-1960).

ANZOO Trimming template for Leica film, model 250 (1936).

ANZUU Variable resistance for using the 250 watt 110 volt lamp connected to the 220 volt mains (1960).

AOBUU Transformer to use the 110 volts 250 watt bulbs on 220 volt (1939).

APDOO Delayed action release for the Leica (1938).

APDUU Projection table for epidiascopes Vp (1960).

APOOM Leather case for delayed action release (1938).

APUUM 250 watt bulb for projector VIII, bayonet mount (1938-1960).

APVII Projection bulb 100 watt 110 volt for projector VIIIc (1949).

AQOOT Extra long release button for all screw mount Leicas when used for reproduction work (1960).

ARHOO Leica model IIIb without spool chamber with Leitz Elmar 5 cm lens, chromium plated (1938).

ARMST Arm for using the Stereoly attachment with the Leica IIIb (1939).

AROOG Standard Leica without spool chamber with Leitz Elmar 5 cm lens until 1938 English catalogue (1936).

ASKOO Delayed action release complete with leather case (1938).

ASKUU Protecting cover for projector (1960).

ASPUL Film winder, hand operated with a crank, to be fixed to a table (1933).

ATOOH Leica model IIIb without spool chamber, without lens, chromium plated (1938).

AUFET Solid leather case for reflecting viewfinder AUFSU (1936).

AUFOR Reflecting viewfinder for the Leica, for lenses of 5 cm focus with leather case (1936).

AUFSU Reflecting viewfinder for the Leica for lenses of 5 cm (1936).

AUOOG Reflecting viewfinder with front lens for lenses of 3,5 and 5 cm focus with solid leather case (1936).

AUTAS Automatic release for the "micro" attachment to the Leica (1933).

AVOOF Intermediate ring for colour accessory on the Focomat enlarger (1960).

AVQOO Complementary condenser for 50 mm lens on enlarger Focomat IIa (1960).

AWOOE Complementary condenser for the enlarging lens 50 mm of the Focomat IIa colour (1960).

AWUUE Slide changer with circular opening of 50 mm diameter for diapositives 3 x 4 cm between 5 x 5 cm glass plates (1936).

AXUOO Complementary condenser for the enlarging lens of 95 mm of the Focomat IIa colour (1960).

AXUUD Spare 100 watt tubular bulb with screw socket for the Small Projector "Standard" model (1936).

AYOOC Reflecting viewfinder with front lens for the Leica for lenses of 3,5 and 5 cm focus, without case (1938).

AYWOO Complementary condenser for enlargers Focomat Ia Ic (1960).

AZOOB Leica model IIIb without spool chamber, with Leitz Summar 5 cm lens, chromium plated (1938).

AZYOO Complementary condenser for enlargers Focomat Ia Colour Ic Colour and Focomator (1960).

B

BANAN Base for the automatic continuous projector attachment for use with projectors equipped with forced ventilation (1939).

BAZOO Universal setting device combining the uses of and parts from BEEOY, BEHOO and BETAB.

BCDOO Plastic box for Hektor 28 Summaron and Elmar 35 (1951).

BCOOA Plastic box for Summarit 50 (1951).

BDFOO Plastic box for Elmar 90 (1951).

BDOOZ Black bakelite box for Hektor 135 mm lens (from 1954 transparent plastic).

BEECH Monla microscope lamp, 6 volt 5 amp.

BEEUL Flexible cable with switch 5 ft long.

BEHOO Auxiliary reproduction device in the ratios of 1:1½, 1:2 and 1:3 for all 50 mm focus lenses.

BEINS Auxiliary reproduction device in the ratio 1:1 with the Elmar 3,5 cm lens.

BEKUR Auxiliary reproduction device in the ratios of 1:1½, 1:2 and 1:3 with the Elmar 3,5 cm lens.

BELOS Illuminating lamp for the auxiliary devices with 25 watt frosted bulb.

BELUN Auxiliary reproduction device in the ratio 1:1 with 5 cm focal Elmar lenses.

BELUN HESUM Auxiliary reproduction device in the ratio 1:1 with Summitar 50 mm lens.

BEMAR Auxiliary reproduction device ratios 1:1½, 1:2 and 1:3 for Elmar 5 cm lens (1933).

BEOON Auxiliary setting device in the ratios of 1:1, 1:1.5 1:2 and 1:3 for all Leica including M types.

BEOOY Auxiliary reproduction device for Leica with 5 cm lenses and supplementary front lenses No. 2 and 3.

BERAT Spare 25 watt bulb for the illuminating lamp BELOS.

BESAL Universal setting device combining the parts of BEMAR, BEVOR and BETAB (similar to BAZOO) (1933).

BESOT As BEKUR but for 5 cm Summar.

BESUM Auxiliary reproduction device in the ratio 1:1 with the Leitz Summar 5 cm lens.

BETAB Four intermediate rods for the setting device BEOOY and BEVOR to be used with supplementary front lens No. 2.

BETRY Three milled legs for converting the device BELUN into the device BESUM.

BEUUY-IZUUS Projection lens Epis 3,6/80 mm with focusing mount (1939).

BEVOR Auxiliary reproduction device to be used with the Elmar and Hektor 5 cm lenses and supplementary lenses No. 2 and 3.

BHOOV Transparent plastic case for Super Angulon 21 mm lens with screw mount.

BISOO Codeword to indicate that the enlarger must be adapted to automatic voltage stabilizer.

BKSOO Plastic box for Elmar or Summitar 50 (1951).

BLITZ Synchronized flash unit model IV with special camera baseplate with contacts eliminating speed dial contacts (1939).

BOOPV Transparent plastic box for Elmar 90 mm lens.

BOORW Transparent plastic box for Hektor 28 mm, Summaron and Elmar 35 mm and Elmar 50 mm lenses.

BOOSI Codeword to indicate that the enlarger must be adapted to a voltage dropping dimmer.

BOOSK Transparent plastic box for Summitar and Summarit 50 mm lenses.

BOOWU Setting device for copying with 50 mm lenses in the ratios of 1:4, 1:6 and 1:9 (screw-mount).

BOOWU-M Setting device for copying with 50 mm lenses M type in the ratios 1:4, 1:6 and 1:9, also called BOWUM (1956).

BOOXZ Extension tube 7 mm for use with ZWTOO and OORES (1939).

BPUOO Resistor for low voltage lamps 50 volts 250 watts for 110 volts current (1939).

BQCOO Blue filter for A36 lenses.

BRACK Bracket for mounting the flash models Synco in a vertical position (1939).

BRUUM Interchangeable condenser for lenses of 5 cm focus for small projectors VIIIa and VIIIi.

BTLOO Flashlight attachment for Leica II, III and IIIa with synchronization via the speed dial.

BTOOK Flashlight attachment for the Standard Leica with synchronization via the speed dial.

BUNOO Flashgun with internal sychronisation through camera baseplate (1939).

BUUEQ Accessory for the episcope Vp 325 when using it at short distance. BUUGR Suitcase projector, easy to carry, complete.

BUUMG Low voltage bulb 250 watts 50 volts for projector VIIIs.

BUUZA Epidiascope Vh with anastigamt lens Epis 400 mm 1:4 for episcopy only.

BWOOG Extra battery container for the flashlight attachment BTLOO.

C

CALFA Calf's leather case for Weston Leicameter (1939).

CALOS Automatic release for the micro attachment to the Leica.

CANOE Automatic continuous projector attachment for showing 12 slides on the VIII type projectors, including base (1939).

CARIR Colour slide carrier for bound 2 x 2 in. colour slides in the Valoy, Vogos, Vamax, Vokom, enlargers (1939).

CASAU Carrying case for automatic projector attachment for continuous showing of 12 slides CANOE (1939).

CASIE Cowhide case for Imarcet Finder (1939).

CASCP Leather case for 135 mm lenses and 127 lens made in USA for Leica (1939).

CAVOO-A Flash attachment, battery operated, folding reflector accessory shoe clip for old type cameras up to III (1951).

CAVOO-B As CAVOO but for model IIIa and IIIb (1951).

CAVOO-C As CAVOO but for model Ic and IIc (1951).

CAVOO-D As CAVOO but model IIIc to No. 392600 (1951).

CAVOO-E As CAVOO but for model IIIc from No. 392601-397000 (1951).

CAVOO-F As for CAVOO but for model IIIc from No. 397001 (1951).

CBOOD Slip-in mask 18 x 24 mm for Focomat II and Vyboo and Vyoos enlargers (later Focomat IIa and Vasex).

CDEOO As CBOOD mask size 24 x 36.

CDOOB As CBOOD mask size 3 x 4 cm.

CELLU Scotch cellulose binding tape 2595 per roll ½ wide for mounting slides (1939).

CENTO Additional cost for a 40 ins. upright in place of the 20 ins. upright for the Valoy enlarger.

CERED As CELLU but tape colour Red (1939).

CEYAL Flashgun CEYOO with the added provision to connect several other flashguns in parallel (1960).

CEYOO Flash attachment, battery operated, folding reflector accessory shoe clip for type IIf and IIIf synchronized (1951).

CFIOO As CBOOD mask size 4 x 4 cm.

CFOOZ As CBOOD mask size 4 x 6.5 cm.

CGLOO As CBOOD mask size 4.5 x 6 cm (1936).

CGOOY As CBOOD mask size 6 x 6 cm (1936).

CHNOO As CBOOD mask size 6.5 x 9 cm (1936).

CHOOX As CBOOD mask size 6 x 9 cm (1936).

CHROM Filter mount 34 mm diameter with set screw and special adaptor ring to fit Wratten filters of 32 mm diameter chromed (1939).

CINLE Adaptor for using the Leica lenses on movie cameras 16 mm C type mount except B & H 70 (USA catalogue) (1939).

CINPY As CINLE but for B & H 70 (1939).

CKOOV Negative mask 24 x 24 mm for enlarger Focomat IIa (1951).

CKROO Spare pilot lamp for colour enlargers (1954).

CLIPP Metal clip or accessory shoe with 3 screws for attaching accessories on cameras other than Leica (1939).

CMEET-XCEES Special mechanical stand USI. Rack and pinion movements on vertical and horizontal rods. (1939).

CMVOO Speed setting dial with fixed contact points for models up to IIIc for electronic flash (1951).

CNOOS Connecting cable as supplied with CEYOO including connector CUMOO (1951).

CNXOO Double connector for the simultaneous use of two flash units (1951).

CODRO Leica developing tank 310 cc complete (1952).

COOAB Short focusing mount for using the Hektor 7,3 cm with the rotating stage plate (1938).

COODQ Knob for turning reel in small type developing tank CODRO (1954).

COOED Short focusing mount for using the Elmar 9 cm with the rotating stage plate (1938).

COOEL Adaptor for using the Elmar 90 in short focusing mount with the COOMI and Focaslide (1939).

COOFR Correx band 12 ft long moulded on one side for the simultaneous development of two films in CORUN (1936).

COOHO Adaptor for using the Hektor 135 mm with the COOMI on the Focaslide (1949).

COOHS Short focusing mount for using the Hektor 13,5 cm with the rotating stage (1938).

COOIF Spare contact piece Vacu for unit CAVOO including cable and plug and connector CUMOO (1951).

COOKT Extension cable 5 ft long with couplings (1951).

COOLG Leather case for sports finders SAIOO, SEROO and SYEOO (1936).

COOMI Adjustable micrometer extension tube (40-60 mm) for copying work (1939).

COONH Leather case for the accessory viewfinder of the twin range Summicron (near focusing) (1960).

COONS Connecting cable between flash and camera with Leica plug (1954).

COONT Special contact piece for Leicas Standard to IIIc to use electronic flash, including cable and CUMOO (1951).

COONY Adaptor for using the 90 mm 4,5 lens (USA model) with the COOMI on the Focaslide (1949).

COOPB Double plug for Chico flashgun (1956).

COOPI Enlarging easel for fixed paper size 2¼ x 3¼ in. for use with paper in roll form (1939).

COOQW Spare test bulb for flash (1951).

COORB Developing tank new type 500 cc capacity (1960).

COORN Apron with both sides mouldings for new developing tank COORB as spare (1960).

COORT Winding knob for developing tank COORB as spare (1960).

COOSE Adaptor for using the 127 mm lens with the COOMI on the Focaslide (1949).

COOSX Flash cable to use Leitz flash with other cameras (1954).

COOTL Short focusing mount for using the Thambar 9 cm with the rotating stage plate (1938).

COOUY Spare adaptor for flash with tubular condenser (1952).

COOVM Spare 22,5 volt flash battery (1952).

COOWQ Focusing mount with one set of adaptor rings for all Micro Summar lenses for macrophotography (1939).

COOWZ Spare adaptor for flash complete with 22,5 volt battery and tubular condenser (1952).

COOXN Leather case for 35 mm viewfinder (1951).

COOYA Leather case for 50 mm viewfinder (1951).

COPIN Sliding focusing copying attachment with Leica holder and special calibrated ground glass for critical focusing (1939).

CORBA Spare celluloid apron for CODRO developing tank with same code name as apron of old type CORDO 1933 (1952).

CORCF Extra lid for Correx tank CORUN model (1939).

CORDO Leica Correx developing tank complete with inner spool and Correx band dimpled on one side, small size 350 cc (1933).

CORET Small thermometer for the tank developer Correx (1931).

COREX Reel as spare for developing tank COORB (1960).

CORID Inner spool for Leica Correx tank CORUN type (1931).

CORLE Empty correx tank, CORDO type and also new type CODRO postwar (1933).

COROL Empty Leica Correx tank of the CORUN type with twisting knob (1931).

CORPE Correx tank only CORUN model without any internal part (1939).

CORSO Spare reel for Leica developing tank CODRO (1952).

CORSU Inner spool for Leica Correx tank, CORDO type (1933).

CORTE Thermometer for developing tank COORB graduated in °C (1960).

CORUN Leica Correx developing tank complete with inner spool and Correx band, but without thermometer (500 cc) (1931).

CORYB Celluloid Correx band with clip and notched on both sides (1931).

COSLA Focusing copying attachment without the sliding Leica device, with special ground glass for critical focusing (1939).

COSTI Twisting knob for Correx tank (1936).

CPBOO Leather case for reflecting viewfinders for 85, 90 and 135 mm lenses (1952).

CPOOQ Leather case for Elmar 90 mm 1:4 collapsible lens bayonet mount, lens shade and two filters (1960).

CSOON Connecting cable for Braun Hobby flash to fit Leica camera synchronized (1956).

CTKOO Connecting cable for Braun Hobby flash to fit Leica M3 (1956).

CTOOM Flash bracket for fitting to camera base without using the accessory slide shoe (1954).

CUMOO Connector fitting extension cables with plug sockets other than Leitz (1952).

CUOOL Connecting cable with plug for Chico flashgun and Leica screw type (1956).

CUUAB Diascope for slides up to 9 x 12 cm lamp 500-1000 watt Dimar lens 200 mm 1:4 (1960).

CUUDQ As CUUAB but with 250 m F4 Dimar lens (1960).

CUUED As CUUAB but with 325 m F3.6 Epis lens (1960).

CUUHS As CUUAB but with 400 m F4 Epis lens (1960).

CUUKT As CUUAB but with 500 F5.7 Dimar lens (1960).

CUUNH As CUUAB but with 600 m F4.5 Epis lens (1960).

CUUYA As CUUAB but with 800 m F4.8 Epis lens (1960)

CUUZO As CUUAB but with 1000 m F6 Epis lens (1960).

CVOOK Connecting cable with plug for Chico flashgun and Leica M3 (1956).

CVOUU As CUUAB but with 700 m F4.8 Epis lens (1960).

CVUUK As CUUAB but with 300 m F4.3 Epnor lens (1960).

CWOOI Negative mask 24 x 36 mm for enlarger Focomat IIc (1960).

CWUUI As CUUAB but with 350 m F4 Epis lens (1960).

CXOOH Negative mask 24 x 24 mm for enlarger Focomat IIc (1960).

CXSOO As CXOOH mask size 3 x 4 cm (1960).

CYOOG As CXOOH mask size 4 x 4 cm (1960).

CYUOO As CXOOH mask size 4.5 x 6 cm (1960).

CZOOF As CXOOH mask size 4 x 6.5 cm (1960).

CZWOO As CXOOH mask size 6 x 6 cm (1960).

D

DAMOT Bindomat device for mounting colour transparencies between glasses, complete with glass and tape (1949).

DBOOF Supplementary ring for using the Agfa Variomat with the Focomat Ic column diameter 40 mm (1960).

DBZOO Intermediate ring 2,5 mm high 40 mm diameter to use the amateur printing board with the Focomat Ic (1956).

DCBOO As DBZOO ring diameter 50 mm (1956).

DCOOE For Focomat 2A ring diameter 50 mm (1960).

DEEMH Iris diaphragm for the MONLA lamp (1939).

DEEQK Illuminating stand, with 110 volt 100 watt lamp, condenser, iris diaphragm, daylight filter, ground glass plate (1939).

DEFOO Spiral developing tank complete with lid, agitator, reel and trimming guide (1938).

DEFUU Lantern slide projector, model IV 250 watt lamp 200 mm lens, for sizes up to 3¼ x 4in. (1939).

DEOOC Chico flashgun, condenser type, folding reflector in plastic case (1954).

DFHOO Special pivoted foot for Chico flashgun with built-in plug that dispenses the need for cable on IIf and IIIf (1954).

DFOOB Pivoted foot as DFHOO but without plug for use on all Leica other than IIf and IIIf (1954).

DGKOO Flash cable to use the flashgun Chico on other camera makes (1954).

DHMOO Plastic case to take the Chico flashgun (as spare) (1954).

DHOOA 22,5 volt battery for Chico flashgun (1954).

DIOOY Diopter selector disc for use by dealers (1955).

DIREKT Self-timer for Leica cameras appears only in the USA catalogue (1932).

DLUUW Front condenser for use of 5 cm Leica lenses on the projector VIII (1938).

DMUOO Intermediate ring for using optical heads of lenses SOSIC and SOMNI on the focusing bellows (1960).

DNWOO Adaptor for using Elmar 50 mm bayonet mount with tilting device in enlargers (1956).

DOOBC Intermediate ring for using the Elmar 50 mm bayonet mount on the Valoy II enlarger (1956).

DOOCQ Focotar copying lens 50 mm f:4,5 with click stops (1954).

DOOGS Repro-Elmar 3,5/50 mm lens, coated (1952).

DOOHF Focotar enlarging lens f 50 mm f:4,5 with click stops (1954).

DOOIT Elmar f 3,5/50 enlarging lens with click stops (1952).

DOOLU Case level, slip on, for panoramic head; painted black (1936).

DOORX Adaptor ring to convert the Repro-Elmar DOOGS into the enlarging Elmar DOOIT and DOOCQ into DOOHF (1952).

DOOSL Upright for the special large foot for the rotating stage plate (1938).

DREUU Carrying case for lantern slide projector model IV (1939).

DRXOO Aluminium box of Leitz film cassette (1952).

DTEOO Green filter for photomicrography (1952).

DUUFE Epidiascope Vh 500 watt lamp slides up to 9 x 12 cm opaque images up to 16 x 16 cm lens Epis 400 mm f.3,6 (1960).

DUUOI Prado 150 projector for 2 x 2 in. slides and 35 mm film without lamp and without lens (1960).

DUUPW Device for reading microfilm in daylight with the Prado 150 equipped with 50 mm lens and film guide (1960).

DUUQK Carrying case with tilting base for Prado 150 projector (1960).

DUUXA As DUUOI but with 100 mm F2.8 Dimaron lens (1960).

DUUYO As DUUOI but with 85 mm F2.5 Hektor lens (1960).

DVUUM Projection lamp 150 watt (1960).

DXOOK Slip proof rubber pad for carrying straps (1956).
DZUUH Complete reading device for Prado 150 with base, lens, film guide (1960).

E

EAWOO Electro automatic printing board, electrically operated paper hold, in four versions, 110-220 volts, DC and AC (1954).
EBDOO Universal carrying case with fittings for one Leica M 50 mm lens, Telyt 200, Visoflex and Hektor 135 (1960).
EBKOO Universal carrying case with fittings for one Leica screw with 50 mm lens, three lenses from 28 to 90 mm Hektor 135 (1960).
EBNOO Internal divisions for universal carrying case for Leica M and five lenses up to 135 mm (as spare) type I (1960).
EBOOH Leather case for universal viewfinder VIOOH (1951).
EBROM Three rolls NPG bromide paper each 64 in. long and 1¼ in. wide (1931).
EBROO Internal divisions for universal carrying case for Leica M, Visoflex, Telyt 200 and 50 and 135 lenses (as spare) (1960).
EBSOO Internal divisions for universal carrying case, screw mount Leica (type III) five lenses to 135 mm, finders (as spare) (1960).
EBYOO Universal carrying case with fittings for Leica M and five lenses up to 135 mm, accessories (1960).
ECOOG Leather case for Summicron 50 mm/2 with viewfinder attachment for near focusing, also for Summicron 35 with finder attachment (1960).
ECUUG Projection lens Dimaron 150 mm/2,8 with tube (1960).
EDCUU Projection lens Hektor 150 mm/2,5 with tube (1960).
EDFOO Ever-ready case for Leica IIIg with exposure meter of viewfinder (1960).
EDOOF Leather case for M type exposure meter (1956).
EDUUF Projection lens Dimar 200 mm/4 with tube (1960).
EFERN Leitz Elmar anastigmatic lens 135 mm/F4.5 screw fix helical focusing mount without range finder coupling (1931).
EFERN CHROM Elmar 135 mm/4,5 lens with chromed parts, coupled to rangefinder, made before the similar Hektor 135 (screw) (1933).
EFGOO Ever-ready case for Leica up to IIIf with lens Summicron or Summitar 50 mm (1954).
EFGUU Projection lens Dimar 250 mm/4 with tube (1960).
EFOOD Ever-ready case for Leica up to IIIf with Summarit 50 mm and universal viewfinder (1954).
EFOOS Ever-ready case for Leica Ig with viewfinder, rangefinder and 50 mm lens (1960).
EFSEL Ever-ready case for Leica with synchronizing baseplate attached, and 50 mm lens (1949).
EGIOO Ever-ready case for Leica up to IIIf and Summicron or Summitar 50 mm lens with fitted exposure meter (1954).
EGIUU Projection lens Hektor 200/2,5 with tube (1960).
EGOOC Ever-ready case for Leica up to IIIf and Summarit 50 mm lens with fitted exposure meter (1954).
EGUUC Projection lens Hektor 250 mm/2,8 with tube (1960).
EHLOO Leather case for the FOKOS rangefinder (1960).
EHLUU Interchangeable condenser 6 x 6 cm for lenses of 150 to 175 mm focal length (1960).
EHOOB Leather combination case with strap, holding one Leica four lenses from 35 to 135 mm, filters, viewfinders etc. (1951).
EIUUA Interchangeable condenser 6 x 6 cm for lenses from 200 to 300 mm focal length (1960).
EKOOL Leather case for Summilux lens 50 mm/1,4 (1960).
EKOOZ Leather combination case for one Leica, six lenses, lens hoods, filters, viewfinders, self-timer, etc. (1954).
EKPUU Small format accessory for the Prado 66 projector, consisting of 2 x 2 in. slide carrier, condenser and Hektor 85 mm/2,5 (1960).
EKURZ Leitz Elmar anastigmatic lens F 3, 5/3, 5 cm screw fix helical focusing mount (1931).
EKUUZ Small format accessory for the Prado 66 projector, consisting of 2 x 2 in. slide carrier, condenser and Dimaron 100 mm/2,8 (1960).
ELANG Elmar 90 mm/4 lens, unitized version black and chrome, later all chromed, screw mount (1936).
ELANG M (Later ELGAM) Elmar 90 mm f 4 lens with M type bayonet mount (1956).
ELCAT Front lens No. 1 for the COMPUR Leica Elmar 3,5/5 cm for distances from 39½ to 21¾ in. (1931).
ELCOM Front lens No. 2 for the COMPUR Leica Elmar 3,5/5 cm for distances from 21½ to 15½ in. (1931).
ELCUR Front lens No. 3 for the COMPUR Leica Elmar 3,5/5 cm for distances from 12¾6 to 10½ in. (1931).

ELDIA Printing apparatus for making contact pictures on film strips and bromide paper size 24 x 36 mm (1931).
ELDOS Three printing Agfa film rolls each 64 in. long (1931).
ELDUR Copying device for making lantern plates 2 x 2 in. from Leica negatives (1933).
ELFOR Combination carrying case, cowhide for Leica and 15 accessories, with strap (1949).
ELGAM As ELANG M (1960).
ELGLA Pressure plate for the ELDUR printer to make contact prints on paper (1933).
ELKIN Film window plate for printing pictures measuring 18 x 24 mm with the ELDIA printer (1931).
ELKOO Elmarit lens 90 mm/2,8 in short mount for use with the Visoflex (1960).
ELLET Window for ELDIA printer 24 x 36 mm Leica negative (as spare) (1939).
ELMAR Leitz "Elmar" anastigmatic lens F 3,5/5 cm with screw and helical focusing mount (1931).
ELMAR CHROM Elmar 50 mm/3,5 lens, chrome finish, coupled to rangefinder, screw mount (when there was also nickel finish) (1933).
ELMAR M Elmar 50 mm f 3,5 with M type bayonet mount (1956).
ELMOM Elmar lens 50 mm/2,8 with bayonet mount in plastic case (1960).
ELMOO As ELMOM but screw mount (1960).
ELOOP Ever-ready case for Leica IIIg with 50 mm lenses and Leicavit attached (1960).
ELPET Front lens No. 3 for Elmar 3,5/50 mm for distances ranging from 12,2 in. to 10,5 in.
ELPIK Front lens No. 2 for Elmar 3,5/50 mm for distances ranging from 21,5 in to 15,5 in.
ELPRO Front lens No. 1 for Elmar 3,5/50 mm for distances ranging from 39,5 in. to 21,75 in.
ELRIM Elmarit lens 90 mm/2,8 with bayonet mount and plastic case (1960).
ELRIT As ELRIM but screw mount (1960).
ELRUU Projection table with tilting platform that permits projector to be used at an angle with three legs 28 in. long (USA catalogue) (1939).
ELRUU Accessory for Prado 66 comprising slide carrier 2 x 2 in., condenser and Hektor 100/2,5 (1960).
ELZEN Elmar 105 mm 6,3 lens, unitized version, black and chrome coupled to rangefinder, screw mount, also chrome type) (1936).
EMOOX Ever-ready case for the Leica with Xenon lens (or Summarit) and rapid wind device.
EMQOO Leather case for Telyt 400 mm with Visoflex, Leica and filters (1954).
EMTOO Solid leather case for the Telyt 200 mm with mirror focusing arrangement (1936).
EMTUU As ELRUU but with 120 mm F2.5 Hektor lens (1960).
EMUUX Table stand for projector VIII about 3 ft 4 in. high (in 1960 codeword used for projector accessory) (USA catalogue) (1938).
EMUUX As ELRUU but with 150 mm F2.8 Dimaron lens (1960).
ENOOR Ever-ready case for Leica IIIg with 50 mm collapsible lenses or wide angle (1960).
ENOOW Leather case for Summarex 85 mm lens (1951).
ENSOO Ever-ready case for Leica IIIg with Summarit lens (1960).
ENVUU Carrying case for combination projector Vp 325 with accessories (1939).
EOUUV As ELRUU but with 150 mm F2.5 Hektor lens (1960).
EOXUU As ELRUU but with 90 mm F2.5 Color-plan lens (1960).
EPNUU Projector VIII-750 with slide changer, projection lens Epnor 300 mm/4,3 (1939).
EPOCH Calf leather pouch (green, blue, red, brown) with bow clips for the Leica camera with one film chamber (1931).
EPZOO Ever-ready case for Leica with Summar 50 mm lens and rapid winder attached (1938).
EQBOO Ever-ready case for Leica Ic and If with Summicron or Summitar lens and attachable rangefinder (1956).
EQOOT Solid leather case with strap for the Thambar 90 mm lens (1936).
ERDOO Morocco leather purse with zipper for the Leica (1938).
ERKOM Elmar 90 mm/4 in. short mount for use with the Visoflex (1960).
EROOS Deerskin purse with zipper for the Leica (1938).
ESFCE Ever-ready case for all Leica cameras up to IIIc with 50 mm lens attached (1949).
ESFOO Ever-ready case for the Leica 250 (1936).
ESFUS Ever-ready case for Leica with Summar 50 mm lens (1936).
ESFUSKIN As ESFUS in Pigskin (1938).
ESMAL Ever-ready case for Leica II or Standard with the right angle finder (1933).
ESMAR Ever-ready case for all Leicas up to IIIc with 50 mm lenses and Imarect finder VIOOH (1949).
ESMOS Ever-ready case of brown leather with velvet liner for the Standard Leica with rangefinder attached.

ESNAR Ever-ready case brown leather with velvet lining for the Leica II and III.
ESNASKIN As ESNAR in Pigskin (1938).
ESNEL Ever-ready case of solid brown leather with shoulder strap for the Leica with focal plane shutter (1931).
ESOOG Ever-ready case for Leica Ic and If with Elmar 50 mm lens and FOKOS rangefinder (1954).
ESOOR Ever-ready case for the Leica with 50 mm lens and rapid winder attached (1954).
ETBIX Leather case for the Leitz Xenon lens or for the Summitar 1:2/50 mm lens.
ETBUL Deerskin purse for Summar 50 mm lens (1936).
ETGAM Square case for the accommodation of Leica camera three or four lenses, universal and angular viewfinder, rangefinder, filters etc. (1931).
ETGUS Leather case fitted for carrying the Leica and five lenses, viewfinder, rangefinder and accessories (1933).
ETHOO Leather case for reflecting viewfinder with negative front lens AYOOC and AHOOT (1936).
ETIFF Leather case with strap for Elmar 105 mm (1933).
ETILA Leather case without strap for Elmar 35 mm (1933).
ETIME Leather case without strap for Elmar or Hektor 50 mm (1933).
ETINI Leather case with strap for Elmar 90 mm (1933).
ETINI M Leather case with strap for Elmar 90 mm F4 with bayonet mount (1956).
ETINX Leather case with strap for Hektor 73 mm (1933).
ETIPO Leather case with strap for Elmar or Hektor 135 mm (1933).
ETISE Leather case for the Elmar 90 mm/4 both in screw and bayonet mount (1960).
ETISY Leather case with strap for two lenses, Elmar 35 mm and Elmar or Hektor 135 mm (1933).
ETKAL Case of coloured calf leather (green, blue, red, brown) for matching covered Leica with one film chamber (1931).
ETMAX Carrying case fitted for Leica and seven lenses, filters, viewfinders and accessories (1933).
ETNEU Leather case with strap fitted for Leica and four lenses, viewfinders, filters and accessories (1933).
ETONO Leather case with strap for Elmar 90 mm F4 lens collapsible with bayonet mount (1956).
ETOOQ Case for HEBOO (1936).
ETOSA Leather case with strap for two lenses, Elmar 35 mm and Hektor 73 mm (1933).
ETRIN Solid brown leather case with handle and shoulder strap for camera, rangefinder and two spare film chambers (1931).
ETROS Solid brown leather case with handle for the camera with COMPUR shutter alone (1931).
ETRUX Solid brown leather case with handle for the camera with focal plane shutter alone (1931).
ETTAS Morocco leather pouch with bow clips for the Leica camera alone (1931).
ETTEL Deerskin pouch with bow clips for the Leica camera alone (1931).
ETTIG Deerskin case for Elmar 35 mm or Elmar 50 mm or Hektor 50 mm lenses (1933).
ETTON Deerskin case for Elmar 90 mm (1933).
ETTOX Deerskin case for Hektor 73 mm (1933).
ETTRE Leather fitted case for Leica and three lenses, universal viewfinder, angle finder or rangefinder (1933).
ETTUM Deerskin case for Elmar 135 mm (1933).
ETTWO Leather case fitted for Leica and two lenses, universal viewfinder and accessories (1933).
ETTYR Deerskin case for Elmar 105 mm (1933).
EUDAL Soft leather bag for the FODUA rangefinder (1931).
EUDIT Solid leather case for the FODUA rangefinder (1931).
EUKAB Deerskin pouch for one filter of the Leitz Xenon lens.
EUKOL Deerskin case for angle finder WINTU (1933).
EUKOS Brown leather case for the FOKOS rangefinder (1933).
EUKUT Deerskin leather case for filters size to suit all Elmar lenses 35/50/90/105 and 135 mm (1933).
EURUS Morocco leather case for angle finder WINTU (1933).
EUSAF Morocco leather case for the Leica with rangefinder (1933).
EUSOR Solid leather case for universal viewfinder VISOR (1931).
EUTEL Soft leather bag for the FOFER rangefinder (1931).
EUVAT Morocco leather case for one filter of the Leitz Xenon lens.
EUVER Solid leather case for the FOFER rangefinder (1931).
EUVIL Morocco leather bag for yellow filter (1931).
EWOON Ever-ready case for the Leica with clockwork motor and Elmar 50 mm lens (1938).
EXOOM Ever-ready case for the Leica with the Xenon lens.

EXPOO Leather case of the ADVOO near focusing device for the Leica IIIg (1960).
EXQOO Deerskin purse for the Xenon 50 mm lens (1938).
EYOOL Leather case for Leica with 50 mm lens 135 mm lens and Telyt 200 with Visoflex and accessories (1936).
EYSOO Ever-ready case for the Leica with clock-work motor and Summar 50 mm lens (1938).
EYZOO Soft leather case for lens hoods of Summitar and Summicron SOOFM and SOOPD (1954).
EZDOO Leather case with shoulder strap for Hektor 125 mm (1954).
EZOOK Ever-ready case for the Leica and Xenon lens and spring drive motor.
EZOOW Leather case with strap for Summicron 90 mm/2 lens (1960).

F

FARBA Colour filter Agfa-Leica 301 for picture taking (1934).
FARLY Scale ring for the panoramic tripod head for lenses of 135 mm focus (1936).
FAROS As FARLY but 35 mm lens (1936).
FARPU Colour filter Agfa-Leica 351 for projection (1943).
FARUX Panoramic tripod head with scale ring for lenses of 50 mm focus (1936).
FASKI As FARLY but for 105 mm lens (1936).
FAVOO Yellow filter medium No. 2 screw in for the Summar 50 mm lens, Hektor 28 mm, Elmar 90 and Hektor 135 (1936).
FAWAG As FARLY but for 73 mm lens (1936).
FAZOY Yellow filter No. 3 for 5cm Summar (USA 1939).
FAXIS As FARLY but for 90 mm lens (1936).
FBOOK As FAVOO but VV filter (1936).
FBUUK Projector Prado 500 with Hektor 85/2,5 lens (1960).
FBXOO As FAVOO but green filter (1936).
FBXUU Projector Prado 500 with Hektor 100 mm/2.5 (1960).
FCKOO Single film holder for cameras Ic, IIc, IIf, IIIc and IIIf up to serial number 590681 (1952).
FCOOI As FAVOO but red filter (1936).
FCUUI Projector Prado 500 with Hektor 120 mm/2,5 (1960).
FCZOO Red filter, light, screw mount for Elmar 35 mm and 50 mm lenses (1936).
FCZUU Projector Prado 500 with Hektor 150 mm/2,5 (1960).
FDBOO Fine focusing adjustment for the Universal Copying device (1936).
FDBUU Diascope IVb special with 1000 watt lamp and fan (1960).
FDOOH As FCZOO but dark red filter (1936).
FDUUH Projector Prado 500 with Hektor 175 mm/2,5 (1960).
FEARM Extra long arm to mount a Leica camera on the FILYT stand for copying purposes (1931).
FEDOO Red filter light, slip on for Hektor 28 and 135 mm and Elmar 35/50/90 mm lenses (1936).
FEDUU Projector Prado 500 with fan with Dimaron 100 mm/2,8 (1960).
FEFFU Baseboard with column 20 in. high from the FILES and FILOY enlargers (1931).
FEHUN Column 40 in. high to be used in place of the 32 in. on the FESSA baseboard (1931).
FELAT Printing board with adjustable masking bands for sizes from 3 x 4 cm to 13 x 18 cm (1933).
FELEU Printing board with adjustable masking bands for sizes up to 30 x 40 cm (1936).
FELIF Sliding arm short for upright of 1¼ in. diameter to carry the Leica camera (1939).
FELIS Printing board as FELAT but with scales in inches (1933).
FELLU Baseboard and 32 in. upright without wiring for copy work (1949).
FELOM Printing board with adjustable masking bands for sizes up to 18 x 24 cm (1933).
FELUK Printing board as FELOM but with scales in inches (1933).
FEMAS Printing frame with adjustable mask up to size 9½ x 7¼ adapted for use with all enlargers (1931).
FEOOG As FEDOO but dark red filter (1936).
FEPRO Reproduction equipment comprising the baseboard FEFFU, the arm FILUM and illuminating equipment STALI (1931).
FESSA Baseboard with column 32 in. high from the FILYT enlarger (1931).
FESTO Reproduction equipment comprising the baseboard FESSA the extra long arm FEARM and the illuminating equipment STALI (1931).
FETRA Printing board size 10 x 8in. with hinged glass plate without border masks for enlargers FILES, FILOY and FILYT (1931).
FEUUG Projector Prado 500 with fan with Dimar 200 mm/4 (1960).
FEUUL Baseboard and 32 in. upright with wiring and switch (1949).
FGHOO Spare lens hood for Hektor 73 mm lens (1936).
FGHUU Dimax 250 mm lens for diascopy projection (1960).

FGOOE Red filter light, screw in for Hektor 73 mm lens (1936).
FHKOO Single film holder for cameras type I, II, III, IIIa and IIIb (1951).
FHOOD As FGOOE dark red filter (1936).
FKOUU Dimax 200 mm lens for diascopy added to DUFFE Epidiascope (1960).
FKUUO Dimax 200 mm lens for diascopy added to diascope BUUZA (1960).
FIAKU Ball jointed tripod head (1931).
FIALT Film holder for single negatives processing (1933).
FIAMA Panoramic tripod head with graduated ring non interchangeable (1931).
FIARO Stereo slide 75mm long (1926).
FIATE Stereo slide 150 mm (6 in.) long with mark at 75 mm (1931).
FIAVI Angular bracket to be used with the panoramic tripod head FIAMA (1931).
FIBLA Case level fitting into the accessory clip, for architectural and panoramic photographs (earlier called DOOLU) (1931).
FIBOB Red filter medium No. 2 screw in for Elmar 35 mm and 50 mm (1933).
FIBOS Shoulder strap with metal snap hooks for Leica camera having eyelets (1949).
FIBYL Illuminating head of the FILYT enlarger, with lamp housing cord, switch, film carriers, tube and lens with iris diaphragm (1931).
FICAT Yellow filter No. 1 to screw into the lens of the COMPUR shutter Leica (1931).
FICFA Chrome flash filter for use with the sunshade and filter holder ADFIK (1949).
FICHR Chrome flash filter slip on A36 mount (1949).
FICOM Yellow filter No. 2 to screw into the lens of the COMPUR shutter Leica (1931).
FICOR Green filter medium, slip on A36 mount (1949).
FICYL Glass cylinder as a spare for developing drum FIMAN (1931).
FIDAX Spindle with handle and spokes of the developing drum FIMAN (1931).
FIDAY Kodachrome type A filter screw in for Summitar 50 mm (1949).
FIDRI Wire release 3 yds. long to screw to the focal plane shutter Leica (1931).
FIEKT Polarizing filter slip on for Hektor 73 mm lens (1949).
FIFLO Kodachrome photoflood filter screw in for Summitar 50 mm (1949).
FIGAM Yellow filter No. 2 to slip on A36 mount (1931).
FIGDA Green filter medium No. 2 for use with the sunshade and filter holder ADFIK (1949).
FIGIL Graduated yellow filter slip on for Hektor 73 mm lens (1933).
FIGLX Lamp housing of VALOY enlarger with cord, lamp and metal mask for negatives, without lens (1939).
FIGRO Yellow filter No. 1 to slip on A36 mount (1931).
FIGUN Yellow filter light No. 1 for use with the sunshade and filter holder ADFIK (1949).
FIHAZ Kodachrome haze filter screw in for Summitar 50 mm (1949).
FIHEL Yellow filter light No. 0 slip on A36 mount (1933).
FIIRL Red filter light No. 1 for use with the sunshade and filter holder ADFIK (1949).
FIKAT Kodachrome type A filter slip on A36 mount (1949).
FIKHA Kodachrome haze filter for use with the sunshade and filter holder ADFIK (1949).
FIKLO Kodachrome photoflood filter, slip on A36 mount (1949).
FIKOZ Kodachrome haze filter slip on A36 mount (1949).
FIKUS Extensible lens hood for lenses of 35/50/90/135 mm focal length (1933).
FIKYB Red filter medium, slip on A36 mount (1933).
FILAR Plain daylight enlarger with fixed focus 65 mm lens for enlargements 5½ x 3½ in. (1931).
FILBY Yellow filter No. 1 to slip on A36 mount (1931).
FILCA Roll film cassette complete as spare (1931).
FILES Variable enlarger, 60 watt lamp, 50 mm 3,5 lens, sizes from 3½ x 2½ to 10 x 8 in. (1931).
FILGE Yellow filter to slip on A36 mount (1931).
FILIF Frosted lamp 60 watt 110 volt for enlarger as replacement (1939).
FILIX Plain enlarger with 100 watt opal bulb, fixed lens 65 mm for enlargements 5½ x 3½ in. (1931).
FILOY Variable enlarger 60 watt lamp, 50 mm variable diaphragm lens, sizes from 3½ x 2½ to 10 x 8 in. (1931).
FILPO Polarizing filter slip on A36 mount (1949).
FILSO Yellow filter No. 1 medium slip on for Hektor 73 mm lens (1933).
FILUM Arm to mount a Leica camera on the FILES and FILOY stands for copying purposes (1931).

FILTU Yellow filter No. 3, A36 (1926).
FILXA Yellow filter No. 3 dark screw mount for Hektor 73 mm (1939).
FILYT Variable enlarger with 75 watt lamp, 70 mm lens, negative size up to 4½ x 6 cm enlargement size up to 10 x 8 in. (1931).
FIMAN Leica developing drum consisting of spindle, cylinder, metal frame, two glass dishes and two clips (1931).
FIMOO Yellow filter light No. 0 screw mount for Summar 50 mm Hektor 28 and 135 mm Elmar 90 mm (1936).
FIMOR Metal frame alone of the developing drum FIMAN (1931).
FIMUU Prado 500 projector with fan with Hektor 85 mm/2,5 (1960).
FINAL Wire release for ealy Leica model (1925).
FINON Polarizing filter slip on for Xenon 50 mm lens (1949).
FINOT Short wire release to screw to the focal plane Leica camera with locking screw for prolonged time exposures (1931).
FINOW Leica camera cable release 10 in. long improved type (1939).
FINUS Yellow filter No. 3 dark screw mount for Elmar 35 and 50 mm (1939).
FIOKO UV filter to screw into the lens of the COMPUR Leica (1931).
FIOLA UV filter to slip on A36 mount (1931).
FIOMU Red filter medium slip on for Hektor 73 mm (1936).
FIONA Orange red filter to be used with the sunshade and filter holder ADFIK (1949).
FIOOC Yellow filter medium No. 1 screw mount for Summar 50 mm Hektor 28 and 135 mm Elmar 90 mm (1936).
FIOPY Yellow filter light No. 0 slip on for Hektor 73 mm (1933).
FIORE UV filter to screw into the Elmar 3,5 and 5 cm lenses of the focal plane Leica (1931).
FIOSI UV filter slip on for Hektor 73 mm (1933).
FIPAN Green filter light No. 1 for use with the sunshade and filter holder ADFIK (1949).
FIPHO Kodachrome photoflood filter for use with sunshade and filter holder ADFIK (1949).
FIPLO Red filter medium screw mount for Hektor 73 mm (1933).
FIPOS Green filter slip on A36 mount (1933).
FIPPA Yellow filter No. 2 dark, slip on, for Hektor 73 mm (1933).
FIQUX Orange red filter light, slip on A36 mount (1939).
FIRAD Graduated yellow filter (sky filter) to slip on in conjunction with the intermediate ring FIRCO (1931).
FIRCO Intermediate collar for using a yellow filter along with a front lens or lens hood on the Leica COMPUR (1931).
FIREG Medium yellow filter screw in for Hektor 73 mm (1933).
FIRGI Intermediate collar for using a slip on filter along with front lenses on the Elmar 3,5 and 5 cm lenses.
FIRHE Yellow filter No. 1 to screw into the Elmar lenses 3,5 and 5 cm focus (1931).
FIRHU Dust cap, screw on type to fit on base of all Leica lenses (1939).
FIRMY Yellow filter No. 2 to screw into the Elmar lenses 3,5 and 5 cm focus (1931).
FIRYX Green filter screw in for Hektor 73 mm (1933).
FISAP Green filter slip on for Hektor 73 mm (1933).
FISEX Wire release 6 yds long to screw to the focal plane shutter Leica (1931).
FISON Lens hood small for Elmar 50 mm (1931).
FISUL Glass dish 13 x 18 cm (5 x 7 in.) for developing drum FIMAN (1931).
FISUM Polarizing filter slip on for Summitar 50 mm (1949).
FISUMMI Polarising filter in slip-on, swing out mount, E39 (USA 1949).
FITAF Kodachrome type A filter for use with the sunshade and filter holder ADFIK (1949).
FITOP Illuminating head of the enlargers FILOY, with lamp housing, cord, switch, film carrier, tube and lens (1931).
FITWO Yellow filter medium No. 2 for use with the sunshade and filter holder ADFIK (1949).
FIUNS Yellow filter light No. 0 slip on A36 mount (1939).
FIUUC Projector Prado 500 with fan with Hektor 100 mm/2,5 (1960).
FIVPL Complete set for technical photography comprising Leica, stand, Visoflex, Elmar 90, extension tubes (USA 1939).
FIWAS Light yellow filter No. 0 for Hektor 73 mm lens with screw mount (1933).
FIWET UV Filter screw mount for Hektor 73 mm (1933).
FIWIG Yellow filter No. 2 screw mount for Hektor 73 mm (1933).
FIXAM Film clip for developing drum FIMAN as a spare (1931).
FIXIO Green filter screw mount for Elmar 35 and 50 mm (1933).

FIXLA Yellow filter No. 3, for 7.3cm Hektor (1933).
FIXTA Yellow filter No. 0 screw mount for Elmar 35 and 50 mm (1933).
FLABU Opal bulb 75 watt for enlarger VALOY (1933).
FLAKO Opal bulb 100 watt for enlarger VALUX (1933).
FLAMI Opal bulb 100 watt for enlarger type FILIX (1933).
FLARA Orange filter in swing mount attachable to the enlargers FILES and FILOY (1931).
FLASH Flash unit model Va for use with the Standard Leica with lower cover and synchronizing device (1939).
FLATY Orange filter in swing mount attachable to enlarger FILYT (1931).
FLAUS Orange filter for enlargers type VALFA and VAKUT (1933).
FLEAR Opal bulb 75 watt for enlargers type FLEOS (1933).
FLECT Dull surface reflector to be used in place of the polished one on SYNCO and flash units (1939).
FLEIN Enlarger for daylight with fixed focus 65 mm lens for enlargements to 3½ x 2½ in. (1931).
FLEOS Plain enlarger with 75 watt opal bulb, fixed lens 65 mm for enlargements to 3½ x 2½ in. (1931).
FLOOA Fluorescent filter for document copying with ultraviolet light with Elmar 50 mm (1941).
FLOOO CHROM Lens sunshade for 35 mm lenses, chromed (1949).
FLOTH Plumb line with attaching clip for ascertaining the centre of the image to be copied with the STARE (1931).
FLQOO Lens hood for the lens Elmar 35 mm (1936).
FLUUA Projector Prado 500 with fan with Hektor 120 mm/2,5 (1960).
FMOOZ Red filter light slip on, for Hektor 73 mm (1936).
FMSOO Red filter, dark, slip on, for Hektor 73 mm (1936).
FNOOY Red filter light, screw in, for Summar 50 mm Hektor 28 and 135 mm Elmar 90 mm (1936).
FNUOO Red filter dark, screw in, for Summar 50 mm Hektor 28 and 135 mm Elmar 90 mm (1936).
FOCASA Complete Focaslide FULEC equipment comprising mangnifier extension and focusing tubes (USA) (1949).
FOCASO Complete Focaslide FULDY equipment comprising maagnifier extension and focusing tubes (USA) (1949).
FODIS Early type of range finder, vertical mounted over the Leica, later called FOFER (1925).
FODUA Rangefinder (1931).
FOERN Leitz rangefinder No. 1F (FOFER) in its solid leather case EUVER (1931).
FOFER Leitz rangefinder No. 1F with large distance scale for the Elmar 13,5 cm lens without case (1931).
FOKAL Holder No. 1H for rangefinder FOKIN (1931).
FOKIN Leitz rangefinder No. 1K for cinematograph cameras in leather case (1931).
FOKOS Short base rangefinder for the Standard Leica (1933).
FOKUX Adjustable holder with universai joint for FOKIN rangefinder (1939).
FONOR Leitz rangefinder No. 1M for medium size cameras with fixing clamp in leather case (1931).
FONOT Wire release for M series 10 in. long (1956).
FOOBD Green graduated filter, slip on, A36 mount (1938).
FOOCR Green graduated filter slip on for Hektor 73 mm (1938).
FOOES Orange filter for Focomat Ic enlarger (1951).
FOOGT Rangefinder FONOR with case (1936).
FOOIU Rangefinder FOKIN with case (1936).
FOOKH Lens hood for Summaron and Elmar 35 mm (1951).
FOOMI Ball jointed tripod head chromium plated (1938).
FOONW As FARLY but for 28 mm lens (1936).
FOOQL As FARLY but for 200 mm lens (1936).
FOORY Printing board FELAT with groove for the clamping device of the Vasex and Focomat enlargers (1938).
FOOUN Printing board FELEU with groove for clamping device of the Vasex and Focomat enlargers (1938).
FOOVA Leica film tank to load the magazine in daylight; contains some 325 ft of film and indicators of length (1939).
FOOXB Filter mount empty A36 (1951).
FOOXC Filter mount empty for Summitar (1951).
FOOXD Filter mount empty for E41 (1951).
FOOXE Filter mount empty for Summarex 85 mm (1951).
FOOXF Filter mount empty for E48 (1951).
FOOXG Filter mount empty E85 (1951).

FOOXH Filter mount empty for E39 (1954).
FOOXK Filter mount empty for E43 (1960).
FOOYP Printing board FELOM with groove for clamping device of the Focomat; scaled up to 18 x 24 cm (1936).
FOSAR Angular bracket for the older reproduction arms to take the auxiliary housing (1933).
FOUUX Projector Prado 500 with fan with Dimaron 150 mm/2,8 (1960).
FOWUU Projector Prado 500 with fan with Hektor 150 mm/2,5 (1960).
FPOOW Orange filter, screw in for Elmar 35 and 50 mm lenses (1941).
FPUUW Projector Prado 500 with fan with Hektor 150 mm/2,5 (1960).
FPYOO Printing board FOOYP with grooves for the clamping device of the Focomat scaled in inches (1936).
FQOOV Orange filter, screw in for Hektor 28, Elmar 90 and Hektor 135 mm lenses (1941).
FRCOO Orange filter, screw in for Hektor 73 mm (1941).
FROOU Printing frame 3 x 4⅛ in. for the Focomator (1954).
FSEOO Orange filter, slip on A36 mount (1941).
FSOOT Printing board with adjustable masking bands as FELEU but scaled in inches (1936).
FTGOO Orange filter snap in for Hektor 73 mm (1941).
FTOOS Swing out orange filter for the VALOY II adjustable (1954).
FUBUX Projector Prado 500 with Colourplan 90 mm/2,5 (1960).
FUECD Extension tubes 12/22/30/60/90 mm set (1939).
FUFIF Extension tube 15 mm long (1949).
FUFOR Extension tube 45 mm long (1949).
FUIOO Printing frame 4⅛ x 5¾ in. for the Focomator (1954).
FULDY Focaslide device for ground glass focusing to be used with Leicas with serial number up to 400.000 (1939).
FULEC Focaslide device for ground glass focusing to be used with Leicas with serial number above 400.000 (1949).
FULET Focusing attachment with removable ground glass that is manually substituted for the camera (1939).
FULFO Extension tube 30 mm long (1936).
FULGX Extension tube 60 mm long (1936).
FULHI Extension tube 90 mm long (1936).
FULIP Metal filing box with cover and sections for holding 25 rolls of Leica film (1939).
FULLS Leica film index containing transparent pockets for holding 36 negatives in strips of three (1939).
FULOR Extension tube 12 mm long (1936).
FUOOR Printing board with masking bands up to 13 x 17 in. and groove for device of enlargers Vasex and Focomat (1939).
FUSEV Extension tube 7 mm long (1949).
FUUKR Epidiascope Vh with anastigmat lens Epis 500/4,3 (1960).
FUULI Heat absorption filter for series VIII projectors as replacement (1939).
FUUMI Lamp 500 watt 110 volt (1960).
FUUOK Lamp 500 watt 220 volt (1960).
FUUXB Projector Prado 500 with long base, fan and Hektor 250 mm/2,8 (1960).
FUUYP As FUUXB but with 250 mm F4 Dimar lens (1960).
FUUZC As FUUXB but with 200 mm F2.5 Hektor lens (1960).
FVLOO Spare 150 watt enlarger lamp (1954).
FVLUU Projector Prado 66/500 with Hektor 200 mm/2,5 (1960).
FVOOQ Intermediate ring 15 mm long for near focusing of Summitar and Summar 50 mm lenses (1951).
FVUUQ Projector Prado 66/500 with Dimar 250 mm/4 (1960).
FWNUU Projector Prado 66/500 with Hektor 250 mm/2,8 (1960).
FWWAL Heat absorption filter for projector VIIIs 400 watt (1939).
FYLOR Swing out orange filter for the enlarger VANOS (1936).
FYLTO Swing out orange filter for the VALOY enlarger (1933).
FYLVA Orange filter, slip on for lens of enlarger VARYL (1933).
FYOON Swing out orange filter for the enlarger Focomat II (1936).
FYOOR Orange filter in special mount for Focomat IIc (1960).
FYROO Printing board with adjustable masking bands as FOORY but scaled in inches (1938).
FYSNE Orange filter for Focomat Ib enlarger (1949).
FYSTY Swing out orange filter for the enlarger Focomat (1936).
FZTOO Printing frame postcard size 3½ x 5½ in. for the Focomator (1954).

G

GBOOM Yellow filter No. 0 screw mount for Summitar (1951).

GBWOO Yellow filter No. 1 screw mount for Summitar (1951).
GCHEO Chrome flash filter screw in for Summitar (1949).
GCOOL Yellow filter No. 2 screw mount for Summitar (1951).
GCYOD Green filter medium No. 2 screw in for Summitar (1949).
GCYOO Green filter screw mount for Summitar (1951).
GDIIK Intermediate adaptor for using the Micro Ibso on Leitz polarizing microscopes with wide tubes (1951).
GDOOK Orange filter screw mount for Summitar (1951).
GECOO Red light filter screw mount for Summitar (1951).
GFEII Clamping ring for draw tubes of 25,4 mm (1 in.) diameter (1951).
GFEOO Red filter medium screw mount for Summitar (1951).
GFOOH Red filter dark screw mount for Summitar (1951).
GHIOO UV protection filter screw mount for Summitar (1951).
GHOOF Graduated yellow filter, screw mount for Summitar (1951).
GIIBR Wire cable release 18 in. long with set screw (1939).
GIIEF Conical extension tube with lens ⅓X for Micro Ibso screw mount (1939).
GIIEF-M As GIIEF but for bayonet mount (1956).
GIIFT Wire cable release 18 in. long for Micro Ibso (1939).
GIIMW Conical extension tube with lens ½X for Micro Ibso screw mount (1939).
GIIMW-M As GIIMW but for bayonet mount (1956).
GIINK Conical extension tube with lens 1X for Micro Ibso (1939).
GIIOX Single exposure camera OLIGO without Ibsor shutter (1939).
GILOO Graduated green filter, screw mount for Summitar (1951).
GLANU Hinged double glass plate 7½ x 4 in. for enlargers VARYL and VANOS (1933).
GLAPA Glass plate 11 x 7½ in; for the printing board FETRA (1933).
GLASI Hinged double glass plate 6¾ x 1½ in. for the VANOS enlarger (1936).
GLAZO Pair of hinged glass plates 1⅜ x 4¾ in. for holding the negative film (1931).
GLOOC Hinged double glass plate 4 x 8½ in. for single negative (1952).
GOOBR Baseboard with ball jointed head for the VAMAX enlarger (1936).
GOOBROKODO Baseboard GOOBR without ball jointed head (1938).
GOOEF Leica IIIg without lens (1960).
GOOEL Leica IIIg with Elmar 2,8/50 mm lens (1960).
GOOFT Baseboard with ball jointed head for the Focomat enlarger (1936).
GOOFTOKGDO Baseboard GOOFT without the ball jointed head (1938).
GOOMI Leica IIIg with Summicron 2/50 mm lens (1960).
GOORM Supporting arm of the Universal Copying device (1938).
GOOSZ Intermediate piece GOOZQ with carrier and rotating plate OORES (1938).
GOOZQ Short sliding arm with tape measure for attaching the rotating focusing device to upright (1939).
GRBOO Upper stage of the Universal Copying device for the use of the Leica 250 (1936).
GROOW Basic outfit of the Universal Copying device, with baseboard and upright, sliding arm and steel tape (1936).
GVKOO Extension ring 30 mm long for using Summitar or Summar 50 mm lens on the focusing stage OOZAB (1951).

H

HATUU Film viewing device (1936).
HEBOO Slow speed attachment for the Leica Standard and II (1936).
HEFAM Hektor 4,5/135 mm chrome plated bayonet mount M (1960).
HEFAR Hektor 135 mm 4,5 lens black or chromed, but only with chromed scale rings, screw mount (1936).
HEFAR-M Hektor 4,5/135 mm lens chrome plated bayonet mount (later HEFAM). (1956).
HEGRA Hektor 73 mm 1,9 in single version with chromed scale rings, screw mount (1936).
HEKON CHROM Lens Hektor 73 mm 1,9 first code word of the type with chromed rings, (later HEGRA). (1933).
HEKOO Lens head of the Hektor 4,5/135 lens (1960).
HEKTO Hektor 2,5/50 mm lens screw mount rangefinder coupled last type chromed (USA catalogue). (1939).

HEKTOR Hektor lens 2,5/50 mm first type nickel plated and without rangefinder coupling (1931).
HEKTORCHROM Hektor 2,5/50 mm lens screw mount chrome (or nickel) plated and with rangefinder coupling (1933).
HEOOL Slow speed attachment HEBOO in leather case (1936).
HEPET Supplementary front lens No. 3 for Hektor 50 mm to focus from 10 to 14 in. (1933).
HEPIK Supplementary front lens No. 2 for Hektor 50 mm to focus from 18 to 22 in. (1933).
HEPRO Supplementary front lens No. 1 for Hektor 50 mm to focus from 22 to 40 in. (1933).
HESUM Summitar 2/50 lens later changed into SOORE (1938).
HFOOK Short base rangefinder FOKOS with clip and shoe, black (1938).
HGOOI Large rear cover for Hektor 125 mm lens (1954).
HIIBE Stand for photography of small objects adjustable in height by rack and pinion and which can be rotated and tilted (1939).
HIIDF Complete set of five illuminating lenses for object stage LUFAS (1939).
HIKOO Hektor 2,5/125 lens in short focusing mount for use with Visoflex (1954).
HKMOO Lens hood (as spare) for Hektor 125 mm (1954).
HMOOD Early separate lens hood for 90 mm f2 Summicron (1957).
HOOAR Yellow filter No. 0 for lenses E39 mount (1956).
HOOBE Yellow filter No. 1 for lenses E39 mount (1956).
HOOCS Red filter light for lenses E39 mount (1956).
HOODF Red filter medium for lenses E39 mount (1956).
HOOET Red filter dark for lenses E39 mount (1956).
HOOFG Green filter for lenses E39 mount (1956).
HOOGU Orange filter for lenses E39 mount (1956).
HOOIV UV protection filter lenses, E39 mount (1956).
HOOKI Blue filter for lenses E39 mount (1956).
HOOPY Hektor 6,3/28 mm nickel plated, screw mount, later from 1938 onward only chrome plated (1936).
HYPOO Extra word to indicate the large baseboard of the Focomat Colour I (22 x 25 in.) (1951).

I

IASOO Ever-ready case for Leica M2 with Elmar 2,8/50 mm lens without exposure meter (1960).
IASUU Polarizing glasses for stereo viewing (1960).
IBSOR Ibsor shutter for use with OLIGO single shot camera and other uses (USA catalogue) (1939).
ICLOR Focomat Ic colour enlarger with enlargement ratio indicator illuminated on the baseboard (1960).
ICOOP Focomat Ic enlarger with 16 x 21 in. base upright 32 in. 75 watt lamp and automatic focusing system (1951).
ICOOP COLOUR Enlarger Focomat Ic as ICOOP but with filter holder for colour work (1951).
ICWOO Focomat Ic enlarger as ICOOP but including Elmar 3,5/50 mm lens, printing board 8 x 10 in. and filter (1951).
ICWOO COLOUR Enlarger as Focomat Ic complete including filter holder for colour work (1951).
IDCOO-N Ever-ready case for Leica M3 with any 50 mm lens and exposure meter attached (1956).
IDYOO Ever-ready case for M type cameras with 50 mm lenses and special finders plus exposure meter (1960).
IDYUU 50 slides for stereo pictures 6 x 6 with two frames 16 x 33 mm separated by a central strip of 3 mm (1960).
IFLEX Microphotography version of Visoflex I with rotating screen holder for two interchangeable screens. (1953).
IFSTA Lifa filter stand for microphotography (1951).
IGEMO Leica M3 body alone (1956).
IGOOL Fully automatic Focomator enlarger for D.C. use (1951).
IHGOO Codeword extra for indicating upright 47 in. tall for Focomat Ic (1951).
IHLOR Focomat Ic with large baseboard 22 x 25 in. and upright 47 in. tall with colour accessories (1960).
IHOOC Focomat Ic as ICOOP but with upright 47 in. tall and baseboard 22 x 25 in. (1951).
IKLOO Enlarger Focomat Ic complete with Focotar 4,5/50 mm lens and orange filter (1954).
IKLOO COLOUR Enlarger Focomat Ic complete with Focotar lens and filter holder for colour work (1954).
IKOOR Focomat Ic colour enlarger complete with Focotar 4,5/50 mm lens and accessories (1960).
ILLUM Improved four-lamp array for 2 inch diameter columns (USA 1939).

ILNOO Elmar 4/90 mm lens in collapsible lens mount, parallel focusing and bayonet mount (1956).
ILNUU Stereo projection device for new type projectors with two Hektor 2,5/85 mm lenses and polarizing filters (1960).
ILOOG Fully automatic Focomator enlarger for A.C. use (1951).
IMARO Leica M3 with Elmar 3,5/50 mm lens (1956).
IMOLO Leica M3 with Elmar 2,8/50 mm (1960).
IMOOP Leica MP bayonet mount, complete with Leicavit but without lens, speeds from 1 sec. to 1/1000 chromed.
IMOOT Leica M3 with Summilux 1,4/50 mm lens (1960).
IMPOO Automatic enlarger with foot control, Focotar 4,5/50 mm lens upright 32 in. tall (1956).
IMPOO COLOUR Automatic enlarger Focovit with foot control with filter holder for colour work (1956).
IMPUU Stereo projection device for old type projectors Prado with two Elmar 3,5/50 mm lenses and polarizing filters (1960).
IMPUU-IZQUU As IMPUU but with screw thread adapter for Prado 250 and 500 projectors.
IPOOC As IMOOP but with 50 mm F2 Summicron.
IPOOM Ever-ready case of brown leather for the Leica MP with Leicavit.
IPOOS As IMOOP but with 50 mm F1.5 Summarit.
IPVOO As IMOOP but with close focus 50 mm F2 Summicron.
IQOOB Film guide 24 x 36 (as spare) for the Focomator enlarger (1954).
IQXOO Film guide 24 x 24 mm for the Focomator enlarger (1954).
IROOA Lens hood for Summaron 35 mm lens (1960).
IROOW Rear cover for Super Angulon 21 mm bayonet mount (1960).
IRZOO Bayonet mount for using the 35 and 50 mm screw mount lenses with M type cameras (1956).
IRZUU Stereo projection device for new type projectors with two Hektor lenses 2,5/100 mm and polarizing filters (1960).
ISAIO Leica M3 with Summarit 1,5/50 mm lens (1956).
ISBOO Bayonet mount for using 90 mm screw mount lenses on the M type cameras (1956).
ISBUU As ILNUU but with two Hektor f2.5, 120 mm lenses.
ISMON Leica M3 with Summicron 2/50 with near focusing device (1960).
ISOOZ Bayonet mount for using 135 mm mount screw lenses on the M type cameras (1956).
ISOUN Leica M3 with Summicron 2/50 non collapsible lens (1960).
ISUMO Leica M3 with Summicron 2/50 mm lens collapsible (1956).
ITDOO Lens hood for Summaron 35 mm and Summicron 50 mm bayonet mount lenses (1956).
ITOOY Lens hood for Elmar 50 mm bayonet mount lens (1956).
IUFOO Lens hood for Elmar 90 and Hektor 135 mm lenses bayonet mount (1956).
IUOOX Single negative mask 24 x 36 for Focomator enlarger (1954).
IVHOO Single negative mask 24 x 24 for Focomator enlarger (1954).
IVZOO Protection cap for camera body bayonet mount (1956).
IWKOO Lens hood for Super Angulon 21 mm lens (1960).
IXMOO All metal film cassette model N in box (1956).
IXOOU Flash socket cover for M3 (1956).
IZQOO Rear cover for lenses with bayonet mount (1956).

J

JASUU Projector VP 325 Model II with EPIS 325 lens and DIMAX 200 mm lens with lantern slide carrier (USA catalogue) (1939).
JBUUG Projector VP 325 model II with EPIS 325 lens only (USA catalogue) (1939).
JSUUZ Carrying case for projector VP 325 model II with accessories (USA catalogue). (1939).

K

KABBI Two electric cords 5ft. long with plugs and sockets for connecting the enlargers (1933).
KABLO As KABBI but 1 cable (1933).
KASAM Leica cassette with parts in velvet, as spare (1933).
KAZWO Two spare cassettes to be added to the Leica C type without lens LENEU to compose LENIX (1931).
KBTOO Electric cord with plug for universal copying device (1933).
KCVOO Electric cord 10ft. long with connection, plug and switch for the X-ray reproduction device (1933).

KGOON Large ball-jointed head (1936).
KIHOO Leica M2 with Elmar 2,8/50 (1960).
KIOOL Leica M2 with Summicron 2/50 (1960).
KLMOO Clamping screws for fixing a printing board to the enlarger (1936).
KNOOG Leica M2 with Summicron 2/50 with near focusing device (1960).
KODIA Universal slide copying device for making glass slides 2 x 2in. or printing on film (1933).
KODRE Film window plate 4 x 4 cm for KOLOM (1933).
KOFIM Positive film transport and housing for KOLOM (1933).
KOGLA Glass slides attachment for plates 2 x 2in. for KOLOM (1933).
KOLOM Base housing of the large slide printer (1933).
KONAF Film window plate 3 x 4 cm for KOLOM (1933).
KOOAS Film carrier for OLEYO (1936).
KOOBF Spool chamber for the Leica 250 (1936).
KOOCT Leica M1 without lens (1960).
KOOEU Leica M1 with Elmar 2,8/50 (1960).
KOOHE Leica M2 without lens (1960).
KOOHI Positive film attachment for 30ft. of film for KOLOM (1936).
KOOLX Copying device KOLOM with accessories KOOHI and KOGLA (1952).
KOORA Large diapositive printer KOLOM complete with positive film holder KOOHI (1936).
KOPAT Large diapositive printer complete with accessories (1936).
KOREF Film window plate 18 x 24 mm KOLOM (1933).
KOSUS Two negative film spools for film 3 x 4 and 4 x 4 cm for KOLOM (1933).
KOTOS Diapositive film attachment for the KOLOM (1933).
KOVIR Glass slides attachment for plates 2 x 2in. and base housing for KOLOM (1933).
KQWOO Mask 18 x 24 mm for the film holder for KOLOM (1954).
KRYUU Polarizing device for vertical projection (1960).
KSOOB Leica M2 with Summilux 1,4/50 (1960).
KSUUB Special condenser for polarized projections (1960).
KUUCT Polarizing device for horizontal projection (1960).
KUUDG Berek type condenser (1960).
KUUGV Iris diaphragm for the projection lens (1960).
KUULX Kit with 16 specimens for demonstration of polarized projection (1960).
KUUML Carrying case for the complete set for polarized projection (1960).
LANCA Case for lantern slides capacity 100 slides 2 x 2in. (1939).

L

LAQOO Leica IIId similar to the IIIc but with delayed action release, with Summar 2/5 cm lens.
LEANE Leica A type with Elmar 3,5/5 cm fixed lens, black with vulcanised covering, with one roll film chamber (1931).
LEANEKALB Leica model A with Elmar 3,5/5 cm fixed lens, black body covered with coloured calf leather, one roll film chamber (1931).
LECOM Leica B type as LECUR black, vulcanised cover Elmar 3,5/5 lens in COMPUR shutter, one roll film chamber and ETROS case (1931).
LECUR Leica model B, with Elmar 3,5/5 cm fixed lens in COMPUR shutter, black with one roll film chamber (1931).
LEDRI Leica C type as LENEU complete with matching Elmar 3,5/3,5 lens in screw mount (1931).
LEFER Leica C type as LENEU complete with matching Elmar 4,5/13,5 lens in screw mount (1931).
LEFFA Lecia outfit comprising camera, three film cassettes and rangefinder FODIS in leather bag (1925).
LEHEK Leica IIIb chrome finish with Hektor 2,5/50 mm (USA catalogue) (1939).
LEICA Leica A type as LEANE black, vulcanised cover, fixed Elmar lens 3,5/50 mm with ETRIN leather case with space for Rangefinder (1931).
LEKAL Leica A type as LEANEKALB black covered with coloured calf leather Elmar 3,5/5 one roll film chamber and ETKAL case (1931).
LELUX Leica model A, body dull gilt and covered with lizard skin, Elmar 3,5/5 cm fixed lens, one roll film chamber and case (1931).
LEMAX Leica Standard with one cassette and Elmar 3,5/50 lens black (1933).
LEMAX CHROM Leica Standard chrome finish with viewfinder, one roll film chamber and Elmar 1:3,5/50 mm lens.
LENEL Leica A type as LEANE black, vulcanised cover, fixed Elmar lens 3,5/5 but with ever-ready case ESNEL (1931).
LENEU Leica model C, for interchangeable lenses, black vulcanised covering, with viewfinder and one roll film chamber (1931).

LENIX Leica C type, black vulcanised cover, without lens, but with three roll film chambers no case (1931).

LENOT Leica Standard with one cassette without lens (1933).

LEOMU Leica C type as LENEU but complete with matching Elmar 3,5/5 lens in screw mount (1931).

LEONI Leica A type as LEANE black, vulcanised cover, fixed Elmar lens 3,5/5 with three roll film chambers (1931).

LEPOK Leica model A type LEANEKALB with matching soft bag of coloured leather (Epoch) (1931).

LESOR Complete set of Leica C type with matching three lenses and accessories in square brown leather case ETGAM (1931).

LESSA Leica A type as LEANE black fixed Elmar lens, with ETRIN brown leather case, three spare film chambers and FOFER range f (1931).

LESSALUX Leica model A gilt LELUX with three roll film chambers coloured crocodile case and gilt range finder FOFER (1931).

LETTO Leica A type as LEANE but with brown solid leather case ETRUX (1931).

LEVIR Complete set of camera, three matching lenses and case as in LESOR with the Hektor 2,5/5 cm lens included (1931).

LEYOO Leica IIIb chrome finish with Elmar 3,5/50 mm (1939).

LFVOO Post-war version of 5x large field magnifier.

LGCOO Simple magnifier 5x for the universal copying device similar to item LOOCG (1938).

LIGOO Leica IIIb chrome finish without lens and case but with one cassette (1939).

LIHIG Leica III black with Hektor 2,5/50 mm (USA catalogue) (1939).

LIMON Leica Manual by Morgan & Lester (1939).

LINID Spare bulb for the MONLA lamp for microscopy (1951).

LKIOO Magnifier holder with large viewing angular magnifier 5x similar to item LOOGI (1938).

LKIUU Transformer to use the 110 volt 1000 watt lamp on the 220 volt system (1960).

LKOOM Leica model 72 without lens for negative size 18 x 24 mm built on IIIa body occasionally on a IIIc or IIIf (1950).

LMOOK As LKOOM but with ELMAR 50 mm F3.5 (1950).

LMUUK Projection table for epidiascope and lamps (1960).

LOOBT Leica IIIb chrome finish with Xenon 1,5/50 mm (1939).

LOOCG Simple magnifier 5x for the universal copying device (1936).

LOODU Leica IIIc with Summitar 2/50 mm (1940).

LOOEL Leica IIc with Elmar 3,5/50 lens (USA catalogue) Leica IIf with Elmar 3,5/50 mm lens (European catalogue) (1949-51).

LOOFV Large viewing magnifier 5x for the universal copying device (1936).

LOOGI Magnifier holder with large viewing magnifier angular 5x for the universal copying device code later used differently (1936).

LOOGI Leica IIIc with Elmar 3,5/50 mm – code word used previously (1940).

LOOHW Focusing magnifier 30x for the universal copying device, later codeword changed and given to other item (1936).

LOOHW Leica IIIc without lens (USA catalogue) Leica IIIf without lens (European catalogue) (1949-51).

LOOIT Leica IIIc with Summarit 1,5/50 mm lens (USA catalogue). Leica IIIf with Summarit 1,5/50 mm (European catalogue) (1949-51).

LOOKX Leica IIIc with Summitar 2/50 mm (USA catalogue) Leica IIIf with Summitar 2/50 mm (European catalogue) (1949-51).

LOOMY Leica 250 black with chambers for 250 pictures, speeds from 1 sec to 1/500 (also 1/1000) rangefinder, no lens.

LOOPN Leica IIIc with Elmar 3,5/50 mm (USA catalogue) Leica IIIf with Elmar 3,5/50 mm (European catalogue) (1949-51).

LOOQA Leica IIIc chrome finish without lens (1941).

LOOSB Leica IIIc chrome finish with Xenon 1:1,5/50 mm lens, one film chamber 1 sec to 1/1000 speeds.

LOOSE Leica IIc without lens (USA catalogue) Leica IIf without lens (European catalogue) (1949-51).

LOOSU Leica IIc with Summitar 2/50 (USA catalogue) Leica IIf with Summitar 2/50 (European catalogue) (1949-51).

LOOTP Leica IIId similar to IIIc but with delayed action release, without lens.

LOOUC As LOOTP but with lens Elmar 3,5/5 cm.

LOOWD As LOOTP but with Xenon 1,5/5 cm lens.

LOOYE Leica 250 black with film chambers for 250 pictures, speeds from 1 sec to 1/500 (also 1/1000) rangefinder, Elmar 3,5/5 cm.

LSZOO Two rings for connecting a microscope tube with the rotating stage plate of the universal copying device (1936).

LUDOO Leica IIIb chrome finish with Summar 2/50 mm (1939).

LUFAS Object stage for photographing small objects in transmitted light (1939).

LUOON Leica IIf with Summicron 2/50 mm lens (1954).

LUOOX Leica IIIf with Summicron 2/50 mm lens (1954).

LVFOO Large viewing magnifier 5x for the universal copying device similar to LOOFV (1938).

LWHOO Focusing magnifier 30x for the universal copying device similar to LOOHW (1938).

LYDRO Leica III black with one cassette without lens (1933).

LYHEK Leica II with Hektor 2,5/50 mm lens, black (1933).

LYKAN Leica II black with one cassette without lens (1933).

LYKUP Leica II black with one cassette and Elmar 3,5/50 mm lens (1933).

LYMAR Leica III black with rangefinder speeds from 1 sec to 1/500 one film chamber and Elmar 3,5/5 cm lens.

LYSTA Leica Standard, black with Elmar 3,5/50 mm and horizontal detachable rangefinder (1939).

LYSUM Leica III black with rangefinder, speeds from 1 sec to 1/500 one film chamber and Summar 2/5 cm lens.

M

MBOOC Auxiliary light cell for the Leicameter, later type (1960).

MBOOW Amplifier cell for the exposure meter Metra of the Leica M type (1956).

MBROO Water proof metal ever-ready case for Leica up to IIIf (1954).

MDVOO Printing board with adjustable mask for sizes up to 18 x 24 cm (1954).

METOO Metal heavy duty printing board, adjustable up to 18 x 24 cm size (1954).

METRA Exposure meter for the accessory shoe of the series M that automatically couples to the speeds dial.

MEUUR Projector model VIII-750 with lens Hektor 2,5/100 mm and slide changer (1939).

MEWOO Metal heavy duty printing board with divisions in inches up to 8 x 10in. (1954).

MEXOO Wooden baseboard with grooves for clamping on enlargers baseboard or for mounting on tilting joint (1954).

MEZOO Metal printing board with adjustable masks for sizes up to 18 x 24 cm (1954).

MFOOS Printing board with fixed masks for the Focomator II enlarger with automatic exposure meter (1960).

MFSSU Projector model VIII-750 without lens and without slide changer or film attachment (1939).

MFUUS-UMEXU Projector model VIII-750 without lens and with slide changer (1939).

MFVVT As MFUUS-UMEXU but with lens Hektor 2,5/8 mm (1939).

MFXXU As MFUUS-UMEXU but with lens Dimas 4,5/120 mm (1939).

MFZOO Mask with 3 mm border for size 10,5 x 14,8 cm (1960).

MGBOO Mask with 3 mm border for size 9 x 14 cm (1960).

MGOOR Printing board with fixed masks for all Leitz enlargers picture size up to 10,5 x 14,5 cm (1960).

MHDOO Mask with fixed border 3 mm for the size 9 x 12 cm (1960).

MHOOQ Mask with fixed border 3 mm for the size 9 x 13 cm (1960).

MIBAC Micro Ibso attachment with optical reducing system ½x with release and eyepiece screw mount (1951).

MICOO Connecting cable for Leica M3 socket to flash DFOOB (1956).

MIKAS Micro Ibso attachment with optical reducing system ⅓x with release and eyepiece screw mount (1951).

MIKKU Attachment for the projection of microscope slides with the projectors VIII complete with micro objectives (1939).

MIOOP Adaptor for using the Leica with a microscope, photo-micrographs to be made with the Leica lens set at infinity (1939).

MKHOO Automatic printing board for the Focomator II with in. border provision and automatic paper ejection (1960).

MKUOO Attachment for the projection of microscope slides with the projectors VIII without objectives (1939).

MLKOO Mask with fixed border of 3 mm for size 7,4 x 10,5 cm (1960).

MLOON Mask with fixed border 3 mm for size 9 x 9 cm (1960).

MLUUN Projector VIII-750 with lens Dimar 4/200 mm slide changer and supporting bracket (1939).

MNUUL Projector VIII-750 with lens Dimar 3,5/150 and slide changer (1939).

MONUU Projector VIII-750 with lens Dimar 4/250 mm slide changer and bracket (1939).

MOOBG Intermediate ring for reproductions in the ratio 1:2 with the universal copying device (1936).

MOODH Intermediate ring for reproductions in the ratio 1:1½ with the universal copying device (1936).

MOOGW Intermediate ring for reproductions in the ratio 1:1 with the universal copying device (1936).

MOOLY Clockwork motor for the Leica to take seqeuence shots (1938).

MOONZ Connecting cable between the flash CEYOO and the M type Leica (1956).

MOORB Extension ring for using the Telyt 200 lens on the rotating stage plate (1938).

MOOSP Intermediate ring 15 mm thick for the Telyt 200 mm (1936).

MOUNT Filter mount 34 mm diameter with set screw and special adaptor to fit Wratten filters of 32 mm diameter (1939).

MQUOO Release operated with mouth operation (1952).

MTOOE Matt diffusing screen for VASEX and Focomat IIa (1938).

N

NAABC Projector VIII-1000 without lens, without slide changer and without film attachment (1939).

NAFOO Distance rod for the ratio 1:1 with the Focomat IIc (1960).

NAGMI Magnifying glass, X 6 magnification for examining the negatives (1931).

NAHNE Focusing magnifier with handle for accurately adjusting the image in the enlarger (1933).

NAKUL Leica negative viewer with handle (1936).

NAMAS Opal glass plate with frame to be used with NAKUL and NATRA viewers (1933).

NATRA Leica negative viewer without handle (1933).

NBBCE Projector VIII-1000 without lens but with slide changer (1939).

NBOOY Anti Newton ring condenser for the VALOY I and Focomat I (1960).

NBQOO Special pressure plate to prevent Newton rings, taking the place of the lower glass plate of the film holder (1956).

NCCDF As NBBCE but with lens Hektor 2,5/85 (1939).

NCOOX Special pressure plate to prevent Newton rings, taking the place of the upper glass plate of the film holder (1954).

NCSOO Condenser with specially treated surface to prevent Newton rings (1956).

NDDGH As NBBCE but with lens Hektor 2,5/100 (1939).

NDOOW Pressure plate with condenser for Focomat Ia and Ic (1954).

NDUOG Condenser in short mount for Focomat Ia and Ic (1954).

NEEJK As NBBCE but with lens Dimax 4,5/120 (1939).

NEOOV Light tight panel for the lamphouse of the Focomat Colour and Focomator when the filter slide is removed (1954).

NESOO Pressure plate in mount to prevent Newton rings (1954).

NEWOO Frame for film to be used in the Focomat I to avoid Newtown rings (1951).

NFFLM As NBBCE but with lens Dimar 3,5/150 (1939).

NFOOU Upper plate glass of the standard negative carrier of the Focomat IIa (1960).

NFYOO Lower plate glass of the standard negative carrier of the Focomat IIa (1960).

NGGNO As NBBCE but with lens Dimar 4/200 (1939).

NGOOT Both plate glass of the standard negative carrier of the Focomat IIa (1960).

NHCOO Condenser N for Focomat Ia Ic and Focomator (1960).

NHHPR As NBBCE but with lens Dimar 4/250 (1939).

NIEOO Single negative carrier for sizes 6,5 x 9 and 7 x 7 cm for the Focomat IIc (1960).

NIIST As NBBCE but with lens Epnor 4,3/300 (1939).

NIOOR Film pressure frame 24 x 36 with specially treated glass to prevent Newton rings (1956).

NKGOO Accessory for manual focusing of the Focomat IIa (1960).

NKOOQ Upper plate glass of the negative carrier NOOIR (1960).

NLIOO Lower plate glass of the negative carrier NOOIR (1960).

NLOOP Pair of glasses of the negative carrier NOOIR (1960).

NOKUM New code name for the NOOKY HESUM, near focusing device for the Summar and Summitar (1960).

NOOAG Intermediate frame for the Focomat IIc and IIc Colour to use the double glass plate (1960).

NOOBU Negative film viewer (1951).

NOOIR Negative carrier for the Focomat IIc 24 x 36 mm with double plate glass with anti Newton surface (1960).

NOOKY Optical near focusing device for the Leica with the Elmar 3,5/50 mm lens (1936).

NOOKY HESUM Optical near focusing device for the Leica with the Summar 2/50 mm lens (1936).

NUBOO Focusing magnifier for accurately adjusting the image in the enlarger (1938).

NUFIR Carrying case for Leica gun with Telyt 400 mm lens (1938).

O

OADGO Leica Ig with Elmar 2,8/50 mm lens and viewfinder (1960).

OAGNO Copy outfit for small objects using PLOOT (1938).

OAPDO Copy equipment for medical specimens (Italy 1939).

OCEGO Leica Ig without lens without finder (1960).

OCLOM Visoflex II bayonet mounts and magnifier 4x (1960).

OCLUX Summilux 1,4/35 mm lens for M2-M4 (1959).

OCMOR Elmar 3,5/65 mm lens to use with Visoflex II (1960).

OCSUX Summilux 1,4/35 mm lens with bayonet mount and viewfinder attachment for M3 (1959).

ODULO Mirror reflex housing PROON plus right-angle 5x magnifier PAMOO (post 1940).

OEFGO Leica If without lens and without finder (1951).

OEGIO Leica model If without lens but with detachable reflecting viewfinder, one metal film cassette and take up spool (1951).

OEINO Leica If with reflecting viewfinder, Elmar 3,5/50 mm lens one metal film cassette and take up spool (1951).

OERDO Summicron 2/90 mm lens in short mount for use with the Visoflex with preset diaphram (1960).

OESBO As OERDO Normal Diaphram (1960).

OESFO Leica Ic with reflecting viewfinder, Summitar 2/50 mm lens one metal film cassette and take up spool (1951).

CFSET Adjustable offset arm for all enlargers up to Focomat I (USA) (1939).

OGILO Leica Ig without lens with viewfinder (1960).

OGSZO Complete outfit for using the rotating stage plate on all columns 32 mm diameter with the Elmar 3,5/50 mm (1938).

OGSZO HESUM As OGSZO but with Summar 50 mm (1938).

OHEBO Hektor 135 mm lens in short mount for use with the Visoflex (1936).

OHIKO Stereo unit complete with Stemar lens, prism and viewfinder (1954).

OHTEO OIPVO + OIFCO

OIASO Stemar stereo attachment comprising a twin Elmar 3,5/33 mm lens with bayonet mount (1960).

OIDYO Reflecting viewfinder for STEMAR (half frame) (1960).

OIFCO Lamp attachment for stereo viewer (1960).

OIGEO Lens shade for STEMAR (1960).

OIMPO Accessory prism for Stereo pictures closer than 10 ft. (1960).

OIPVO Stereo viewer (1954).

OIRZO As OHIKO, but with addition of stereo lens hood OIGEO.

OOVIW Adaptor ring to use Diax lenses with Leitz enlargers (1956).

OIWKO Lens cap with bayonet for Stemar.

OOVKY Adaptor ring to use Exacta screw mount lenses with Leitz enlargers (1956).

OIZQO Rear cover for prism OIMPO.

OKARO Orange filter for the rangefinder of the IIIb model (1936).

OKBZO Correcting lenses for near and farsightedness for Leica IIIg (1960).

OKGDO Additional codword for the baseplates GOOBR and GOOFT without the ball and socket head (1938).

OKLMO Connecting bracket for the column of the repro device Focomat I (1960).

OKVCO Correcting lenses for anastigmatism for the viewfinder of the Leica IIIg (1960).

OKYNO Carrying arm of the VALOY II with locking device (1960).

OKZPO Upright 65 cm high with rectilinear guide (1960).

OLDER Enlarger film holder for making 35 mm copies with the enlarger, accomodated all type up to Focomat I (1939).

OLEYO Leica accessory for single exposures with small Ibsor shutter (1934).

OLIGO Leica accessory for single exposures with large Ibsor shutter (1934).

OLLUX Sunshade for Summilux 1,4/35 mm lens (1959).

OLORA Single exposure housing without shutter (USA 1936).

OMEXO-ROOYH Portable copying stand with focusing stage and canvas bag (1951).

OMIFO Optical near focusing device for Elmar 4/90 mm lens with fixed reproduction ratio of 1:4 (USA) (1949).

ONLIO Canvas bag for the copying equipment Omexo (1951).

OOBAZ New focaslide for all the Leicas with screw mount, slide alone (1960).

OOEUK Light box size 36 x 40 cm (1954).

OOEVM Light box size 18 x 24 cm (1951).

OOFRC Remote winding and shutter release for the Leica (1936).

OOGAN New focaslide for screw mount Leicas with helical ring, magnifier, and accessories for Elmar 2,8/50 mm (1960).

OOGIT As OOGAN but using the Elmar 3,5/50 mm (1960).

OOGUM As OOGAN but with Focotar 4,5/50 mm lens (1960).

OOMAP as OOGUM for the Focotar 4,5/50 for bayonet mount cameras (1960).

OOMEX Focoslide complete with helical focusing ring, diaphragm setting ring, magnifier and accessories for the Elmar 2,8/50 (1960).

OOMYL As OOMAP but with Summicron 2/50 lens (1960).

OORES Upper stage (rotating plate) of the universal copying device (1936).

OOTGU Focoslide for use of bayonet mount lenses (1960).

OOVBH Adaptor ring to use Finetta lenses with Leitz enlargers (1956).

OOVCK Adaptor ring to use Akarette lenses with Leitz enlargers (1956).

OOVDM Adaptor ring to use Contax lenses with Leitz enlargers (1956).

OOVFQ Adaptor ring to use Exakta bayonet mount lenses with Leitz enlargers (1956).

OOVGS Adaptor ring to use Prominent lenses with the Leitz enlargers (1956).

OOVHU Adaptor ring to use Robot lenses with Leitz enlargers (1956).

OOVIW Adaptor ring to use Diax lenses with Leitz enlargers (1956).

OOVKY Adaptor ring to use Exacta screw mount lenses with Leitz enlargers (1956).

OOVMC Adaptor ring to use Lordonat lenses with Leitz enlargers (1956).

OOVNE Adaptor ring to use Praktica lenses on the VALOY II (1960).

OOVPI Adaptor ring to use Robot Royal bayonet lenses on the VALOY II (1960).

OOZAB Focusing stage of the Reprovit and similar outfits (1951).

OOZEG Folding stand of the portable copying equipment OMEXO (1951).

OOZIS Simple table reproduction device consisting in a column and several masks indicating the area covered (1939).

OOZKU Set of five adaptor rings of different lengths for the copying device OOZIS (1939).

OOZMY Focusing stage of the copying equipment OMEXO (1951).

OPDUR Combined supports OPFAS and OPRYL for technical picture taking (1933).

OPFAS Leica support against the chest with scope finder and two 500 watt lamps (1933).

OPKOM Flexible release 20in. long for OPDUR (1933).

OPRTO Correcting lenses for near and farsightedness for the models IIc, IIIc, IIf, IIIf (1951).

OPRYL Lower support to be used with OPFAS (1933).

OPSVO Correcting lenses for astigmatism for Leica models IIc, IIIc, IIf, IIIf (1951).

OQWCO Lens cap for Summicron 90 mm (1960).

OQZIO Near and farsightedness correcting lenses for LVFOO and PEGOO (1960).

ORAKO Orange filter, slip on for the rangefinder of the Leica III (1936).

ORBMO Eyesight correcting lenses for viewfinder of Leica models up to IIIa (1941).

ORESO Revolving stage plate with special tripod foot (1936).

ORIFT Lens cap for Elmar 3,5/50 mm first type (1933).

ORLEO Correcting lenses for anastigmatism for the Leica M3 (1956).

ORMGO Eyesight correcting (including astigmatism) for the Leica models up to IIIa (1941).

OROBA Cap for lens hood XOOIM for Summilux 50 mm (1960).

OROBI Cap for lens hoods IWKOO, IROOA, ITOOY, IUFOO (1960).

OROLF Turret revolving for three screw lenses for Leica M2 and M3 (1960).

ORPNO Spare lens cap for Summarex 85 mm (1951).

ORQDO Lens cap for the Summicron 50 mm lens (1954).

ORQPO Lens hood for Summarex 85 mm (1951).

ORSTO Spare lens cap for Summitar 50 mm (1951).

ORSUM Lens cap for Summitar 2/50 mm (later ORSTU) (1949).

ORTOX Correcting lenses for near and farsightedness for the Leica M 3 (1956).

ORTUX Eyesight correcting lenses to be added to the viewfinder (1933).

ORTVO Aperture cover for screwing into the Leica body when no lens is on (1938).

ORUXO Eyesight correcting lenses for astigmatism for the Leica models II and III (1938).

ORVZO Lens cap for lenses Elmar 3,5/50; 35 mm and similar (1936).

ORWBO Lens cap for Elmar 105 mm black (1936).

ORWYB Correction lenses for the view and range finder of the Leica IIIb to correct near and far sightedness (1939).

ORXDO Lens cap for Hektor 73 mm black, later used for cap of Xenon and Summarit 50 mm (1936).

ORXDO Lens cap for the Summarit 1,5/50 mm similar to the former Xenon 1,5/50 lens cap (1951).

ORYCE Correction lenses for the view and rangefinder of the Leica IIIb for the correction of astigmatism (1939).

ORYFO Rear cover for all Leica lenses screw mount (1951).

ORZHO Lens cap for Thambar 90 mm and Telyt 200 mm early type lens, black (1936).

ORZIT Lens cap (black) for Telyt 4/200 (1960).

OSBLO Eyepiece to be used 50 and 90 mm Leica lenses allowing them to be used as telescopes (1954).

OSERO Astigmatism correcting lens for magnifiers LVFOO and PEGOO (1960).

OSIZO Rotating stage plate with special tripod foot including ball-jointed head and intermediate thread with adapting rings.

OSIZO HESUM Rotating stage plate with special tripod foot for use with the Summar 2/50 mm (1938).

OSLAM Spare 15 watt lamp for the Kodia copier (1933).

OSNIT Nitraphot 500 watt lamp as spare (1933).

OSROT Spare red lamp for the Kodia copier (1933).

OTDYM Visoflex bayonet mount without magnifier (1960).

OTEMO Stereo separation prism for Wetzlar wartime stereo system.

OTPLO Telyt lens 4,5/200 mm without mirror reflex housing (1936).

OTQNO Adaptor to use the Elmar 90 mm at close range with the Visoflex II (1960).

OTRPO Adaptor to use Elmar 65 mm Elmarit 90 mm and Hektor 135 mm at close range with Visoflex II (1960).

OTSRO Adaptor to use the optical group of the Hektor 135 mm with the Visoflex (1960).

OTVXO Magnifier 5x for Visoflex II (1960).

OTXBO Magnifier 4x with prism for Visoflex II (1960).

OTYDO Visoflex II screw mount without magnifier (1960).

OTZFO Adaptor to use Elmar 65 mm Elmarit 90 and Hektor 135 mm with the Visoflex II (1960).

OUAGO Adaptor to use Elmar 90 mm with the Visoflex II (1960).

OUBIO Adaptor to use Hektor 125 mm Hektor 135 mm Telyt 200 mm and Telyt 400 mm with the Visoflex II (1960).

OUCLO Visoflex II with screw mounts and magnifier 4x (1960).

OUFRO Adaptor to use 35 and 50 mm lenses, Hektor 125 and 135 mm Telyt 200 and 400 mm at close range with Visoflex II (1960).

OUTSO Projection head of the Reprovit I and II (1951).

OUUEW Projection lens 2x on the large micro adaptor (1960).

OUUIY Projection lens 4x on the large micro adaptor (1960).

OVAFO Column of the Reprovit I with baseboard (1951).

OVURO Baseboard and upright of the Valoy II with upright 32in. (1960).

OWMAN Repro Summar lens 4,5/24 mm for copying (1960).

OZIXO Mirror reflex device with 5x magnifier (1951).

OZTNO Intermediate piece for using wire releases of the normal type with the Leica M3 (1956).

OZTOM Double cable release for bayonet cameras and Visoflex I.

OZUDU Film carrier for size 8 x 11 mm for the Valoy II and Focomat Ia and Ic enlargers (1960).

OZUPO Visoflex I without magnifier (1951).

OZVUO Valoy II enlarger without lens with upright 32in. high (1960).

OZWTO Double wire release for the Visoflex (1951).

OZXOM As OZYXO, but with bayonet mount.

OZXVO Screw in cable release link for reflex housing OZYXO (1954).

OZYXO Visoflex I with 5x vertical magnifier LVFOO (1951).
OZYXO-M Visoflex housing for M type cameras complete with 5x focusing magnifier (1956).

P

PAGES Extra pages for the loose leaf file (USA catalogue) (1939).
PAMOO Focusing magnifier 5x right angle (1951).
PBAAG Light tight box for enlarging paper size 8 x 10in. (1939).
PBEED As PBAAG but paper size 11 x 14in. (1939).
PBOOC As PBAAG but paper size 18 x 24 cm (1936).
PCOOB Slip on yellow filter No. 0 for Thambar 90 mm and Telyt 200 mm (1936).
PEGOO Focusing magnifier 45° presenting the image laterally correct (1951).
PEOOZ As PCOOB but yellow filter No. 1 (1936).
PEZEN Periplanatic eyepiece for photomicrography (1951).
PFOOY As PCOOB but yellow filter No. 2 (1936).
PGOOX As PCOOB but graduated yellow filter (1936).
PGYOO As PCOOB but graduated green filter (1939).
PHOOW As PCOOB but UV filter (1936).
PIOOV As PCOOB but green filter (1936).
PKOOU As PCOOB but red filter light (1936).
PLGOO As PCOOB but orange filter (1941).
PLGUU Carrying case for episcope 325 (1960).
PLOOT Mirror reflex housing with two magnifiers and double cable release unit (1938).
PMOOS As PCOOB but red filter medium (1936).
PNLOO Plastic box for Super Angulon 21 mm bayonet mount (1960).
PNOOR Slip on red filter dark for Thambar 90 mm and Telyt 200 mm (1936).
POFLA Kodachrome flash filter E48 (USA 1949).
POLAR Equipment for the projection of stereo pictures with the Stereoly through polarizing filters (1939).
POLMO Plastic box for 35 mm lenses with bayonet mount (1956).
POLWO Plastic box for all 50 mm lenses bayonet mount (1956).
POLXO Plastic box for Elmar 90 mm bayonet mount (1956).
POLYO Plastic box for Elmar 90 mm collapsible bayonet mount (1956).
POLZO Plastic box for Hektor 135 mm bayonet mount (1956).
POOAH E48 yellow filter No. 0 (1936).
POOBV E48 yellow filter No. 1 (1936).
POOCI E48 yellow filter No. 2 (1936).
POOCQ E48 blue filter (1956).
POODW E48 green filter (1936).
POOEK E48 red filter medium (1936).
POOEL Polarizing filter A36 mount with numbered scale (1951).
PPOFX E48 UV filter (1936).
POOAY Type "A" Kodachrome filter E48 (USA 1949).
POOGL E48 red filter light (1936).
POOHY E48 red filter dark (1936).
POOIM Vertical 5x and 30x magnifier assembly for PROON (post 1940).
POOKZ Orange filter screw in for the Telyt 200 mm (1951).
POOLU Polarizing filter in rotating mount A36 (1941).
POOMA Polarizing filter slip on mount A36 (1939).
POORE Polarizing filter for Summitar 50 mm lens (1951).
POORQ Double cable release for mirror reflex housing (1949).
POOSD Transparent plastic case for standard size filters (Summitar) (1951).
POOTR Polarizing filter E39 (1960).
POOUE Plastic container for Summarit filters (1954).
POOVS Plastic box for filters up to 43 mm diameter (1960).
PQUUO Prism for projection on a table with the large micro accessory (1960).
PROCU Protection cup for Leica cameras up to model IIIb (USA catalogue) (1939).
PROGBAN Connecting cable for the old projectors when the low voltage lamp was used (1933).
PROON Mirror reflex housing without magnifier (post 1940).

Q

QCPOO A36 dark yellow filter (1939).
QBOOE Dark yellow filter for lenses Hektor 28 and 135 mm Summar 50 mm and Elmar 90 mm (1939).

R

RAMET Mask for the 105 and 135 focal lengths to be used with RASUK (1933).
RASAL Large frame finder with mask RAMET (1933).

RASUK Large frame finder (1933).
RCOOF Dark slide to use in the Valoy and Focomat enlargers for copying slides on film and glass plates (1951).
RDOOE Universal copying device complete for Elmar 3,5/50 mm (1938).
RDOOE HESUM As RDOOE but for Summar 2/50 mm (1938).
RDQOO Diaphragm operating lever and guide for the lens of the Reprovit II (1951).
REAFU Transformer for 220 volt A.C. (1931).
REAMO Variable resistance for supply voltages 110 to 250 volt (1931).
REDIG BEEUL Resistance for MONLA lamp with connecting cable BEEUL (1952).
REDUK As REDIG-BEEUL but for 220 volt (1951).
REDYX Transformer 220-110 volt for the MONLA lamp (1939).
REFUG Mains transformer type ETL for 220 volts (1933).
REGET AC regulating set comprising a resistance, transformer and connecting cables (1933).
REGIR Resistor 50 ohms for the regulating set REGET and REGNO (1933).
REGLU DC regulating set comprising a primary resistance a secondary resistance and connecting cables (1933).
REGMI Resistance for 200-240 volts AC and DC with voltmeter for regulating the brightness of the reading desk image (1936).
REGNO Regulating set for AC and DC with one resistor and connecting cable (1933).
REGOL Resistor 50 ohm for DC regulating set (1933).
REGYD Supplementary resistance for DC regulating set REGLU (1933).
RENAX Resistance combined for 110 and 220 volt DC or AC for ULEJA and ULIOS (1931).
RENIA Resistance for a 220 volt DC or AC for ULEJA or ULIOS (1931).
RENNI As RENIA but for 110 volt (1931).
RENUM Transformer combined for 110 and 220 volt AC or DC 60 cycles (1931).
REOOD Universal copying device complete (1956).
REPOO Light tight box for copying with the Focomat IIc on film or plates size 6,5 x 9 or 7 x 7 cm (1960).
RESOO Upper stage of the universal copying device (1936).
RFOOC Special assembling tool for Reprovit II (1950).
RFUUO Resistance for the ring illuminator of the universal copying device (1936).
RGOOB Regulating resistance with 70-240 volt voltmeter (1936).
RGWOO Framing box for size 297 x 420 mm (11⅝ x 16⅜in.) DIN A3 (1951).
RHEOS Photoflood rheostat control for controlling illumination in enlargers (USA catalogue) (1939).
RHYOO Double stage with compensating device for Reprovit (1950).
RIFLE Leica gun for use of the camera with Visoflex and Telyt 200 and 400 mm lenses (1938).
RIFUN Carrying case for Leica gun with Telyt 200 or Hektor 135 mm (1938).
RIOOX Baseboard with double column of the Reprovit II with arm and steel tape measure (1950).
RIOOZ Ring illuminator for the universal copying device (1936).
RIPBO Leica gun complete including Hektor 135 mm lens, Visoflex Leica camera model IIIb and special camera baseplate (1938).
RITEL As RIPBO but with Telyt 400 mm lens (1938).
RITOO As RIPBO but with Telyt 200 mm lens (1938).
RKCOO Four lamps illuminating system for the Reprovit II (1950).
RKOOY Mask size 6 x 6 cm for the accessory REPOO (1960).
RKOOZ Mask size 5 x 5 cm for the accessory REPOO (1960).
RMOOW Adaptor ring for printing in the ratio 1:2,5 with the Focotar 60 mm lens (1960).
ROLBA Ruled steel tape 1.5 metres long (1933).
ROLUU Accessory for slides size 8,5 x 10 and 9 x 12 cm for the episcope Vh 400 with Dimax lens 250 mm (1960).
ROOAI Special focusing stage for Reprovit II (1950).
ROOAM As ROOAI but with bayonet mount (1960).
ROOEL Regulating resistance with 70-240 volts voltmeter and connecting cable (1936).

ROOFU Carrying arm for the focusing stage fitting 40 mm column (1951).
ROOKA Large copying device complete (1936).
ROOMB Extra long arm for the universal copying device with 40in. upright (1936).
ROONP Supporting arm for focusing stage fitting 32 mm column (1951).
ROOPQ Extra long arm for the column Vesta, is substituted in some catalogues by a similar arm VEHAL (1939).

ROOQD Framing box for size 210 x 297 mm (8¼ x 11 in.) DIN A4 (1951).
ROOSE Basic Reprovit I equipment comprising baseboard and upright, arm, focusing stage, projection head (1950).
ROOTS Film holding device for Focomat II and Vasex supplied subsequently for the VANOS and VADUM (1938).
ROOVZ Adaptor ring to use the Micro Summar 4,5/24 mm lens on the Reprovit II (1952).
ROOXU Basic Reprovit II equipment with baseboard and column focusing stage, lens, lamps, tool (1951).
ROOYH Extension ring REPRO (26 mm) (1952).
ROSOL Frame finder similar to RASAL but with frames for lenses of 50, 85, 90 and 135 mm (1951).
ROXUM As ROOXU but with bayonet mount (1960).
RPNOO Micro adaptor for focusing stage and Reprovit (1951).
RPOOT Micro adaptor for Reprovit similar to RPNOO but without lateral eyepiece and release (1956).
RQPOO Screw mount blue filter for Summitar 50 mm (1954).
RSOOQ Rapid winding device for special Leica RUXOO meant for X-ray photography; serves as lower camera cover (1940).
RSTOO As RPOOT but with optical system ½x (1956).
RSTUU Adjustable transformer 220-110 volts 500 watts (1960).
RSUUQ As RSTUU but 1,000 watts (1960).
RTOOP Support tube and adaptor of camera to X-ray screen (1940).
RTSOO As RPNOO but with optical system ½x (1956).
RTVOO Device for connecting the rapid winding mechanism (1940).
RUUKA Epidiascope Vh with Dimax 250 mm lens with slide accessory (1960).
RUXOO Leica X-ray camera 24 x 24 format, without viewfinder and lower cover (1940).
RVOON Steel cable for rapid winding mechanism, as spare (1940).
RVZOO Solid leather case for the wide-angle viewfinder SUOOQ (1938).
RWBOO Deerskin purse for the frame finder RASAL and ROSOL (1936).
RXDOO Leitz Xenon lens 1,5/5 cm without focusing mount and without diaphragm, mounted in tube RTOOP (1940).
RXOOL Adaptor ring to use the micro tubes on the slide with Leica M type bayonet (1960).
RYOOK Complete outfit for X-ray photography with special Leica 24 x 24 camera and Xenon 1,5/5 cm lens (1940).
RZHOO Support for winding control (1940).

S

SAIOO Sports finder for the 73 mm lens (1936).
SAMWO Summicron 2/35 mm lens for M3 with viewfinder attachment (1960).
SAWOM Summicron 2/35 mm lens for Leica M2 (1960).
SAWOO Summicron 2/35 mm lens screw mount (1960).
SBKOO Reflecting viewfinder for Super Angulon 4/21 mm (1960).
SBLOO Reflecting viewfinder for 35 mm lenses (1951).
SBOOI Reflecting viewfinder for 50 mm lenses (1951).
SBUUI Film guide with automatic release for projectors VIIIc (1939).
SCNOO Rapid winder for the Leica early type (1936).
SCNUU Slide changer for glass slides 5 x 5 cm (1939).
SDOOG Tripod head with spring catch (1936).
SDUUG Simple carrier for glass slides 5 x 5 cm (1939).
SELAN Angle bracket to use SELSY and SELIS on side of Leica (1949).
SELBA Flash unit with syncronizer for multiple flash use (1949).
SELCA Connecting cord to use with SELAN (1949).
SELEX Connecting cord 10ft. long (1949).
SELIS Flash unit for Leica models IIIc and IIc (1949).
SELLO Connecting cord 6ft. long (1949).
SELOR Special three way socket to connect up to three lamps to the synchroniser (1939).
SELSY Flash unit for cameras having serial numbers higher than III.450 except models IIIc and IIc (1949).
SEOOF Summicron 2/90 mm lens screw mount (1960).
SEOOM Summicron 2/90 mm lens bayonet mount (1960).
SEROO Sports finder for 90 mm focus lens (1936).
SEVUE Sports viewfinder for the 90 mm lenses (USA catalogue) (1949).

SFTOO Frame finder for Telyt 200 mm (1936).
SFTUU Spare lamp 30 volts 100 watts for VIIIc projectors (1939).
SFUUE Carrying case for projectors series VIIIc (1939).
SGOOD Reflecting viewfinder for 85 mm lenses (1951).
SGUUD Spare lamp for projectors VIIIc (1939).
SGVOO Reflecting viewfinder for 90 mm lenses (1951).
SGVUU Condenser lens next to objective in condenser No. 1 of projector VIIIc (1939).
SHADE Lens shade for THAMBAR 2,2/90 mm lens (USA catalogue) (1939).
SHOEE Accessory shoe for using Lecia accessories on other cameras (1939).
SHOLD Non-slip shoulder pad for camera neck strap (USA 1950).
SHOOC Reflecting viewfinder for 135 mm lenses (1951).
SHUUC Viewing desk for use with projectors VIIIc and PRADO 150 (1939).
SHXOO Shutter adjusting knob 13,8 mm diameter with fixing knob (1936).
SIMOM Summaron 2,8/35 mm lens for Leica M1 and M2 (1960).
SIMOO Summaron 2,8/35 mm lens screw mount (1960).
SIMWO Summaron 2,8/35 mm lens bayonet mount for Leica M3 with viewfinder attachment (1960).
SIUUB Projector VIIIc 'Parvo' for film strip with Hektor 2,5/85 mm lens with 100 watt lamp (1939).
SIUUB GLAS As SLUUB but for glass slides (1939).
SIZOO Folding type viewfinder for 10.5cm lens (1935).
SKBUU Interchangeable 3 lens condenser 73 to 100 mm for projectors VIIIc (1939).
SLDUU As SKBUU for Elmar 500 mm lens (1939).
SLOOZ Reflecting viewfinder for 28 mm focus (1960).
SLUUZ Slide changer for 5 x 5 cm slides on the PRADO 150 (1960).
SMFUU Condenser lens next to objective in condenser II for projector VIIIc (1939).
SMUUY Projector VIIIc 'Parvo' for glass slides, without lens with 100 watt lamp (1939).
SMYOM Rapid winder Leicavit MP for Leica models M1 and M2 (1960).
SNEEX Projector VIIIc in simplified form like SNUUX for the USA market (1939).
SNHOO Adaptor ring to use E39 on the Summitar 50 mm (1960).
SNHUU Interchangeable 3 lens condenser to use Summar 2/50 and Hektor 2,5 mm lenses on the projector VIIIc (1939).
SNOOX Summaron 5,6/28 mm screw mount (1960).
SNUUX Projector VIIIc 'Parvo' in simplified version with Dimenar 4,8/85 mm lens fixed for glass slides (1939).
SOMKY Near focusing device for Leica M models with most of the 50 mm lenses (1960).
SOMNI Summicron 2/50 mm lens with viewfinder attachment for close range focusing (1960).
SOOAW Cradle type viewfinder for 7.3cm lens (1943).
SOOBK Lens hood for Summaron 5,6/28 mm lens (1960).
SOOCX Summarex 1,5/85 mm lens chromed (1951).
SOODL As SOOLB but for 5cm.
SOOEY Adaptor ring to use Summitar and Summarit filter on E39 lenses except the 21 mm Super Angulon (1960).
SOFIT Tubular lamp 25 watt for the large light box of the X-ray reproduction device (1933).
SOOFM Lens hood for the Summicron 50 mm (1954).
SOOGZ Adaptor ring for E39 filters on A36 lenses (1960).
SOOHN Lens hood for Hektor 28 mm (1936).
SOOIA Summarit 1,5/50 mm lens (1951).
SOOIA M Summarit 1,5/50 mm lens in bayonet mount (1956).
SOOIC Summicron 2/50 mm collapsible, screw mount (1954).
SOOIC M As SOOIC in bayonet mount (1956).
SOOKY Near focusing device for Summicron 2/50 mm screw mount (1954).
SOOLB Cradle type viewfinder for 8.5cm lens (USA 1950).
SOOME Summilux 1,4/50 mm lens bayonet mount (1960).
SOOMP Lens hood for the Summar 50 mm lens (1936).
SOONC Summaron 3,5/35 mm screw mount (1951).
SOONC M As SOONC in bayonet mount (1956).
SOOPD Lens hood for Summitar 50 mm collapsible (1951).
SOOQR Screw in adaptor to use Summitar filters on the lens (1954).

SOORE Summitar 2/50 mm lens (1951).
SOOTF Adaptor ring to use Summitar and Summarit filters on A36 mount (1954).
SOOUT As SOOAW but for 9cm.
SOOWU Tape measure fitting arm ROOMP (1951).
SOOYV As SOOAW but for 13.5 cm.
SOREI Flexible release soft and improved type for all Leica models up to IIIc (1949).
SOSIC Summicron 2/50 mm lens rigid bayonet mount (1960).
SOUUW Projector Q VIIc 'Parvo' for film strips with Hektor 2,5/100 mm lens and 100 watts lamp (1939).
SOUUW GLAS As SOUUW but for glass slides (1939).
SPECS Polaroid spectacles for looking at stereo projection (1939).
SPMOO Special large foot with baseboard for the rotating stage plate (1936).
SPMOO DOOSL Large horse shoe stand for copying devices (1938).
SPMUU Height adjuster for projectors VIIIc (1939).
SPOOM Spare spool for Ig, IIIg, M1, M2, M3, MD (1955).
SPOOV Special tripod for the rotating stage plate of the universal copying device (1936).
SPOOV Special tripod foot for the rotating stage plate of the universal copying device (1938).
SPUCA Centre spool of the roll film chamber (1931).
SPULM Take up spool of the Leica camera (1931).
SPUUV Projector VIIIc 'Parvo' for film strip, without lens with 1000 watt lamp (1939).
SQTOO Special finder for Telyt 400 mm (1954).
STABU Spare 40 watt bulb for the illuminating device (1933).
STAFO Four lamp illuminating device for the large copying device (1933).
STALI Illuminating equipment comprising two 40 watt opal bulbs with reflectors, wire and plug and support rod (1931).
STAMA Steel tape measure for the special copying device (1933).
STAOT Copying stand collapsible STARE in canvas bag complete with plumb line FLOTH (1931).
STARE As STAOT but without FLOTH (1931).
STERO Stereoly stereo accessory for the Leica IIIb (1939).
STOOR Four lamp illuminating device for the universal copying device (previously called STAFO) (1936).
STUOO Steel tape measure for the universal copying device (previously called STAMA) (1936).
STYYX Illuminator for copying with 4 adjustable lamps (1939).
SUMAN Microsummar lens for macrophoto, 24 mm, 4,5 with diaphragm (1939).
SUMAN-ROOVZ As SUMAN with three Repro rings (1954).
SUMAR Summar 2/50 mm lens in Rigid mount (1936).
SUMAX Micro Summar 4,5/35 mm lens (1939).
SUMEX As SUMAX with diaphragm (1939).
SUMIT Micro Summar 4,5/42 mm lens (1939).
SUMMY Micro Summar 4,5/100 mm lens (1939).
SUMOM Super Angulon 4/21 mm lens bayonet mount (1960).
SUMOR Micro Summar 4,5/80 mm lens (1939).
SUMOS Micro Summar 4,5/65 mm lens (1939).
SUMUR Micro Summar 80 mm 4,5 with diaphragm (1939).
SUMUS Summar 2/50 mm lens in collapsible mount (1936).
SUMZO Micro Summar 4,5/120 mm lens (1939).
SUNGO Sunshade for Telyt 4,5/200 replacement (1939).
SUOON Super Angulon 4/21 mm lens screw mount (1960).
SUOOQ Special finder for the Hektor 28 mm lens (1936).
SUUAW Window for 18 x 24 mm size for projectors VIIIc (1939).
SUUBK Accessory condenser and lens mount for projectors SNUUX and SUUEY (1939).
SUUCX Supplementary condenser SUUBK with Hektor 2,5/85 mm projection lens for projectors SNUUX and SUUEY (1939).
SUUEY Projector VIIIc 'Parvo' in simplified version with fixed Dimenar 4,8/85 mm lens for film strips (1939).
SUUPD Code word for fitting fan to projectors (1960).
SUUZI Film guide 24 x 36 mm for projectors PRADO (1960).
SUWOO Simple finder for a 50 mm lens (similar to the one used on the Standard Leica) (1936).
SVOOP Take up spools for cameras prior to type IIIg with catch spring button (1960).
SYBAT Battery case extension for the SYNCO and flash units (1939).
SYEOO Sports finder for the 135 mm focus lens (1936).

SYNCO Flash unit for the Leica that attaches to the lower base of camera with upper synchronising contact (1939).
SYOOM Leicavit for cameras above 400.000 (1952).

T

TAHOO Daylight developing tank for 35 mm film (1938).
TBKOO Intermediate for photomicrography with the Universal copying device (1936).
TEEAH Carrying case for projectors series VIII 750 and 1000 (1939).
TELOO Telyt 4/200 mm lens with lens hood for Visoflex (1960).
TEOOH Leitz Agfa Rondinax daylight developing tank (1951).
TEQOO E85 orange filter (1951).
TEQUU GLAS Projector VIII 250 with slide changer and Hektor 2,5/100 mm lens (1939).
TFOOG E85 light yellow filter No. 0 (1938).
TFSOO E85 yellow filter No. 1 (1938).
TFUUG Objective carrier tube for lenses of 175 mm focus (1960).
TGOOF E85 yellow filter medium No. 2 (1938).
TGUOO E85 red filter light (1938).
THMOO Lens hood (replacement) for Telyt 5/400 mm (1951).
THOOE E85 red filter medium (1938).
THWOO E85 red filter dark (1938).
THWUU Projection lens Hektor 2,8/250 mm (1960).
TIOOD E85 UV filter (1938).
TIYOO E85 yellow green filter (1954).
TIYUU Hektor 2,5/85 mm projection lens with tube (1939).
TKUUC Hektor 2,5/100 mm projection lens with tube (1939).
TLCOO Telyt 5/400 mm lens for Visoflex (1960).
TLCUU Projection lens Hektor 2,5/175 mm (1960).
TLOOB Telyt 5/400 mm lens complete with mirror reflex housing (1938).
TLUUB Resistor for 75 volts 375 watts lamp when used on 110 volts (1939).
TMEOO Lens hood for Telyt 5/400 mm (second type) (1954).
TNGOO Lens hood (replacement) for Telyt 4,5/200 mm (1951).
TNOOQ Spare lens cap for Telyt 400 mm (1951).
TNOOZ Spare lens cap for Telyt 200 mm (1951).
TNUUZ Condenser lens No. 3 for projectors type VIII (1938).
TOIUU Carrying case for projectors type VIII with resistance (1938).
TOODY Thambar 2,2/90 mm lens (1936).
TOOLP Telyt 4,5/200 mm lens complete with mirror reflex housing (1936).
TOOLP M Telyt 4,5/200 mm with bayonet mount Visoflex (1956).
TOOQE Table stand TOOUG with tripod head FOOMI (1951)
TOOSF Table stand for the Leica (1936).
TOOUG Folding table tripod (1949).
TOTEL Telyt 400 mm f:5 lens in focusing mount with Mirror reflex housing (1938).
TOWIN Device for coupling together two Leica IIIc (USA catalogue) (1949).
TPUUX Viewing table for projectors series VIII 250 and 400 (1939).
TREPL Equipment for photomicrography with microscope, Leica, and Mirror Reflex Housing (1938). Apparatus for ophthalmic photography with special 9cm Elmar in long tube (1953).
TROOV Wrist strap to carry a Leica (1938).
TROOV Wrist strap to carry a Leica (1941).
TRPOO Neck strap for Leica camera with patent hooks (1951).
TRPOO M Neckstrap with patent hooks for Leica M (1956).
TRPUU Condenser No. 1 for projectors type VIII (1938).
TRVZO Internal condenser No. 2 removable for replacement (1939).
TSFUU Projection lens Hektor 2,5/175 mm (1960).
TSOOV Neck strap with split rings (1960).
TULOR Focomat II c enlarger as TUOOS with added TWOOQ and TWZOO (1960).
TUOOS Focomat II c enlarger with accesories (1960).
TUSOO Tape measure for ROOFU (1951).
TUUAK Projector VIII-250 for using Leica lenses and projecting film strips 35 mm (1938).
TUUBA Dimar 3,5/150 mm projection lens (1939).
TUUBX Epner 4,3/300 mm projection lens (1939).
TUUCL Removable gate for glass slides 3,5 x 12 cm (1939).
TUUDY Basic outfit of projectors VIII (1938).
TUUEL Slide changer for glass plates 3,5 x 12 cm for the projector VIII (1938).
TUUEM Interchangeable automatic film carrier for the projectors VIII (1938).
TUUFZ IZUUS Hektor 2,5/100 mm projection lens (1939).

TUUGN Simple slide changer for positives 3 x 4 cm in glasses 5 x 5 cm (1938).
TUUIO Projector VIII 250 for using Leica lenses and projecting 5 x 5 glass slides (1938).
TUUKB Dimar 4/200 mm projection lens (1939).
TUULP GLAS Projector VIII 250 with slide-changer and Dimar 3, 5/150 mm lens (1939).
TUUMC GLAS as TUULP GLAS but with Dimar 4/200 mm lens (1939).
TUUNQ Intermediate support for using the Telyt 200 mm lens with the projectors series VIII (1938).
TUUOD Interchangeable slide changer for 5 x 5 glass diapositives for the projectors series VIII (1938).
TUUPR As TUULP GLAS but with Epis 3,6/80 mm lens (1939).
TUUQE As TUULP GLAS but with DINAX 4,5/120 mm lens (1939).
TUURS As TUULP GLAS but with Hektor 2,5/85 mm lens (1939).
TUUVE GLAS As TUULP GLAS but with Dimar 4/250 mm lens (1939).
TUVOO Accessory for the VIOOH viewfinder bringing the field to the 28 mm focus lens (1951).
TVOOR Automatic enlarger Focomat II with turret with Elmar 3,5/50 mm lens and Focotar 4,5/95 mm lens (1951).
TVOOR COLOR Automatic Enlarger Focomat II as TVOOR but with also Agfa filters carrier (1951).
TVUUR Dimar 4/250 mm projection lens (1939).
TWOOQ Enlarging ratio indicator with two scales for Focomat IIc enlarger (1960).
TWZOO Filter holder for filters 12 x 12 cm for the Focomat IIc enlarger (1960).
TXBOO Intermediate collar for using the Telyt 200 and 400 mm lenses on the Leica M without reflex housing, with viewfinder shoe (1956).
TXOOP Enlarging ratio indicator for Focomat IIa (1960).
TYDOO Focomat IIa complete with accessories (1951).
TYDOO COLOR As TYDOO but with colour head Agfa colour (1951).
TYUUO Projection lens Hektor 2,5/200 mm (1960).
TYZOO Focomat IIa complete new codeword (1954).
TYZOO COLOR Focomat IIa colour complete new code word (1954).
TZFOO Extension tube for Telyt lens on screw camera.
TZOON Intermediate collar for using the Telyt 200 and 400 mm lenses directly on the Leica without reflex (1951).

U

UASKU Interchangeable mask 18 x 24 mm for projector V (1939).
UBAFE Lantern slide attachment for the UDIMO projector with thread for Leica lenses (1936).
UBAHO Slide changer of the UBODI projector with projection lens Milar 80 mm (1933).
UBAHOMAX Slide changer of the Obodimax projector with projection lens Dimax 120 mm (1933).
UBAZU Condensers for lenses of 150 and 175 mm focus (1960).
UBEAF Cine socket lamp 30 volts 100 watts (1933).
UBECD Extension tube 22 mm long (1936).
UBEHO Condensers for lenses of 400 and 500 mm focus (1960).
UBEHU Condensers for lenses of 85, 100 and 120 mm focus (1960).
UBELA Small projectors VIIIa with film attachment (1936).
UBELABIKU Projector UBELA set for use of Leica Elmar 105 mm and 135 mm lenses (1933).
UBELADAKI Projector UBELA set for use of Leica Hektor 73 mm and Elmar 90 mm lenses (1933).
UBELADOKO Projector UBELA set for use of Leica Elmar 50 and Hektor 50 mm lenses (1933).
UBEMI Cine socket lamp 100 watt for direct connection to mains (1933).
UBEOL Mask with window 18 x 24 mm of the film carrier UBEPU (1933).
UBEPU Film carrier with window 18 x 24 mm for the UBELA projector (1933).
UBFKU Condensers for lenses of 200 and 300 mm focus (1960).
UBIKU Interchangeable condenser for projectors to be used with 105 and 135 mm lenses (1933).
UBIRN Special 500 watt lamp partially silvered for 100 or 110 volts as spare (1931).
UBMWU Heat filters for Prado projectors (1960).
UBODI Projector type VIIIb for slides 5 x 5 cm with Milar 80 mm lens (1933).
UBODIMAX As UBODI but with Dimax 120 mm lenses (1933).
UBYMO Electric cord with switch 7ft. long (1960).
UCDEU Pradovit f projector for 220/50 hz or 110/60 hz mains with Hektor 2,5/85 mm lens: other 6 lenses available (1960).

UCHRU Projector cover for Pradovit lenses up to 120 mm (1960).
UCMYU Pradovit f projector for 220/50 hz or 110/60 hz mains with Hektor 2,5/85 mm lens; 6 other lenses available (1960).
UCSHU Control cable for projectors 13ft. long (1960).
UDAKI Interchangeable condenser for projectors with lenses from 73 to 90 mm focus including Milar 80 mm (1933).
UDALU Slide changer for projector for glass slides 3,5 x 12 cm (1933).
UDANO Small projector VIIIa for glass slides 5 x 5 (1933).
UDANOBIKU Projector VIIIa UDANO for 105 and 135 mm lenses (1933).
UDANODAKI Projector VIIIa UDANI for 105 and 135 mm lenses (1933).
UDANODOKO Projector VIIIa UDANO for 50 mm lenses Elmar and Hektor (1933).
UDAOB Projection lens Milar 80 mm (1933).
UDAPA Slide changer with round opening 43 mm diameter for 5 x 5 cm glass slides (1933).
UDGKU Carrying case for Pradovit projectors with lenses up to 150 mm (1960).
UDHUS Semi automatic film changer for the projector UBELA (1933).
UDIAS Lantern slide front attachment with 230 mm focal lens and pairs of frames 3¼ x 3¼; 4 x 3¼ and 4¾ x 3½ (1931).
UDIMO Projector VIIIa without film attachments (1933).
UDKQU Double heat filter for using a 500 watts lamp in the Prodovit f projectors (1960).
UDOKO Interchangeable condenser for the UBELA projector with 50 mm lenses. (1933).
UDOOL One hundred folding paper masks with window 24 x 36 mm for sliding mounting (1951).
UDOZU Tubular lens carrier to be screwed into the film and lens carriers (1933).
UDQCU Table projecting device for Prado 250/500 (1960).
UDRUK Press switch inserted in short flexible twin wire to the supply circuit (1931).
UDSGU Screen and shield for using with UDQCU (1960).
UDVNU Complete reading device (1960).
UDWPU Plastic box for two slide magazines (1960).
UDXRU Plastic box with two slide magazines (1960).
UDYGE Slide changer with a hole 50 mm diamter for picutres 3 x 4 cm size in 5 x 5 cm slides (1933).
UDYTU Prado 250 projector with Hektor 2,5/85 mm lens six other types with lenses up to Hektor 2,5/150 mm (1960).
UEOOK Ring of the lens shade UZEOM of the bellows UXOOR when using A36 objectives (1960).
UEOXU Magazine for 30 slides (1960).
UEPOO Lens shade ring for E39 Lenses for bellows UXOOR (1960).
UEYSU Projection lens Dimaron 2,8/100 mm (1960).
UFBXU Box with 5 magazines for slides (1960).
UFEDU IZUUS Projection lens Hektor 2, 5/85 mm in focusing mount (1939).
UFGEU Projection lens Colorplan 2,5/90 mm (1960).
UFIUC Prado 500 projector with Colorplan 2,5/90 mm lens (1960).
UFKOU Projection lens Hektor 2,5/120 mm (1960).
UFOWU Projection lens Hektor 2,5/85 mm (1960).
UFPYU Projection lens Dimaron 2,8/150 mm (1960).
UFSEU Projection lens Hektor 2,5/100 mm (1960).
UFTGU Two 50 slides magazines in cardboard box (1960).
UGECU Prado 250 projector without lens (1960).
UGKNU Projector Prado 500 without lens (1960).
UGLAS 100 glass plates 35 x 120 mm suitable for use with ULEJA, ULVOR and ULONG (1931).
UGLIT 100 glass plates 5 x 5 cm suitable for use with ULIOS, ULASE and ULOSU (1931).
UGLYR 100 glass plates 35 x 120 mm for mounting 3 pairs of stereo pictures (1931).
UGPXU Control cable for projectors 33ft. long (1960).
UGQZU Control cable for projectors 50ft. long (1960).
UGRBU Control cable for projectors 66ft. long (1960).
UHAUS Lamphouse with 500 watt lamp and three lens condenser of 155 mm diameter (1931).
UHPWU Multi contact plug for connecting the Pradovit to a tape recorder (1960).
UKABY Projector type VIIIb with semi automatic film transport device and Milar 80 mm lens (1933).
UKABYMAX As UKABY but with Dimax 120 mm lens (1933).
UKAMS Wooden box for the projector UBELA with a spare lamp and lens (1933).
UKEDU Leica film attachment with tube for the lens on UBELA projector (1933).

UKESO Film carrier device for the projector UKABY with Milar 80 mm lens (1933).
UKESOMAX Film carrier device for the projector UKABYMAX with projection lens Dimax 120 mm (1933).
UKGDU Connecting cable for operating the projector via a tape recorder (1960).
UKLIB Double slide changer for the UBELA projector (1933).
UKLON Small standard projector with 100 watt lamp to be used with the Elmar 2, 5/50 mm lens (1939).
UKMOU Electric fan to be added to projectors (1960).
UKUHL Cooling chamber round 10 cm diameter as spare (1931).
UKYLA Carrying case for the small projector UBELA with the slide changing magazine WEDYA (1933).
ULANI 100 watt 30 volt low voltage lamp as spare (1931).
ULASE Leica front attachment for slides 5 x 5 cm and projection lens 80 mm focus (1931).
ULAVA 100 watt 110 or 220 volt lamp as spare (1931).
ULEDO Projector for Leica 24 x 36 film three lens condenser 100 watt 110 or 220 volt lamp, 80 mm focus lens (1931).
ULEJA As ULEDO but with 30 volt lamp (1931).
ULFEN Film gate 18 x 24 mm for use with ULVOR and ULONG (1931).
ULFIX Film gate and guides for lantern slides for use with ULVOR AND ULONG 24 x 36 mm (1931).
ULIGU Variable resistor 500 watts (1960).
ULIOS As ULEJA but for lantern slides 5 x 5 cm (1931).
ULIUM As ULEJA but 110 or 220 volt lamp (1931).
ULNUR Extension twin wire 11ft. long with coupling and plug (1931).
ULONG Film attachment similar to ULVOR but with 120 mm lens (1931).
ULOSU Lantern slide attachment for 5 x 5 cm lens of 120 mm focus (1931).
ULOUB Rheostat adjustable for 375 watt lamps T5 volts for mains voltage from 100 to 250 volt (1939).
ULSIT Wooden folding table top 31½ x 11¼in. inclinable front and rear and with intermediate shelf (1931).
ULSOB One dozen of glass plates contrast 5 x 5 cm for slides (1939).
ULSMA As ULSOB but medium grade glass (1939).
ULSPU Metal spool to take 5ft. 3in. of film as spare for the projectors ULEJA, ULVOR and ULONG (1931).
ULVOR Film front attachment comprising the collecting lens, film gate and projection lens 80 mm focus (1931).
ULWAK Additional codeword if the small projector are desired with 30 volt lamp (1933).
UMASK 100 paper mask opaque size 5 x 5 cm with opening 24 x 36 mm (1931).
UMDOO Mounting kit for slides consisting of 25 frames, 25 masks, 50 glass plates and case (1939).
UMERN Easel desk projection screen 16 x 16in. with washable surface and cover (1939).
UMEXU Carrier with flange for screw mount lens for projector use (1939).
UMGBU Pradovit f projector for mains from 110 to 240 volts with Hektor 2, 5/85 mm lens: 6 other lenses available (1960).
UMKLE Gummed binding paper, black for binding diapositive slides, roll of 110 yards length (1931).
UMLED Soft leather case for the easel UMERN (1939).
UMOQU Electric fan to be added to projectors for universal voltages (1960).
UNHCU Metal frame with anti heat filter and condenser for lens from 85 to 120 mm focus (1960).
UNKGU As UNHCU but for 150 mm lenses (1960).
UNOPU Carrying case for the Prado 66 projector with 150 mm lens (1960).
UNOOB Lower stage of the universal copying device (1934).
UNOOB YSMOO Lower stage of the universal copying device to use the Summar 50 mm (1937).
UONMU 1000 watts lamp 110 volt only (1960).
UOOND Adaptor ring for the bellows for fitting bayonet mount lenses (1956).
UOOPE Voltage dimmer for the Focomat allowing to focus at reduced voltage and exposing at full voltage (1951).
UOORF Adaptor ring for optical groups of SOSIC and SOMNI to be used with the SOMKY (SOOKY-M) (1960).
UOOST Codeword for Combination of UOOYW + UOOVH (1952).
UOOTG Two parts adaptor for Elmar 90 mm on the universal focusing bellows (1952).
UOOVH Adaptor for Hektor 135 lens head to screw mount (1952).

UOOWV Adaptor ring for mounting the Elmar 90 mm on the universal focusing bellows (1951).
UOOXI Adaptor ring for using the Hektor 125 mm with the bellows (1956).
UOOYW Milled adaptor ring for UXOOR bellows with screw mount lenses (1954).
UOOZK Adaptor ring to use the optical group of the Summicron 2/90 mm lens on the UXOOR bellows (1960).
UPEOB Projection lens Dimax 120 mm focus (1933).
UPEOB-IZUUS As UPEOB with focusing mount (1939).
UPOOZ E58 yellow filter No. 0 (1951).
UQMOO E58 yellow filter No. 1 (1951).
UQOOY E58 yellow filter No. 2 (1951).
UROOX E58 green filter (1951).
USERU Projection lens Hektor 2,5/150 mm (1960).
USNAL Tilting plate with two milled screws for tilting the small projectors (1933).
USOOW E58 orange filter (1951).
USQOO E58 red filter (light) (1951).
USTAN Wooden box to carry the projector UDANO with Leica lens and one spare lamp (1933).
USTOL One hundred silvered paper mask with 24 x 36 mm aperture for slides (1933).
UTAHU Lens carrier for 150 mm focus lenses (1960).
UTBKU Lens carrier for 85, 100 and 120 focus lenses (1960).
UTCMU Connecting ring for device UDQCU (1960).
UTDOU Lens tube for Pradovit for lenses 85 to 120 mm (1960).
UTEQU Lens tube for the Pradovit for 150 mm lens (1960).
UTFSU Lens tube for the Pradovit f for lens from 85 to 120 mm (1960).
UTHWU As UTFSU but for 150 mm lens (1960).
UTOOV E58 red filter (medium) (1951).
UTSOO E58 red filter (dark) (1951).
UUDMK Cover for episcope 500/330 (1960).
UUPMI External interchangeable condenser for lenses of 200 250 and 300 mm (1939).
UUPNL Removable front with carrier for the projection lens and condenser of the projector V (1939).
UPPTX Lens carrier with lens Milar 4, 5/65 mm for projector V (1939).
USFLA Kodachrome flash filter E58 (USA 1949).
USOAY Type "A" Kodachrome filter E58 (USA 1949).
UUPWD Universal attachment complete for lantern slides, film strip and micro projection for projector V (1939).
UUQKD Securit glass as spare for eipiscopes diascopes (1960).
UUQVF Dispositive accessory for the episcope Vh 500 with Dinor 330 mm lens (1960).
UURAK Projection lens Dimax 250 mm with accessories (1960).
UURZH Supporting table for the episcopes Vz and epidiascopes Vh (1960).
UUSDP Cover for episcope 400/250 (1960).
UUZOB Low tension lamp 375 watt 75 volt for projectors VIIIs 400 (1939).
UVFLU Slide changer magazine feed for the Prado 150 with two magazines (1960).
UVFUN Projection lens Dinor 330 mm with accessories (1960).
UVIDI Projector composed of the lamphouse UHAUS and front attachment ULASE (1931).
UVIRI Projector composed of the lamphouse UHAUS and Leica film attachment ULVOR (1931).
UVOOF E58 UV filter (1951).
UVWOO Four way connector for using four lamps to illuminate objects (1951).
UWOOS Bracket for fitting the Leica focusing stage on the VALOY II (1954).
UWYOO Adaptor plate for using the focusing bellows on the carrying arms ROONP and ROOFU (1951).
UXOOR Universal focusing bellows with adaptor for Hektor 135 mm (1951).
UYCOO Bayonet adaptor for the Elmar 50 mm for the universal focusing bellows (1951).
UYOOQ Fitted fibre case for the universal focusing bellows, Focaslide and accessories (1951).
UZEOM Lens shade of the UXOOR bellows for objectives of 42 mm diameter (1960).
UZEOO Extensible lens shade with masks for the universal focusing bellows, screw mount (1951).
UZEOOM Extensible lens shade with interchangeable masks for the universal focusing bellows with bayonet mount (1956).
UZISU New codeword of the standard small projector (1938).
UZWIK Intermediate ring used on projector VIIIa to reduce the image size for colour slides Agfa Leica system (1934).
UZOCU Projection lamp 300 watts (1960).

V

VABAN Negative carrier size 28 x 40 mm for enlargers up to Focomat I (1939).
VABBA Negative carrier size 4½ x 6 cm for the VACUB Flashgun (USA 1934).
VARYL enlarger (1933).
VADAL VAMAX enlarger with ten printing boards for various sizes and tilter for correcting distorted lines (1933).
VADIV Additional illuminating arrangement for the VANOS enlarger for fully diffused light (1936).
VAFFE As VABBA but 4 x 6½ cm (1933).
VAFOO Baseboard and upright for the universal copying device (1936).
VAKES As VABAN but 4 x 4 cm (1952).
VAKOP Negative carrier size 4 x 4 cm for the VEKUX enlarger (1933).
VAKUT Enlarger with 32in. upright, 100 watt bulb and fixed 4,5/75 mm lens (similar to VALFA but for the lamp) (1933).
VALAU Slip on ring for operating the diaphragm when using the Elmar 3,5/50 mm lens on the enlargers (1933).
VALFA Enlarger with 32in. upright 75 watt bulb and fixed 4,5/75 mm lens (1933).
VALKY Negative carrier size 4 x 6½ cm for the enlargers VALFA and VAKUT (1933).
VALLI As VABBA but 4 x 4 cm (1933).
VALME As VALKY but 4 x 6½ cm (1933).
VALOO Diaphragm actuating ring for the Elmar 3,5/50 mm when used with Reprovit (1949).
VALOY Enlarger with upright 20in. for sizes up to 4 x 4 cm allowing the use of Leica interchangeable lenses (1933).
VALOY CENTO Enlarger as VALOY but with upright 40in. instead of the standard 20in. (1938).
VALOY OKTCO Enlarger as VALOY but with upright of 32 in. (1938).
VALUX Enlarger as VALOY but with 100 watt lamp instead of 75 watt and double condenser (1933).
VAMAX Big enlarger similar to VALOY but with upright 48in. large baseboard and long arm (1933).
VAMMO As VABBA but 3 x 4 cm (1933).
VANNU As VABBA but 24 x 36 mm (1933).
VAPPO As VABBA but 6 x 6 cm (1933).
VAREN Vamax enlarger with eight printing boards English sizes and tilter for correcting distorted lines (1936).
VARIP Large copying device with baseboard and upright, arm and focusing device with 4 lamps 40 watt (1933).
VARKU Large lamp carrier for a 100 watt lamp to be used with enlargers FILES, FILOY or FYLAB (1933).
VAROB Enlarging lens Elmar 3,5/50 mm with diaphragm and exposure factors table (1933).
VARSO As VALKY but 3 x 4 cm (1933).
VARYL Enlarger for negatives up to 6 x 9 cm with upright 80 cm 75 watt lamp and Leitz 4/90 mm lens (1933).
VASIX As VALKY but 24 x 36 mm (1933).
VASON Vamax enlarger with six printing boards and tilting device for correcting distorted lines (1936).
VASOX Single negative carrier for size 24 x 24 mm for enlargers VALOY and Focomat (1933).
VATIF Plate carrier size 4 x 6½ cm for the enlargers VALFA and VAKUT (1933).
VATOX Vamax enlarger with six printing boards continental sizes and tilting device for correcting distorted lines (1933).
VATUS As VATIF but 4 x 4 cm (1933).
VAVIR Negative carrier size 3 x 4 cm for the VALOY enlarger (1933).
VAWOL Enlarging lens 4,5/50 mm (USA Catalogue) (1939).
VAXKO As VATIF but 3 x 4 cm (1933).
VAZEL Film window plate for single Leica negatives with double glass for the VALOY enlarger (1933).
VAZIS Negative carrier size 4 x 4 cm for the enlargers VALOY and VAMAX (1933).
VAZOF Hinged double glass plate 5 x 16 cm for the enlargers VALOY and VAMAX (1933).
VAZUP As VAZIS but 3 x 4 cm (1933).
VAZYK Single negative carrier size 24 x 36 mm for the enlargers VALFA and VAKUT (1933).
VBHOO Bayonet collar for the Elmar 3,5/50 when used in conjunction with eliminating distortion device (1951).
VBOOP Mask 24 x 36 mm for the Focomat enlarger (1936).
VDMOO Film slide 24 x 36 mm for enlargers VALOY and Focomat (1936).
VDOON Film slide for the standard cine size for the Leitz special enlarger (1938).
VEARM Extra long arm for attaching the Leica to the upright of the large copying device (1933).
VEBOL Printing board with hinged boarder mask for the American size 14in. x 11in. (1931).
VEBYL Illuminating head from the FILYT but with longer arm suitable for use on the VIATS base in place of the VETOP (1931).

VEBYX Enlarging Easel fixed size 11 x 14in. with grooves for clamps of enlargers Focomat and VASEX (USA catalogue) (1939).
VECAR Printing board with hinged masks for size 9 x 14 cm (1933).
VECOF Projector head of the VYBOO enlarger for use on the VAMAX enlarger (1936).
VECUP Projector head of the VAMAX enlarger with arm and VAROB lens (1933).
VEDER Printing board with hinged border mask for size 6½ x 4¾ (half plate) (1931).
VEDRI As VEDER but 13 x 18 cm (1931).
VEDUK Electric cable 12ft. long with plug for the X-ray copying device (1933).
VEFIV As VEDER but 5½ x 3½ins. (1931).
VEFOR As VEDER but 4¼ x 3¼in. (1931).
VEGIT As VEDER but 8½ x 6½in. (1931).
VEGRO As VEDER but 40 x 50 cm with two clamping scres (1933).
VEGUR As VEDER but 20 x 16in. (1931).
VEHAL Arm for attaching the Leica to the upright of the X-ray reproduction device (1933).
VEHIG Ground glass auxiliary housing for focusing with the special copying devices (1933).
VEKAS Illuminating box 20 x 16in. with six frosted lamps ground glass plate, opal glass plate and loose glass (1931).
VEKIP Tilting angle of metal for straightening converging lines (1931).
VEKOT Light box size 13 x 18 cm for the X-ray reproduction device (1933).
VEKUX Illuminating head for enlarger like VECUP but with a 100 watt lamp and a double condenser (1933).
VELAN As VEDER but 5 x 3½in. (1931).
VELIF Arm for attaching the Leica to the small copying device (1933).
VELOK As VEDER but 18 x 24 cm (1931).
VELTU Baseboard for the large copying device with 40in. upright (1933).
VELUM Arm for fixing the Leica on the enlarging apparatus VITAS for copying purposes (1931).
VELVE As VEDER but 15 x 12in. (1931).
VELYP Glass plate for holding the film flat on the light box VEPUT (1933).
VENTY As VEDER but 24 x 30 cm (1931).
VENUM As VEDER but 9 x 12 cm (1931).
VEOOM Vamax enlarger without the enlarging lens (1938).
VEPOS As VEDER but 10.5 x 14.8 cm (1933)
VEPUT Light box 30 x 40 cm for the X-ray reproduction device (1933).
VERAP X-ray reproduction device complete with 40 x 50 cm box but without Leica camera (1933).
VERBE Base board of the VALOY enlarger (1939).
VERON Copying set for X-ray and film comprising the column VESTA, arm VELUM, box VEKAS and cable VEDUK (1931).
VERUP Metal upright 32in. long for the VALOY enlarger (1939).
VERYK Glass plate for holding the film flat on the light box VEKOT (1933).
VESEX As VEDER but 6½ x 9 cm (1931).
VESIR As VEDER but 7 x 5in. (1931).
VESTA Base board with 48in. upright of the VAMAX and VITAS enlargers (1933).
VETIN As VEDER but 18 x 8in. (1931).
VETOP Illuminating head of the enlarger VITAS with arm, lamp housing, film carrier, cable, switch and lens (1931).
VETRU As VEDER but 30 x 40 cm (1931).
VETWO As VEDER but 3½ x 2½in. (1931).
VEUUM Ventilating unit with electric blower for the series VIII projectors (1939).
VEVAX Enlarger head for sizes up to 4½ x 6 cm with 75 watt lamp and enlarging Leitz lens 4,5/75 mm (1933).
VEVIL As VEVAX but with 100 watt lamp (1933).
VEZEN As VEDER but 10 x 15 cm (1931).
VEZUK Circular lateral holder to protect the lid of the Leica when it is used on the copying devices (1933).
VFOOL Spare lamp 100 watt for the 4 lamp illuminating device of the reprovit (1951).
VGSOO Adapting arm for converting the X-ray device into a combined enlarging and projection device (1933).
VHOOI Ring for use of the Agfa Variomat on the Focomat IIc with column diameter of 60 mm (1960).
VIDAL Enlarger VITAS complete as in VITOY plus three printing boards: VENUM, VEZEN, VETRU (1931).
VIDEO Multiple viewfinder for 3,5-5-9-13,5 cm lenses black without parallax correction (1932).
VIDNY Leitz exposure meter of the extintion type to be fitted on top of camera (1939).
VIDOM Universal viewfinder (first type) with adjustable field and parallax correction (1933).
VIEIN Solid leather case for the universal finder type VIUNA, VIZWO and VITRE VIFUR (1933).
VIFUR Universal viewfinder for lenses of 35, 50 and 135 mm focus (1933).

VIHAK Small copying device with base board and 20in. upright and 4 lamp illuminating system (1933).

VIKUL Light box 24 x 30 cm for the X-ray reproduction device (1933).

VILUI Solid leather case for the universal viewfinder VIDOM (1933).

VIOAD 28 mm adaptor to screw in front of Imerect finder VIOOH (1949). Also TUVOO.

VIOOH Universal viewfinder for lenses from 35 to 135 mm focus with correct sided image and parallax correction (1949).

VIPRO Light protection tube for the upright of the Focomat Ib enlarger (1949).

VIREN Vitas enlarger with the complete set of eight printing boards English sizes and tilting angle (1931).

VIROT Copying set as VERON but comprising also camera LEANE release FINT, finder WINKO, WICAP and ELPRO, ELPIK, ELPET (1931).

VIRUP Glass plate for holding the film flat on the light box VIKUL (1933).

VISAM Enlarger VITAS complete with set of six printing boards American sizes and tilting angle of metal (1931).

VISIL Multiple viewfinder for 3,5-5-7,3-10,5 cm lenses black without parallax correction (1932).

VISOR Universal viewfinder for the lenses of 3,5 cm 5 cm and 13,5 focus (1931).

VISUS As VISOR but in solid leather case EUSOR (1931).

VITAS Enlarger with 4ft. column, 60 watt lamp, baseboard 20 x 24 in Leitz lens 50 mm 3,5 with iris diaphragm (1931).

VITOY Enlarger VITAS with set of six european printing boards and tilting angle VEKIP (1931).

VITRE Universal viewfinder for lenses of 35, 50 and 105 mm focus (1933).

VIUNA Universal viewfinder for lenses of 35, 50 and 73 mm focus (1933).

VIUSA Focomat enlarger model Ib (1949).

VIWOO Automatic enlarger Focomat complete but without lens (1936).

VIWOO VAROB As VIWOO but with enlarging lens 3,5/50 mm (1938).

VIWOO YOOSV Automatic enlarger Focomat with 40in. upright and light protecting shield (1938).

VIZWO Universal viewfinder for lenses of 35, 50 and 90 mm focus (1933).

VKOOK Spare bulb for illuminating box 36 x 40 cm 60 watt (1951).

VLOOF Folding segmented reflector of the CAVOO and CEYOO flash (1951).

VMCOO Adaptor to use the supplementary front lenses of the Elmar 3,5/50 mm on the Summar 2/50 mm (1936).

VNAOO Film guide for size 18 x 24 mm for enlargers VALOY II and Focomat Ic (1954).

VNEOO As VNAOO but 24 x 36 mm (1954).

VNIOO As VNAOO but 24 x 24 cm (1954).

VNOOD Film slides size 24 x 24 mm for the enlargers VALOY and Focomat (1951).

VNOOU As VNAOO but 3 x 4 cm (1954).

VNUOO As VNAOO but 4 x 4 cm (1954).

VOBIT Additional illuminating lens (condenser) for use in enlargers with extra powerful lamps (1936).

VODDA Projector VIII 400 watt with slide changer without lens (1939).

VOEEB As VODDA but with Hektor 2,5/85 mm lens (1939).

VOFFC As VODDA but with Epis 3,6/80 mm lens (1939).

VOGGM As VODDA less slide changer (1939).

VOGOS Enlarger with horizontally rotating film stage for negative size up to 4 x 4 cm without lens (1936).

VOHHD As VODDA but with Hektor 2,5/100 mm lens (1939).

VOJAL Accessory for the VOGOS enlarger to use it as a projector (1936).

VOJEK Enlarger VOGOS without bulb (1936).

VOJJE As VODDA but with Dimax 4,5/120 mm lens (1939).

VOKKF As VODDA but with Dimar 3,5/150 mm lens (1939).

VOKOM Combined enlarging and projection apparatus with reading desk (1936).

VOLAM Projection lamp type A 100 watt (1936).

VOLES Reading desk arrangement for the combined apparatus VOKOM (1936).

VOLIG Projection apparatus of the combined VOKOM but without mirror (1936).

VOLLG As VODDA but with Dimar 4/200 mm lens and supporting bracket (1939).

VOMIR Mirrors with supporting joint for VOPRO device of the VOKOM combined device (1936).

VOMMH As VODDA but with Dimar 4/250 mm lens and supporting bracket (1939).

VONNI As VODDA but with Epnor 4,3/300 mm lens and supporting bracket (1939).

VOOAL Lamp housing of the enlarger VOGOS (1936).

VOOBY Lamp housing for the enlarger VOGOS but with a 100 watt projection lamp (1936).

VOOCM Accessory parts to make an X-ray reproduction device into a projection apparatus similar to VOPRO (1936).

VOODZ As VOOCM less mirror (1936);

VOOEN Accessory parts to transform an X-ray device into a reading desk similar to VOLES (1936).

VOOLA Diaphragm setting ring for the Elmar 50 mm to operate diaphragm with a filter attached to lens (1956).

VOOLQ Slip on ring to operate the diaphragm of the Hektor 2,5/50 mm lens when used on the enlargers (1939).

VOOLY Enlarger VALOY II special model with adaptor to use it on the stand of the Reprovit equipment (1954).

VOOMD Double glass plate 3,5 x 12 cm for the Focomat (1936).

VOONR Hinged doube glass plate 5 x 16 cm for the Focomat (1936).

VOOPS Combined enlarger with reading desk (1938).

VOOQF Column 31½in. tall for the VALOY II enlarger (1954).

VOORT Enlarging lens 95 mm focus for the VANOS and VOOWI enlargers (1936).

VOOSG Enlarging head and reading desk equipment to be used with the upright and baseboard VESTA (1938).

VOOWI Focomat enlarger model II for all negative sizes up to 6,5 x 9 cm including VOORT lens (1936).

VOOWI VAROB Focomat IIa enlarger with two enlarging lenses of 50 mm and 95 mm focal length (1938).

VOOZX Supplementary condenser for direct illumination in the VALOY II enlarger (1954).

VOPRO Projection apparatus of the combined device VOKOM (1936).

VOPUL Picture viewing box for the reading desk arrangement of the VOLES (1936).

VORGI Adaptor ring to use additional lenses HEPRO, HEPIK and HEPET with the Summar F.2 lens.

VOROD Stereoly for II, III, & IIIa (USA 1938).

VORSA Leica 'stereoly' front attachment in leather case, with viewfinder (1931).

VORSTAN Stereo attachment 'stereoly' for the Leica standard old code (1933).

VORUF Arm for attaching the 'stereoly' to the Leica II and III (1939).

VORYM Ventilating ring for the enlargers if the more powerful 100 watt lamp is used (1936).

VOSTN As VORSA new code (1936).

VOTIV Stand for supporting the VOTRA stereoscope (1931).

VOTRA Leica stereoscope for positives taken with the VORSA stereo attachment, in case (1931).

VSPOO Helical focusing mount for using the optical group of the Summicron 2/50 mm in short range (1956).

VTOOX Diaphragm regulating ring for the Elmar 2,8/50 when used in the near focusing devices (1958).

VTROO As VTOOX but with the Summicron 2/50 mm (1956).

VUCAS Carrying case for the desk film viewer VUDFS (1949).

VUDFS Desk viewer for 2in. square slides and film strip (1949).

VUFIL Film holder for using 35 mm positive or negative film in the VUDFS viewer (1949).

VULPE Focusing magnifier for accurately focusing the image in all enlargers except the VAMAX (1933).

VULVI As VULPE but for VAMAX (1933).

VUOOW Valoy II enlarger complete with film guide for 24 x 36 mm size, lamp 75 watt upright of 25¼in. (1954).

VUROO Baseboard and column 65 cm high of the VALOY II (1960).

VUSOO Valoy II last type with upright 65 cm high, 75 watt lamp and screw mount for Leica lenses (1960).

VUTOO Special model of the Focomat enlarger with upright 48in. and baseboard 25 x 24in. (1936).

VUTOO VAROB Special model of the Focomat I enlarger with the Leitz 3,5/50 lens (1938).

VUUEN Regulating resistance for the low voltage lamp of the projector VIII-250 (1938).

VWOOU Repro N ring to use with the Summicron 2/50 optical group in the ratios from 1:1,9 to 1:1,1 (1956).

VWXOO Screw mount ring for filters (1960).

VXOOT As VSPOO but for the Elmar 3,5/50 mm lens (1958).

VXZOO As VSPOO But with bayonet adaptor (1958).

VYBOO Enlarger for all sizes up to 6,5 x 9 cm with 32in. upright and Elmar 4/95 mm lens (1936).

VYOOS Enlarger for all sizes up to 6,5 x 9 cm upright 48in. and Elmar 4/95 mm lens (1936).

W

WINAT Leather case for the angular viewfinder WINTU (1933).

WINEK As WINKO plus case WITUI.

WINKO Angular viewfinder (90°) without prism for the Leica standard (1931).

WEDYA Slide changing magazine for Leica glass slides 2 x 2in. (1933).

WEISU Special finder for the Elmar 3,5/35 mm lens (old type) (1933).

WENOO Projector head from the VAMAX enlarger without lens (1936).

WESCA Soft leather case with zipper for the Weston Leicameter (1939).

WESTO Weston Leicameter direct exposure reading scale (1939).

WICAB Holder for attaching the angular viewfinder to the standard model when making reproductions (1936).

WICAP Holder for fixing the angular finder on the lens of the Leica camera when copying (1931).

WINTU Angular viewfinder (90°) with prism for the Leica II or III (1933).

WIOOK Solid leather case for the angular viewfinder WINKO (formerly WITUI) (1936).

WIRIN WINTU with leather case (1933).

WITUI Solid leather case for WINKO viewfinder.

WIVOO Solid leather case for angular viewfinder WINTU (formerly WINAT) (1936).

WOOCZ Projector head VECUP with press switch (1936).

WOOIC Projector head VECOF with press switch (1936).

WOOLD As WINKO, but with additional internal prism (1938).

WOOSU As WINTU, but with additional internal prism (1938).

WUUBM Projector PRADO 500 with lens Hektor 3,5/100 (1960).

WUUCZ As WUUBM but with Hektor 2,5/120 lens (1960).

WUUDN As WUUBM but with Hektor 2,5/150 lens (1960).

WUUEA As WUUBM but with Dimar 4/200 lens (1960).

WUUFO As WUUBM but with Hektor 2,5/200 lens (1960).

WUUGB As WUUBM but with Hektor 2,5/175 lens (1960).

WUUNE Elmar 3,5/50 without diaphragm in special mount (1960).

WUURG As WUUBM but with Colorplan 2,5/90 lens (1960).

WZCOO Holder for attaching the angular viewfinder for models II and III when making reproductions (1936)

X

XADEE Special stand for ophthalmic and dental photography (1939).

XBEET Dove-tail slider with tripod screw to fit the camera to CMEET-XCEES. Available post-war for fitting Focoslide to pillar stands. (1939).

XDQII Sliding arm for the upright with ball bearing movements in all directions to carry the rotating focusing stage (1939).

XEMOO Leitz Xenon lens 1,5/50 mm chrome finish screw mount.

XENCA Lens cap for Xenon 50 mm (1939).

XGQOO Light protecting metal sheet for the Focomat I enlarger (1938).

XIOOM Folding lens shade for the Leitz Xenon lens.

XOOAM Yellow Filter 'O' with bayonet mount for the Leitz Xenon lens.

XOOBZ As XOOAM but yellow filter '1'.

XOOCN As XOOAM but yellow filter '2'.

XOODA As XOOAM but graduated yellow.

XOOFB As XOOAM but ultraviolet filter.

XOOGP As XOOAM but green filter.

XOOHC As XOOAM but graduated green.

XOOIM Lens hood for Summilux 50 mm (1960).

XOOIQ As XOOAM but light red.

XOOKD As XOOAM but medium red.

XOOLR As XOOAM but dark red.

XOOME As XOOAM but orange filter.

XOOMT As XOOAM but yellow filter dark No. 3 (1939).

XOONS Lens hood for Summarit 50 and Xenon 50 mm (1951).

XOOPT E41 yellow filter very light No. 0 (1951).

XOOQG E41 yellow filter light No. 1 (1951).

XOORU E41 yellow filter medium No. 2 (1951).

XOOSH E41 yellow green filter (1951).

XOOUI E41 red filter light (1951).

XOOVW E41 red filter medium (1951).

XOOWK E41 red filter dark (1951).

XOOYL E41 UV filter (1951).

XOOZY E41 orange filter (1951).

XPGOO E41 graduated yellow filter (1951).

XPOOF E41 graduated green filter (1951).

XQIOO E41 Polarizing filter with numbered scale (1951).

XQOOE E41 blue filter (1951).

XUUME Double heat filter for the Prado 250/500 projector to use a 750 watt lamp (1960).

XWTVS Intermediate focusing mount for Summar and Summitar on the Focaslide (1949).

XYFOR Projection lamp 400 watt 110 volt (1939).

XYSET Projection lamp 750 watt 110 volt (1939). XYTHA Projection lamp 1000 watt 110 volt (1939).

Y

YACUU PRADO 66 projector with DIMARON 2,8/150 lens (1960).

YBEEO No. 0 yellow filter, E43 (1959).

YBEUU Slide carrier 7 x 7 cm for the PRADO 66 projector (1960).

YCGOO E43 yellow filter No. 1 for Summilux 50 mm screw mount (1960).

YDIUU Slide carrier 6 x 6 cm for the PRADO 66 projector (1960).

YDUUT Accessory 6 x 6 for the PRADO 250/500 projector with Hektor 2,5/150 lens (1960).

YELOO E43 green filter (1960).

YEUUS As YDUUT but with Dimaron 2,8/150 lens (1960).

YFNUU As YDIUU but 5 x 5 cm for 24 x 36 mm (1960).

YGPOO E43 red filter (1960).

YHROO E43 infrared filter (1960).

YHRUU As YACUU but with Hektor 2,5/150 lens (1960).

YKUUN Carrying case for the PRADO 66 projector with 150 mm lens (1960).

YLUUM Carrying case for the PRADO 66 projector with 175 mm lens and transformer RSTUU (1960).

YLXOO E43 orange filter (1960).

YMOOL E43 blue filter (1960).

YMZOO E43 UV filter (1960).

YOOBN Codeword to indicate printing boards with threaded nut for the device for correcting distorted lines (1936).

YOOCA Codeword for plug in socket in the base board of enlargers to regulate the exposure with a time switch (1938).

YODUU As YDUUT but with Dimar 4/200 lens (1960).

YOOQU Intermediate ring for use of the single exposure device with the universal copying device (1936).

YOOSV Codeword to indicate that the Focomat enlarger is required with a 40in. upright (1936).

YRKOO Rack and pinion movement for the sliding arm, permits greater accuracy of movement in focusing (1949).

YROOF Rack and pinion movement for focusing devices on sliding arm similar to YRKOO but finer adjustment (1951).

YQHOO Intermediate piece for the collapsible upright of the universal copying device (1936).

YQHUU Heat filter 6 x 7 for the PRADO 250/500 projector (1960).

YQUUG Aspherical condenser 6 x 6 for the PRADO 250/500 projector to be used with the 6 x 6 accessories (1960).

YSMUU As YDUUT but with Dimar 4/250 lens (1960).

YSOOE Adaptor for sport finders SAIOO, SEROO and SYEOO when used on the Leica Standard (1939).

YUUCA Prado 66 projector with Dimar 4/200 lens (1960).

YUUFP As YUUCA but with Hektor 2,5/175 lens (1960).

YUUHQ Prado 66/500 projector with Hektor 2:5/175 lens (1960).

YUUID As YUUHQ but with Dimaron 2,8/150 lens (1960).

YUUKR As YUUHQ but with Hektor 2,5/150 lens (1960).

YUULE As YUUHQ but with Dimar 4/200 lens (1960).

YUURH As YDUUT but with Hektor 2,5/175 mm lens (1960).

YUUSV As YDUUT but with Hektor 2,5/200 lens (1960).

Z

ZBDUU As YDUUT but with Hektor 2,8/250 lens (1960).

ZBUUX Prado 66 projector without lens without lamp (1960).

ZDHUU Carrying case for the PRADO 66/500 projector with long base (1960).

ZDUUV Carrying case for the PRADO 66/500 projector with transformer attached to base (1960).

ZEKUU ZGUUS Complete projector model IVf with accessories 500 watt 110 volt lamp (USA Catalogue) (1939).

ZEOOU Tilting device for the negative carrier of Focomat Ic (1952).

ZESOO Device for correcting distortions for the VALOY II and Focomat I enlargers comprising ZHOOR + ZFNOO + ZFOOT (1960).

ZFNOO Hinged negative carrier for the Focomat Ic (1952).

ZFOOT Printing board tilter with joint and base plate (1952).

ZHOOR Tilting device for the negative carrier for the VALOY II Focomat I enlargers (1960).

ZIOOQ Supplement for the accessory shoe of the Leica If when using flash and the viewfinder SBOOI (1951).

ZISOO Device for correcting distortions for Focomat Ic complete and consisting of ZEOOU-ZFNOO and ZFOOT (1952).

ZISUM New codeword for ZWTOO (1960).

ZISUU Carrying case for the IVf projector (1939).

ZLUUO Episcope VZ 2 with Epis 3,6/325 lens and for 500 watt lamp with fan (1960).

ZLWUU As ZLUUO but with 4/400 mm lens (1960).

ZOCUU Episcope VZ similar to ZLUUO but without fan (1960).

ZOKEG Adaptor ring to transform a short 135 Hektor into a normal screw mount one with rectilinear focusing mount (1960).

ZOKEM As ZOKEG but bayonet mount (1960).

ZOMUK Long mount to use a short Summicron 2/90 OESBO or OERDO with bayonet M cameras (1960).

ZOSUM Focusing mount and three rings for the Focaslide ZISUM + BOOXZ + FVOOQ + GVKOO (1960).

ZOOAN Short focusing mount for fitting the Hektor 135 mm lens to the reflex housing (1938).

ZOOBA Adaptation of Hektor 135 mm lenses with serial number below 241.000 which are to be used on the reflex housing (1938).

ZOOEP Short focusing mount to use the Summicron 2/90 lens SEOOM or SEOOF on the Visoflex II (1960).

ZOOKE Intermediate mount with rangefinder coupling to change OHEBO into HEFAR screw (1936).

ZOOKEM As ZOOKE but to bayonet mount (1956).

ZOOMF Intermediate ring 50 mm long for using the Hektor 135 mm in short mount (ZOOAN or OHEBO) with the Focaslide (1951).

ZOONT Helical mount for older type Elmar lenses 50 mm to be used on the Focaslide (1951).

ZOOSI HESUM Intermediate thread ZWTOO HESUM and rings BOOXZ-FVOOQ and GVKOO to use Summitar and Summar 50 with the Focaslide (1951).

ZOOUK Long mount to use a Summicron 2/90 short OESBO or OERDO with screw mount cameras (1960).

ZOOVX Adaptor to fit FOCATAR to ZOOXY.

ZOOWL Helical focusing mount as ZOOXY but with special thread to take the Focotar 50 mm lens (1956).

ZOOXY Helical focusing mount for using the Elmar 50 mm (only) on the Focaslide (1951).

ZOOYM Adaptor with bayonet mount for using the Elmar 2,8/50 with he Focaslide (1960).

ZOUUL Episcope VZ similar to ZLWUU but without fan (1960).

ZPOOK Clamp to fasten the upright of the VALOY enlarger to a table and use it for reproduction work (1956).

ZQGOO Helical focusing mount with interchangeable ring with screw or bayonet mount (1956).

ZQGUU Plastic cover (transparent) for the Episcope VZ 2 (1960).

ZRIOO Device for correcting distorted lines when printing (1936).

ZRIOO VOOND Distortion eliminating device for printing, comprising ball joint for printing board and tilting negative carrier (1939).

ZRIUU Carrying case for episcopes ZOCUUL and ZOUUL (1960).

ZROOH Extension tubes set of 7 mm, 16 mm, 25,4 mm, 41 mm (1939).

ZRUUH Carrying case for episcope VZ 2 (1960). ZSLOO Collapsible upright for the universal copying device (1936).

ZSOOG Intermediate piece for using the ball jointed heads of former construction with tilting tops tripods (1938).

ZTNOO Set of two adaptors ZTOOF and ZVOOD (1938).

ZTOOF Large adaptor for converting English tripod heads to Continental (1938).

ZUPOO Turret head for flashgun BTLOO (1937).

ZUUAN 500 watt lamp with bayonet mount (1960).

ZUUBA Accessory for diapostive projection 85 x 85 and 85 x 100 for the Episcope 325 VP (1960).

ZUUCO 500 watt lamp with screw mount (1960).

ZVOOD Large adaptor for converting Continental tripod heads to English (1938).

ZWMQX Adaptor to use the Micro Summar lenses on the focusing device ZWTOO HESUM (1939).

ZWMYY Helical focusing mount with adaptor for the lenses of the Micro Summar series (1939).

ZWOOC Intermediate thread and four intermediate rings for using the Elmar 50 mm lens on the universal copying device (1936).

ZWOOC HESUM Intermediate thread and four intermediate rings for using the Summar 50 mm lens on the universal copying device (1936).

ZWTEL Intermediate focusing mount for 3,5/50 mm lenses on the Focaslide (1949).

ZWTOO Intermediate thread for using the Elmar 50 mm lens on the universal copying device (1936).

ZWTOO HESUM As ZWTOO but for F2 Summar (1936).